Leaders in Philosophy of Education

LEADERS IN EDUCATIONAL STUDIES

Volume 6

Series Editor: Leonard J. Waks, *Temple University, Philadelphia, USA*

Scope:
The aim of the *Leaders in Educational Studies* Series is to document the rise of scholarship and university teaching in educational studies in the years after 1960. This half-century has been a period of astonishing growth and accomplishment. The volumes in the series document this development of educational studies as seen through the eyes of its leading practitioners.

A few words about the build up to this period are in order. Before the mid-twentieth century school teaching, especially at the primary level, was as much a trade as a profession. Schoolteachers were trained primarily in normal schools or teachers colleges, only rarely in universities. But in the 1940s American normal schools were converted into teachers colleges, and in the 1960s these were converted into state universities. At the same time school teaching was being transformed into an all-graduate profession in both the United Kingdom and Canada. For the first time, school teachers required a proper university education.

Something had to be done, then, about what was widely regarded as the deplorable state of educational scholarship. James Conant, in his final years as president at Harvard in the early 1950s, envisioned a new kind of university-based school of education, drawing scholars from mainstream academic disciplines such as history, sociology psychology and philosophy, to teach prospective teachers, conduct educational research, and train future educational scholars. One of the first two professors hired to fulfil this vision was Israel Scheffler, a young philosopher of science and language who had earned a Ph.D. in philosophy at the University of Pennsylvania. Scheffler joined Harvard's education faculty in 1952. The other was Bernard Bailyn, who joined the Harvard faculty in 1953 after earning his Ph.D. there, and who re-energized the study of American educational history with the publication of *Education in the Forming of American Society: Needs and Opportunities for Study* (University of North Carolina Press, 1960). The series has been exceptionally fortunate that Scheffler provided a foreword to the volume on philosophy of education, and that Bernard Bailyn provided a foreword for the volume on the history of American education. It is equally fortunate that subsequent volumes have also contained forewords by similarly eminent scholars, including James Banks of the University of Washington, who has been a creative force in social education for decades and the prime mover in the field of multi-cultural education.

The *Leaders in Educational Studies* Series continues to document the growing and changing literature in educational studies. Studies conducted within the established academic disciplines of history, philosophy, and sociology comprised the dominant trend throughout the 1960s and 1970s. By the 1980s educational studies diversified considerably, in terms of both new sub-disciplines within these established disciplines and new interdisciplinary and trans-disciplinary fields.

Curriculum studies, both in general and in the particular school subject matter fields, drew extensively from work in philosophy, history and sociology of education. Work in these disciplines, and also in anthropology and cultural studies among others, also stimulated new perspectives on race, class and gender.

This volume, like previous volumes in the series, brings together personal essays by established leaders in a major field of educational studies. Subsequent volumes in the series will continue to document other established and emerging disciplines, sub-disciplines and inter-disciplines in educational scholarship.

Leaders in Philosophy of Education

Intellectual Self-Portraits (Second Series)

Foreword by Jane Roland Martin

Edited by

Leonard J. Waks
Temple University, Philadelphia, USA

SENSE PUBLISHERS
ROTTERDAM / BOSTON / TAIPEI

A C.I.P. record for this book is available from the Library of Congress.

ISBN 978-94-6209-756-8 (paperback)
ISBN 978-94-6209-757-5 (hardback)
ISBN 978-94-6209-758-2 (e-book)

Published by: Sense Publishers,
P.O. Box 21858, 3001 AW Rotterdam, The Netherlands
https://www.sensepublishers.com/

Printed on acid-free paper

All rights reserved © 2014 Sense Publishers

No part of this work may be reproduced, stored in a retrieval system, or transmitted in any form or by any means, electronic, mechanical, photocopying, microfilming, recording or otherwise, without written permission from the Publisher, with the exception of any material supplied specifically for the purpose of being entered and executed on a computer system, for exclusive use by the purchaser of the work.

TABLE OF CONTENTS

Foreword   vii
Jane Ronald Martin

Introduction: Leaders in Philosophy of Education after 1980   1
Leonard J. Waks

From Experimentalism to Existentialism: Writing in the Margins of Philosophy of Education   13
Gert Biesta

From Existentialism to Virtuality   31
Megan Boler

The Personal and the Philosophical   49
Nicholas C. Burbules

My Life in Philosophy   59
Randall Curren

Still Facing the Torpedo Fish   75
Ann Diller

Liberalism and Education: Between Diversity and Universalism   89
Penny Enslin

My Life as a Vixen   103
Morwenna Griffiths

On Wonder   117
David T. Hansen

An Unlikely Philosopher?   133
Kenneth R. Howe

Tacking Toward the Subjective   151
Donna H. Kerr

Hungry for Insubordinate Educational Wisdom   163
Susan Laird

TABLE OF CONTENTS

The Freedom of Paradox *Lars Løvlie*	175
Pedagogue and/or Philosopher? Some Comments on Attending, Walking, Talking, Writing and ... Caving *Jan Masschelein*	197
An Accident Waiting to Happen: Reflections on a Philosophical Life in Education *Peter Roberts*	211
A Kind of Spiral Thinking: Philosophy of Education Through the Eyes of a Fellow Traveller *Paul Smeyers*	231
Philosophy in Its Place *Richard Smith*	245
Making Sense of Moments *Barbara S. Stengel*	255
Learning From and Living With Life's Rough Threads *Sharon Todd*	269
Afterword: A Path Forward *Leonard J. Waks*	279

JANE ROLAND MARTIN

FOREWORD

In his Foreword to the first *Leaders in Philosophy of Education* Israel Scheffler told us that he joined the faculty of the Harvard Graduate School of Education in 1952 under a Rockefeller grant designed to introduce new perspectives to the field of Education. It is my pleasure to report that 62 years later, new perspectives are still being introduced into the Philosophy of Education.

Jurgen Habermas, Hans-Georg Gadamer, Michel Foucault, Hannah Arendt, Jacques Derrida, Emmanuel Levinas, Paulo Freire, Louisa May Alcott, Luce Irigaray: this is a bare sampling of the people scarcely mentioned in the first *Leaders* whose ideas have had a profound influence on the philosophers of education included in the Second Series. The presence in the pages to follow of scholars from Europe, Australia, and New Zealand is another sign of the continued reinvigoration of our field, and a third indication is that eight out of the eighteen contributors to this volume are women.

One new to our profession will not know what a sea change the near gender parity of authorship represents. At the first meeting of the Philosophy of Education Society I ever attended – this was 1960 and analytic papers were still not allowed on the official program – I, a graduate student, was one of only two women there. In the first *Leaders* volume Patricia White wrote that in Britain in the early 1960s she knew of no women working analytically in the philosophy of education until she happened upon my article in the 1961 B. Othanel Smith and Robert Ennis collection *Language and Concepts of Education*. That book was the exception. Scan the Table of Contents of the other landmark collections of analytic work in our field – Scheffler's 1958 anthology *Philosophy and Education*, its second edition published in 1966, and R. S. Peters' 1967 *The Concepts of Education* – and you will see that the works contained therein are all written by men. Having firsthand knowledge of the historical record, I was duly impressed that as many as six out of twenty-four of the essays in the first *Leaders* were by women and rejoice that in this volume close to one-half of them are.

A newcomer may not realize either that in a matter of decades English language philosophy of education has twice been transformed. Although the analytic philosophy that Scheffler, Peters, Smith and Ennis introduced into our discipline and that I as a student enthusiastically embraced met strong resistance from the philosophy of education "establishment," analytic approaches soon came to dominate our field. These memoirs testify, however, that the one intellectual revolution quickly gave way to what is perhaps most aptly described as methodological pluralism. I roundly applaud this development and admire the deep commitment to philosophical modes of thinking that shines through every essay in this volume. The new pluralism does, however, present a number of challenges.

In his Introduction, Editor Leonard Waks refers to "the philosophy of education conversation." Each of these leaders has clearly engaged in conversation with philosophers past and present. To what extent they have met the challenge of talking to, listening to, and learning from one other across the very different philosophical approaches or methodologies is a question for readers to judge.

In view of the near parity of male and female authors in this volume it might be thought that where the philosophy of education is concerned, issues of gender will from now on take care of themselves. Pluralistic conversation is, however, facilitated when the various parties are acquainted with one another's theoretical perspectives, and here there is a notable gender disparity. Whereas just about all the leaders in this Second Series seem to have been influenced by continental philosophy and most of the women appear to have been deeply affected by feminist theory and scholarship: very few of the men seem even to be acquainted with the feminist literature. I hasten to add that this gender imbalance is more than matched in these autobiographical accounts by the paucity of references to philosophical perspectives rooted in continents other than Europe and North America.

If the first challenge of the new pluralism is to talk across different methodologies, a second one is to resist the centrifugal forces inherent in pluralism and find shared concerns on which the very different approaches can be brought to bear. When a multitude of approaches co-exist within a single discipline, it is all too easy for each one to lay claim to its own small patch of land rather than seek out common ground to cultivate. Again I leave it an open question whether these leaders are talking with one another about issues of concern to all.

Yet a third challenge is to keep the conversation focused on significant educational questions and here, past philosophical conversations about education can be helpful. I trust that in 2014 it scarcely needs saying that the membership of the "official" old philosophy of education conversational circle was not nearly as representative as it could and should have been. Nonetheless, many – perhaps most – of the educational issues that Plato, Comenius, Locke, Rousseau, Pestalozzi, Froebel, Dewey and the rest took up are as pressing today as they ever were and could easily supply the new pluralism with material for common cause for years to come.

Of course there is nothing sacred about the ideas of the distant or even the recent past. On the contrary, one good reason for reclaiming and joining in conversations about education in which the "old-timers" in our discipline participated is that the ideas of yore need to be scrutinized, analyzed, and revised, over and over again. Another reason is that a discipline that treats the cultural wealth it has so far produced as a living presence does not have to reinvent the wheel. And last but not least, when the history of educational thought is passed down to each new generation of philosophers of education as a living legacy rather than a dead relic, newcomers to our field can take pride in the knowledge that they have entered a discipline with a distinguished past.

As for the present, I thank Leonard Waks for this second series of *Leaders in Philosophy of Education*. These memoirs give me great delight. They testify that the field I entered so many decades ago, and fell madly in love with, continues to thrive.

Jane Roland Martin
Professor of Philosophy Emerita
University of Massachusetts, Boston
April 2014

LEONARD J. WAKS

INTRODUCTION: LEADERS IN PHILOSOPHY OF EDUCATION AFTER 1980

This volume of the *Leaders in Educational Studies* series presents the self-portraits of 18 philosophers of education influential after 1980. They are selected from the United States, Canada, the United Kingdom, New Zealand, the Netherlands, Belgium, and Norway. While I make no claim that these individuals are *the* leaders, taken as a group they represent the vibrant state of the field today.

The first volume of *Leaders in Philosophy of Education* (Waks, 2008) presented autobiographical essays by 24 philosophers of education writing in English who entered the field in the 1960s and 1970s. The authors were all situated in North America or the United Kingdom. At that time the field was dominated by analytical philosophy. Richard S. Peters, a leading British philosopher, spent a year with Israel Scheffler at Harvard in 1960 prior to taking up his professorship at University of London's Institute of Education, and the two scholars forged a vision of the field which soon became dominant. Their students took up philosophy of education posts and saw themselves as working on a common intellectual project. They formed graduate programs and created new scholarly journals for the field. Warm collegial relationships and personal friendships were forged across the Atlantic.

Those working in Australia and New Zealand were excluded from that volume, as I lacked sufficient awareness of developments there, though had I been more in tune with them James Marshall would surely have been included.[1] Michael Peters and Denis Phillips, both originating 'down under,' had taken up positions in the United States (Peters had first moved to Glasgow) and were influential figures at the time of publication. Leading philosophers of education working on the European continent who came of age in the 1960s and 1970s were also excluded, because, again, I lacked sufficient awareness of European work and because on the whole European philosophers of education were not influential in the English language conversation in the field at that time.

Those entering the field in the 1980s – and included in this volume – have faced a very different situation. First, scholars from Australia and New Zealand have been more effectively linked to the Anglo-American conversation, which has also clearly expanded to include scholars working on the European continent. Second, European philosophy – and especially the post-modernist trend represented by Derrida, Levinas and Foucault – is now as potent an intellectual source in that discussion as Anglo-American philosophy. Third, those entering the field after 1980 entered a discussion profoundly shaped by the 1968 student revolts, the women's movement and new generations of feminist thought, the Vietnam War, and economic globalization, among other events. Philosophy of education has taken an exacting critical stance toward educational projects of the neo-liberal state, and perhaps partly in response, the institutional support for philosophy of education as a field of study has suffered. The course in philosophy of education has been all but eliminated from undergraduate teacher preparation programs, and in many cases senior professors in the field have not been replaced upon retirement. Paradoxically, a considerable number of very talented young people have entered the field, although many have obtained university positions in posts not explicitly labeled 'philosophy of education.'

I begin by situating the contributors to this volume, and where relevant, indicating how they came to join the in the conversation of philosophy of education. Then I will tease out some of the main themes in the works of the contributors, and suggest a way for the field to move forward from here.

THE PATH TO PHILOSOPHY

Each contributor has his or her own path of entry to the professional conversation in philosophy of education. This is a relatively esoteric field; even philosophy majors are unlikely to encounter it in their university studies as it is, for the most part, stuck away in schools or departments of education; even the links tentatively formed after 1960 with department of philosophy have frayed in recent years. How did the authors in this volume find their way to this field of study?

Many speak of the tortuous, contingent, serendipitous path that led them to this field. Most started as unusually bookish and inquisitive children who fell in love with philosophy at first sight. Boler writes, "I have always believed I was born a philosopher and it has been a primary identification in the world, even beyond more materialist ones including gender, race and class." Burbules' questions about how to be a good person led first to the study of religion, and then existential philosophy. Curren was attracted from a young age to libraries and bookstores; reading "set his mind on fire." Diller had a "lifelong penchant for philosophical speculation;" Hansen, a recurring but "unanticipated feeling of wonder" that led to a study of "philosophy as the art of living." Howe became "infected with philosophy" early on, while Laird "fell in love with wisdom" while attending a broad church-related secondary school imbued with existential theology. Lovlie took joy in reading as "the door to freedom" leading to "a journey of wonderment." Roberts loved to read and ponder existential questions from childhood. Stengel felt a "calling" to philosophy and to challenging limiting expectations. Todd took deep pleasure in reading as "feeling her way into situations and allowing them to speak to her."

This love of reading and learning led many toward the study of either education or philosophy in their baccalaureate years. Boler, Curren and Howe majored in philosophy as undergrads. Smeyers, Masschelein, and Roberts majored in educational studies programs with strong philosophical components. Biesta became a teacher, earned a teaching certificate, and enrolled in university with a major in Pedagogics that had a strong philosophical component. Smith studied classics and philosophy, became an uncertified teacher, and like Biesta took a certificate course and then undertook formal work in educational studies. Some took disciplinary detours: Burbules, Diller, and Stengel came to philosophy by way of religious studies; Hansen came to philosophy of education from history, Todd from art history, Laird from architecture, Kerr and Griffiths from Physics.

Eventually, the Anglo-American contributors found their way to the conversation of philosophy of education. Boler was introduced to philosophy of education by Deanne Bogdan, who directed her to the journal *Educational Theory* and to PES, where she met such fellow grad sudents as Cris Mayo and Natasha Levinson as well as more senior scholars including Nick Burbules, Jim Garrison (first series of *Leaders in Philosophy of Education)*, and Lynda Stone. Burbules in turn studied at Stanford under Denis Phillips (first series of *Leaders in Philosophy of Education*) and Arturo Pacheco (who had been my student during my Stanford years). Curren, who had been a teacher and enthusiastic reader of the education literature, earned a doctorate in philosophy and obtained a joint appointment in philosophy and education at Rochester; he soon enjoyed lively conversations with Emily Robertson and Thomas Green (first *Leaders*) at nearby Syracuse University. Diller worked in religious education, and encountered Israel Scheffler and Jane Roland Martin (first *Leaders*) when she went to Harvard for graduate studies. Griffiths became a teacher, took evening courses in philosophy at the University of Bristol, and then a Masters with Gordon Reddiford, who had studied at the University of London's Institute of Education with Richard Peters and Paul Hirst (first *Leaders*). Hansen did a Masters in teaching, and then a doctorate in philosophy of education with Philip Jackson and Sophie Haroutunian-Gordon (first *Leaders*). Kerr was a doctoral student of Jonas Soltis (first *Leaders*), who like Jane Martin and Harvey Siegel (first *Leaders)* had earned his doctorate at Harvard with Israel Scheffler. Laird studied philosophy of education at Cornell with Bob Gowin, but was led into the contemporary conversation by Ann Diller and Jane Roland Martin. Roberts studied education at the University of Auckland under Colin Lankshear, James Marshall, and Michael Peters (first *Leaders*), and was introduced to both the Anglo-American and European traditions in philosophy and philosophy of education even as an undergraduate. Smith studied Anglo-American philosophy at Oxford, and analytical philosophy of education during his teacher training course at the University of London's Institute of Education, before doing his doctorate under Robert Deardon, who had studied under Richard Peters and Paul Hirst. Stengel learned European philosophy during her graduate work in Religious Studies at Catholic University, and Anglo-American philosophy and philosophy of education at University of Pittsburgh, where she studied under David Engle, who like Kerr had studied with Jonas Soltis at Teachers College. Howe did a bachelors and masters in philosophy, and a joint philosophy and education doctorate with a thesis on the logic of evaluation; he connected himself more closely to the professional conversation in philosophy of education through active participation in the Philosophy of Education Society.

THE EXPANDED CONVERSATION

The European and Anglo-American traditions in educational philosophy and theory have been quite distinct. Although drawing on a common trunk of classical texts – from Plato and Aristotle through Locke, Rousseau and Kant, they had earlier divided (with many exceptions) into Continental vs. English Empiricist schools by the eighteenth century and branched out even more during the twentieth century. Contemporary Europeans have drawn heavily upon German phenomenology from Husserl to Heidegger, the German Frankfurt School of critical theory, and French existentialism. Americans have grounded their work in pragmatism, and after 1960, in the British analytical philosophy school shaped by Richard Peters, Paul Hirst and Israel Scheffler. As Paul Smeyers notes in his chapter, the Europeans have largely regarded analytic philosophy as trivial, while the Americans and British have largely rejected twentieth century European philosophy as unphilosophical – and incoherent – rubbish. So how did this chasm get crossed after 1980? How has philosophy of education in English been able to draw from both traditions?

First, some Europeans with prior training in European philosophy were attracted to the Anglo-American approach, came to the United States or United Kingdom as visiting scholars, and remained active in the Anglo-American conversation. Biesta studied pedagogics at the University of Leiden, where he took an additional one year program in philosophy, not least because he was inspired by the work of Ben Spiecker, a figure very much at home in Anglo-American philosophy of education – he had, for example, presented at PESGB and contributed to the *festschrift* for Israel Scheffler. Biesta earned a masters and doctors degree in pedagogics at Leiden, writing theses on John Dewey under the direction of Siebren Miedema, who urged him to link with English language scholars. In addition he studied philosophy in Rotterdam, also earning a masters. Biesta then spent time as a visiting scholar in the United States studying Dewey and Mead, re-located to the United Kingdom, and finally returned to Europe in 2012. Although Biesta consciously remained at the margins of British philosophy of education when working in the U. K., he has been an influential figure in the United States, serving on the board of the John Dewey Society and as president of the Philosophy of Education Society (the first president not based in North America).

Lovlie was educated in the German critical tradition, but "became an Anglophile." He contributed to the Norwegian critique of positivism, which connected him to the work of Karl Popper, an Austrian philosopher teaching in London, whose work had become central to Anglo-American philosophy of science. Lovlie' teacher Hans Skjeivheim, the "spiritual father of Norwegian philosophy of education," engaged him in a critique of American experimental psychology – an off-shoot of positivism – that in Skjeivheim's work extended as well to Dewey. Lovlie later went to Cambridge as a visiting scholar, where he met

Paul Hirst (first *Leaders*) and Terry McLaughlin, two leaders in English philosophy of education.

Smeyers did his bachelor's degree in pedagogics, a field grounded in European philosophy, but then chose to write his master's thesis on Richard Peters and his doctoral thesis on Wittgenstein. He attended University of London's Institute of Education as a visiting scholar, and has subsequently been active in the American Philosophy of Education Society, PESGB, and the International Network of Philosophers of Education (INPE), and on the editorial boards of the *Journal of Philosophy of Education, Educational Theory, Educational Philosophy and Theory, Studies in Philosophy and Education*, and *Ethics and Education*. Smeyers has also been active in study groups spanning North America, the U.K., and the European continent, and has brought other Europeans – including Jan Messchelein – into the broader conversation.

How has the European tradition in philosophy, and especially the post-modern trend, entered the conversation. One might think that the Europeans simply brought it with them as they joined the international discussion, but that would not be accurate. In some cases, the ground was laid by Anglo-American contributors' earliest engagements with philosophy. Burbules notes his early interest in existentialism and his encounters under Art Pacheco's influence with the Frankfurt school; Diller, Laird and Stengel mention introductions to existential theology in religious studies; Hansen his engagement with Nietzsche, Sartre and Camus in college. Beyond that, two bridging figures – James Marshall and Paul Smeyers – have been particularly influential. It was Marshall, Roberts' teacher at Auckland, who got Biesta interested in Derrida, and connected to Smeyers through mutual interests in Wittgenstein and post-modern ideas. Smeyers in turn was central to the growing interest in post-modern philosophy in the U.K., maintaining a study group with Nigel Blake, Paul Standish and Richard Smith that led to many publications including the *Blackwell Handbook in Philosophy of Education* (Blake et al., 2003) – a reference volume that put a Anglo-European frame around the field. Editor-in-Chief positions at both of the journals explicitly founded to give voice to the Anglo-American analytic philosophy program – *The Journal of Philosophy of Education* and *Studies in Philosophy and Education* – both were taken up by philosophers of education influenced by European post-modern ideas: Smith and Biesta.

The feminist movement in philosophy of education – with its focus on difference, otherness and relatedness – themes explored by Derrida and Levinas – has also been an important factor in the spread of post-modern thinking in the field. Derrida's diagnosis of binary thinking and his strategy of inverting binaries, for example, have been important moves in 'third generation' feminist thought. Feminist philosophy study groups in both North America and the United Kingdom have been significant sites for the spread of such ideas. Jane Roland Martin and Ann Diller, both students of Israel Scheffler, were influential in the PHEADRA study group in the United States; Griffiths in a feminist reading group in philosophy in England. All three had been trained in analytic philosophy, but the feminist philosophers they met also drew upon phenomenology and existentialism and post-modernist/ post-structuralist philosophy. It was in such groups that Laird and Griffiths – and other feminist philosophers of education – first encountered Foucault, Derrida and Levinas as well as Luce Irigaray and Judith Butler, feminist philosophers influenced by them.

CURRENT THEMES

The contributors to this volume have emphasized some themes in their work. Here I indicate a few of these. Readers will probably discover others.

1. The desire for a more personal diction, a language and tone for philosophy writing that more adequately captures the unique, personal intent of individual philosophers and speaks to the more intimate, personal dimension of their readers.

Several contributors note their attraction to philosophy as resulting from personal questions arising in childhood or adolescence. Burbules turned to philosophy to learn how he could become a better person, Curren to gain insight into the racial injustice sustained by his own family, Hansen to sustain his sense of wonder and offer a guide to the art of living.

Many found sustenance in literature and existential philosophy, but not always in the philosophical diction of professional philosophers of education. Kerr came to philosophy from physics, and found the transition easy because she could do analytic philosophy the same way she had done math and physics – operating as an arbitrary point in space rather than a unique person. Kerr withdrew from philosophy writing when she could no longer find herself – her own distinct voice – in it and had no way of assisting her graduate students express their distinct selves in their graduate student writing. Some of our contributors found their voices through new post-modern philosophical dictions and the risks they encouraged, or by incorporating literary sources directly into their work. Kerr, for her part, developed a form of subjective pedagogy – starting with each student's self and its pre-professional philosophy problems and concerns, and then blending in philosophical texts – generously read – as sources of personal solutions.

2. A re-positioning or de-positioning with respect to analytic philosophy of education.

Biesta, though drawing on American pragmatism, chose to remain marginal to British philosophy even after relocating to England. Burbules, though trained by analytic philosopher Denis Phillips, rejected the style of analytic philosophy discussion – the "shoot out at the O. K. corral" approach; he has sought to understand dialogical approaches to discussion and their limits, drawing on Habermas, Gadamer, and other European sources. Curren, who was drawn to the study of education through Kozol's *Death at an Early Age* and Freire's *Pedagogy of the Oppressed*, had from the start distaste for philosophical abstractions typical of analytic philosophy; like Burbules, Diller and Howe, he has favored educational scholarship firmly situated in practical realities. Although trained in analytic philosophy, Griffiths never quite 'fit the mold.' Kerr, whose first books were models of analytic philosophy, withdrew from philosophy writing when she found she could not bring herself as a unique person into her work. Laird's doctoral study of co-education was blocked when her advisor insisted that 'co-education' was not a "concept" and hence could not be subjected to conceptual analysis. Smith was trained in analytic philosophy of education but rejected it because in his words, (i) the leading practitioners were not clear about what a 'concept' was, their analyses were, in his view, linguistic legislation in disguise; (ii) they saw their modest or inconsequential conclusions as a 'plus,' and (iii) because work in analytic philosophy of education was 'pedestrian.'

3. The attraction of 'deconstruction' as a new method or anti-method, a way of reading, a conscious attempt to tease out and confront binaries hiding implicit comparative value judgments, and intervening to invert them.

No fewer than 8 of the seventeen contributors – Biesta, Laird, Lovlie, Masschelein, Roberts, Smeyers, Smith, and Stengel cite Derrida as a significant influence, while Griffiths speaks more generally of French post-modernist influences. Biesta speaks of Derrida as affirming not just what is excluded (i.e., the de-valued component of the binary), but also of what lies outside the currently conceptualizable –what Derrida calls "the incalculable." Derrida's attempt to make room for the arrival of what cannot currently be expressed is, Biesta says, a "thoroughly educational gesture." Lovlie finds reading Derrida a "relief from the relentless rationality" of other philosophical texts (he mentions Habermas, but might well include analytic philosophy). He appreciates Derrida's deconstructive way of making "forms of life tremble and dissolve from within," like "organisms and their own autoimmunity." Like Biesta, he sees this move as opening the way for experiences without origins or finalities – openings for the new and unprecedented (connecting his concerns with those of Hannah Arendt). Masschelein, on the other hand, finds Derrida's notion that we are all captured by language, especially when coupled with Foucault's idea that we are all disciplined by omnipotent power structures implicit in the language of power/knowledge, a path toward nihilistic impotence; he seeks construction of new 'languages' and new possibilities of expression and understanding.

4. A recognition prompted by Levinas of the opacity and ultimate unknowability of other persons, combined with recognition of the claims each one makes upon me.

Seven of our contributors – all of those mentioning Derrida as an influence except Laird – also mention Levinas.

Biesta mentions Levinas and Arendt as influencing his "ethico-political turn," which had already been waiting in the wings in his earlier writings; although he doesn't expand upon this here, his recent work on 'pragmatic readings of pragmatism' suggests that his early focus on Dewey and Mead had already prepared him for his more radical embrace of the primacy of the practical. In particular, Levinas helped him to understand uniqueness as irreplaceability, because the claims made upon me 'single me out' and so in taking up responsibility for them I can realize my unique singularity. Masschelein came to Levinas, on the way to Buber and later Ranciere, in exploring emancipatory pedagogy. For Todd, Levinas was useful in facing the sense of mystery in encounters with works of art and with other people. He helped her with her struggle to "put into words things for which I never had a language."

4. A rejection of the initiation metaphor central to Richard Peters' conception of education, and a new interest in radical beginnings – and hence in the philosophy and educational writings of Hannah Arendt.

Biesta makes this rejection clearest in his essay "Education, Not Initiation" (1996), but the theme also echoes through his book *Beyond Learning*, where he sets out a critique of humanism as placing limits on human nature. The Peters – Hirst "forms of knowledge" curriculum, positing seven distinct (and at least relatively fixed) logical structures within which thinking is confined, certainly appears to limit humanity's possibilities. As Biesta explains in his contribution to this volume, Arendt helped him "think of education in terms of how newcomers come 'into the world.'" He adds,

> Education as 'coming into the world' not only gives educators a responsibility for the new beginnings, but also for the plural or 'worldly' quality of the world, as it is only 'under the condition of plurality' (Arendt) that everyone has a possibility to bring their beginnings into the world.

The contrast between the Peters-Hirst program, with its already fixed forms of knowledge and thinking, and its view of education as initiation into the long-standing cognitive activities and practices that embody them, on the one hand, and Arendt's concern with the emergent, with new possibilities in individuals and new beginnings in practice, could not be starker. If education is about how 'newcomers' with emergent possibilities come into an open world, then as Biesta had already argued, it can have nothing much to do with initiation. I'll have more to say about this contrast in the Afterword to this volume.

Masschelein sees Arendt, along with Foucault, as guides in dropping the 'critical judgmental attitude' of conventional philosophy, an attitude that seeks to check and limit others and tell them how to think. Instead, these philosophers saw their works as "experiments" – ways to think and live in the world "otherwise." This phrase places the emphasis on stepping beyond the given and coming into unique new possibilities of existence – living otherwise.

For Todd, Arendt holds a special place because she acknowledges the "miracle of birth" – that is, of coming into existence as an actor within the polis, a birth that can only be realized in relation to others. Individuality as relatedness is taken up again in the next theme.

5. A critique of ontological individualism, and recognition of the connected or distributed nature of human selves, knowledge, thinking and understanding.

The idea Todd associates with Arendt that individuals are constituted by their relations, has been prominent in feminist accounts of teaching and scholarship. As mentioned earlier, study and writing groups have also been characteristic of feminist intellectual practice, as noted by Diller, Laird and Griffiths. And these study groups provide concrete, public and political reference points for the relations that shape the individualities of these participants. But these recognitions of relatedness are not restricted to feminism. Lovlie's essay brings out the notion of mind as distributed intelligence in Dewey, while Masschelein also highlights co-production of knowledge and understanding through dialogue – "the need for others for thoughts to come – one cannot think by oneself." For Masschelein the general term for such co-productive relations is 'friendship,' and in his writing practice he has turned to collaborative authorship as an "articulation of friendship," a notion that echoes formulations in the works of both Dewey and Ivan Illich Perhaps the most radical expression of this view has recently been expressed by Stephen Downes, in his "connectivist" theory of learning, according to which only networked groups can think or know; individuals can only do so in a derivative sense, *via* their participation in networks.

6. An ever-deepening recognition of chance, contingency, complexity, and with it, a deeper critique of educational schemes based on tight means-ends reasoning – not merely because they are reductive or harmful, but because they are 'pure fantasy.'

All contributors to this volume, and perhaps all educational scholars trained in the humanities disciplines, reject – perhaps even detest – the imposition of technocratic norms in education: specific learning objectives, high stakes standardized tests, evaluation and award of merit pay to teachers based on test scores. This rejection was already marked in the analytic philosophy period; Petrie, Strike, Waks and others established themselves in the field by making trenchant arguments for the irrationality of such approaches, but framed the flaws as primarily philosophical or logical. The current group of leaders extends these earlier critiques. They locate these technocratic moves as components of the neo-liberal project – of rendering knowledge and teaching as commodities within capitalist markets, and introducing market mechanisms in education to achieve market efficiencies in learning. Teachers and schools are, in this logic, set in competition to one another and to alternative means including new information technologies, in supplying knowledge(s) to student consumers as market goods. Researchers are, in turn, viewed as competing to supply new knowledge(s) to markets where they may be converted into "intellectual property," capitals that can be patented and copyrighted, bought and sold. The neo-liberal approach eliminates the 'social' – the idea that education serves society by coordinating common learning so that we can get along as civic friends, cooperate despite our many differences, and contribute to a common pool of social goods including non-rival knowledge shared and used by all, common public goods that should be provided by socially – through efforts of the state and civil society outside of market mechanisms.

Our contributors, on the whole, reject the neo-liberal project in education. But, with a growing appreciation of contingency, chance, and complexity in human affairs, many have come to regard the dream of controlling learning by adjusting techniques to obtain highly specific learning objectives as insane, based on delusions of grandeur that rival those of petty dictators. Bill Doll, who first placed the notion of complexity into the heart of educational studies, pointed Biesta toward a deeper study of complexity. Todd adds that "one of the rough threads of life has to do with chance and serendipity." Smith speaks of the "particular irony (of) relishing (Martha Nussbaum's) emphasis on the inevitability of chance in human life while the educationists around me spoke insistently of school effectiveness and education as a totally reliable technology."

Readers will find additional themes, and perhaps question my interpretations. I invite further commentary on the upshot of these essays. In an Afterword I suggest a path forward for our field.

A NOTE ON SELECTION

In selecting the contributors to the current volume I was greatly assisted by a number of colleagues and friends – in senior, mid-career, and junior positions in North America, the United Kingdom, Europe and Australasia. I asked for lists my correspondents considered the most influential voices, and then considered for selection only those mentioned on at least two lists. I excluded those who had entered the field after the mid-1990s (making an exception for Sharon Todd, who was 'nominated' by many colleagues, and who has certainly been an influential voice in the field). Most of the contributors were born in the 1950s – making them a decade younger (or more) than those featured in the first series of *Leaders*.

The volume would be more balanced had it included contributions by Eammon Callen, Harry Brighouse, and Paul Standish. Callen, however, declined to participate due to health concerns; Brighouse and Standish initially expressed interest but did not submit essays – perhaps they may be included in a later series. The contingent of younger philosophers of education – those who were born in the 1960s and 1970s, and entered the field in the 1990s and early 2000s, includes many talented scholars – I mention Rene Arcilla, Eduardo Duarte, Judith Suizza, Suzanne Rice, Kathleen Knight Abowitz, Michael Hand, Claudia Ruitenberg, Andrea English, Brian Warnick, David Waddington, Michele Moses and Dianne Geruluk merely to provide a flavor for this generation, as there are many others making significant contributions. This generation displays a great abundance of talent and energy. But it will also require a lot of savvy and considerable luck for them to restore philosophy of education to a prominent institutional position in schools of education and teacher education programs, and to make its impact felt in public deliberations about the future direction of educational policy and practice.

NOTES

[1] Bruce Haynes included a brief self-portrait by Marshall in his special issue celebrating the 40th anniversary of the Philosophy of Education Society of Australia. *Educational Philosophy and Theory*, *41*(7), 774-776.

REFERENCES

Biesta G. (1996). Education, not initiation. In *Philosophy of Education 1996*, online at http://ojs.ed.uiuc.edu/index.php/pes/article/view/2247/942

Biesta G. (2009). How to use pragmatism pragmatically?: Suggestions for the twenty-first century. *Education and Culture*, *25*(2).

Blake, N, Smeyers, P., Smith, R., & Standish, P. (Eds.). (2003). *The Blackwell guide to the philosophy of education*. Oxford: Blackwell.

Waks, L. (2008). *Leaders in philosophy of education*. Rotterdam: Sense Publishers.

GERT BIESTA

FROM EXPERIMENTALISM TO EXISTENTIALISM

Writing in the Margins of Philosophy of Education

EARLY YEARS: 1957-1990

I was born in Rotterdam, the Netherlands, in 1957, twelve years after the end of the Second World War, and grew up in a city centre that was still largely empty as a result of the May 1940 bombings. My daily walk to school thus took me along many building sites and the sound of pile drivers was constantly in the background for many years to come. I cannot deny that I had an early fascination for education. As a child one of the first jobs I imagined I wanted to have, was that of an architect in order then to become a teacher of architects. While my (Montessori) kindergarten and (regular) primary school were rather easy and uneventful, secondary school turned out to be more challenging, so I only just managed to get through. As economics was one of the very few subjects in which I had done well, I decided to study it at university. I soon found out, however, that it was not really 'my' subject, so after a year I switched to theology. This was a much more enjoyable experience, but a rather serious car accident two years into my studies put an abrupt end to it. This put me in a position where I had to reconsider my options, and I decided to look for work rather than continuing at university. I found a job in a hospital and took courses to become a radiographer.

After I had obtained my diploma I had the good fortune of being asked to contribute to the teaching of radiographers. For the next 10 years I taught physics to student radiographers. In the first years I did this alongside my job as a radiographer, but after having completed a two year part-time teacher certification programme, I was eager to deepen my knowledge of education, so I decided to return to university, now to study education. Whereas in most English speaking countries the study of education tends to happen in the context of teacher education, in the Netherlands education – in Dutch: pedagogiek – exists as an academic discipline in its own right and it was this discipline that I focused on for the next four years at the University of Leiden. My initial plan was to specialise in curriculum and instruction, but I became increasingly interested in the theoretical and historical aspects of education, and thus decided to focus on this area instead.

It was here that I became interested in philosophy, first and foremost through the work of Ben Spiecker, Professor at the Free University Amsterdam, who had written a number of exciting essays on Wittgenstein and education. In the second year of my studies I followed an additional one year programme in philosophy. This covered the philosophical 'basics,' and I particularly enjoyed logic, epistemology, philosophy of science, and Greek philosophy, including a superb course on Aristotle. The third year in Leiden was devoted again to pedagogiek, although I was able to make connections with my developing interest in philosophy. Through courses from Vygotskij-specialist René van der Veer I became interested in Piaget's genetic epistemology, while Rien van IJzendoorn, stimulated my interested in the philosophy of educational and social research. Courses from Siebren Miedema not only fuelled my interest in critical theory (Habermas), critical pedagogy (both the German and the North American variety), and the theory and philosophy of educational and social research, but also brought me into contact with the work of John Dewey. Dewey's work had been largely absent from the educational conversation in the Netherlands since the early 1950s and had only received sporadic attention from Dutch philosophers. I eventually decided to write a Master's thesis on Dewey under Siebren's supervision.

I further pursued my interest in philosophy through a newly established programme in the philosophy of the social sciences at Erasmus University Rotterdam, which I started in my final year as a pedagogiek student, and finished successfully three years later. My studies not only allowed me to deepen my understanding of logic, epistemology and the philosophy of science, but also brought me into contact with analytic philosophy, phenomenology, existentialism, postmodern and post-structural philosophy (particularly the work of Foucault), and – just emerging at the time – the neo-pragmatism of Richard Rorty. Rorty's Philosophy and the Mirror of Nature (Rorty, 1979) formed the framework for the thesis I wrote, which focused on paradigmatic pluralism in educational research in the Netherlands. Whilst still studying philosophy, I was fortunate to receive a four year studentship to conduct PhD research on Dewey, focusing on his views about the relationship between knowledge and action and the implications for educational and social research. I conducted my PhD research at Leiden University under the supervision of Siebren Miedema and Rien van IJzendoorn. I worked closely with Siebren, particularly on the study of Dewey, and many of my early publications were co-authored with him, including a joint book (Miedema & Biesta, 1989). I obtained my PhD in 1992 (Biesta, 1992), but again was lucky in having been selected for a lectureship in education at the University of Groningen before I had finished my PhD. I thus started my academic career there in the summer of 1990, teaching courses in pedagogiek and in the philosophy of educational and social research.

An important aspect of the early years of my career was the fact that I did not develop my intellectual and academic identity within philosophy or philosophy of education, but within pedagogiek. That is why up to the present day I prefer to refer to myself as an educationalist (or in Dutch: a pedagoog) with a particular interest and expertise in philosophy, and not as a philosopher and only hesitantly as a philosopher of education – my hesitation having to do with the fact that 'philosopher of education' remains a rather imperfect translation of my identity as a pedagoog and my commitment to pedagogiek. The question of the differences between pedagogiek and philosophy of education has continued to intrigue me, and became even more of an issue when I moved from the Netherlands to the UK (in 1999) and was faced in very concrete ways with the differences between the Continental and the Anglo-American 'construction' of the field – something I have explored since in a number of publications (for example, Biesta 2011a). This is why I have always felt to be working more in the margins of Anglo-American philosophy of education – and perhaps even more so with regard to the British variety than the one in North America – rather than at its centre.

The context in which I was a student of pedagogiek and philosophy was one of a rapid and radical transformation of the field of Dutch educational research and scholarship. If there was a 'Positivismusstreit' in educational research in the 1980s in the Netherlands – and I think there was – it was between two fundamentally different conceptions of empirical research, one that made a case for quantitative-explanatory research as the only properly scientific mode of research and one that tried to make a case for qualitative-interpretative research. The fact that quantitative-explanatory research – in the Dutch context often referred to as 'empirical-analytical' research – 'won,' is particularly significant when compared to developments in the English-speaking world. There the debate between 'quantitative' and 'qualitative' approaches was mainly about attempts from the side of qualitative approaches to overcome the hegemony of quantitative research so as to make a case for methodological pluralism. In the Netherlands, in contrast, there had actually been a long and flourishing tradition of interpretative research, particularly the phenomenology of the Utrecht School where, in the areas of education and developmental psychology, M.J. Langeveld was for a long time the leading figure. In the Netherlands the debate thus went in the opposite direction, that is, of quantitative-explanatory research trying to replace qualitative-interpretative research. The 'Streit' that was going on in the Netherlands was not only a battle about the 'right' or 'proper' form of empirical research, but was also directed against non-empirical forms of inquiry. It was as a result of this that theoretical and philosophical traditions became increasingly marginalised. Over time this led to what, in hindsight and from a distance, I would characterise as an academic mono-culture that, unlike what I was going to experience in the UK, left little room for other forms of empirical research and for non-empirical modes of inquiry and scholarship.

The transformation of educational research in the Netherlands also brought with it a strong push towards internationalisation. This definitely had an impact on my own formation as a researcher since I was encouraged early on to make connections with researchers and scholars in other countries and, given my interest in Dewey, particularly in North America. In 1988, the first year of my PhD, I attended the AERA conference in New Orleans and visited the Centre for Dewey Studies in Carbondale, then under the directorship of Jo-Ann Boydston, who was extremely helpful in the early stages of my PhD research. Since Dewey's collected works had not yet all been published, and since this was well before the age of the internet, my visits to Carbondale, and also to archives at Teachers College Columbia University and the University of Chicago, provided me with access to unique materials for my PhD. They also formed the beginning of my networks in North America, a process in which the John Dewey Society was particularly important.

THE NETHERLANDS: 1990-1999

The years in Groningen were stimulating and enjoyable, not only because there was a group of supportive colleagues who were willing to put trust in a relatively inexperienced lecturer, but also because in my teaching I could focus on 'my' subject, that of pedagogiek. This allowed me to deepen my understanding of Continental educational theory (and here I would particularly highlight the work of Dutch educationalists such as M.J. Langeveld, Nic. Perquin, Ben Spiecker and Jan Dirk Imelman, and of German theorists such as Klaus Mollenhauer and Klaus Schaller), and also of the forerunners of North American critical pedagogy, particularly the 'social reconstructionism' of authors such as George Counts. My main task during the first two years in Groningen was the completion of my PhD. Part of the work I did was a more or less straightforward reconstruction of Dewey's views on the relationship between knowledge and action. Yet I did not want to present Dewey's ideas as 'just another philosophical position' that either could be adopted or rejected. There was much in Dewey that I considered to be important for the discussion about the status of social and educational research – a discussion that, at the time, was still strongly influenced by the work of Karl Popper. Yet what troubled me about Dewey was the metaphysical framework that seemed to come with his ideas, a framework that was clearly rooted in secular naturalism and ultimately went back to Darwinism (something which Dewey explicitly acknowledged in his autobiographical essay From Absolutism to Experimentalism; Dewey, 1984[1930]).

My concerns partly had to do with Darwinism itself, which I saw as a rather limited and ultimately limiting understanding of the human condition, and partly with the scientism it seemed to bring in through the backdoor, something which Max Horkheimer in his book Eclipse of Reason indeed had identified as the main problem of Deweyan pragmatism (Horkheimer, 1947). I eventually found a way to resolve these issues through a paper Dewey had written relatively late in his career – called Experience, Knowledge and Value: A Rejoinder (Dewey, 1991[1939]) – which was a response to essays written about his work published in The Philosophy of John Dewey, edited by Paul A. Schilpp. This paper helped me to identify the problem that had motivated Dewey's intellectual and political 'project,' and thus allowed me to provide a pragmatic reading of Dewey's work, that is, to see it as an attempt to address a problem rather than as the articulation of a philosophical position (see also Biesta, 2009a). I could show that Dewey's philosophy was actually motivated by a critique of scientism – that is, a critique of the idea that science is the only valid kind of knowledge – and a critique of a cognitive worldview in which it is assumed that knowledge is the only 'real' way in which we are connected to the world. That is why, in my reconstruction of Dewey's work, I made the case that 'crisis in culture' to which he was responding had to be understood as a crisis in rationality, and that his ultimate project was aimed at restoring rationality to all domains of human experience rather than to confine it to the domain of cognition or, even worse, to the domain of scientific knowledge.

What was particularly interesting about Dewey's work was that he was able to criticise the hegemony of scientific rationality without having to reject the technological and practical 'fruits' of what goes on under the name of 'science.' Dewey thus opened up a third way between a wholesale rejection of science on the one hand and a wholesale acceptance of science on the other. This became an important theme in my own thinking as it allowed for a much more precise critique of the hegemony of the scientific worldview and scientific rationality, and also a much more mature engagement with the possibilities and limitations of what goes on under the name of 'science.' This line of thought was further reinforced through my reading of Bruno Latour's *Science in Action* (Latour, 1987), an author whose work has continued to play an important role in my work on knowledge and the curriculum (for example Biesta & Miedema, 1990; Biesta, 2002, 2012a), well before a rather watered-down version of his ideas became fashionable as 'actor-network theory.' While over the years I have become increasingly critical of key-aspects of Dewey's work – particularly his views on democracy, which I have characterised as social more than as political (see Biesta, 2007a, 2010a), and the totalising tendencies in his conception of communication (see Biesta, 2010b) – I find Dewey's wider project still very valuable for an effective critique of contemporary forms of scientism (for example, Biesta, 2009b, 2011b).

During my work on the PhD I had increasingly become interested in the educational dimensions of pragmatism, particularly with regard to the theory of communication in Dewey's work, and this topic became a central interest in the years following my PhD. In the first paper I wrote on the topic (Biesta, 1994) I explored the relationships between critical theory (Habermas) and pragmatism (Dewey, Mead) around the idea of 'practical intersubjectivity.' Inspiration for this partly came from my own readings of Dewey, partly from the work of Hans Joas on Mead (see Joas, 1985), and also from Jan Masschelein's PhD thesis on Habermas, communication and education (Masschelein, 1987). I presented a first version at AERA in 1993. It was here that I met Jim Garrison – a meeting that formed the start of many important conversations about Dewey and pragmatism in the years to come. The paper was accepted for publication in *Educational Theory*, my first journal article in English. Jim Garrison subsequently invited me to contribute to a book he was editing on the new scholarship on Dewey, and in my contribution I further pursued my interests in the implications of Dewey's understanding of communication for education (Biesta, 1995a).

In 1993 I had moved from Groningen to the University of Leiden to take up a lectureship in the department where I had studied pedagogiek and done my PhD. Fairly soon after I had started the opportunity arose to apply for a senior lectureship in pedagogiek at the University of Utrecht. As this would allow me to focus more strongly on pedagogiek and work more closely with Jan Dirk Imelman in the theory of education and Brita Rang in the history of education, I decided to apply. My application was successful so I moved to Utrecht in the spring of 1995 (unfortunately Imelman took early retirement soon after I had arrived, and Rang left for a Professorship in Frankfurt). In the autumn of 1994 I had submitted an application for a Spencer Postdoctoral Fellowship with the National Academy of Education USA – encouraged and endorsed by Jim Garrison and Ben Spiecker – and early in 1995 I learned that I had been selected. For the next two academic years I was therefore able to spend a considerable amount of time on research. In hindsight I would say that these years were truly formative for the development of my academic 'habitus.' The project I had submitted extended my explorations of pragmatism to the work of George Herbert Mead. I spent part of the time in the Netherlands but also at Virginia Tech with Jim Garrison. I also was able to study the George Herbert Mead papers at the University of Chicago. Here I discovered an unpublished set of lecture notes of a course Mead had given on the philosophy of education. I eventually managed to publish the lectures in English and in German translation, co-edited with Daniel Tröhler (Mead, 2008a, 2008b). The Spencer project led to the publication of a number of articles on Mead (Biesta, 1998, 1999) – who I actually found a stronger theorist than Dewey. 1994 was also the first year that I attended the annual conference of the Philosophy of Education Society USA, and I have returned almost every year up to the present day.

Perhaps the most significant event during my time as a Spencer postdoc was the invitation I received from Jim Marshall in New Zealand to contribute a chapter on Derrida in a collection he was editing. At the time I had only heard of Derrida, but had never had had a chance to read his work properly. I told Jim that although I had no special knowledge of Derrida I would be very happy to take on the challenge. Jim took the risk and this set me off on a sustained period of reading. The encounter with Derrida's work had a profound impact on my thinking. Whereas up that point I had hoped that pragmatism could provide an 'answer' to the postmodern critique of the modern 'philosophy of consciousness' (Habermas) by replacing a consciousness-centred philosophy with a communication-centred philosophy, Derrida helped me to realise that the point was not to find a new and better starting-point or foundation for philosophy, but rather to question the very possibility of articulating and identifying such a foundation. Derrida also showed me, however, that the way out of this predicament was not to become anti-foundational – the route taken by Rorty and other anti-foundational (neo)pragmatists – as such a rejection of foundations would end up with the same problem, namely that it also had to rely on some fixed and secure place from which foundations could be rejected. What I found in Derrida was the suggestion that as soon as we go near a foundation – either to accept it or reject it or to use it as a criterion to identify performative contradictions – we find a strange oscillation between the foundation and its rejection; an oscillation that cannot be stopped. It is this oscillation that Derrida referred to as 'deconstruction,' thus highlighting that deconstruction isn't a method and cannot be transformed into one (Derrida, 1991, p. 273), but that it is something that occurs or, as he put it, "cannot manage to occur ... wherever there is something rather than nothing" (Derrida & Ewald, 2001, p. 67).

The work of Derrida not only helped me to put pragmatism in perspective but also made it possible to articulate more clearly some of the problems I always had had with metaphysical readings of pragmatism that would just end up as another form of foundationalism. I thus started to argue that we needed a more radical understanding of intersubjectivity (Biesta, 1999) and eventually came to the conclusion that the only possible pragmatism would thus be a deconstructive pragmatism, one that acknowledges that communication is always 'in deconstruction' (Biesta, 2010b). The encounter with Derrida also allowed me to create an opening in the discussion about critique – both in philosophy and in education – showing both the problem with dogmatic forms of critique that relied on a (fixed) criterion or a (fixed) truth about the human being, and with transcendental forms of critique that relied on a similar foundational gesture by highlighting the occurrence of performative contradictions, that is, contradictions between utterances and their conditions of possibility. With Derrida I could show that the latter form of critique – quite prominent in the educational literature on critical thinking – relied on the assumption that it is possible to identify conditions of possibility, whereas Derrida would argue that such a gesture would at the same time reveal conditions of impossibility and can therefore not achieve what it intends (and pretends) to achieve (see Biesta & Stams, 2001). The shift from critique to deconstruction was particularly significant in light of my interest in North American critical pedagogy. I had been following the important work of its main proponents – Henry Giroux and Peter McLaren – for a good number of years, and was now able to raise some more precise concerns about the question as to what it actually means to be critical in and 'for' education (see Biesta, 1998).

Derrida's work also helped me to see that the point of deconstruction was not negative or destructive, but thoroughly affirmative, not just of what is excluded but more importantly from what is excluded from a particular 'system' or 'order' and yet makes such a 'system' or 'order' possible. That meant that deconstruction is not just affirmative of what is known to be excluded, but also of what lies outside of what is (currently) conceptualisable – something to which Derrida in some of his writings referred to as the 'incalculable.' I slowly began to see that to prepare for the arrival of the incalculable could be seen as a thoroughly educational gesture (Biesta, 2001) and also began to connect Derrida's suggestion that the affirmative 'nature' of deconstruction means that deconstruction is (driven by) justice with educational concerns and themes (Biesta, 2003).

The final way in which the encounter with Derrida was important for my further trajectory had to do with the fact that Derrida did not position deconstruction in epistemological terms but rather put ethico-political considerations at the (de)centre of his writings. This helped me to articulate more clearly what I had always thought that the postmodern turn was after (see Biesta, 1995b), namely that it did not want to replace epistemological objectivism with epistemological relativism – a misreading of postmodern thought that goes on until the present day – but rather wanted to call for a shift from an epistemological worldview where knowledge of the world is the first and final 'thing,' towards an ethico-political 'attitude' that puts ethical and political concerns at the centre of our being-in-the-world and sees knowledge always in relation to and derivative of it, rather than that it founds ethics and politics on some deeper knowledge about the world and/or the human being. Derrida thus helped me to achieve (or perhaps I should say: complete) an ethico-political 'turn' that, in a sense, had always already been waiting in the wings of my writings. With regard to this 'turn' two other philosophers became increasingly important and influential, one being Hannah Arendt and the other – who I had already encountered early on in my career but whose thought needed time to 'arrive' – being Emmanuel Levinas.

Looking back, the seven years after finishing my PhD in 1992 allowed me to explore a number of different themes and issues and engage with a number of different theorists and philosophers, so as to eventually arrive at a position where I felt that I was beginning to find my own voice and my own trajectory. The next period of about seven years – culminating in the publication in 2006 of my first monograph, *Beyond Learning* (Biesta, 2006; to date published in Swedish, Danish and Portuguese) – allowed me to pursue a number of these lines more confidently. Whereas in the 1990s my interest had been more strongly philosophical, educational themes, issues and concerns began to become more central in my reading, writing and research. Two further important events happened during this period. One was meeting Bill Doll who introduced me to complexity theory and provided generous enthusiasm for my work during a period where I was still searching for its direction. Through Bill I met Denise Egéa-Kuehne. Our shared interest in Derrida let to the publication of the first book length study on his work and education, simply titled *Derrida & Education* (Biesta & Egéa-Kuehne, 2001). The other was the invitation from Jim Garrison to take over as editor-in-chief of *Studies in Philosophy and Education*. I started to work on this behind the scenes in 1999 and became the journal's next editor in 2001.

Although my job in Utrecht provided me with interesting opportunities and interesting colleagues – including Bas Levering who, at the time was one of the few people in the country who continued to work within a much broader tradition of educational research and scholarship with clear connections back to the Utrecht School – I increasingly felt the need for a different, more plural intellectual context. Having briefly considered a move to North America, I was lucky to find a job in England. In the autumn of 1999 I thus took up a senior lectureship at the University of Exeter.

ENGLAND AND SCOTLAND: 1999-2012

My job in Exeter was designated as a senior lectureship in post-16 education, and thus had a clear focus on vocational and adult education. My teaching was partly connected to teacher education in those fields and partly involved working with teachers on masters and doctoral programmes. Unlike in the Netherlands, where universities are hierarchically structured and much time is spent making sure that everything has its 'proper' place – which creates difficulties for those individuals or areas of research that do not fit in such a system – what I encountered in Exeter was a much more open and much more horizontal academic culture where there was far less eagerness to tell others what they should do or be. This not only created a much greater degree of intellectual freedom but also made my own academic identity less fixed, which allowed me to pursue both theoretical-philosophical and empirical lines of work. I had the good fortune to work with Martin Bloomer, who eventually became Professor of Post-16 Education, and Rob Lawy, who had just started in Exeter as a postdoc. With Rob I began to develop my work on citizenship and democracy, resulting in a number of empirical studies on young people's citizenship (see, for example, Biesta, Lawy, & Kelly, 2009; Lawy et al., 2010) and more theoretical work on education, democracy and citizenship (for example Biesta & Lawy, 2006; Lawy & Biesta, 2006). The work on theory and policy of citizenship education and civic learning eventually ended up in a short book, published in 2011 (Biesta, 2011c – to date translated into Danish and Japanese).

Martin was key in developing my research interests in vocational education and adult education and generously involved me in a research proposal on learning and the life-course. The project was originally conceived as one on learning and identity; I suggested adding the theme of 'agency,' as I was interested in what people can do with their learning, rather than just who they become. Martin very sadly died in 2002, just after he had completed and submitted the proposal for what was to become the Learning Lives project (Biesta et al., 2011), still the first large-scale longitudinal study into learning, identity and agency in the life-course. At the time of his death, Martin was also co-directing a large scale study into the Further Education sector, called Transforming Learning Cultures in Further Education (see James & Biesta, 2007). I was asked to replace Martin on the project team. This not only meant that for the next 6 years I was strongly involved in major empirical projects working closely with a range of interesting and highly committed colleagues. It also brought me in touch with the overarching national research programme within which both projects were funded, the Teaching and Learning Research Programme (TLRP). All this work taught me a lot about the joys and the complexities of large-scale collaborative research, and provided a unique opportunity to connect with many educational researchers in the UK. Given my own predilections for theory and philosophy, these projects also convinced me of the need for the closer communication between empirical and theoretical work, rather than to think that theoretical – and perhaps even more so: philosophical – work should be conducted from the sideline, only referring to itself. My experiences not only showed me that such connections were possible, but also that they were necessary for the healthy development of the field of educational research.

In 2002 the University of Exeter promoted me to Professor of Educational Theory and soon afterwards I became Director of Research of the School of Education – a position that provided me with valuable insights in the running of higher education institutions and the more political dimension of higher education policy in the UK. Under the leadership of vice-chancellor Steve Smith Exeter developed a clear sense of direction, and it was enjoyable and instructive to experience the transformation of the university at a close distance. Although administration, empirical research and research management took a significant amount of my time, I was able to continue my theoretical and philosophical work as well. *Derrida & Education* (Biesta & Egéa-Kuehne, 2001) appeared in 2001 and *Pragmatism and Educational Research*, co-authored with Nick Burbules, in 2003 (Biesta & Burbules, 2003). For the development of my more theoretical work I benefitted tremendously from a visiting professorship at Örebro University, Sweden (from 2001 until 2008) followed by a similar post at Mälardalen University, Sweden (from 2006 until 2013). The focus of the work was on education and democratic citizenship and the many courses for doctoral students I taught there allowed me to explore key aspects of the discussion in detail with great students and great colleagues, particularly Tomas Englund and Carsten Ljunggren. The collaboration with Carl Anders Säfström had already started in the 1990s, and his move to Mälardalen University made it possible to establish an institutional basis for our collaboration. I had met Tomas and Carl Anders in the early 1990s when Siebren Miedema and I organised a small conference on pragmatism in Europe. Lars Løvlie, from Oslo University, was one of the other participants and he has been an ongoing source of support and inspiration throughout my career. Also significant were my yearly visits to the annual conference of the USA Philosophy of Education Society and the American Educational Research Association, particularly to participate in activities of the Philosophical Studies SIG, of which I became programme chair and, after that, chair, and the John Dewey Society (of which I was a board member).

Publication-wise, I was particularly pleased with the appearance of *Beyond Learning: Democratic Education for a Human Future* (Biesta, 2006), which I consider to be my first 'real' single-authored book. Theoretically the book took up a theme I had already been working on in the 1990s, namely the postmodern critique of humanism, often referred to as the issue of the 'death of the subject' (see Biesta, 1998). While in popular readings of postmodernism the theme of the death of the subject is often seen as a critique of the very idea of human subjectivity, the point I tried to convey in the book was that the critique was actually aimed at philosophical humanism, that is, at the idea that it is possible and desirable to identify the essence of the human being and use this knowledge as the foundation for a range of theoretical and practical 'projects,' including education and politics. In the book I not only showed the ways in which humanism had influenced modern educational thought and practice, but also argued how it had put limits on what education could achieve by basing education on a 'template' about what the human being is and thus of what the child should become.

In *Beyond Learning* I developed an alternative set of educational concepts that did not focus on the nature or essence of human beings but rather on their existence. More specifically I focused on the question how 'newcomers' might come 'into presence.' With the help of Hannah Arendt I suggested that coming into presence is ultimately a public and hence a political process in the literal sense of the word political, that is, as 'occurring in the polis,' in the presence of others who are not like us. That is why I eventually suggested that we should think of education in terms of how newcomers come 'into the world.' Education as 'coming into the world' not only gives educators a responsibility for the new beginnings, but also for the plural or 'worldly' quality of the world, as it is only 'under the condition of plurality' (Arendt) that everyone has a possibility to bring their beginnings into the world.

The other concept I put forward was that of 'uniqueness.' Taking inspiration from the work of Emmanuel Levinas and his translator Alphonso Lingis, I developed a distinction between uniqueness-as-difference – which is about our identity or essence, that is, about how I differ from others – and uniqueness-as-irreplaceability. The latter approach – which can be characterised as existential rather than essential – moves from the question as to what makes me unique to the question when my uniqueness matters, that is, the question when it matters that I am I and no one else. Such situations, so I suggested with the help of Lingis's idea of the community of those who have nothing in common (Lingis, 1994), are situations where an appeal is made to me, where I am being addressed by another human being, and where I cannot be replaced because the appeal is made to me – not just to anyone. These are situations where I am literally 'singled out' by a question, by a request, by an appeal. It is then still up to me whether I respond or not, that is, whether I take up the responsibility that is waiting for me, so to speak, and thus 'realise' my unique singularity, my singular existence in that particular moment.

My hope with thinking about education in existential terms was to make it possible again (that is, after the death of the subject), to make a distinction between education as socialisation and education orientated towards freedom, a dimension to which in later publications – particularly my 2010 book *Good Education in an Age of Measurement* (Biesta, 2010c) – I started to refer to as 'subjectification.' In a sense *Beyond Learning* became a 'turning point' in my career, not only because it brought together much of the work I had been doing in previous years but also because it set the agenda for much that was to follow, particularly an increasing focus on educational questions and issues and an ambition to engage with such questions in an educational way, that is, through the development of educational forms of theory and theorising.

In the next period of about seven years I thus turned increasingly to what I saw as key educational questions and issues, particularly questions concerning education, freedom and emancipation. Here – but only here (see Biesta, 2013a) – I found the work of Jacques Rancière helpful, as it made it possible to (re)turn to the question of emancipation in a way that was significantly different from how it had been engaged with in critical theory and critical pedagogy (see Biesta, 2010d). Together with Charles Bingham I published a book on Rancière's work (Bingham & Biesta, 2010) in which the question of emancipation was a central theme. Questions concerning the nexus of education, freedom and emancipation also were central in a short text I wrote with Carl Anders Säfström, which we published under the title *A Manifesto for Education* (Biesta & Säfström, 2011a). The Manifesto attracted a lot of attention in many countries, not only from academics but also from students and teacher. The first translation was actually published by a Norwegian teacher union (Biesta & Säfström, 2011b).

The other line that emerged during these years focused on educational policy and practice, particularly in order to show the extent to which and the ways in which educational issues were increasingly being sidelined, either by replacing an educational language with a language of learning – which was one of my reasons for arguing that in order to bring educational questions back into view we needed to go 'beyond learning' (see also Biesta, 2004, 2013b) – or by pushing education into a logic of production, that is, of predictable connections between educational 'inputs' and outputs.' One paper I published in relation to these tendencies focused on the shift from professional-democratic responsibility to technical-managerial accountability in education (Biesta, 2004). Another paper focused on the calls to turn education into an evidence-based profession (Biesta, 2007b – to date my most cited paper – and also Biesta, 2010e). The fact that both papers attracted quite a lot of attention, gave me an indication that the topics were important and that some of my reflections were seen as relevant and helpful. This gave me the motivation to focus more explicitly and more 'positively' (rather than just critically) on questions of good education, that is, questions about what education should be like and aim for. I brought a number of the papers I wrote on this together in Good Education in an *Age of Measurement* (Biesta, 2010). In the book I continued with some of the main themes from *Beyond Learning*, but I put them in a wider perspective – partly by connecting them to developments in educational policy (accountability; evidence) and partly by taking a broader view on the functions and purposes of education, through a distinction between three domains of educational purpose: qualification, socialisation and subjectification (Biesta, 2010, chapter 1). While the distinction itself was simple, it proved to be a useful heuristic device for making discussions about what education is for more precise and concrete – which was also recognised by the fact that the book was rather quickly translated into a number of languages (to date into Swedish, Danish and Dutch).

The stronger focus on educational theory and policy was also supported by my move, in 2007, to the University of Stirling in Scotland. In the Teaching and Learning Research Programme projects I had worked closely and productively with two professors from Stirling, John Field and Richard Edwards, and when a position opened up in Stirling I decided to try my luck. I had five wonderful years in Stirling. Together with Julie Allan and other colleagues from the Institute of Education we tried to further the case for theory in education through the establishment of the Laboratory for Educational Theory. This was an exciting adventure albeit not without difficulties, partly because we were doing something new for which there was little (research) expertise available. We nonetheless managed to stir the discussion about theory a little, both nationally and internationally, through seminars and symposia, a number of international conferences and a doctoral summer school. We also managed to give the question of theory some prominence in ongoing discussions in the UK about research capacity building (Biesta, Allan, & Edwards, 2011) and brought together a group of international scholars in an edited volume on the theory question in education and the education question in theory (Biesta, Allen, & Edwards, 2014). Another fruitful collaboration in Stirling was with Mark Priestley and focused on curriculum research and theory, a field that particularly in England had led a marginal status since the introduction of the National Curriculum in the 1990s. The work with Mark resulted, amongst other things, in an edited collection on the new curriculum, analysing curriculum trends in Scotland against the background of wider international developments (Priestley & Biesta, 2013).

Three significant other events during my time in Scotland were the publication of a short edited book on complexity and education (Osberg & Biesta, 2010), on which I worked with Deborah Osberg, with whom I had already published a number of papers on the topic. Unlike much literature on complexity and education we particularly tried to highlight the political dimensions, potential and implications of thinking education through complexity. Through the efforts of Maria de Bie of the University of Ghent and Danny Wildemeersch at the University of Leuven I was, in 2011, awarded the International Interuniversity Francqui Professorship by the Francqui Foundation in Belgium. This allowed me to spend about half a year at the University of Ghent in the spring of 2011 to work with colleagues from Ghent and Leuven on questions concerning education, social work, democracy and citizenship. This was another project that proved the importance of connecting theoretical and empirical work and really helped to push my own thinking on the topics forward, and probably did the same with many of the people involved in the activities around the chair (see Biesta, De Bie, & Wildemeersch, 2013). The greatest recognition I received from my peers was my election as president of the USA Philosophy of Education Society for 2011-2012 – the first president of the society from outside of North America. One of the prerogatives of the president is to invite the speaker for the Kneller Lecture (a lecture at the society's annual conference sponsored by an endowment from George F. Kneller). I was extremely grateful that John D. Caputo accepted my invitation, not only because of his standing as a philosopher but also because his scholarship has had a significant impact on my own work. Caputo also provided inspiration for the title and some of the content of the book in which I brought together much of my most recent work on education, namely The Beautiful Risk of Education (Biesta, 2013c – with a translation in Danish on its way).

LUXEMBOURG: 2013 AND BEYOND

At the time of writing, my latest job move is still in its initial stages. After working for nearly 14 years in the UK I felt a need to (re)turn to the Continent, partly because over the years I had come to realise how strongly my work and my academic identity has been shaped by Continental philosophy and educational theory, and partly out of curiosity for a very different institutional, intellectual and linguistic environment. I was lucky to be selected for the post of Professor of Educational Theory and Policy at the University of Luxembourg (a tri-lingual university), which will allow me to concentrate on two areas that, over the years, have indeed become central in my work. What Luxembourg will bring lies in the future, but there are still a number of issues I wish to pursue, not only because they are important for me but also because I sense that they can be important for the direction in which educational research and practice seem to be moving internationally.

I see myself not only getting further away from the discourse of learning, but also turning increasingly towards teaching. An essay I recently published – Giving teaching back to education (Biesta, 2012b) – provides an indication of work that still needs to be done here. The distinction I operate within the essay – between 'learning from' and 'being taught by' – not only has important practical implications for how we think about teaching and how we might do it, but also has a wider theoretical potential as it provides two very different ways of thinking about the way we are in the world with others: one where we see others as resources for our own growth and development and one where others are addressing us and where this address (literally) 'opens up' opportunities for a very different way of being human. The distinction between 'learning from' and 'being taught by' is therefore not just a micro-matter for how teachers and students might conduct themselves in the classroom, but hints at much wider ethical, political, existential and educational themes and issues. My more recent collaborations with Herner Sæverot from the University of Bergen and with colleagues from NLA University College in Bergen are particularly important in the exploration of the existential dimensions of these challenges.

There are two further aspects of the 'turn' towards teaching that require further work. One has to do with the educational significance of the experience of resistance – the resistance of the material world and the resistance of the social world – and suggests a need to return to the rather old educational theme of the education of the will, that is, the question how the will can come to a 'worldy' form (Biesta, 2012c; see also Meirieu, 2007). The other concerns the need for the development of an informed critique of constructivism and the articulation of a viable alternative, so that we can understand what it means to know no longer just in terms of (our own) constructions but also, and perhaps first of all, in terms of reception, that is, as something that is given to us. This is a line with many theoretical, philosophical and political challenges, but nonetheless important in order to challenge what seems to have become a new 'dogma' of contemporary education. A further theme has to do with developing a critical understanding of the transformation of the field of educational research and scholarship, also in order to be able to interrupt the ongoing rise of an Anglo-American definition of educational research and scholarship – one that is increasingly marginalising other, what we might call 'indigenous' forms of theory and research in education. And if I can find the time, I would also like to explore in more depth the educational significance of the idea of 'metamorphosis,' particularly to challenge the dominance of linear modes of thinking and doing that seem to suggest that we just need to start earlier and earlier with our educational 'interventions' – a way of thinking that puts an enormous amount of unwarranted pressure on (young) children and their teachers.

What might emerge from all this (and in a sense is already emerging from it) is a conception of education that is thoroughly 'world-centred' – an education for 'earthlings' (Lingis, 1994, p. 117), we might say – which is focused on the possibilities for 'newcomers' to exist in the world with others who are not like them. Questions about subjectivity, freedom, emancipation, and democracy are likely to play an important role in this wider ambition, as will be the question of the education of teachers in a world that seems to want to take all that matters educationally out of education in order to turn it into the risk-free production of pre-specified identities and learning outcomes.

Finally: the title of this chapter is an attempt to capture my intellectual and scholarly trajectory. This trajectory started with pragmatism, and I have indicated the ways in which I am still indebted to pragmatism. But the encounter with philosophers such as Derrida, Arendt, and Levinas and with educational thinkers such as Langeveld, Mollenhauer, and Meirieu, has convinced me that the most important challenge for education today lies in the question how we can be 'at home in the world,' as Arendt so beautifully has put it. This, as I have come to realise, is ultimately not a matter of theory or philosophy but a matter of existence, so that there is the ongoing challenge not to let theory and philosophy get in the way of life, not to let it get in the way of what matters and what should matter most in our existence as 'earthlings.'

FAVORITE WORKS

Publications That Have Been Important for My Own Work

Arendt, H. (1958). *The human condition.* Chicago: The University of Chicago Press.
Bauman, Z. (1993). *Postmodern ethics.* Cambridge, MA: Basil Blackwell
Caputo, J. D. (2006). *The weakness of God: A theology of the event.* Bloomington and Indianapolis: Indiana University Press.
Derrida, J. (1976). *Of grammatology.* Baltimore & London: Johns Hopkins University Press.
Dewey, J. (1929). *The quest for certainty: A study of the relation of knowledge and action.* New York: Minton Balch & Company.
Latour, B. (1987). *Science in action.* Cambridge, MA: Harvard University Press.
Levinas, E. (1981). *Otherwise than being or beyond essence.* The Hague: Martinus Nijhoff.
Meirieu, P. (2007). *Pédagogie: Le devoir de résister.* Issy-les-Moulineaux: ESF éditeur.
Mollenhauer, K. (1964). *Erziehung und Emanzipation* [Education and emancipation]. Weinheim: Juventa.
Mollenhauer, K. (1983). *Vergessene Zusammenhänge. Über Kultur und Erziehung* [Forgotten connections: On culture and education]. München: Juventa.
Rorty, R. (1979). *Philosophy and the mirror of nature.* Princeton, NJ: Princeton University Press.

Some Key Publications

Biesta, G. J. J. (2006). *Beyond learning. Democratic education for a human future.* Boulder, CO: Paradigm Publishers.
Biesta, G. J. J. (2010). *Good education in an age of measurement: Ethics, politics, democracy.* Boulder, CO: Paradigm Publishers.
Biesta, G. J. J. (2013). *The beautiful risk of education.* Boulder, CO: Paradigm Publishers
Biesta, G. J. J. (2007). Why 'what works' won't work. Evidence-based practice and the democratic deficit of educational research. *Educational Theory, 57*(1), 1-22.
Biesta, G. J. J. (2012). Giving teaching back to education. *Phenomenology and Practice, 6*(2), 35-49.

REFERENCES

Biesta, G. J. J. (1992). *John Dewey: Theory & praktijk*. Delft: Eburon.
Biesta, G. J. J. (1994). Education as practical intersubjectivity. Towards a critical-pragmatic understanding of education. *Educational Theory, 44*(3), 299-317.
Biesta, G. J. J. (1995a). Pragmatism as a pedagogy of communicative action. In J. Garrison (Ed.), *The new scholarship on John Dewey* (pp. 105-122). Dordrecht/Boston/London: Kluwer Academic Publishers.
Biesta, G. J. J. (1995b). Postmodernism and the repoliticization of education. *Interchange, 26*, 161-183.
Biesta, G. J. J. (1998). Pedagogy without humanism. Foucault and the subject of education. *Interchange, 29*(1), 1-16.
Biesta, G. J. J. (1999). Radical intersubjectivity. Reflections on the "different" foundation of education. *Studies in Philosohpy and Education, 18*(4), 203-220.
Biesta, G. J. J. (2001). "Preparing for the incalculable." Deconstruction, justice and the question of education. In G. J. J. Biesta & D. Egéa-Kuehne (Eds.), *Derrida & education* (pp. 32-54). London/New York: Routledge.
Biesta, G. J. J. (2002). How general can Bildung be? Reflections on the future of a modern educational ideal. *British Journal of Philosophy of Education, 36*(3), 377-390.
Biesta, G. J. J. (2003). Jacques Derrida. Deconstruction = Justice. In M. Peters, M. Olssen, & C. Lankshear (Eds.), *Futures of critical theory: Dreams of difference* (pp. 141-154). Lanham, MD: Rowman and Littlefield.
Biesta, G. J. J. (2004). Against learning. Reclaiming a language for education in an age of learning. *Nordisk Pedagogik, 23*, 70-82.
Biesta, G. J. J. (2006). *Beyond learning. Democratic education for a human future*. Boulder, CO: Paradigm Publishers.
Biesta, G. J. J. (2007a). Education and the democratic person: Towards a political understanding of democratic education. *Teachers College Record, 109*(3), 740-769.
Biesta, G. J. J. (2007b). Why 'what works' won't work. Evidence-based practice and the democratic deficit of educational research. *Educational Theory, 57*(1), 1-22.
Biesta, G. J. J. (2009a). How to use pragmatism pragmatically: Suggestions for the 21st century. In A. G. Rud, J. Garrison, & L. Stone (Eds.), *John Dewey at 150. Reflections for a new century* (pp. 30-39). Lafayette, IN: Purdue University Press.
Biesta, G. J. J. (2009b). What kind of citizenship for European Higher Education? Beyond the competent active citizen. *European Educational Research Journal, 8*(2), 146-157.
Biesta, G. J. J. (2010a). "The most influential theory of the century." Dewey, democratic education and the limits of pragmatism. In D. Troehler, T. Schlag, & F. Osterwalder (Eds.), *Pragmatism and modernities* (pp. 197-213). Rotterdam: Sense Publishers.
Biesta, G. J. J. (2010b). "This is my truth, tell me yours." Deconstructive pragmatism as a philosophy for education. *Educational Philosophy and Theory, 42*(7), 710-727.
Biesta, G. J. J. (2010c). *Good education in an age of measurement: Ethics, politics, democracy*. Boulder, CO: Paradigm Publishers.
Biesta, G. J. J. (2010d). A new 'logic' of emancipation: The methodology of Jacques Ranciere. *Educational Theory, 60*(1), 39-59.
Biesta, G. J. J. (2010e). Why 'what works' still won't work. From evidence-based education to value-based education. *Studies in Philosophy and Education, 29*(5), 491-503.
Biesta, G. J. J. (2011a). Disciplines and theory in the academic study of education: A comparative analysis of the Anglo-American and continental construction of the field. *Pedagogy, Culture and Society, 19*(2), 175-192.
Biesta, G. J. J. (2011b). How useful should the university be? On the rise of the global university and the crisis in higher education. *Qui Parle: Critical Humanities and Social Sciences, 20*(1), 35-47.
Biesta, G. J. J. (2011c). *Learning democracy in school and society: Education, lifelong learning and the politics of citizenship*. Rotterdam: Sense Publishers.

Biesta, G. J. J. (2012a). Knowledge/democracy. Notes on the political economy of academic publishing. *International Journal of Leadership in Education, 15*(4), 407-420.
Biesta, G. J. J. (2012b). Giving teaching back to education. *Phenomenology and Practice, 6*(2), 35-49.
Biesta, G. J. J. (2012c). The educational significance of the experience of resistance: Schooling and the dialogue between child and world. *Other Education, 1*(1), 92-103.
Biesta, G. J. J. (2013a). *Don't be fooled by ignorant schoolmasters.* Presentation at the Discourse, Power and Resistance 2013 Conference. London, 9-11 April 2013.
Biesta, G. J. J. (2013b). Interrupting the politics of learning. *Power and Education, 5*(1), 4-15.
Biesta. G. J. J. (2013). *The beautiful risk of education.* Boulder, CO: Paradigm Publishers.
Biesta, G. J. J., & Burbules, N. (2003). *Pragmatism and educational research.* Lanham, MD: Rowman and Littlefield.
Biesta, G. J. J., & Egéa-Kuehne, D. (Eds.). (2001). *Derrida & education.* London/New York: Routledge.
Biesta, G. J. J., & Lawy, R. S. (2006). From teaching citizenship to learning democracy. Overcoming individualism in research, policy and practice. *Cambridge Journal of Education, 36*(1), 63-79.
Biesta, G. J. J., & Miedema, S. (1990). Pedagogy of science: The contribution of pedagogy to the philosophy of science. *Phenomenology and Pedagogy, 8,* 118-129.
Biesta, G. J. J., & Säfström, C. A. (2011a). A manifesto for education. *Policy Futures in Education, 9*(5), 540-547.
Biesta, G. J. J., & Säfström, C. A. (2011b). Et manifest for utdanning. *Første Steg, 3* (September/October), i-iv.
Biesta, G. J. J., & Stams, G. J. J. M. (2001). Critical thinking and the question of critique. Some lessons from deconstruction. *Studies in Philosophy and Education, 20*(1), 57-74.
Biesta, G. J. J., Allan, J., & Edwards, R. G. (2011). The theory question in research capacity building in education: Towards an agenda for research and practice. *British Journal of Educational Studies, 59*(3), 225-239.
Biesta, G. J. J., Lawy, R. & Kelly N. (2009). Understanding young people's citizenship learning in everyday life: The role of contexts, relationships and dispositions. *Education, Citizenship and Social Justice, 4*(1), 5-24.
Biesta, G. J. J., Field, J., Hodkinson, P., Macleod, F. J., & Goodson, I. F. (2011). *Improving learning through the lifecourse: Learning lives.* London/New York: Routledge.
Biesta, G. J. J., De Bie, M., & Wildemeersch, D. (Eds.). (2013). *Civic learning, democratic citizenship and the public sphere.* Dordrecht/Boston: Springer Science+Business Media.
Biesta, G. J. J., Allan, J., & Edwards, R. G. (Eds.). (2014). *Making a difference in theory: The theory question in education and the education question in theory.* London/New York: Routledge.
Bingham, C., & Biesta, G. J. J. (2010). *Jacques Rancière: Education, truth, emancipation.* London/New York: Continuum.
Derrida, J. (1991). Letter to a Japanese friend. In P. Kamuf (Ed.), *A Derrida reader* (pp. 270-276). New York: Columbia University Press.
Derrida, J., & Ewald, F. (2001). "A certain 'madness' must watch over thinking." Jacques Derrida's interview with François Ewald (Trans. Denise Egéa-Kuehne). In G. J. J. Biesta & D. Egéa-Kuehne (Eds.), *Derrida & education* (pp. 55-76). London & New York: Routledge.
Dewey, J. (1984[1930]). From absolutism to experimentalism. In J. A. Boydston (Ed.), *John Dewey. The later works, 1925-1953. Volume 5: 1929-1930* (pp. 147-160). Carbondale & Edwardsville: Southern Illinois University Press.
Dewey, J. (1991[1939]). Experience, knowledge, and value: A rejoinder. In J.-A. Boydston (Ed.), *John Dewey. The later works (1925-1953), Vol. 14: 1939-1941* (pp. 3-90). Carbondale & Edwardsville: Southern Illinois University Press.
Horkheimer, M. (1947). *Eclipse of reason.* New York: Oxford University Press.
James, D., & Biesta, G. J. J. (2007). *Improving learning cultures in further education.* London: Routledge.

Joas, H. (1985). *George Herbert Mead: A contemporary re-examination of his thought*. Cambridge: Polity Press.

Latour, B. (1987). *Science in action*. Cambridge, MA: Harvard University Press.

Lawy, R. S., & Biesta, G. J. J. (2006). Citizenship-as-practice: the educational implications of an inclusive and relational understanding of citizenship. *British Journal of Educational Studies, 54*(1), 34-50.

Lawy, R., Biesta, G. J. J., McDonnell, J., Lawy, H., & Reeves, H. (2010). The art of democracy. *British Educational Research Journal, 36*(3), 351-365.

Lingis, A. (1994). *The community of those who have nothing in common*. Bloomington IN: Indiana University Press.

Masschelein, J. (1987). *Communicatief handelen en pedagogisch handelen* [Communicative action and educational action]. PhD Thesis. Leuven: KU Leuven.

Mead, G. H. (2008a). *Philosophie der Erziehung. Herasugegeben und eingeleitet von Daniel Tröhler und Gert Biesta*. Bad Heilbrunn: Verlag Julius Klinkhardt.

Mead, G. H. (2008b). *The philosophy of education. Edited and introduced by Gert Biesta and Daniel Tröhler*. Boulder, CO: Paradigm Publishers.

Meirieu, P. (2007). *Pédagogie: Le devoir de résister*. Issy-les-Moulineaux: ESF éditeur.

Miedema, S., & Biesta, G. J. J. (1989). *Filosofie van de pedagogische wetenschappen* [Philosophy of the educational sciences]. Leiden: Martinus Nijhoff.

Osberg, D. C. & Biesta, G. J. J. (Eds.). (2010). *Complexity theory and the politics of education*. Rotterdam: Sense Publishers.

Priestley, M., & Biesta, G. J. J. (Eds.). (2013). *Reinventing the curriculum. New trends in curriculum policy and practice*. London: Bloomsbury.

Rorty, R. (1979). *Philosophy and the mirror of nature*. Princeton, NJ: Princeton University Press.

MEGAN BOLER

FROM EXISTENTIALISM TO VIRTUALITY

I have a secret history of burying birds, an oddly hopeful childhood ritual. Some of the birds were my own but most were wild, found in the dark leaves or wet grass during times we lived in the hills or woods of Northern California, or by the side of buildings when we lived in San Francisco. At ten, I created an entire graveyard in the dank dark of the steep south-facing hill underneath our house on 23rd Street in Noe Valley.

Beneath the back porch was hard sandy clay where no sun ever reached. Here neighborhood cats fought out turf battles, leaving tufts of fur and cat spray, but I had no alternative – no back yard, no fields nearby. It was difficult for me to dig deeply, and the place was not graced by any natural beauty but was to the contrary hard to get to and difficult to perch in, and once I was there next to the graves it was simply damp and potently acrid, but I was committed. Each small, feathered creature deserved its own burial box, grave, prayers, and blessings. If a bird had been dead for awhile, I did feel a sense of revulsion at the cold body and frigid claws, whereas if it was still warm I was able to hum the final hymns with greater tenderness. I used shoeboxes for coffins, filled the box with a bed of grass, placed the bird's feathered body into the box with yellow sourgrass flowers and orange nasturtiums as a gentle cover, and began to dig. I saw myself as their minister. I didn't know any prayers, nor a single religious invocation, so I made up songs to sing to them. Their passing thus marked not by liturgy but blessed with my most sacred sense of loving thoughts and appreciation of the life they had lived flying in the sky.

This rite grew from no church, since we went to only one church for one night in my entire growing up, but from a tender love of the meek and the vulnerable. Stray dogs and cats, birds and rodents all found a place in my life. Whether domestic, captive or befriended, I found animals and they found me. Sometimes I found them only once they were dead and became their keeper and minister for only this short time. One and all, they found places not only in my heart but in my digging of soil to bury each one the best I could, with small bare hands.

I have always believed I was born a philosopher and it has been a primary identification in the world, even beyond more materialist ones including gender, race and class. One may not be born a woman, but perhaps one may be born existentialist? The characteristics of philosophical thought are of course learnt as much as they are inherent, but there is a strong indication that those of us drawn to this field of enquiry have strong predispositions to it, not unlike artists and writers show early proclivities for their own ways of seeing the world. For me, these

L.J. Waks (ed.), Leaders in Philosophy of Education, 31–48.
© 2014 Sense Publishers. All rights reserved.

indicators were there from the beginning, and remain strongly present in all the diverse areas of philosophical enquiry that draw me. The connection between studies of emotion and affect, and my studies today of the philosophy of media and technology mirrors my childhood bird-burying ritual, in sharing a concern with what is silenced, which the marginalized and muted, with the ways in which power shapes what is heard and unheard, seen and hidden.

My discovery of philosophy of education as a 'field' or discipline is a story of good fortune, persistence and perhaps of circumstance. My earliest love in philosophy (although I didn't know it was philosophy at the time) was existentialism, an orientation I come by naturally, the child of two poets each intimately familiar with experiences of the world's darker side. As a result, I grew up exposed to a certain misanthropy, a sensibility arguably well-captured by the affective demeanor of much existentialist writing. Today, it is more popular and increasingly recognized as a scholarly pursuit to speak of animals in this context and their manner of existence and comportment; and clearly from a very early age I was acutely aware of a certain preference for the non-human species. Such bonds were the salvation of my growing up, and continue to be through the tumult of human folly, deeply impactful relationships and forms of communication and exchange that kept me thriving and provided a sense of hope when witnessing man's inhumanity to man.

While I didn't encounter 'philosophy proper' until my first year of college, my entire childhood and adolescence was spent reading and engaged in creative writing. The absence of television as well as our nomadic lifestyle made reading an ideal semi-controlled space and place to escape to, and also kept my mind genuinely engaged, and I have continued to be an avid reader of literature and fiction year in and year out – my absolute favorite leisure activity. In grade six, I decided to read 100 novels outside of school in that year and kept them listed in a special notebook. By the age of ten I had written a few novellas, and upon reflection now I see that the themes were of suffering, turning hardship to triumph, and questions of agency and freedom – the same that have accompanied my philosophical explorations since that time. My extensive reading, our frequent moves (I attended at least 16 public schools in the course of growing up in California), my exposure to diverse cultural experiences, the artists and creative relatives in my family, and deeply traumatic experiences as well, cultivated in me an acute sense of social justice – though still perhaps most keenly on behalf of the welfare of animals, still informed by a philosophical reflection on agency.

At the age of 7 in Berkeley I was bussed to a primarily African American school. At the age of 8, I made a classroom stand against an anti-Latino teacher. Riding on a New York City bus with my grandmother one autumn evening at the age of 10, I saw from the bus window both homeless persons as well as stray animals. Thinking that while both situations were deeply unjust, I felt the suffering of animals more keenly due to the animals' lack of agency and their vulnerability caused largely by human failure.

My high school years were characterized by both an awakening of the pleasures of intellectual pursuits but also of great suffering, both of which have informed my

FROM EXISTENTIALISM TO VIRTUALITY

life as a philosopher. I survived my third high school, my senior year, by enrolling almost entirely in independent studies with teachers who recognized both my gifts and I suppose a degree of alienation. During this period I also experienced the permanent disappearance of my very close cousin who lived with us at the time, which only compounded an inherited capacity for seeing into the dark side. Alex herself was an artist and though only a few years older than me, seemed to be one of the wisest souls I knew and perhaps amongst my first real friends; her loss was devastating.

Yet there were also moments of great meeting, sometimes unspoken, and almost always amidst intellectual pursuits. An important figure at school during this period was a teacher and writer by the name of Gregory Lum, who kindly and with few direct words allowed me to escape English classes for my last year and a half of high school and take credits through independent study with him; with him I shared volumes of bad adolescent poetry and observations during the darkest years of loss in my life. Yet in this last year of high school I also managed to pursue tap-dancing, characteristic of my resilience and more creative pursuits.

A fellow tap-dancer turned out to be a young socialist, which is how I came to know about the ongoing events at the I-Hotel. My interest in politics began to come alive, revealing my colors as a young inadvertent rabble-rouser when the International Hotel[1] incident events led me to more ongoing engagements with the young socialists. My teacher of politics and social studies, Mr. Lewbin, a wonderfully smart, well-read and cultured teacher, was highly supportive of my explorations. I suggested to Mr. Lewbin that we invite these young socialists to speak to our class, to which he agreed. This resulted in my first encounter with fighting for social justice and human rights, in this instance freedom of expression within a bureaucratic and institutionalized public setting; my teacher and I had to make strong and careful argument to the school administration to get permission for their visit.

I see in these moments as well as important others the unlikely characteristic of both a contemplative philosopher but one who will take serious action when she believes justice is threatened – a characteristic nurtured in me by the adults in my formative years.

UNDERGRADUATE EDUCATION

By the age of 17, the ideas in Sartre's *Being and Nothingness* resonated profoundly and felt like translations of my own ontological experience. Roquentin's experience of alienation as described in *Nausea* captured my own.

I also had the good fortune for Sartre's ideas to be introduced into my developing philosophical study at the birth of women's studies, so once in college was exposed to feminist thinking and early investigations of gender. I was also powerfully influenced by Simone deBeauvoir's *After the Second Sex*, bell hooks' first book *Ain't I a Woman*, Descartes' *Meditations*. I remember comparing come passage to the original French and seeing what I suspected to be serious issues with the translation – and as it has turned out, some controversy surrounds the translation of this text. I also had the pleasure of interdisciplinary reading in then-new area of quantum physics. With the *Tao of Physics* in one hand and Sartre's tome on the other, I devoured hungrily. I added to this, via another favorite series of literature courses, *Zen Mind, Beginner's Mind*, in terms of what I consider its existentialist philosophy, and the resonance of such texts with certain traditions of American literature. The synthesis of these texts for me would come, some Saturday mornings, when I would find myself contemplating alternative ways of conceptualizing a kind of visualized metaphysics – spirals intersecting with spirals, where points of connections represent how 'units of analysis' – ranging from individual to social to political and historical – intersect in the strange continuums (or not) of space and time.

My undergraduate studies included a major in philosophy, which for good or bad I chose at the expense of being a music major. My grandfather David Broekman was a renowned composer and conductor who had emigrated from Holland to New York in the 1920s, and as they say musical talent skips generations, I often wonder if that road not taken might not have led to greater joy and day to day equilibrium, in contrast to the angst that seems part of being a dedicated 'thinker' and dissector of ideas and concepts. Philosophy is a heady business and while there is great pleasure when certain 'dots connect' and concepts forge in new iterations, the work involved in 'getting there' can be fraught with anguish, a deeply-felt sense of being mired in sometimes dark places before finally emerging into fresh air and sunlight. My own choice also begs the question of why I felt I had to choose, why both weren't feasible. There was a literal sense of being torn apart, as if I couldn't balance the two quite different logics and processes.[2]

In addition to studying philosophy at Mills College, I spent my junior year at University of California, Santa Cruz, and thus studied with additional professors of philosophy. The study of existentialism, phenomenology, and an early exposure to Descartes, Plato, epistemology, and ethics was pivotal in my development of thinking through the nature of being, embodiment 'versus' virtuality, and intersubjectivity, yet in the end there was something I yearned for from philosophy, as much of it seemed to me not to take into account what to my own thinking were key, ontologically-defining features of existence, such as the interaction between organisms and environment, private and public, emotional and rational – or even material and discursive considerations, as Karen Barad would now articulate it (2007).[3]

GRADUATE STUDIES – AND MY SEARCH FOR AFFECT AND EMOTION

In 1983, I entered a graduate consortium program in Philosophy, hosted at Bryn Mawr College. This program allowed students to study not only at Bryn Mawr but also to take courses at Villanova, University of Pennsylvania, and Temple University. I studied existentialism and phenomenology with the greatest interest, as well as early Greek and medieval philosophy. The nascent areas most exciting to me at the time were the contemporary texts in philosophy of science, ranging from Thomas Kuhn to Nelson Goodman, Richard Rorty to Richard Bernstein.

The boundedness of Western philosophy felt increasingly stifling; the questions that were not posed, that were silenced or dismissed, particularly around the epistemological queries I had regarding the subject, subjectivity, epistemological and ontological questions of the place of emotions and affect in how we experience, perceive, and interpret the world, how these become ethical and moral values. I found I needed a new context, aware I would not survive as a student of philosophy, a field that I felt at times was too narrowly understood and too narrowly considered.

This persistent concern with feelings, emotion and affect dogged me and went from being a pebble in my shoe to being the focus of my doctoral study and book *Feeling Power*. This biographical detail continues to be instructive to me: as a philosopher, particularly in education, I try to remember that the questions that most perturb us, most preoccupy my students and myself, are usually the doorways into new knowledge, and into new ways of understanding the power and need for philosophy in education - both applied and theoretical.

I had first become interested in emotion's absent-presence as a student of philosophy. Theories of subjectivity and epistemology were undergoing radical change as philosophies of science had begun to question the ubiquity of scientific production of knowledge. Positivism and scientific approaches committed to the possibility of objectivity were being increasingly challenged at this rapidly-evolving and exciting time. Yet even these challenges rarely explored emotion. I became deeply interested in why these new theories and theorists neglected to explore the role emotions play in shaping our perceptions, our selection about what we pay attention to, and our values that in turn play such a large role in our life trajectories. In the many years since that awakening to emotion's absence, I have seen a rise in scholarly concerns with emotion as it relates to affect, and yet I continue to search for the undeniable impact and distinct weight of emotion itself; to this day, I continue to come up empty-handed, despite important and valuable progress in related fields.

Yet it continues to seem evident that emotion's exclusion from philosophy and science is not a coincidence. As I noted in my earliest scholarship, this exclusion of emotion remains part of a long scholarly tradition in western discourses. Since the originary moment of Western and Greek philosophy, emotion had been positioned on the 'negative' side of a false ontological binary division that has remained inexorably tied to gender, and it still is in today's western paradigms. It seems in the fifteen years since I published *Feeling Power*, the fight for the legitimacy of emotion (and indeed of women) in the academy continues apace. Then I only knew I craved new horizons and rigorous intellectual engagement.

Midway through my year of graduate studies in philosophy, I had the opportunity to attend what would turn out to be a life-altering conference entitled 'After the Second Sex' in Philadelphia in 1984. I became aware again of the work of Donna Haraway through a presentation by Evelyn Fox Keller who had recently published *Gender and Science*. Also at this time I had the pleasure of attending the East Coast Society for Women in Philosophy – another tremendously validating experience, since feminist philosophers like Naomi Scheman (another author on emotions and philosophy) was in attendance; so there was, of a sudden, a beginning sense of recognition of the value of emotions in scholarly examination of philosophy. Having applied already once, I was re-inspired to apply again for admission to the History of Consciousness (HC) graduate program, and this time clearly outlined my desire to explore emotions as a site of power and social control, and to study this topic under the mentorship of Donna Haraway.

Accepted for admission into the HC cohort of 1985, I began my true immersion and career in interdisciplinary scholarship that would help me to analyze emotions in the socio-cultural and historical contexts which had not yet been brought to bear on this topic, and which would eventually lead me into philosophy of education (achieved through persistence, an important lesson indeed in this business). To this day I continue to recognize again and anew what a gift it was to be part of this intellectual milieu. So I began my doctoral studies in 1985 with Donna Haraway as my first mentor, and I completed my dissertation in 1993: *Feeling Power: The Discourses of Emotion in Higher Education*. It would be an additional several years of revising the dissertation to become *Feeling Power: Emotions and Education* – the three years in my first tenure-stream position at the University of Auckland, and one year after arriving at Virginia Tech, my second tenure-track position, the book finally held in my shocked hands in 1999.

SEEKING EMOTION

In the History of Consciousness milieu in which Hayden White's wisdom included teaching us about the "meta" questions of all things, I was taught to read not only as an activity for absorbing information and ideas but simultaneously to question texts as representations of far more than a uni-dimensional transmission of supposed truths. I learned to investigate how meanings, truths, and authority are produced: Who is the intended audience? How is the book itself, as a material product, being marketed? What does its cover, blurbs, picture, categorization, price, publishing location tell us? What is the author assuming? What contradictory agendas and ideologies shape the text itself? How do countless cultural values, teachings, assumptions, and ideologies mediate our interpretations of the text? Exposed to interdisciplinary approaches, I began to acquire the tools I needed to pursue emotion's absent-presence.

Much of my acute attention to affect in education began with the teaching profession: nearly all graduate student at UCSC worked as teaching assistants teaching two discussion sections per quarter, so six courses a year pus summer teaching if we could get it (myself in the fields of women's studies, philosophy, sociology, American Studies, and Core required freshmen courses such as "Arts and Heritage in a Multicultural, Society," and soon in my career, two sole responsibility courses each term. A short time after I began in the program, I also was appointed as a "Teaching Assistant Trainer," through a new program in California universities, and this opportunity opened up wider questions of the ethical and epistemological implications of (higher education) pedagogies as well as a professional side to my interest in education.

Further, by the end of my years as a graduate student I had become sole instructor in teaching composition and rhetoric. It was my colleagues in the field of composition and rhetoric who were thinking through cutting edge questions of pedagogy, power, and voice, issues that were only just surfacing as topics of scrutiny within critical frameworks. Journals such as *College English* provided insightful analyses of pedagogy and politics. I discovered the work of such scholars as Valerie Walkerdine through the mentoring of Professor Helene Moglen, and thinkers such as Paulo Freire through seminars taught by Donald Rothman. These experiences gave me the space to begin doing my own real intellectual work of forming original ideas about educational theory and educational philosophy, in conversation with those scholars around me – a crucial stage for any emerging intellectual.

My graduate studies were privileged to benefit from studying with– in addition to Donna Haraway – Helene Moglen, Hayden White, Jim Clifford and the constantly vibrating atmosphere of the History of Consciousness program in the 1980s at its pinnacle, which represents a remarkable legacy (one I am working to document through a project with Zoe Sofoulis, Chela Sandoval, Saron Traweek, and Chris Hables Gray) and from the many pivotal public talks and seminars held on the University of California Santa Cruz campus between 1985-1992 by Gayatri Spivak, Stuart Hall, Fredric Jameson, Wendy Brown, Oliver Sacks, Joan Scott, Sandra Harding, June Jordan, Patricia Hill Collins, Cherrie Moraga, Gloria Anzaldua, Judith Butler, bell hooks, Teresa DeLauretis, and Angela Davis among many others. And, in History of Consciousness, we were much influenced by our peers – for example, Gloria was a peer and fellow writing-group member, as well as other friends and colleagues such as Ruth Frankenberg, Katie King, Lata Mani, Zoe Sofoulis, Chela Sandoval, Chris Hables Gray, Ron Eglash, Vince Diaz, and so many more.

When I think back on this epoch of intellectual and scholarly history, it is fair to say that this convergence of factors, this fecund period for so many, reflects a remarkable emergence of concerns about discourse and its functions, operation, and circulation, about the politics of knowledge and representation. Scholars of the late 20th century were in the midst of perhaps the most fertile and thorough cross-disciplinary investigation about the assumptions and premises of the disciplines in which they worked, whether in the disciplines of history, sociology, semiotics, or biology – or indeed feminist theory and cultural studies as informed by all of these and many other disciplines. From the vantage point of our present neoliberal era of dismantling the humanities and social sciences, of cutbacks and decimations of departments of comparative literature, communications, queer theory, gender studies, and feminist scholarship, I realize yet again how deeply fortunate I was, and how profoundly this cultural and scholarly atmosphere contributed to the development of my own thinking and scholarly identity. I was truly fortunate I have been to have benefited from these giants of the American intellectual landscape.

PHILOSOPHY OF EDUCATION

My HistCon colleague Julia Creet had studied at the Ontario Institute for Studies in Education, and introduced me near the end of my studies to Professor Deanne Bogdan, which is where my story of "philosophy of education" genuinely begins.

A visiting scholar at UCSC, at our lunch meeting overlooking West Cliff of the Pacific Ocean in Santa Cruz, she introduced me to the journal of *Educational Theory* and the proceedings of the Philosophy of Education Society (PES) which opened a whole new world for me. What a relief to find there had been a name for what I had been working to articulate in my dissertation these past years, and that was philosophy of education. Thanks to Deanne's encouragement of my project and interests, I attended PES for the first time in 1991 in New Orleans, where I met others who would come to be lifelong colleagues and mentors in this field, including scholars who were fellow graduate students at the time: Cris Mayo, Natasha Levinson, Zelia Gregoriou. We not only slept on floors given graduate student life at conferences but by the next year, I submitted my first paper to PES and in Charlotte had the opportunity to present "The Risks of Empathy"[4] to a standing room only gathering. For the first time I saw, despite the many doubts that plagued me from the beginning of my work on the unpopular topic of emotion, the question of emotion in philosophy was one that scholars were hungry to hear about. Through PES I met many others who would provide mentoring and collegiality through the years to come, including Suzanne DeCastell, Audrey Thompson, Nick Burbules, Jim Garrison, Barbara Stengel and Lynda Stone.

Also while completing my dissertation in Santa Cruz, thanks to the gracious hosts of the California Association of Philosophy of Education and its members including Michael Katz, Nel Noddings, and then doctoral student Ron Glass – who has been a primary influence on me as a role model of commitments to social justice in his thinking and scholarship and community engagement – I was invited to give a paper at the meeting held at Stanford. That night, Nel Noddings in her traditional generosity provided warm hospitality, along with a salon atmosphere, and couches and beds for it seemed over a dozen keen graduate students in philosophy of education from all over the Bay Area.

It might be said that philosophers of education as a community of scholars have perhaps more modesty and consequently often quite good senses of humor – somehow the combination of choosing both the identity of 'philosopher' – not a big party topic as is – combined with 'education,' which happens to be the discipline lowest on the totem pole of the ivory halls of academe – well this combination might be said to make for a humbling mix. Perfect: Thus commenced a warm and welcoming experience of finding one of my 'tribes,' and a key intellectual home that was yet committed to praxis and to discerning just aims and goals in learning and education writ large, using diverse critical and philosophical lenses to work, as I say, 'in the trenches' – the undervalued space of education – in part through its gendered association with women – especially in the United States but of course, around the globe. A place where social justice is frequently valued, and worked through as a challenge to bring theory and praxis to achieve what

Donna Haraway describes as the problem of "how to have simultaneously an account of radical historical contingency for all knowledge claims and knowing subjects, a critical practice for recognizing our own 'semiotic technologies' for making meanings, and a no-nonsense commitment to faithful accounts of a 'real' world, one that can be partially shared and friendly to earth-wide projects of finite freedom, adequate material abundance, modest meaning in suffering, and limited happiness" (1991, p. 187).

Towards the end of my dissertation writing, a friend introduced me to Professor Deborah Britzman, who had just published *Practice Makes Practice*. Deborah provided a strong influence on my thinking during this period, as she was the first scholar I had met who also read in the areas of post-structuralism, feminist theory, education, and critical and social theory.

Finally, my connection with Maxine Greene provided a source of sustenance and inspiration during the later part of my dissertation writing and throughout my early career. I boldly wrote a letter of introduction to Maxine Greene while a doctoral student, having just read her book *The Public School and the Private Vision: A Search for America in Education and Literature* (1965), which impressed me as prescient insight into the tensions that are only increasing between public and private values and spheres. Some ways into our correspondence, I inquired whether she would be willing to allow me to record her autobiographical oral history of her own graduate studies and entry into academe. Whenever I traveled to New York, during those years, she generously opened her home to me for visits which remain some of my most cherished memories. We would share meals, talk for hours, and she provided me a bedroom for these stays in New York (where incidentally my mother was raised and I used to visit my grandmother). Sitting at her living room table, discussing all matters of philosophy of education, my awe and respect grew as I learned of the trials and tribulations of being a woman in philosophy also interested in aesthetics – and how hard she had to work to gain a place at the table of (solely) men occupying philosophy of education. Being with Maxine gave me a sense of history and place in philosophy of education.

CONTRIBUTION OF FEELING POWER AND PEDAGOGY OF DISCOMFORT

When I use this book in my graduate teaching today, students ask about the writing of it. I feel it provides a reality check for their own writing (within the neoliberal context in which humanities and philosophy students are expected to complete a dissertation in four years) to confess that it took me eight years to complete my dissertation and another substantial number of years to revise the book for publication to my satisfaction. And I do find myself saying that 'never again' will I invest such sweat, blood, tears, and time into one monograph. But the rewards have made the suffering worth it, as I realize over time that the book has made a significant contribution and opened up spaces for other scholars. This is particularly gratifying, because the years of writing it, and then seeking a publisher, were marked by a profound loneliness and sometimes despair. Nowhere could I find a blueprint. The closest I found in those days were essays such as Peter

Lyman's 'The Politics of Anger,' sociologist Arlie Hocshchild's *The Managed Heart* (1983), and finally – by the later 1980s – the work of feminist philosophers such as Alison Jaggar who had begun to take up questions of emotion.

I continue to receive letters and emails from students and scholars thanking me for how *Feeling Power* has impacted their lives, made another vista and approach to dissertation scholarship possible, validated their ideas and thinking, all of which is immensely humbling. Perhaps most satisfying is that certain ideas from the book continue to spark scholars to push into new territories of exploration, extending the lenses of *Feeling Power* into new areas of excavation. I recently received a letter asking:

> I'm a graduate student in Indigenous Governance at the University of Victoria, B.C. I just read your chapter on the pedagogy of discomfort and am wondering if you have ever engaged this idea with Canadian colonialism/ decolonization? Or do you know of anyone doing this work right now? I know Paulette Regan briefly engages with pedagogy of discomfort in "Unsettling the Settler Within" however this is on the context of residential schools. I'm a non-Indigenous woman in this program so your ideas on discomfort really resonated with me. I think it was the realization of this discomfort that got me interested in Indigenous issues in the first place.

Sometimes it has been through these colleagues, students, reviewers and even strangers that I have come to know more about *Feeling Power* than when I was writing it. For example, the ways in which the book offers a "persuasive example of the power of Boler's method of discourse analysis" (Houston, 2002, p. 206), of the power of testimonial reading over "passive empathy" (p. 206), and of my key concept of a 'pedagogy of discomfort' as "a pedagogy that makes emotions a site of political resistance and a catalyst for social change" (p. 206) were all great insights noted by Houston that helped me place the work in its wider context. It is moving to see noted the ways in which I have extended my fellow (feminist) scholars and those who have come before me including Elizabeth Spelman (1989, 1991), Alison Jaggar (1989), Sandra Bartky (1990), and Sue Campbell (1997) to "develop a theoretical framework for revealing and explicating the myriad ways in which the " politics of emotion," (206) shaped by different scholarly disciplines, functions in public education to enforce social control of the nation' s citizens" (Houston, 2002, p. 206).

I have become aware of the impact of *Feeling Power* and its notion of a pedagogy of discomfort within medical and health education, by scholars such as Julie Aultman, and I continue to receive keynotes and workshop invitations on this topic regularly. The book also received enormous generosity and support from senior colleagues in philosophy of education at the time of its publication, including a symposium panel at PES featuring Maxine Greene and Barbara Houston amongst others. Early reviewers too helped develop my thinking about the book and its contribution by noting, for example that: "Perhaps most importantly, Boler asks us to consider the potential risks we take when we ignore emotion" (Driscoll, 1999, p. 717), and that my "larger intent to theorize a discourse of the emotions that steers away from terms that bias our reading" (p. 718) was recognized.

Another early review of *Feeling Power* highlights a seed in that work that is more fully developed in my current work on truth/truthiness as reflecting a lifelong preoccupation the nature and enactment of truth: "Testimonial reading ... realizes that Socratic self-reflection can easily ignore differences. Such reasoning queries the truth. It calls for witnesses to testify. It multiplies perspectives and requires us to participate in the unending co-construction of 'truth'" (Garrison, 1999, p. 33). The sense of accomplishment I derive from this and other generous responses have demonstrated to me the value in having persisted in such a challenging line of enquiry, and I use it as an example to my students in trying to nurture persistence in them.

When I completed my PhD and went on the job market, I interviewed for jobs in philosophy, women's studies, and education. As luck would have it, I entered the discipline and world of education through my first tenure-track position at the University of Auckland in New Zealand in 1995. It was an honor to work with that dynamic Department and School of Education which most immediately included Alison Jones – one of my first professional mentors, to whom I will always be indebted – and my immediate colleagues Michael Peters, Jim Marshall, Peter Roberts, and in the just-burgeoning and now well-established Maori Studies program I had as well the great fortune to work closely with Linda Tuhiwai Smith and Graham Smith. At the time that Linda and I applied and were awarded a Marsden Research Award, she was in the midst of completing her groundbreaking book *Decolonizing Methodologies* (1999).

POLITICAL PHILOSOPHY OF COMMUNICATION, TECHNOLOGIES AND DIGITAL MEDIA

My scholarly interests and research turned after 1999 significantly towards the rising phenomenon of digital media in relation to participatory democracy, its impact on education, and philosophies of technology. In my reading and in my teaching I began to cultivate my longstanding interest in representation and the politics of representation, particularly the shifting role of news media and journalism in relation to the constitution of publics, counterpublics, ways of thinking, discourses, what is named and what is not. My interest in this topic is not solely intellectual but has always reflected my activist histories and interest in developing theory as a response to a problem: as Stuart Hall stated in a public seminar at U.C. Santa-Cruz in the 1980s, theory is something we "turn into when we are stuck." It is indeed the praxis-oriented aspects of philosophy of education that compel me most about the field.

One of my particular interests lies in media and communication studies and correspondingly in media education and literacy. The agenda-setting power of news and the complex role of media in democracies and other governmental regimes interests me both as a longtime activist and as a complex question that requires interdisciplinary tools for analysis, intervention, and the understanding of effective dissent and dialogue or participation with governmental and institutional structures.

My scholarship and teaching have also maintained a focus on semiotics, cultural studies (including importantly the work of Raymond Williams and Stuart Hall), feminist and queer theory as well as extensive use of independently-produced documentaries and other media. These I have taken as opportunities not only to use films and videos as teaching texts for their content, but also for their production values, aesthetics, and as artifacts of cultural production. Further, my interest in alternative media and questions of justice in representational politics has always been fundamentally concerned with freedom of thought and expression.

The latter of my years at UCSC corresponded with the first Persian Gulf War, and importantly to my scholarship and thinking, I began to archive even then, perhaps in more ways than I knew. Drawn to a discourse analysis of how the news represented war in times of war, and more importantly how it did not, my interest in social justice continues to extend to questions of fairness in access to the means of production and distribution; indeed, my interest in the philosophy of technology has taken root particularly in the forms of media production and circulation that do not rely on corporate funding, but are publicly or independently funded.

These are questions about the principles of democracy and forms of engaged 'civic participation' that persistently engage scholarly and philosophical commentators, who see that these desperate times are in serious need of both public intellectuals and activist collectivities, as do I. Noam Chomsky's 1966 essay on the social responsibility of the public intellectual remains central in part because the topic is not frequently taken up in scholarly discourse:

> Intellectuals are in a position to expose the lies of governments, to analyze actions according to their causes and motives and often hidden intentions. In the Western world, at least, they have the power that comes from political liberty, from access to information and freedom of expression. For a privileged minority, Western democracy provides the leisure, the facilities, and the training to seek the truth lying hidden behind the veil of distortion and misrepresentation, ideology and class interest, through which the events of current history are presented to us. (Chomsky, *The Responsibility of Intellectuals*, 1967, p. 3)

As a tenured academic scholar, I take this role seriously. Particularly in times of war, of threats to civil liberties and institutions of democracy, I have taken such matters to heart and increasingly shifted my research to questions of media. I understand media as a social and cultural sector, landscape, and set of practices which function both as primary curriculum which should be of great concern to education, and as complex materialized and representational practices (in terms of print, broadcast, and now web-based news and social media) that effectively govern and delimit social thought and inscribed habits of (in)attention within so-called democratic states. However, there is considerably more room in the field of education for attention to media and technologies engaging the lenses of the humanities, social sciences, and arts, and all of these in greater collaboration with fields ranging from computer science and engineering to instructional and learning technologies. And for those of us in teacher education, as most teachers will testify, popular culture and informal learning using media ranging from YouTube to Instagram offer arguably a more potent site of learning than much of formal schooling. Yet questions of media as foundational to citizenship are too often mentioned only in passing.

Also in this essay in *The Methodological Dilemma*, I cite C. Wright Mills who encourages my media collaborators of the need for scholarship that offers what I aim to do, and which is mentioned in this review of my edited book *Digital Media and Democracy* (2008): "… a rare engagement with decidedly practical political concerns, addressed it seems, as much to activists as to academics. More than many other comparable volumes, *Digital Media and Democracy* foregrounds the voices and concerns of individuals actually engaged in using all kinds of digital media for practical political uses" (Xenos, 2009).

CURRENT INTERESTS AND PROJECTS

Irony as Political Method

My interest in speaking back to the power catalyzes my interest in the roles that satire can play in political environments and mediascapes. I am especially excited about the work I have published but have several other essays on satire as well as on digital dissent which was the focus of my first funded project. I hold particular admiration for the theoretical and philosophical work of Linda Hutcheon on parody, Claire Colebrook on irony, and Cris Mayo on humor.

I recall Donna asking me about humor when I would bring drafts of my dissertation on emotions to her, the role of humor within affect and how wonderful it would have been to explore that more fully with her, as she loves to laugh and has a very quirky, sharp and witty sense of humor. And, she speaks of its importance in her pedagogy. As she wrote in the opening of the *Manifesto*,

> Irony is about contradictions that do not resolve into larger wholes, even dialectically, about the tension of holding incompatible things together because both or all are necessary and true. Irony is about humor and serious play. It is also a rhetorical strategy and a political method, one I would like to see more honored within socialist-feminism. (Haraway, 1991, p. 149)

My commitment to questions of media stems from my interest in how education can instill curiosity and critical reflective skills Dewey and Freire recognized as requisite for democracy. Beyond the relative silence on media as a site of curricula or tool of social control that necessitates central understanding for those in educational studies, educational scholars only too rarely assess how to insert their research into the public sphere, including into news media. A century ago, John Dewey and Walter Lippmann debated this relationship of scholarship to news media; I place myself in that lineage and take my responsibilities to current and future generations seriously.

Patriotism and Political Satire

Philosophical and theoretical areas that I am eager to develop further include: "inscribed habits of (in)attention" (Boler, 1999) and how this concept can be further explored to analyze the now widely-used notion of attentional economies; and, the role of satire and creativity in social movement practices. Similarly with my more recent work, there is significant interest and I am able to cross the boundaries accomplishing what my present institution UT terms "knowledge mobilization" but I prefer to think of as public intellectualism – witnessing rallies such as the writing about political satire which I have found satisfying to try and engage in news and op-ed context, thought an article I wrote criticizing the film Borat for not meeting the standards of political satire drew significant hate mail in response.

We never know when the work we do may tap into a vein, a significant event or pulse. But it is fair to say in retrospect that my intuition serves me well in terms of catching the zeitgeist of ideas early on – for example, my work in the 1980s and 1990s looking for scholars to discuss emotion and affect (a wave that seems finally to be hitting with the current Affective Turn); writings on patriotism, nationalism and war since 1991 to publishing "On the Spirit of Patriotism" with Michalinos Zembylas in 2002 – a period when it was quite challenging and risky for anyone to speak up against the war in Afghanistan; pursuing what I saw to be the value of user-generated content and "microblogging" (my reason for commencing the project that resulted in *Digital Media and Democracy*, and for conducting interviews with scholars such as Robert McChesney and Geert Lovink and journalists including Amy Goodman and Hass Ibrahim) while others dismissed so-called user-generated content; my work with Matt Ratto producing a conference in 2010 entitled *DIY Citizenship: Critical Making and Social Media*; and my interest in studying how young people are engaging new modes of participatory democracy as turned out to be the case as rebellions and protests spread from the Cairo to Greece, London to Wall Street in NY. Two web-based achievements I feel especially proud of are *Critical Media Literacy in Times of War* and a collaboratively produced study guide to accompany the documentary *The Corporation*.

IN SUMMARY

My intellectual history and relationship with philosophy of education bears parallels with my childhood ritual of burying birds. Both seem to me oddly but infinitely hopeful practices, grounded in the usefulness and very embodied need of the everyday, not abstractions at all. The connection between studies of emotion and affect, and my political philosophical interrogation of media and activist practices, share a concern with what is silenced, which choices are muted, how power shapes what is heard and unheard.

Today I recognize (with collaborator Zoe Sofoulis in the History of Consciousness Legacies project) the extraordinary intellectual training many of us received that has laid the groundwork for my philosophical work today and that of many others who emerged out of that program. It helps me see, for example, a significant shift from an epistemology of truths to an ontology of making sense, tied deeply to technological mutations. Its rapidly evolving nature ascribes this work to margins and overlaps, as my earlier work in emotion did at that time. If given my preference, I would name the field I am currently working in as something akin to: *"Understanding Subjectivity, Agency, Politics, Power, Semiotics and Bodies through Studies of Media Communications and Technology."*

Part of the contribution of my work as both a scholar and public intellectual is to remind my readers of need and persistence of such interdisciplinary lines of inquiry including a concern for how the unheard, sometimes unspoken, voices and perspectives are marginalized by the powerful and dominant forces of such institutions as higher education, media, and even government and corporate decision-making bodies. This work is never more necessary than today, and brings the philosophy of education and public culture from the theoretical into applied realms. The focus of much of my work over the last 15 years has been on what might be likened to a Foucauldian analysis of media and power, voices and the view from below, margin and center, heard and the unheard as Ranciere says, and as feminists have theorized from the get go.

A further but absolutely central aspect of my work today as a scholar is a commitment to serving as a public intellectual if and when I am able. Whether that includes as a public scholarly, media or online go-to real time commentator, writing for journalistic venues, or circulating and sparking ideas and conversation in the public domain for alternative and independent media and social action, I consider my history of philosophical privilege now to be of service to the common good.

A lot has changed since Jaggar called out the myth of 'dispassionate investigation' in scholarship and charged that "Western epistemology has tended to view emotion with suspicion and even hostility" (1989, p. 161). And fifteen years before affect and Deleuze became an area-du-jour for scholarly study, in 1993 I completed a dissertation on our deep need of attention to emotion in education and the cost of denying it. Since then, scholarship on affect and its relation to emotion has built to a crescendo and has moved on from representing the gendered landscape and discourses of difference that Jaggar's and my texts made visible. Yet has this wave of affect theory really answered Jaggar's call to overturn the myth of scientific objectivity? As Zoe Sofoulis maintains, positivism is better than alive and well – it is thriving, and monstrous in a Frankensteinian sense. Perhaps its legacy is not so much in understanding desire (as Massumi might have us believe) so much as its potential for pushing into "good thinking and stubborn love" (Alexander & Jones, 2013, p. 251).

A politically-engaged philosophy of both education and digital media offer ways of understanding the threshold experience of the Other, a way of entering the space of social inclusion and activism for those like our students whose lives most often do not (yet) depend on it, at least not in material terms, but certainly do in emotional and intellectual ones; of "learning in other words what it means to live in the shadow world of non-recognition and how best to counter it ethically, legally and politically" (Butler, 2013, n.p.).

Throughout my career, I have articulated the desire to transcend embodiment as a "new digital Cartesianism" (2002, p. 331), replacing an older turn to God for "ideal rationality" with an ironic "turn to the body as the final source of epistemological certainty" (p. 331). My work in the philosophy of technology today continues this contribution, exploring more broadly the possibilities and difficulties of virtuality that includes ecological, posthuman, non-human and digital. I continue to expand on my earlier understandings of a virtuality that encourages a Cartesian duality between logos and pathos. Today, I am joining my earlier work in affect and emotions with the virtual, in exploring the ways in which the virtual may return us to the threshold of embodiment (and by extension of love) in ever-more-certain ways – to the place where the unseen and the seen become one. To do so, I map the uneasy passage between reflection and action, imagination and creativity, interiority and intersubjectivity.

My research presently focuses on how individuals and collectivities engage affect, social media, and creativity in struggles for social change, in such forms as the Occupy Wall Street Movement and other global uprisings (see for example Boler et al., 2014). Declaiming is not enough, neither for the scholar or the activist, and collectivities can be surveilled and disbanded. The most radical gathering of virtual embodiment may be the loneliest number, but the most effective activist cell. Judith Butler similarly today troubles the thresholds between work/love, public/private and scholarship/activism, which – once again – appear to converge in the ever-urgent need for more than public intellectualism, into radical collectivism. Paolo Freire couldn't have said it better himself:

> Even as we seek to affirm ways of acting and transforming the world, we also have to affirm ways of being thoughtful, ways of reading listening learning ... and to take those critical practices with us onto the street, into those spaces of work and love, and into our public lives.
>
> For as important as freedom of expression is, and it
> most.
> surely.
> is.
> So too it is important to know what we want to express.
> And why.
> As important as freedom of assembly is, and it surely is ...
> It remains equally important to know it is why we assemble and for what purpose.
> (Butler, 2013b)

For me, philosophy of education is a road that has taken me to many strange and wondrous lands, and continues to do so in ever more diverse modes and incarnations. Yet its power continues to lie expressly in its capacity to remind me of Butler's imperative, to return us to the collective *for what purpose*, and the ways in which a philosophy of education can address this question with a greater capacity for robust criticality and meta-view than any other.

ACKNOWLEDGMENT

I wish to dedicate this essay to the memories and pioneering works of Maxine Greene and Roger I. Simon.

My heartfelt thanks to Dr. Anne Harris for keen and supportive editing and feedback that enabled the composition of this essay.

NOTES

[1] An infamous moment in San Francisco as well as protest history. For further history and reading, see "The Battle for the International Hotel" by James Sobredo http://foundsf.org/index.php?title=The_Battle_for_the_International_Hotel retrieved September 15, 2014.

[2] Certainly some do balance the two: this was a topic I ended up discussing at length with one of my first colleagues in philosophy of education – Professor Deanne Bogdan – who as an Emeritus professor now pursues both music and philosophy as a highly accomplished pianist.

[3] And yes, to this day at the forefront of scholarship in affect as well as myriad other fields are questions of how to outwit the power of such binaries: the prisonhouse of language as Fredric Jameson puts it.

[4] The later publication of this essay in the journal Cultural Studies, is thanks to the generous reading and encouragement of Roger I. Simon. Roger is yet another early mentor (who, years later, would also become my colleague at OISE/UT), whom I first met at the American Educational Studies Association Conference in 1993, the final months of writing my dissertation; after his delivery of the R. Freeman Butts Invited Lecture, I approached him recognizing he might be one of the few scholars I had met who appreciated the question of emotion and affect in education. He kindly offered to read my early version of "The Risks of Empathy". I am forever grateful to these correspondences with Roger, written from his Ontario summer cottage, and his humble generosity of spirit and intellect.

FAVORITE WORKS

The Works of Others

De Beauvoir, S.(1962). *The Second Sex, Translated and Edited by HM Paishley.* London.

Greene, M. (1988). *The Dialectic of Freedom.* New York: Teachers College Press.

Hall, S. (1993). Encoding, decoding. *The Cultural Studies Reader*, edited by Simon During, pp. 90-103. London: Routledge. 3rd ed.

Haraway, D. (1991). *Simians, Cyborgs, and Women: The Reinvention of Nature.* London and New York: Routledge.

Sartre, J. P. (1956). *Being and Nothingness*, trans. Hazel E. Barnes. New York: Philosophical Library.

My Own Work

Boler, M. (1997). The Risks of Empathy: Interrogating Multiculturalism's Gaze, *Cultural Studies*, Vol. 11, No. 2, 253-273.

Boler, M. (1999). *Feeling Power: Emotions and Education.* New York: Routledge.

Boler, M. (1999). Emotional Quotient: The Taming of the Alien, *Discourse: Journal for Theoretical Studies in Media and Culture*, Vol. 21, Iss. 2, Article 4.

Boler, M. (2000). An Epoch of Difference: Hearing Voices in the Nineties (Decade Review of 1990-99 for Special 50th Anniversary Issue), *Educational Theory*, Vol. 50, No. 3, 357-381.

Zembylas, M. and M. Boler. (2002). On the Spirit of Patriotism: Challenges of a "Pedagogy of Discomfort," *Teachers' College Record*, Special Online Issue on Education and September 11, Fall 2002, http://www.tcrecord.org/content.asp?contentid=11007

REFERENCES

Barad, K. (2007). *Meeting the universe halfway: Quantum physics and the entanglement of matter and meaning*. Durham, NC: Duke University Press.
Boler, M. (1999). *Feeling power: Emotions and education*. New York/London: Routledge.
Boler, M. (2002). The new digital Cartesianism: Bodies and spaces in online education. In Scott Fletcher (Ed.), *Philosophy of education society* (pp. 331-340). Champaign, IL.
Boler. M. (2004). *Democratic dialogue in education: Troubling speech, disturbing silence*. New York: Peter Lang.
Boler, M. (2007). Hypes, hopes, and actualities: Representations of bodies and difference in text-based digital communication. *New Media and Society*, 9(1), February.
Boler, M. (2008a). Making claims: The responsibilities of qualitative researcher. In Kathaleen Gallagher (Ed.), *Methodological dilemmas of qualitative research*. Routledge.
Boler, M. (Ed.). (2008/2010). *Digital media and democracy: Tactics in hard times*. Cambridge: MIT Press (Critics Choice Award, American Educational Studies Association, 2010).
Boler, M., Macdonald, A., Nitsou, C., & Harris, A. (2014). Connective labor and social media Women's roles in the 'leaderless' Occupy movement.*Convergence: The International Journal of Research into New Media Technologies*, 1354856514541353.
Bozalek, V., Leibowitz, B., Carollissen, R., & Boler, M. (Eds.). (2013). *Discerning critical hope in education*. London: Routledge.
Butler, J. (2013a). McGill Honorary Doctorate address, available at: http://www.youtube.com/watch?v=1F1GS56iOAg
Butler, J. (2013b). Informal talk at McGill on the public intellectual. Available at: http://www.youtube.com/watch?v=4ECjyoU6kGA
Chomsky, Noam. (1966). *The responsibility of intellectuals*.
Driscoll, Jennifer. (1999). Feeling power: Emotions and education (Review). *JAC*, 715-720.
Garrison, Jim. (1999). Responding to the paradoxes of feeling power. *Educational Researcher* (Book Reviews), December, 33-34, 43.
Haraway, D. (1991). The Cyborg Manifesto: Science, technology, and Socialist-feminism in the late twentieth century. In *Symians, cyborgs and women: The reinvention of nature* (pp. 149-181). New York, NY: Routledge.
Haraway, D. (2003). *The companion species manifesto*. Chicago, IL: University of Chicago Press.
Houston, Barbara. (2002). Feeling power (Review). *Hypatia*, 17(1), Winter, 205-209.
Jaggar, A. (1989). Love and knowledge: Emotion in feminist epistemology. In Alison M. Jaggar & S. R. Bordo (Eds.), *Gender/body/knowledge: Feminist reconstructions of being and knowing* (pp. 145-171). New Brunswick/London: Rutgers University Press.
Massumi, B. (2002). *Parables for the virtual: Movement, affect, sensation*. Durham, NC: Duke University Press.
Ratto, M., & Boler, M. (Eds.). (2014). *DIY citizenship: Critical making and social media*: Cambridge, MIT Press (forthcoming).
Reilly, Ian, & Boler, Megan. (2014). Satire and social change: The rally to restore sanity and the future of politics. *Communication, Culture and Critique* (forthcoming).
Smith, L. T. (1999). *Decolonizing methodologies: Research and indigenous peoples*. Zed books.
Xenos, M. A. (2009). Review of M. Boler (Ed.), 'Digital media and democracy: Tactics in hard times.' *Information, Communication & Society*, 12(8), 1268-1269.
Zembylas, Michalinos, & Boler, Megan. (2002). On the spirit of patriotism: Challenges of a "pedagogy of discomfort." *Teachers College Record*, August 12.

NICHOLAS C. BURBULES

THE PERSONAL AND THE PHILOSOPHICAL

I have always had the attitude that, perhaps more than any other field of endeavor, philosophy as a life's work involves a set of personal questions and issues that are partly being worked out in one's professional undertakings.

I would not ordinarily write about my upbringing and events from my personal life – this is certainly the first time I have ever done so. But it is necessary here as a context, or explanation, for the kind of philosophy I do and the outlook through which I view educational problems.

It would have been difficult to predict an academic career from my family background or early years in school. I was born in 1954 and grew up in a working class, mixed ethnic family on the South Side of Chicago. I went to very good public schools, I had many excellent teachers, and I performed well academically, but I was wild and often in trouble. My teachers must have despaired over how to help this bright kid learn to control himself, and this perception was perhaps reinforced by the fact that they knew my home life was very troubled, sometimes violent. I grew up in-between a loving but dysfunctional domestic situation and the very strict moral and religious influence of my grandparents, with whom my sister and I spent a great deal of time when it wasn't safe to be in our home.

The point I want to draw out of this background is that from a certain time in my life I was preoccupied with the question of whether I was a good person, and whether it was within my capacity to become a better person. I was troubled by the anger and intemperance I saw in myself. By the time I was in high school, in the 1970s, these self-doubts took me in the direction of a passionate, intense, but brief engagement with that strange brew of Pentecostalism and countercultural values that was called the Jesus Freak movement (or as I called it, "Jesus as the ultimate hippie"). This seemed to me a way of reconciling my anti-Vietnam war activities, my growing curiosity about drugs, and my desire for a rebirth, a fresh start, and a Higher Power who could help me quell the demons that made me question my worth as a human being.

My involvement with religion carried forward into college and I declared a religious studies major the day after I arrived there. Yet, as it played out, probably nothing did more to drive me away from my personal beliefs than turning religion into an object of academic study. What drew me into religion was a "passionate intensity," a desire to be cleansed and carried forward in the company of a close-knit community who helped me form a new sense of who I was. It was non-, even anti-intellectual, and I thought that was what I needed. But studying the history of Christianity and the origins of the gospel (a narrative so full of strange historical circumstances and paths that could have gone another way, along with the diverse sects and the debates over what it even meant to be a Christian), made it impossible for me to believe in the inevitability and rightness of the "One Way" I had been inculcated with. Studying comparative religions and the world-wide diversity of spiritual faiths made it impossible for me to believe that I, and people who believed what I did, were "saved," while everyone else – including the billions who were not, and could not be, even exposed to these "truths," were inevitability doomed to hell.

It is an oversimplification to say that I faced a conflict between mind and heart, and chose mind. But during this time I started taking more philosophy courses, and fewer religion courses. I started noticing that there were a lot of good people who weren't religious, and a lot of religious people who weren't very good. I studied ethics, I studied existentialism; I started to realize that my core question, How does one live a good life? wasn't necessarily a religious question. And so, my interest in philosophy sprang from the same origins as my interest in religion. I have always been moved by the well-known quote from Ludwig Wittgenstein:

> What is the use of studying philosophy if all that it does for you is enable you to talk with some plausibility about some abstruse questions of logic, etc., and if it does not improve your thinking about the important questions of everyday life .... You see, I know that it is difficult to think well about "certainty," "probability," "perception," etc. But it is, if possible, still more difficult to think, or try to think, really honestly about your life and other people's lives.

At the same time, I started to want to understand certain authors and texts, I started to exercise my writing as a form of self-expression, I started to discover the strange joy of copying notes and quotations out of stacks of books in the library, and then trying to arrange them in a meaningful way. I didn't realize it, but I was cultivating the dispositions of an academic. I had professors who reshaped my outlook on the world, and I started to think, this is what I want to be able to do for others.

AN EXISTENTIAL OUTLOOK

It is only with hindsight that I can recognize how much of my philosophical outlook was shaped early on by existentialism. Camus and Kierkegaard were some of the first philosophers I studied in college. I remember being deeply moved by the image of Sisyphus in Camus' essay: destined to push a rock up the hill, never able to succeed, finish, and rest, but ceaselessly striving against the obstacle. I remember the force of Kierkegaard's injunction to stay in the moment of difficulty, not to seek to resolve or escape it. This is philosophy not in the technical sense of developing systematic theory, but in portraying a vision of life and human endeavor that is the opposite of triumphant. It is a vision that is profoundly sobering – not pessimistic, I would say, but tragic (which is not the same thing). Success and failure are never very far apart. Modesty about one's provisional achievements is a virtue: especially, I have argued, in education.

In my own mind there is a direct link between these early formative readings and experiences and the themes of my later work. Karl Popper is reputed to have said, "We learn from mistakes, therefore our aim in life should be to make mistakes as often as possible." It's a quip, of course, but it has always struck me as taking entirely too sanguine a view of what making a mistake is actually like. Of course we can learn from our mistakes, and ought to; imperfection is a condition of human life. But the experience of making a mistake – a big mistake, a failure of character, a harm toward others, a neglect to live up to one's own standards – is not something one shrugs over and simply resolves to learn from. That comes later, perhaps. But in the moment, these can be experiences of deep self-disappointment, doubt, confusion, regret, anger, and guilt. There is nothing redemptive about them. They hurt. The best that can be said about them is that they help strengthen the resolve to live our best selves, and not to fail again. But of course we will fail again.

And so, the thread in my essays that deal with themes of tragedy, doubt, aporia, and getting lost as learning moments. I think that no one has captured this central theme in my work as well as Andrea English:

> Nicholas Burbules offers a further way of understanding our encounters with the unfamiliar and unexpected. He uses the term aporia to describe "an experience that affects us on many levels at once: we feel discomfort, we doubt ourselves ... Aporia is a crisis of choice, of action and identity, and not just of belief. When I have too many choices, or no choice; I'm stuck. I do not know how to go on." In these moments in our experience, we are "lost," as Burbules states, and this sense of being lost can lead to a different kind of doubt than the doubt that arises merely as a transitional phase between a wrong answer and a predetermined right answer. This different kind of doubt is part of the experience of the "movement towards an unknown destination." As he suggests, this sense of being lost makes a different kind of growth possible; it engenders new inquiries, exploration, and the posing of "questions that make a new understanding possible." This experience of being lost points to the space of the in-between of learning (as I have described throughout this book), a space that allows for learning in ways we could not have imagined without this experience.

One can never control how others read one's work, and sometimes even the creative potential of misreading can help you see aspects of your work that you never intended or fully understood yourself. But it has always bothered me when readers characterize this line of my work as pessimistic or gloomy. What I have always tried to emphasize, and what readers like English appreciate, is that these moments and experiences of difficulty are potentially productive – and more to the point, productive of understandings and insights that could not be achieved in any easier or more direct way. You cannot tell anyone else what the experience of failure is like, or what it can teach you. Of course our students, our children, and others have to be able to make their own mistakes. That is almost a truism. But they also need to experience what making a mistake feels like, and how to move on. That is even more important, in what it can teach us.

CRITICAL STUDIES

In graduate school I had two primary mentors and influences, Arturo Pacheco and Denis (D.C.) Phillips. They were both strong personalities, inspiring teachers, and generous supporters for me. I did research with both, I was a teaching assistant with both, and later in my PhD, when both were on leave at the same time, I covered some courses for each of them. Each socialized me into a strong orientation toward critical philosophy – but different orientations, which I struggled to reconcile.

In Art Pacheco's classes, I was reading the critical theory of post-Marxian writers, particularly the Frankfurt School. In these traditions, critique meant questioning constructions of norms and knowledge against the background of institutional dynamics of power: it meant critiquing ideologies (including educational ideologies, like meritocracy or equal opportunity) as legitimating frameworks that led people to accept their roles, whether privileged or underprivileged, as the proper working-out of social processes of selection and advancement that were fair and in the wider interests of all. I remember the shocking impact of books like Samuel Bowles and Herbert Gintis's *Schooling in Capitalist America* (1976) which argued (after the hopefulness of the civil rights movement and compensatory educational reforms like Head Start, Title I, and school integration) that schools functioned much more as perpetuators, even reinforcers, of inequality than as avenues of escape from it – and that this wasn't merely an unfortunate failure of schools to fulfill their ideals, but actually just what schools in a capitalist society were designed to do. It was during this period, in the United States, Britain, and elsewhere, that criticizing schooling as an institution became a legitimate area of scholarship and teaching within schools of education.

In Denis Phillips's classes, I was introduced to a very different critical tradition, the emphasis on identifying formal and informal logical fallacies and distorted, sloppy uses of language that came to be described as analytical philosophy of education. This mode of critique was not (overtly) political in nature; the idea was that the philosopher was a nonpartisan referee, trying to enforce the rules of clear speaking and rigorous argumentation on all points of view. This mode of critique was equally rigorous, sometimes almost devastating in its dismissal of nonsense (I like to say that in Denis's classes I first learned the term "bullshit" as a technical term in philosophy!) As I started going to conferences, I saw that this methodological stance was often reinforced in practice by a hyper-aggressive – and in some cases ruthlessly dismissive – attack style that one could hardly avoid recognizing as linked to a conflict between male egos. To be sure, men were hardly the only wielders of these weapons (many of us remember an epic showdown between Harvey Siegel and Jane Roland Martin at the 1983 Philosophy of Education Society meeting), but I and others struggled with how to earn respect and credibility in a domain where the Shootout at the OK Corral seemed to be the model for good, rigorous, philosophical debate.

Something else was happening during this period, and in years to come: the discovery within the educational domain of Michel Foucault's work, and later other poststructural writers, both feminist and of other stripes, who used the tools of critical language analysis, not primarily in defense of clarity and precision, but as a critique of discourse, that is, language in use: how meanings get overlaid with social and political significance; how struggles over different meanings, and who gets to decide them, are part of wider social and political struggles; how hidden meanings or ambiguities operate as tools of manipulation, and not only as offenses against philosophical standards of clarity.

These were the influences that formed me in graduate school. My dissertation, *Ideology and Radical Educational Research* (1983) was a 450 page, overstuffed attempt to reconcile these different traditions into a coherent theory. I would not say that I was successful. But a number of my papers and projects since then have tried to keep these different meanings of "critical" in engagement with each other. I have tried to maintain this multisided conversation, in my own mind at least, even as others have characterized these traditions as either/or opponents, and rushed to take sides.

One of the areas in which I have tried to reconcile these critical models is in my work on dialogue in education. From Plato to Freire to Habermas and Gadamer, philosophers have focused on the normative value of dialogical communication as a model of teaching and learning. I share this normative commitment, in theory and in my own Socratic teaching; but over the years I have been increasingly influenced by the critical work of scholars like Elizabeth Ellsworth, Alison Jones and others – sometimes in direct criticism of my work – who, in line with the critical discursive approach described previously, want to ask different kinds of questions about where, when, and how dialogue happens, and who benefits or fails to benefit from those interactions. Putting dialogue in context is an important corrective to tendencies to idealize or abstract dialogue's potential. Real social asymmetries, different cultural styles of communication, and histories that influence and frame the communicative interactions between people, and between groups of people, all need to be taken into account – and the result, I think, has been an increased scepticism in my work toward the celebratory way in which dialogue in education has often been championed. It is never easy being criticized, but this is one area in which criticism pushed me into taking my ideas in new directions.

Finally, part of this work on dialogue has been carried out with Suzanne Rice. One of our core ideas, which has been sketched but not yet fully developed, is the idea of communicative virtue. What are the actual capacities and dispositions that enable effective dialogue, and what are the circumstances under which they can be formed, internalized, and sustained (or, conversely, what are the circumstances that discourage and undermine them)? It is all well and good to praise the values of dialogue, listening, open-mindedness, etc., in general; but these are also situated, embodied activities, carried out by real people in real situations, and as such they are themselves implicated in dynamics of encouragement, discouragement, punishment, and risk that can make the exercise of these virtues much harder – one might even say more dangerous – for some participants than for others. This recognition needs to be drawn into a fuller theory of dialogue, without (I would say) abandoning a normative commitment.

TECHNOLOGY STUDIES

During the 1990s I came to realize that new technologies, including the Internet, were not just the latest fad in education, but an enduring, transformative influence. I never went into this field to be a technology scholar, but during this decade and since it has become perhaps my most visible body of work.

At a deeper level, the way in which I have tried to engage technology has involved a working-out of other longstanding philosophical questions, in a domain to which I see them as especially relevant. For me, the most interesting aspects of these new hypertextual media are how they exemplify the themes of navigation, exploration, serendipity, and getting lost – which are both interesting metaphors for the journeys of learning, while at the same time very concrete experiential dimensions of the ways in which we interact with these media. The wonders and the frustrations of navigating links – or making links – in decentralized knowledge systems like blogs and wikis, and how we can evaluate credibility when the status or authority of the author are inscrutable, or where these is no single author, or where the "reader" is also an "author" – all overlay my ongoing interests in doubt, uncertainty, and aporia.

I have long felt that in the field of education, technology issues have been given too little attention by philosophers, which has ceded the terrain to psychologists, engineers, and computer scientists. Technological questions in education have therefore been framed as predominantly utilitarian: How do we teach with new technological tools; Which modes of instructional design are most effective; Where can new technologies create greater efficiency and productivity; and so on. Whereas the philosopher's questions: How do these new technologies change us; How do new technologies influence how we think about knowledge, where it comes from, and how it is validated; What ethical problems or dilemmas does this new domain of social interaction and communication confront educators with, have been neglected.

At the same time, there seems to be an ongoing struggle among educators with how to assess the wider impact of these new technologies: Are they exciting transformative resources that will unlock the potential of new learning, reaching new audiences and liberating them from the confines of the classroom? Or are they dystopic influences that foster "shallow" thinking, instant gratification, weaker social ties, and even greater corporate influence over the methods and content of teaching? And so there are second-order questions about how we are supposed to think about these technologies. For me, and my "tragic" outlook, the answer is always "both." If there is a hallmark to my work in this area, it is that we need to keep both the possibilities and the dangers of these technologies always in mind.

We need to be attuned to the inevitability of unintended consequences. We need to operate in that uncomfortable space of embracing the potential of these new technologies, and trying to move them toward more productive and equitable educational pathways, while also expecting that in ways foreseeable and unforeseeable these will yield up new problems and inequities. A useful manual for documenting the tensions and paradoxes of this sort of outlook is Edward Tenner's *Why Things Bite Back*.

SITUATED PHILOSOPHY OF EDUCATION

The exchanges with critics around my work on dialogue, and a larger body of reading and thinking about the notion of practice (some of it with my colleague Paul Smeyers), has caused me to think differently about the ways we go about doing philosophy of education. The prescriptive tradition is a powerful influence on us: that what we do as philosophers is to propose what education should be about, what an educated person is, how education should best proceed, how education can lead us to a better society. Even the analytical tradition, which characterized itself as nonpartisan on various substantive issues surrounding teaching and learning, but simply devoted to encouraging the standards of reasoned argument and clearer uses of language, was at another level simply another prescriptive endeavor. People have questioned whether these normative conceptions of reason and clarity of language are in fact generalizable or neutral, or whether they actually import tacit assumptions that privilege certain kinds of substantive claims over others. And they have questioned whether the exercise of these analytical tools manifests cultural (ethnic, racial, national, or gendered) styles of thought and expression that are in practice exclusionary or biased against non-dominant styles of thought and expression.

As a result of these concerns, I have recently worked with Kathleen Knight Abowitz in positing a "situated" approach to philosophy of education: one that reimagines our own activities as philosophers as a kind of practice: and as a practice, one that is always carried out by actual people; with their own characteristics and positionality; in actual circumstances; applied to actual problems and with actual consequences at stake. This pragmatic self-awareness should not cause us to abandon the normative stance – otherwise philosophy becomes only a kind of sociology of knowledge. But in exchanges with Harvey Siegel and many colleagues over the years I have become convinced that prescribing normative aims without also engaging the question of whether, how, and under what circumstances people might be able to achieve them, is an example of what Thomas Nagel called "the view from nowhere." For situated philosophy of education the philosopher is always somewhere, and aware of himself or herself as such. In my 2001 PES presidential address I called this a "binocular" perspective, and emphasized the importance (and the difficulty) of keeping both points of view in mind at once.

A PHILOSOPHER IN-BETWEEN

The self-portrait I have painted here, as I re-read it now, has a recurring theme of someone continually in-between outlooks in tension: religion and philosophy; analytical and continental conceptions of critical philosophy; the prescriptive and the deconstructive takes on dialogue; hope and doubt as perspectives on learning; a tragic view of both the possibilities and the dangers of technology, and this final "binocular" perspective on the nature and purpose of philosophy itself. The story I tell myself is that this is a creative, fertile dialectic, not the rationalizations of someone who wants to have it both ways, or who cannot make up his mind.

It is the strand of John Dewey that most appeals to me, that when we are confronted with an untenable dichotomy, the resolution is not to make a forced choice between the alternatives, but to seek a new perspective that reframes the choice. Wittgenstein, my other favorite philosopher, says something similar.

I have to leave it to others to judge whether I have been at all successful.

FAVORITE WORKS

Personal Favorites

Burbules, N. C. (1990). The tragic sense of education. *Teachers College Record*, 91(4), 469-479.

Burbules, N. C. & Rice, S. (1991). Dialogue across differences: Continuing the conversation. *Harvard Educational Review*, 61(4), 393-416.

Burbules, N. C. (1993). *Dialogue in teaching: Theory and practice*. New York: Teachers College Press.

Burbules, N. C. (1996). Postmodern doubt and philosophy of education. In A. Neiman (Ed.), *Philosophy of education 1995* (pp. 39-48). Urbana, IL: Philosophy of Education Society.

Burbules, N. C. (1997). A grammar of difference: Some ways of rethinking difference and diversity as educational topics. *Australian Educational Researcher*, 24(1), 97-116.

Burbules, N. C. (2000). Aporias, webs, and passages: Doubt as an opportunity to learn. *Curriculum Inquiry*, 30(2), 171-187.

Burbules, N. C. (2002). A philosophical odyssey. In S. Rice (Ed.), *Philosophy of education 2001* (pp. 1-14). Urbana, IL: Philosophy of Education Society.

Burbules, N. C. (2005). Rethinking the virtual. In J. Weiss, J. Nolan, & P. Trifonas (Eds.), *The international handbook of virtual learning environments* (pp. 3-24). Dordrecht: Kluwer Publishers.

Peters, M. A., Burbules, N. C., & Smeyers, P. (2008). *Showing and doing: Wittgenstein as a pedagogical philosopher*. Boulder, CO: Paradigm Publishing. Revised and reissued with a new Preface and Postscript (2010).

Burbules, N. C. & Knight Abowitz, K. (2009). A situated philosophy of education. In R. Glass (Ed.), *Philosophy of education society yearbook 2008* (pp. 268-276). Urbana, IL: Philosophy of Education Society.

Major Influential Texts

Dewey, J. (1916). *Democracy and education: An introduction to the philosophy of education*. New York: The Free Press.

Foucault, M. (1977). *Discipline & punish: The birth of the prison*. New York: Vintage.

Freire, P. (1970). *Pedagogy of the oppressed*. New York: Continuum.

Marx, K., & Engels, F. (1970). *The German ideology.* New York: International Press.
Noddings, N. (1984). *Caring: A feminine approach to ethics & moral education.* Berkeley: University of California Press.
Rorty, R. (1980). *Philosophy and the mirror of nature.* New York: Cambridge University Press.
Wittgenstein, L. (1958). *Philosophical investigations.* Oxford: Blackwell.

RANDALL CURREN

MY LIFE IN PHILOSOPHY

My earliest memory, at the age of three months, is of the bright interior of an airplane, and being carried into the dark, chill air of what I later learned was Kalamazoo, Michigan, in December 1955, for Christmas with my father's family. I remember the following Easter gazing across a sun drenched room as my uncle, visiting from Kalamazoo, spoke and our "colored" maid stood quietly ironing what might have been my father's white shirts. That was in our apartment, one of 1,114 in the Parkchester development in Gentilly, the lowest lying neighborhood in New Orleans, at a time when having a maid was common and no doubt abetted by racial barriers to more desirable employment. This is my earliest image of fellow human beings and of a person working, and I have later memories of our maid greeting me and walking me to a store for treats after school. We moved into a "GI starter home" in nearby Gentilly Woods before I began kindergarten, and I remember vividly my parents' heated discussion of the impending enforcement of Brown v. Board of Education. Why were they upset that black and white children would go to school together? Nothing they said about race on that or any other occasion made sense.

How could I not dwell upon these experiences years later in my philosophical encounters with contentions surrounding the role of ancient Athenian pedagogues – the household slaves in whose care children were entrusted as they walked through the city from one teacher's lessons to another's? How could I not bring my experience of the first wave of desegregation in New Orleans schools, and the importance of the personal connections I made, to my years of work on Aristotle's defense of common schools in which children from all parts of a city would be educated together as equals in civic friendship, to cooperate in ruling and being ruled in the common interest, sharing enough in common to all believe in a common good and common justice? There is nothing idle in my references to the failures of schools that serve urban youth, unjustifiably harsh, punitive treatment of juvenile offenders, "the role of racial injustice and hostility in undermining an equitable administration of criminal justice," and the school to prison pipeline (2000, 2002a, 2002b, 2002c, 2014b; quoting 2000, p. 246).

I have other vivid childhood memories of streets in Gentilly Woods flooded too deep by rain for me to walk through, the failing mark in reading in first grade that prompted a truce between my warring parents long enough for my father to help me learn to read, my father moving out when I was seven, my pleasure in teaching my brother arithmetic on a weekend in my father's apartment, my mother's suicide when I was eight, realizing at the age of ten that I was somehow much older than

L.J. Waks (ed.), Leaders in Philosophy of Education. 59–74.
© *2014 Sense Publishers. All rights reserved.*

my peers, and the enduring, perverse manifestations of my father's personality disorder. It is hard to grasp what is notable or abnormal in the social and environmental circumstances of one's early existence, without an independent measure of what is normal or reasonable to expect. Finding and overcoming one's blind spots in the course of time requires access to wider circles of acquaintance and thought. Could I write about the wish of homeschooling parents to be unchallenged in their exclusive determination of what their children will learn and with whom (Curren & Blokhuis, 2009), and not reflect on what I know of the difficulties parents can have in grasping their own limitations, the importance of good public institutions to overcoming the moral and prudential hazard to which our epistemic dependence subjects us all (Buchanan, 2004), and the importance of such institutions in my own early life? What remains now of the hallway, house, and neighborhood where my parents argued about desegregation is the crumbling pavement of a world of unacknowledged hazard washed away. When I began to lecture and write about climate change and sustainability in the aftermath of hurricanes Katrina and Rita (Curren, 2009a, b, 2010a, b, c, 2011, 2013a; Curren & Metzger, forthcoming), it was with an acute sense that I would never be going home again. I would like it to be true that, by thinking and writing about these matters with as much moral clarity as I can muster, I might do something in service to humanity.

I regard myself as lucky to have been contemplative by nature and driven to understand everything, but my parents' mental illness was impossible to fathom at the time, and the weight of survivor guilt filled my veins like lead through much of high school. It helped that I had by then become a reader in diverse subjects and found philosophy, and I had the presence of mind to take out a subscription to *Psychology Today* and read R. D. Laing's *Sanity, Madness and the Family* and D. H. Lawrence's *Sons and Lovers*, the latter no less an exploration of the dark corners of family life than the former. Having been taught little by my parents and left to ripen in Rousseau's garden as I might, I had also enjoyed more than a little freedom to explore, invent, and pursue my interests as I pleased. I never felt so intensely alive as I did on fire with ideas.

It was in libraries and bookstores especially that I found well-ordered spaces to make my own, beginning with the public library that opened when I was ten after the swamps teeming with crawfish and armadillos around our new apartment on the suburban edge of New Orleans were cleared and developed. I became interested in science and by the middle of junior high school I was supplementing family subscriptions to *National Geographic* and *Natural History* magazines with my own subscription to *Science Digest*. Barry Commoner's ecological classic, *Science and Survival*, arrived in the fall of 1967 as a supplement to *Natural History* and I read with keen interest its warnings of the unintended consequences of large-scale technologies – disruption of ecological systems, nuclear winter, "the possible influence of atmospheric carbon dioxide on the earth's temperature" (Commoner, 1967, p. 64) – as I began junior high school thinking pointedly about what I would do with my life. I had already abandoned the idea that I might become a petroleum geologist like my father, having been cautioned by him that the oil would be gone before there was any chance of me having a career. The peak of U.S. oil production arrived in 1971, much as he predicted, and his description of efforts within Texaco to hide this as "playing musical chairs on the Titanic" made a lasting impression. I read Leslie Groves' monumental *Story of the Manhattan Project* about the making of the atomic bomb, George Gamow's marvelous *Thirty Years That Shook Physics*, and many related works and histories of science and biographies of scientists and mathematicians, beginning with Marie Curie and Albert Einstein. The logic of explanations, experiments, and systems interested me, and reading those biographies of lives I perceived as exemplary and rewarding, I began to envision such a life for myself. I made my way to philosophy in part, but not entirely, through science and mathematics.

An early step on that journey was my first attempt at public speaking, in the sixth grade. I chose alchemy. The readings I found explained the Aristotelian four element theory of matter (earth, air, fire, and water) on which alchemy rested, and the history of discovery and invention through which the Aristotelian theory was replaced by the atomic theory of matter and modern understanding of chemical elements. It was a wonderful story. If lead and gold are manifestations of the same element, earth, why should it not be possible to transmute the former into the latter? Yet, it wasn't, and seeing that it wasn't suggested the need for a better theory of elements. I did well enough to return to my seat feeling elated, so I remember this as much for the lesson I learned about what I could do as for the story – a story that is one strand of the progressive replacement of an Aristotelian theory of science in seventeenth and eighteenth century philosophy, which I would find myself teaching university students fifteen years later.

Another step in my turn toward philosophy began in the summer of 1970, as I was working my way through a three-volume survey of physics and a shelf of math books in our neighborhood library. I read Henri Poincaré's classic, *Science and Hypothesis*, and found the chapter on infinity absolutely riveting. The idea of a proof by mathematical induction and the use of such proofs in demonstrating theorems about infinite series was the most amazing thing I had ever encountered. Browsing in a bookstore a few weeks later I came upon a review of Poincaré's book in Bertrand Russell's *Philosophical Essays*, and it dawned on me that *Science and Hypothesis* was as much philosophy as mathematics. I soon read Alfred North Whitehead's *Introduction to Mathematics*, also as much philosophy as mathematics, and took great delight in its recounting of the introduction of zero and the controversy associated with there being nothing it could refer to. *Philosophical Essays* was one of dozens of philosophy books I bought and devoured in the course of high school, using the money intended for my school lunches. One of those was a large book called *Ethics* with an image of the Parthenon on its cover. I bought it, read enough to learn the basics of utilitarian moral philosophy, and lay awake that night thinking through its implications. That was immensely exciting, and it led me to adjust my conduct in light of calculations that it would be little trouble to leave the world a bit more pleasing than I was finding it.

I was soon so obviously and persistently occupied with Russell's works in the precincts of my school, that three years after my graduation my younger brother complained that an English teacher, who had released me to the library to study David Hume's *Enquiry Concerning Human Understanding* for a full marking period, would sometimes confuse the two of us. Apparently concerned that I might object to something she had said, she would pull up short and ask, "Tyler, what would Bertrand Russell say about that?" He did not find this amusing. My reading of Russell's works included *Problems of Philosophy*, a few of his serious philosophical essays, the autobiography, numerous popular works, and parts of *Principles of Mathematics* and the *Essay on the Foundations of Geometry*. I learned geometry as a deductive system in my first (sophomore) year of high school, and it was far and away my favorite class – no less so for my encounters with Russell's *Essay* and Poincaré's chapter on non-Euclidean geometries. By junior year, I was listing "epistemologist" as my intended vocation on the class cards we filled out for each teacher.

I special ordered a copy of Einstein's collection, *Ideas and Opinions*, in the summer of 1971, and its eight short pieces on education were my introduction to thoughtful reflection on this topic that has so occupied me. Einstein's insistence on a broad and humanistic education for independent thought and judgment, education for peace and international solidarity in the nuclear age, and centrality of what we now refer to as intrinsic motivation in healthy schools, lives, and societies, sharpened and validated some of my own intuitions. Rereading his words now, I am struck by continuities with my present general account of education (Curren, 2006b, 2008a, 2014a, 2014b, forthcoming; Curren & Metzger, forthcoming: ch. 5), internationalist perspective on patriotism and civic education (Curren, 2009d, 2010a; Curren & Dorn, forthcoming), and occupation with motivation and well-being in education (Ryan, Curren, & Deci, 2013; Curren, 2015a, 2015b).

I cannot resist mentioning – as I sit writing this at my desk in the Institute for Advanced Study on Einstein Drive, in Princeton, and having recently accepted a professorship in the Royal Institute of Philosophy, co-founded by Russell in London – that by the end of high school I had affixed to the wall above my desk at home large black and white posters of both Einstein and Russell. These intimidating three foot by four foot titans looked down on a bedroom floor that was a sea of plexiglass, brass and aluminum tubing and spheres, high-voltage cables, capacitors and gauges, industrial corona suppressants, a half-fabricated 65,000 volt generator of my own design, an operational 40,000 volt generator I had built, and tools and materials, in which I had substantially lost interest as I discovered myself as a writer.

With this, we come now to my first adventure in philosophy of education, in the form of Whitehead's 1929 classic, *The Aims of Education*, and an impertinent little essay I wrote. Having been drawn by friends into co-editing the first issue or two of an unauthorized school newspaper we called *Essay*, I got the attention of my teachers by publishing this piece in which I critiqued the school's testing practices on the basis of Whitehead's three-stage theory of the cycle of learning. According to this theory of the "rhythm" of mental growth, learning is properly initiated in "romance," proceeds through a stage of "precision," and is consummated in "generalization." Whitehead notes that "we tend to confine [education] to the second stage of the cycle" and fail to arouse the imagination and achieve the deeper understanding that can long outlast the recollection of one or another detail (Whitehead, 1929, p. 18). I argued this failing was evident in the nature of what was and was not being tested in our school. Sales of *Essay* were forbidden yet brisk, and a copy soon sat in plain view on every teacher's desk. If there was any sense of crisis among the staff, it was well addressed by Ms. Lenyard, with whom I had classes in both trigonometry and calculus. Taking me aside, she asked how I was with the slide rule, confided she had never used one, and invited me to teach the upcoming slide rule unit and write, administer, and grade the test. The slide rule was a form of mechanical analog computer invented in the seventeenth century on the basis of John Napier's work on logarithms, and knowing some history of mathematics and being reasonably well practiced in the art of slide rule calculations, I accepted the offer. I taught and tested the history, underlying mathematical principles, operation, and skills as a package, instinctively adopting a kind of history and philosophy of mathematics approach to the teaching of mathematics. Let me offer a word of advice: When you do practical philosophy, take pains to get it right. Someone, maybe even you, may be asked to test your ideas on live, non-consenting, human subject, children. It did go rather well, I thought, and it will not surprise you to learn that I have devoted some of my more recent efforts in philosophy of education to understanding and improving grading and testing practices (Curren, 1992, 1995a, 1995b, 2004, 2006a, 2008b, 2009c, 2013b) and defending an integrated historical and philosophical approach to instruction in science, mathematics, and technology (Curren & Metzger, forthcoming).

I can write this now with an air of inevitability, but it is really somewhat unexpectedly that I have come to recognize my philosophical work as a gathering together of loose ends of my life, in which ever more aspects of my lived experience are sources of motivation and objects of puzzlement and concern. A passion for philosophy, and the associated grip of specific philosophical problems, typically owe much to encounters with philosophical writings and conversation. They may also owe something to experiences that puzzle, trouble, and linger in the mind.

HIGHER LEARNING

I began college in the fall of 1973 at the University of New Orleans, considering both philosophy and sculpture as possible majors. The sea that stretched from bed to closet and door to desk had begun to part and form itself into art, by means alternately constructive and reductive, as the shape of my impulses to design and make things was itself shifting. Those impulses had been strong in me from the age of about five onward but remained almost entirely unschooled. My philosophical impulses were similarly irresistible but unschooled. I knew by the end of high school that I could speak, teach, and write, but could I be good at philosophy? I could design and make, but could I be good at art? My father thought either major would be fine, noting how senseless it is to spend one's life doing something one doesn't like.

The pivotal educational experience of my undergraduate years arrived the following fall in the form of Norton Nelkin's seminar on Ludwig Wittgenstein's celebrated *Tractatus Logico-Philosophicus*. Norton had worked through the *Tractatus* with Wittgenstein's disciple, Norman Malcolm, in the context of an intensive seminar at Cornell, and his style was to put questions to us, wait long enough to get answers that satisfied him, and let the works that followed challenge those earlier in the series, rather than challenge them himself. We spent the semester working line by numbered line through the 73 pages of the *Tractatus*, and as I thought my way through its account of the relationships between language, thought, and the world I came to think it was true, if any such theory could be true (T. 6.54). About once each week a class would end with the assignment of a two-page interpretive essay due the next meeting, to be written without recourse to secondary sources – which might well have been wrong, and would in any case have been further works to interpret – until the time came to read Wittgenstein's *Blue Book* on our own and write a twenty-page paper on what it had to say about a central feature of the *Tractatus*. I was able to understand the *Blue Book* well enough to be shocked and awed by its destruction of what was so impressively constructed in the *Tractatus*. What a valuable educational experience that was! Norton graded on a 100 point scale, except that he reserved 100 for the notional possibility of a paper that would reveal itself as the singularly best any student would ever write for him. Sometime after the papers were due, he let us know that he was very disappointed that no one had understood the *Blue Book* at all, and my heart sank along with everyone else's, though he noted in closing that there were one or two papers he hadn't read yet. Mine was 26 pages, typed with half-inch margins to minimize the page count, and the prospect of reading that much may have landed it at the bottom of the stack. It came back a 99, and that persuaded me I could do philosophy well enough to make a go of it.

I signed up for Norton's seminar on Wittgenstein's *Philosophical Investigations* the following term, and wrote as much on the *Remarks on the Foundations of Mathematics* as the *PI* itself. Before long, Norton brought me by the department office and persuaded Carolyn Morillo, the department chair, to give me a job as office assistant. It was their way of adopting me, and it contributed more than a little to the quality of education I received on that former air force base re-commissioned in 1958 as New Orleans' first public university. My hours on the department clock, spent primarily in philosophical and wider conversation with the faculty, provided a wealth of personal attention and mentoring unimaginable for an undergraduate in these far more hurried times. Norton also hosted philosophical discussions in his home and Jerry Nosich and his wife, Jean, were extraordinarily generous in welcoming me into theirs for numerous gatherings, including at least one evening of listening to music with philosopher and cellist John Tice leading us through the score, commenting on phrasing, ornamentation, and the like. My course work in literary classics and music history were a footnote to what I learned from those three.

Well into that spring of 1975, I was both firmly committed to continuing in philosophy and confronted with the prospect of being cut off by my father if I did not change my major to mechanical engineering, a possibility we had never discussed. He was anxious for my future and ashamed at the prospect of a son doing work portrayed as useless and unmanly in the *Wall Street Journal* articles he passed along to me. (You never see "MEN AT WORK" signs posted around philosophy departments, do you? Do you?) Norton offered the cautious judgment that it only makes sense to pursue a life in philosophy if you feel you could not be happy doing anything else, and he suggested I read Virginia Woolf's *To the Lighthouse*, for its portrayal of how unhappy a life in philosophy can be. A charming, German born and educated Dean of Engineering wagered I would not last long in mechanical engineering, philosophy being the field to which his majors most often fled the monotony of "machines, machines, machines," as he put it. He noted with pride that he required two philosophy courses of all engineering majors, it being essential to a good education. I signed up for a pair of engineering foundation courses as an experiment that summer, felt myself absurdly out of place among students who spoke only of the hotness of cars and "chicks" (think "babes"), switched within a week to classes in intermediate logic and French, and braced myself for the fight of my life. I belonged with philosophers and thought I would rather die than spend my life among shallow, sexist jerks.

I graduated two years later with a major in philosophy and undeclared minor in psychology, taking the bus alone across town to the diploma ceremony were I accepted a round of anonymous applause for being one of two *magna cum laude* graduates, second in the college of arts only to the lovely and mysterious Paula Lawrence I had known in high school. I had undertaken courses and seminars in philosophy of mind, science, and social science, epistemology, the history of analytic philosophy, Quine, utilitarian moral theory, Aristotle's *Nicomachean Ethics*, social philosophy, and Rationalism, taught by faculty who had studied with well-known philosophers at the University of Michigan, Stanford, Cornell, Princeton, and the like. I had supplemented those with allied courses in abstract arithmetic, linguistic anthropology, history of social radicalism, economics, and enough psychology and computer science to prepare me well for work in philosophy of mind, psychology, and artificial intelligence as a doctoral student at the University of Pittsburgh. Jean Piaget's genetic epistemology fascinated me, and I was deeply impressed by the work of Jerome Bruner, whom I later encountered at meetings of the National Academy of Education, and Michael Walzer, whom I have come to know this year at the IAS. In the end, I was most occupied with understanding human agency, freedom, and responsibility in a physical world. If rationality is presupposed by attributions of belief and desire, how can attributions of irrationality be justified? When does irrationality undermine attributions of responsibility? I had chosen akrasia as the topic for my term paper in John Tice's seminar on the *Nicomachean Ethics*, and made connections to the work of Elizabeth Anscombe, Donald Davidson, and G. H. von Wright.

John invited me to travel with him and his daughter to Florence that summer of 1977, and I thereby enjoyed a semblance of the education a Grand Tour of Europe was understood to provide. I also felt a great weight of oppression lifted from me and began to grow again in the most literal, physical sense, not having done so for six years. Within a few months, I was an inch and a half taller. After some weeks of travel on the continent, I was in residence at Exeter College for a summer course in politics, philosophy, and economics, with a room above Broad Street looking out on Blackwell's bookshop, where I spent many happy hours and pounds. From Oxford, I made my way to Pittsburgh to begin my doctoral studies in philosophy, with a copy of R. S. Peters' Oxford Readings collection, *The Philosophy of Education*, among my acquisitions.

The first term at Pitt, I was enrolled in advanced metalogic, a seminar on imagination with Annette Baier, Ancient Greek philosophy with Alexander Nehamas, and an extraordinary seminar on reference and ontology with Joe Camp, in which he led us through the perplexities addressed in his 2004 book, *Confusion*, and launched seven dissertations. Joe had published little besides his deflationary theory of truth (Grover, Camp, & Belnap, 1975), but he was a legendary force of nature in the world of Pitt philosophy, sponsoring more dissertations than half the faculty combined, including many that were nominally directed by Wilfred Sellers – storied slayer of the "myth of the given," analytic pragmatist son of Roy Wood Sellars, and guiding light of the Pittsburgh school of social practice philosophy. Pitt was a place of philosophical glory where we could ask Wilfred at the start of class whether Richard Rorty was right that he (Wilfred) had put an end to epistemology (no, because traditional forms of foundationalism do not exhaust the possibilities); could share an elevator with Wilfred, Quine, and Carl Hempel as they chatted like regular guys; would listen spellbound to Joe on a roll through sunset, as darkness filled the seminar room and no one dreamed of making a move for the light until he paused. Writing a dissertation with Joe typically involved pulling at least one "all-nighter" with him, fuelled by large pots of whatever he was cooking. It was a supportive environment in which faculty spent a lot of time with graduate students and everyone was expected to succeed. Where else could my son, born on Bertrand Russell's birthday in 1982, have played with Russell Brandom, named after Bertrand, while Bob and I talked philosophy and teething biscuits?

In the spring of that first year I studied epistemology with Wilfred, philosophy of law with Kurt Baier, the nature of time with Adolf Grünbaum, and twentieth century Marxism with Holly Graff, who left after the election of Ronald Reagan to serve as a founding national chair of Michael Harrington's Democratic Socialists of America. What was most new to me in all of this was falling in love with Plato's dialogues, the study of racial equality and criminal justice in American law with Kurt, and the effect of reading thousands of pages of classical and twentieth century Marxism. Holly did not turn me into a socialist – I was never optimistic enough to be a socialist – but her seminar was extremely valuable in enabling me to think my way out of some conventions of thought I still hadn't recognized as conventions. In that respect, it was deeply educational in much the way my encounter with the *Blue Book* had been.

Having had no break from school since beginning school, I went off for a year to work and travel, with copies of Jonathan Kozol's *Death at an Early Age*, and Erik Olin Wright's *Politics of Punishment* in my bag. I could not read Kozol without feeling that I must do something to right the educational injustices of the world, and I was soon on my way back to New Orleans to work in schools serving the Fischer Projects, a copy of Paulo Freire's *Pedagogy of the Oppressed* in hand, but with little idea of what I might actually accomplish. What my substitute teaching proved to be was a series of lessons in what I did not know about children and how to help them. I audited a masters level course in educational foundations, read widely in educational theory, sociology, and revisionist history, and developed a profound distaste for educational scholarship that struck me as doctrinaire or grounded in theory but not reality. My greatest satisfaction that year was in guessing correctly that my students in the riverside "Olaf Fink School for the Trainable Mentally Retarded" could find pleasure in poetry and seeing aspects of their day transformed in poetry. I found the school's cramped vision of vocational training and unimaginative "sentences of the day" unbearable. It was a happy day when we walked the levee of the Mississippi as laden barges passed, and could all understand that

> When we walk together in the sun
> our shadows are like barges of silence.
> (Strand, 1968: Seven Poems, 3)

In the course of that year, I also had an opportunity to see Jerry Nosich teach critical thinking and discussed with him the approach he was developing in *Reasons and Arguments*. Years later I would find myself teaching school of education courses in critical thinking theory and pedagogy, and joining my epistemologist colleague, Richard Feldman, in preparing philosophy student interns to teach critical thinking in Rochester city schools.

There was no place for philosophy of education in the doctoral work in philosophy I resumed in September 1979, though Kurt and I discussed his work on moral education and Annette's reading group on Carol Gilligan's book, *In a Different Voice*, offered a valuable perspective on a work that would soon make waves in educational studies. After a pair of seminars with Hempel, three more with Sellars, Aristotle with John Cooper, seminars on Habermas and Hegel with Bob Brandom, moral theory with Kurt Baier and David Gauthier, seminars on Russell and Wittgenstein with new arrivals from Princeton, causation in science and the law in the History and Philosophy of Science department, and extensive work in modern philosophy and philosophy of psychology and psychoanalysis, I returned more or less to where I had left off in my B.A. studies with a lengthy paper for Alexander Nehamas in which I interpreted some features of Aristotle's views on akrasia as consequences of the presuppositions of three different forms of explanation, and suggested a general approach to the attribution of irrationality.

That proved to be the basis of a dissertation on responsibility and explanation, in which I developed an alternative to MacIntyre's explanation of how moral agents "became ghosts," defended an Aristotelian account of responsibility, and drew lessons for modern negligence law. My unusually large and wonderful committee was a reflection of the project's multi-faceted character: Joe Camp (chair), Kurt Baier (second reader), Carl Hempel, Alexander Nehamas, Annette Baier, John Haugeland (philosophy of psychology), and Tom Gerety (law). As the project developed, it seemed to steer itself toward education, inasmuch as I identified a relational appropriateness condition for blame associated with formative responsibility: in a naturalistic framework, such as Aristotle's, the formative responsibility of human communities for how children develop.

Pressing farther into Aristotle's *Politics* in the years that followed provided the basis for addressing relationships between education, law, and citizenship; and a series of invitations to conceptualize the shape of philosophy of education (Curren, 1998a, 1998b, 2003, 2007) nudged me toward the more comprehensive account of education, justice and the human good that I have more recently pursued (Curren, 2014a, 2014b, forthcoming). What my book, *Aristotle on the Necessity of Public Education*, revolves around is the burdens of formative responsibility for all children that societies bear collectively in order to create any semblance of a just system of social cooperation under a common rule of law, let alone a form of democracy we could admire. This is a responsibility that is inalienable, hence one that cannot without due diligence and oversight be assigned to parents or any other private entities (Curren & Blokhuis, 2009), and it entails education and broader social justice sufficient to enable every child to become a full civic equal. The case for public and common schools, the civic purposes of education, and the role of education in enabling children to become rationally self-governing, "effective" agents (Curren, 2006b) are central to this work. I conceive of the major divisions of philosophy of education as pertaining to educational aims, responsibilities, authority, content, and manner (see Curren, 2007, pp. 3-4). Aristotle places the promotion of human flourishing at the center of educational aims and content, and in recent years I have been largely occupied with developing a philosophically defensible and psychologically informed account of the nature of flourishing, or living in a way that is both admirable and personally rewarding, and how education can promote flourishing. An important aspect of my view is that schools will not succeed through standards and accountability schemes predicated on the idea that teachers and students need to be externally motivated; if we want students to leave school able to live well, schools must be places in which they experience progress in living well. "What will sustain students in real learning and teachers in real teaching is the meaning, satisfaction, and energy of engagement associated with doing work one can see is good, in a setting where that is expected and appreciated" (Curren, 2014b). A second important aspect of my view is that education must prepare students to live well in the world they will inherit. The unfolding world of accelerating climate change, impaired ecosystems, and profound energy insecurity will present challenges like nothing any of us has faced. In this context, I argue that an adequate education in sustainability is something every student is owed, and that one of its components must be preparation for the global citizenship and cooperation without which there will be no solution to the problems we face (Curren, 2009a, 2010a; Curren & Dorn, forthcoming).

CAREER TO DATE

I headed to the California Institute of Technology in 1985 as an Andrew Mellon Postdoctoral Instructor in philosophy of law, and developed various aspects of my dissertation project in an atmosphere more interdisciplinary and strongly focused on actual practices in domains of philosophical inquiry (legal, political, professional, scientific) than Pitt had been. Every lecture in the Division of Humanities and Social Sciences was for everyone in the Division, and when Brian Barry or Jim Woodward convened the philosophers and philosophically interested for weekly evening discussions of our work in progress, there were not just other world class philosophers like Alan Donagan present, but often colleagues in law, classics, environmental quality, computational neuroscience, or experimental economics. Caltech was an extraordinary place to be for three years, and with my interest in philosophy of education rekindled by teaching great books sequences on classics of moral and political thought, I was ready to accept a joint position at the University of Rochester in which I could continue to work in a multidisciplinary environment while also being half in a philosophy department with a doctoral program.

Arriving in Rochester in 1988, in an era when all new hires in the school of education were split equally with departments in the College of Arts and Sciences, I had supportive colleagues in both philosophy and education, and felt at home in the strong cohort of disciplinary education faculty recruited from Harvard, Chicago, Princeton, and Columbia. How could I not also feel at home in the department of Lewis White Beck, Deborah Modrak, and Richard Feldman, on a campus dominated by a library bearing the name of a philosopher, Rush Rhees (see Wittgenstein, 1958), and with the names Plato, Aristotle, Augustine, Descartes, and Kant engraved in its entablature?

I was and remain the only philosopher of education at Rochester, but I soon met Emily Robertson and Tom Green, who were not far down the road in Syracuse, and introduced myself to Harvey Siegel at an American Philosophical Association (APA) meeting. The three of them welcomed me to the world of philosophy of education and made it a world to which I could happily belong. I was soon presenting papers at both the Philosophy of Education Society (PES) and the Association for Philosophy of Education (APE), a satellite of the APA, and getting to know Ken Strike, Denis Phillips, Sharon Bailin, Walter Feinberg, David Carr, Fran Schrag, Sophie Hartounian-Gordon, Gary Matthews, Doret de Ruyter, and many others. Tom made himself my sponsor, inviting me to meetings of the National Academy of Education, where he introduced me to Israel Scheffler and other luminaries. He read and commented on almost everything I wrote, and was wonderfully supportive in many ways. I hosted Maxine Greene, Matthew Lipman, and some years later Eamonn Callan and Bill Galston, on my own campus.

Conversations with Rochester education and psychology colleagues led, in time, to collaborations with lawyers Tyll van Geel and our former student, Jason Blokhuis, psychologist Richard Ryan, and historians Bruce Kimball and (with much help and encouragement from Harold Wechsler) Jon Zimmerman and Chuck Dorn. A graduate school connection led to a five-year collaboration with University of Chicago psychometrician Darrell Bok and the California Golden State Exams Biology Assessment. A convergence of interests with a high school friend, Ellen Metzger, a Professor of Geology and long-time Director of Science Education at SJSU, inspired an ongoing collaboration in sustainability and climate education.

Having found my way in the field with so much help, I recognized as my teachers began to exit the stage that it was becoming time for me to accept responsibility for the continued success of the professional associations in which I had found homes. With friends in high places, there was no shortage of opportunities. I happily served as Harvey's Eastern Division Vice-President of the APE for four years, then as President for another four years, working with Gary Matthews, Tom Wren, Bob Fullinwider, James Dwyer, Jonathan Adler, and Larry Blum. I was similarly happy to serve as Emily's PES Program Chair and Yearbook Editor when she was President in 1999, bringing the diverse worlds of philosophy of education a little closer together by including philosopher friends who wrote on education but moved in different orbits: Michael Slote, Peter Markie, Ken Westphal, and Laura Purdy. Getting to know Bill Mann through the APE led to four years of service as chair of the APA Committee on Teaching, and my encounters with Harry Brighouse led to a decade of collaboration in editing Theory and Research in Education and other ventures, with him, Meira Levinson, Sigal Ben-Porath, Elaine Unterhalter and other members of the editorial team we gathered, and the authors whose work has enabled us to make a distinctive contribution to the field. I have found other rewarding platforms for collaboration and service in the Association for Practical and Professional Ethics (APPE), where Brian Schrag and Michael Pritchard led a group of philosopher-administrators in addressing issues in the ethics of academic administration (having become chair of philosophy in 2003, I qualified; see Curren, 2008a, 2010b); with the Communitarian Network, when Bill Galston was serving in the Clinton administration and he and Amitai Etzioni were hosting White House conferences on character building and gathering panels to develop position papers; with the Philosophy of Education Society of Great Britain (PESGB) and its IMPACT pamphlet series; and through the Spencer Foundation initiative in philosophy of education policy and practice, so ably led by Michael McPherson. Jon Zimmerman and I launched a History and Philosophy of Education (HPE) series of co-authored books with the University of Chicago Press in 2010, a platform for sustained collaboration that will likely occupy us for a decade or more to come.

My role in the school of education at the University of Rochester has been greatly diminished in the years since I became chair of philosophy and the educational foundations faculty dispersed, but new opportunities beckon. My appointment as Chair of Moral and Virtue Education in the Jubilee Centre at the University of Birmingham provides an institutional connection to colleagues in philosophy of education for the first time in my career — Kristján Kristjánsson, David Carr, Ben Kotzee, and Michael Hand, no less — and a leadership role with multi-disciplinary research teams in virtue studies. What more could I want?

It is impossible to do justice in a few words to how much these many diverse collaborations have meant to me both professionally and personally, in expanding the reach of what I have been able to do and be. *Theory and Research in Education*, the HPE book series, and the Jubilee Centre are all predicated on the belief that philosophy and philosophers cannot go it alone and flourish.

LESSONS LEARNED

My teachers, colleagues, students, friends, and family have been more important to me than they know, and I am indebted to them as much for what they have endured as for what they have done, since I am all too often, in the grip of an idea, not the most agreeable company one might keep. The rewards of doing what we do together, reaching across divides that separate us, are in many ways indispensable, if also challenging, in philosophy as in life. Whatever your preferred philosophical language may be, strive to outgrow it and bridge the conceptual divides between the disciplinary silos that will otherwise prevent you from facing big questions in all their daunting complexity. Strive for rigor, but understand the value of a Crude Look At the Whole, and CLAW away at the things that matter. Engage the world and focus your energies in the creative space where life and philosophy tangle, knot, and occasionally weave a more attractive picture of what is to be done and how to live wisely and well in the face of madness, loss, and the hazards of our own handiwork. As darkness falls, someone really must make a move for the light.

FAVORITE WORKS

Personal Favorites

Curren, R. (1995). Coercion and the ethics of grading and testing. *Educational Theory*, 45(4), 425-441.

Curren, R. (1996). Aretê. In J. J. Chambliss (Ed.), *Philosophy of education: An encyclopedia* (pp 29-30). New York: Garland.

Curren, R. (1999). Cultivating the intellectual and moral virtues. In D. Carr & J. Steutel (Eds.), *Virtue theory and moral education* (pp. 67-81). London: Routledge.

Curren, R. (2000). *Aristotle on the necessity of public education*. Lanham, MD: Rowman & Littlefield.

Curren, R. (2003). Theory. In J. Collins & N. O'Brien (Eds.), *The Greenwood dictionary of education* p. (p. 355). Westport, CT: Greenwood Press.

Curren, R. (2008). Cardinal virtues of academic administration. *Theory and Research in Education*, 6(3), 337-363.

Curren, R. (2009). Academic standards and constitutive luck. In M. Eckert & R. Talisse (Eds.), *A teacher's life: Essays for Steven M. Cahn* (pp. 13-32). Lanham, MD: Lexington Books.

Influential Works

Buchanan, A., & Brock, D. (1989). *Deciding for others*. Cambridge: Cambridge University Press.

Deci, E., & Ryan, R. (1985). *Intrinsic motivation and self-determination in human behavior.* New York: Plenum Press.
Dennett, D. (1981). *Brainstorms: Philosophical essays on mind and psychology.* Cambridge, MA: The MIT Press.
Foot, P. (2001). *Natural goodness.* Oxford: Clarendon Press.
Frankfurt, H. (1988). *The importance of what we care about.* Cambridge: Cambridge University Press.
Green, T. (1980). *Predicting the behavior of the educational system.* Syracuse, NY: Syracuse University Press.
Gutmann, A. (1987). *Democratic education.* Princeton: Princeton University Press.
Kozol, J. (1967). *Death at an early age.* New York: Houghton Mifflin.
Kraut, R. (1984). *Socrates and the state.* Princeton: Princeton University Press.
Kraut, R. (1989). *Aristotle on the human good.* Princeton: Princeton University Press.
Rackham, H. (1934). *Aristotle, The nicomachean ethics.* Cambridge, MA: Harvard University Press.
Rawls, J. (1971). *A theory of justice.* Cambridge, MA: Harvard University Press.
Tainter, J. (1988). *The collapse of complex societies.* Cambridge: Cambridge University Press.

REFERENCES

Buchanan, A. (2004). Political liberalism and social epistemology. *Philosophy & Public Affairs, 32*(2), 95-130.
Camp, J. (2004). *Confusion.* Cambridge, MA: Harvard University Press.
Commoner, B. (1967). *Science and survival.* New York: Viking.
Curren, R. (1992). *A rationale for the use of multiple process category scales in measuring achievement in biology.* Consultant's report commissioned by the Methodology Research Center, NORC, University of Chicago.
Curren, R. (1995a). *Essay items in standardized testing: Current uses, methods, and research on item format effects.* Consultant's report commissioned by the Methodology Research Center, NORC, University of Chicago.
Curren, R. (1995b). Coercion and the ethics of grading and testing. *Educational Theory, 45*(4), 425-441. Reprinted in P. Hirst & P. White (Eds.) (1998), *Philosophy of education: Major themes in the analytic tradition,* Vol. 4, pp. 381-389. London: Routledge. Reprinted in D. Fenner (Ed.) (1999), *Ethics in education,* pp. 199-221. New York: Garland Publishing. Reprinted in R. Curren (Ed.) (2007), *Philosophy of education: An anthology,* pp. 465-476. Oxford: Blackwell. Reprinted in *Critique & Humanism, 26* (2008), 59-76.
Curren, R. (1998a). Education, philosophy of. In E. J. Craig (Ed.), *Routledge encyclopedia of philosophy* (Vol. 3, pp. 231-240). London: Routledge.
Curren, R. (1998b). Education, history of philosophy of. In E. J. Craig (Ed.), *Routledge encyclopedia of philosophy* (vol. 3, pp. 222-231). London: Routledge.
Curren, R. (2000). *Aristotle on the necessity of public education.* Lanham, MD: Rowman & Littlefield.
Curren, R. (2002a). Moral education and juvenile crime. In S. Macedo & Y. Tamir (Eds.), *Nomos XLIII: Moral and political education* (pp. 359-380). New York: NYU Press.
Curren, R. (2002b). Public education and the demands of fidelity to reason: A response to Dwyer, Feinberg, Hourdakis, Pendlebury, Robertson, Strike, and White. *The School Field, 13*(1/2), 81-107.
Curren, R. (2002c). Civic education in the liberal and classical traditions. *The School Field, 13*(1/2), 108-120. Reprinted in Slovenian, in J. Pikalo (Ed.) (2011). *Državljanstvo in globalizacija: k državljanska vzgoja za sodobni svet* [Citizenship and globalisation: Towards citizenship education for a modern world]. Ljubljana, Slovenia: Zalozba Sophia.
Curren, R (Ed.). (2003). *A companion to the philosophy of education.* Oxford: Blackwell. (2011) *Simplified character,* Chinese edition (Transl. Peng Zhengmei). Shanghai: East China Normal University Press.

Curren, R. (2004). Educational measurement and knowledge of other minds. *Theory and Research in Education*, 2(3), 235-353.
Curren, R. (2006a). Connected learning and the foundations of psychometrics: A rejoinder. *Journal of Philosophy of Education*, 40(1), 17-29.
Curren, R. (2006b). Developmental liberalism. *Educational Theory*, 56(4), 451-468.
Curren, R. (Ed.). (2007). *Philosophy of education: An anthology*. Oxford: Blackwell.
Curren, R. (2008a). Cardinal virtues of academic administration. *Theory and Research in Education*, 6(3), 337-363. Reprinted in E. Englehardt et al. (Eds.), *The ethical challenges of academic administration* (pp. 63-86). Dordrecht: Springer.
Curren, R. (coordinating author). (2008b). *APA statements on the profession: Outcomes assessment*. Newark, DE: American Philosophical Association. On-line at: http://www.apaonline.org/APAOnline/About_The_APA/Statements/Issues/Outcomes_Assessment.aspx
Curren, R. (2009a). *Education for sustainable development: A philosophical assessment*. London: PESGB, Impact Series. On-line: http://onlinelibrary.wiley.com/doi/10.1111/imp.2009.2009.issue-18/issuetoc
Curren, R. (2009b). The big uneasy. In Rich Hayes (Ed.), *Thoreau's legacy: American stories about global warming* (pp. 94-95). Cambridge, MA: Union of Concerned Scientists and Penguin Classics. On-line at http://www.ucsusa.org/americanstories/.
Curren, R. (2009c). Academic standards and constitutive luck. In M. Eckert & R. Talisse (Eds.), *A teacher's life: Essays for Steven M. Cahn* (pp. 13-32). Lanham, MD: Lexington Books.
Curren, R. (2009d). Education as a social right in a diverse society. *Journal of Philosophy of Education*, 43(1), 45-56. Published in Spanish (2009), La educación como un derecho social en una sociedad plural. In José Antonio Ibáñez-Martin (Ed.), *Educación, conocimiento y justicia* (pp. 145-159). Madrid: Dykinson.
Curren, R. (2010a). Education for global citizenship and survival. In Y. Raley & G. Preyer (Eds.), *Philosophy of education in the era of globalization* (pp. 67-87). London: Routledge.
Curren, R. (2010b). Academic freedom and integrity: The firestorm over 'salvage logging' at Oregon State. In E. Englehardt et al. (Eds.), *The ethical challenges of academic administration* (pp. 192-196). Dordrecht: Springer.
Curren, R. (2010c). Sustainability in the education of professionals. *Journal of Applied Ethics and Philosophy*, 2, 21-29. Online at: http://ethics.let.hokudai.ac.jp/ja/files/jaep_vol2.pdf
Curren, R. (2011). Sustainable development. In D. Chatterjee (Ed.), *Encyclopedia of global justice*. Dordrecht: Springer.
Curren, R. (2013a). Defining sustainability ethics. In M. Boylan (Ed.), *Environmental ethics*, 2nd ed. Oxford: Wiley-Blackwell.
Curren, R. (2013b). Formative and punitive assessment. In C. Ruitenberg (Ed.), *Philosophy of Education 2012*. Urbana: Philosophy of Education Society.
Curren, R. (2014a). Judgment and the aims of education. *Social Philosophy & Policy*, 31(1).
Curren, R. (2014b). A neo-Aristotelian account of education, justice, and the human good. In K. Meyer (Ed.), *Education, justice, and the human good* (pp. 80-99). London: Routledge.
Curren, R. (2015a). Virtue ethics and moral education. In M. Slote & L. Besser-Jones (Eds.), *Routledge companion to virtue ethics*. London: Routledge.
Current, R. (2015b). Motivational aspects of moral learning and progress. *Journal of Moral Education*.
Curren, R. (forthcoming). *The philosophy of education*. Lanham, MD: Rowman & Littlefield.
Curren, R., & Blokhuis, J. C. (2011). The prima facie case against homeschooling. *Public Affairs Quarterly*, 15(1), 1-19.
Curren, R., & Dorn, C. (forthcoming). *Patriotism and civic education*. Chicago: University of Chicago Press.
Curren, R., & Metzger, E. (forthcoming). *An education in sustainability*.
Einstein, A. (1954). *Ideas and opinions*. New York: Crown Publishers.
Freire, P. (1978). *Pedagogy of the oppressed*. New York: The Seabury Press.

Gamow, G. (1966). *Thirty years that shook physics: The story of quantum theory.* New York: Doubleday.
Gilligan, C. (1982). *In a different voice.* Cambridge, MA: Harvard University Press.
Grover, D. L., Camp, J. L. Jr., & Belnap, N. D. (1975). A prosentential theory of truth. *Philosophical Studies, 27,* 73-125.
Groves, L. (1962). *Now it can be told: The story of the Manhattan project.* New York: Harper.
Hume, D. (1963). *An enquiry concerning human understanding and other essays.* New York: Washington Square Press.
Kozol, J. (1967). *Death at an early age.* New York: Houghton Mifflin.
Laing, R. D. (1969). *Sanity, madness and the family.* London: Penguin.
Lawrence, D. H. (1966). *Sons and lovers.* New York: Viking Compass.
Nosich, G. (1982). *Reasons and arguments.* Belmont, CA: Wadsworth.
Peters, R. S. (1973). *The philosophy of education.* London: Oxford University Press.
Poincaré, H. (1904). *Science and hypothesis.* New York: Walter Scott Publishing.
Russell, B. (1897). *An essay on the foundations of geometry.* Cambridge University Press.
Russell, B. (1903). *Principles of mathematics.* Cambridge University Press.
Russell, B. (1910). *Philosophical essays.* London: Langmans, Green.
Russell, B. (1912). *Problems of philosophy.* London: Williams and Norgate.
Ryan, R. M., Curren, R., & Deci, E. L. (2013). What humans need: Flourishing in Aristotelian philosophy and self-determination theory. In A. S. Waterman (Ed.), *The best within us: Positive psychology perspectives on Eudaimonia* (pp. 57-75). Washington, DC: American Psychological Association.
Strand, M. (1968). *Darker.* Cambridge, MA: Atheneum.
Walzer, M. (1971). *Obligations: Essays on disobedience, war, and citizenship.* New York: Touchstone.
Whitehead, A. N. (1929). *The aims of education and other essays.* New York: Free Press.
Whitehead, A. N. (1948). *An introduction to mathematics.* London: Oxford University Press.
Wittgenstein, L. (1958). *The blue and brown books,* with a preface by R. Rhees. Oxford: Basil Blackwell.
Wittgenstein, L. (1961). *Tractatus logico-philosophicus.* London: Routledge & Kegan Paul.
Wittgenstein, L. (1968). *Philosophical investigations,* 3rd ed. New York: Macmillan.
Wittgenstein, L. (1975). *Remarks on the foundations of mathematics.* Cambridge, MA: The MIT Press.
Woolf, V. (1927). *To the lighthouse.* New York: Harcourt Brace.
Wright, E. O. (1973). *The politics of punishment.* New York: Harper & Row.

ANN DILLER

STILL FACING THE TORPEDO FISH

As far back as I can remember, I have been a philosopher. And, in my mother's oft-repeated words, I "took to school like a duck to water." Wonderful teachers, in school and out of school, came my way, occasionally appearing just in the nick of time when I was feeling "torpified" from what I call "Facing the Torpedo Fish."[1] This phrase, derived from Plato's Meno, refers to the shock of suddenly realizing we do not know what we thought we knew. My lifelong penchant for philosophical speculation continues to land me in torpedo fish experiences; hence my title. I did not, however, discover Philosophy of Education per se until after I had completed my Master's degree and had begun my first career as a Director of Religious Education.

EARLY YEARS & SCHOOLING

I grew up in what one of my sons aptly described, decades later, as a "nice little village" – a small town, beside a small lake, surrounded, during my childhood, by woods and fertile farmland. Its well-educated citizenry supported the town's public schools and able teachers. In the midst of this farm country, my paternal grandmother, twice-widowed, commuted to a rural elementary school, where she reigned as their Teaching-Principal. Back in town, I frequented the attic of her house that overflowed with books. When I turned seven, my grandmother gave me two liberating gifts – my first Library Card and my first two-wheeler bicycle. The library card nourished my propensity for voracious reading. The bicycle facilitated my access to our town woods, where I practiced peripatetic philosophy.

As soon as I was free to go on solitary excursions into the local woods, I would stroll along the woodland paths, talking out loud to myself creating monologues and dialogues. I do not recall the precise content of these musings; I do remember their frequency and the philosophical tone dominated by ethical concerns and spiritual perplexities. When I learned about the Athenian philosophers walking about talking philosophy, I felt an instant kinship.

My youthful philosophizing was not limited to solitary ramblings. During elementary school I selected "best friends" according to their willingness to join me in "deep" discussions.

During high school, I discoursed for hours with philosophically-minded peers. I also sought out adults who seemed wise. These adults included my Great Uncle Frank, Miss Greene our formidable second grade teacher, Mr. Montgomery principal and sixth grade teacher, Mrs. Wells a relentless literature teacher, a few members of my church community, and my own mother, a wise woman and a schoolteacher before her marriage.

I entered upon my first systematic study of philosophy and religion as a college undergraduate. Maryville College, nestled in the Smoky Mountains of eastern Tennessee, founded in the early nineteenth century by Scotch Presbyterians, provided us with strong introductions to the philosophy of western Europe, of England and, of course, Scotland. Not much attention was given to North American, Eastern, or Middle-Eastern Thought, except through the study of Comparative Religions. During my senior year I reveled in the honor of being an assistant to one of the philosophy professors, grading papers for an introductory course; and I remember first stirrings, during that time, of an interest in teaching philosophy myself.

As an undergraduate I again sought out fellow students to engage in philosophical dialogue and energetic disputation. One of my favorite disputants, John Gilmore, went on to become a popular professor of philosophy. Two of my dearest friends, Jeanne and Stan Stefancic, provided memorable introductions to the New England Transcendentalists. Jeanne reveled in reading aloud from Thoreau, while her husband Stan propounded the superiority of Emerson, often quoting illustrative passages. Our admiration for New England philosophical traditions – Pragmatists as well as Transcendentalists – may have contributed to the fact that Jeanne and Stan, along with my husband and me, all ended up moving to Cambridge, Massachusetts for our graduate studies.

During my college years I also made my first foray into a sustained study of mystical literature. The topic of my senior honors thesis: "Main Themes and Variations in Christian Devotional Literature" provided the vehicle for a systematic reading of Christian Mystics, including Meister Eckhart, Brother Lawrence, St. John of the Cross, and Theresa of Avila. More than three decades would then go by before I retrieved this thread and wrote an entry on "Mysticism" for J. J. Chambliss's *Philosophy of Education: An Encyclopedia* (1996).

One of the reasons I attended Maryville College was financial. I had received a full scholarship, including tuition, room and board, that enabled me to attend any Presbyterian College (that accepted me) within the United States. Because I admired some local MC graduates and knew high school classmates who planned to attend, MC became my college of choice. I am glad I did choose it; and I am grateful for the considerable financial support provided for my education by various institutions, starting with the Presbyterian Church. Without that aid, I could not have attended a residential college. I continued to receive substantial financial assistance throughout graduate study, including truly reasonable graduate school loans.

During my year of Master's study in Philosophy and Religion at the University of Tulsa (again financed by a generous fellowship) two professors made a strong impression on me. Professor Paul Brown's brilliant pedagogy and persuasive introductions to the American Pragmatists won me over almost instantly, especially to William James. I latched onto James with enthusiasm and tenacity, reading everything I could find – his writings, his letters, his biography.

In the next few years as my liberal Christian theology, of a Princeton-educated Presbyterian variety, felt increasingly untenable, I turned to James's writings, in particular to his *Varieties of Religious Experience* as well as to popular essays such as "The Will to Believe." After moving to Cambridge I discovered Paul Tillich's *The Courage To Be* and found Tillich's way of replacing 'God' talk with references to 'the ground of being' a reassuring companion to James's writings – and a temporary 'theological' resting place for my rational soul.

Right alongside Paul Brown and the pragmatists came Professor Walter Steuermann and the magic of Symbolic Logic. I believe Professor Steuermann was genuinely "in love" with symbolic logic. And somehow I caught this affection. I would spend hours happily hunched over problem sets with lines of symbols. I even assisted Steuermann, briefly, at his request, with the textbook that he and Brown were co-authoring at the time. This knowledge would stand me in good stead a few years later when, in my first seminar with Israel Scheffler, I detected a blatant (but hitherto unnoticed) logical fallacy staring up at us from the central text for the seminar. My display of logical acumen sufficiently impressed Scheffler that he encouraged me to apply to his program. But that gets me ahead of my story, first we need to move to Harvard Square.

DISCOVERING PHILOSOPHY OF EDUCATION

September in Harvard Square during the 1960s felt full of warm sunshine and whirling fields of mental energy. As the Director of Religious Education for Christ Church, my office and apartment were right around the corner – a handy location for taking advantage of the open auditing opportunities at Harvard. My only difficulty arose around the matter of choice – I wanted to study everything! It was a heady, exciting time not only for civil rights and peace movements, but also for philosophical inquiry. I found myself simultaneously absorbed in studying Plato alongside the American pragmatists, fascinated by British analytic philosophy and by French existentialism, intrigued and perplexed by the recent trends in English-speaking ethics.

Inside the gates of Harvard "Yard" I would join philosophy students and auditors of all ages as we made our way into Emerson Hall. One of my more memorable bouts of auditing occurred over a sequence of semesters when familiar faces kept filling the same lecture hall waiting attentively, almost breathlessly, to hear what John Rawls had to say, in his halting, captivating, speech, about the most recent revisions on his manuscript for A Theory of Justice. The open attentive way Rawls received questions and his thoughtful responses to questioners left me with a strong respect for him as a person even when I felt critical toward his theories.

Meanwhile, I was facing the realization that gender was a difference that made a huge difference in even the most liberal of Protestant churches, where women were confined to the lower echelons. If I had been a man, I might have become a Protestant Pastor or a leader in Religious Education, but these were not options for me as a woman; and I needed a larger horizon. Then someone told me about a "new program" created by Professor Israel Scheffler at the Harvard Graduate

School of Education (HGSE) that combined the study of philosophy and education. I discovered, upon further inquiry, that Scheffler was about to teach a seminar focused on a contemporary author who set forth a "rational basis" for ethics. Scheffler granted me permission to audit on the one condition that I be a full participant. I eagerly agreed and found myself able to participate fully, thanks to my longstanding interest in ethics and my graduate work in symbolic logic. Very soon thereafter I became officially enrolled as a student in the Philosophy of Education Program at HGSE, where we divided our studies between courses in the Philosophy Department and in the "Ed. School."

Along with Israel Scheffler, two other faculty – Jane Roland Martin and Frederick Olafson – were full time members of the HGSE Philosophy of Education Program. I found these three a wonderful trio for my studies. I have already written at some length about my work with Scheffler and my appreciation for his support.[2] An even longer essay, as yet unwritten, would be required to do justice to Jane Roland Martin's influence.

When, as a Graduate Assistant, I first stepped into Jane Roland Martin's classroom, I could not have imagined or guessed how significant and long-term her influence, colleagueship, and friendship would be for me and for my work in philosophy of education. But already her very presence standing there at the lectern, the only woman philosopher on the Harvard University faculty, signaled a far-reaching influence. Jane stood there as a most promising model: a woman, a mother with two sons, and a professor in my new field of study. She soon became a mentor whose supportive encouragement and insightful critiques continued long after I graduated. It was Jane Martin who shepherded me to my first PES meeting. It was Jane who served as the steady, most mature active participant in our circle of women philosophers known as PHAEDRA, formed during our members early struggles with dissertations and professional presentations. Over the course of decades, Jane and I continued our philosophical conversations, sometimes walking and talking for long stretches along the Charles River.

Back in the 1960s, conceptual analysis was in the ascendancy; and Jane was working on *Explaining, Understanding, and Teaching*. I myself, still under the sway of my affection for symbolic logic, thrived on acquiring more skills of surgical precision that could "cut through" conceptual confusions and clarify ambiguous terminology. Scheffler's work on *The Language of Education* and other handy distinctions such as those that differentiated 'broad definitions' from 'narrow definitions,' or mapped out Wittgensteinian 'family resemblances,' all felt useful and reassuring.

While I enjoyed the precision and clarity gained from conceptual analysis, my philosophical interests continued to range widely. Thus I appreciated Professor Frederick Olafson's courses on European philosophy. His erudite introduction to existentialism helped to balance my headlong leap into the works of Sartre and Simone de Beauvoir. Olafson also generously agreed to a private tutorial for my reading of Kant. I still remember the kindness of his gentle response when I, with graduate student hubris, told him my idea of attempting to read Kant in German. Without betraying any sign of incredulous amusement, Frederick Olafson diplomatically suggested that I might make better use of my time by studying Lewis White Beck's commentary.

Not all my graduate school reading was as ponderous as Kant's Critiques. In fact, in my eagerness to read as much as possible I would gulp down whole books in one sitting. I remember sitting on sunny autumn afternoons in the quad outside Longfellow Hall, oblivious to my surroundings, speeding my way through library reserve copies of enticing "educational romantics" such as John Holt, A. S. Neill, Carl Rogers, Rousseau, Tolstoy, etc.

From page-turners like Holt to demanding texts such as Kant's, I read widely and somewhat haphazardly. Nor was my learning confined to reading and classrooms. Again, as in college, I grew intellectually from my exchanges with other students. One of my favorite forums for intense dialogue at this time occurred around the table in the *Harvard Educational Review* Board Room. Here we sat, a group of eager doctoral students, determining the selection of articles for forthcoming issues. Defending our choices, critiquing the opposition, we argued, pondered, and re-considered, long into the night. What I learned from participating in these heated exchanges and delicate decision-making processes gave me a decided advantage a few years later when, as a young assistant professor, I began to initiate gender-sensitive academic programs and policies. But before that came – the dissertation – a great opportunity for multiple "facing the torpedo fish" experiences.

TWO BIG TORPEDO FISH: DISSERTATION WRITING AND PARENTING

Writing my dissertation took what felt like a very long time, partly because it coincided with the birth of my first child. Although this 'reproductive labor' wreaked havoc with my envisioned schedule for dissertation production, the direct experiences of conscious, and conscientious, parenting began to create sea changes in my entire philosophy of education. For example, suddenly, educational treatises such as Rousseau's *Émile* and Charlotte Perkins Gilman's *Herland* captured my attention. John Dewey's extensive writings rose in my estimation. Dewey's conceptual framework now appeared both persuasive and useful. I began to notice how much learning inevitably happens all the time, under all sorts of conditions, how the whole "situation" (social, physical, emotional, etc.) requires our deliberate attention, how the "transactions" between the child and his or her environment can easily turn 'miseducative' in spite of our best intentions.

As a new parent I started studying a new genre – books by Adele Faber and Elaine Mazlish, Haim Ginott, T. B. Brazelton were high on my list. I sought out other graduate students with young children. I compared parenting notes with my "dissertation buddy" Nancy Glock, also a new mother. In fact, Nancy and I mapped out an entire book, chapter by chapter, on philosophy of education for parents, entitled *The Free Child*. Our book would unpack the details for distinguishing 'freedom' from 'license' and 'facilitation' from 'permissiveness'; we would explicate Dewey's concept of 'freedom of intelligence' and its relationship to 'freedom of movement' and so forth. We never did write that book, but we did finish our dissertations.

I began to embrace broad definitions for education and for teaching, in contrast to a narrow construal that sometimes seems to trivialize or dismiss informal educational labor as mere 'socialization' or happenstance. I gained a new respect for 'progressive' and 'alternative' school approaches, a respect that would be further enhanced when, in New Hampshire, I served as a school board member, and parent, for a local alternative elementary school, where I discovered first-hand that elementary school students can, indeed, start being philosophers of their own education.

I realize, in retrospect, that my research focus and styles of expression were evolving and unfolding in new ways during this often tortuous dissertation writing process, as I moved closer to forms of expression that felt alive to me as their author. My conception of education and of the realm of educational philosophy kept expanding until it burst wide open. By the time I completed my dissertation I was turning to exemplary teaching done by parents in informal settings as salutary cases. For instance, my essay "On a Conception of Moral Teaching" built around J. D. Salinger's depiction of a mother-child dialogue[3] is based on a culminating chapter in my dissertation.

Other long term benefits from this period of prolonged dissertation writing showed up a couple of decades later. In the midst of creating our new Ph.D. in Education Program, I remembered how much I had benefited from two informal sources of assistance: (1) meeting on a regular basis to "check in" with a dissertation-writing 'buddy'; and (2) getting together with a small group of other dissertation writers, at scheduled meeting times with a semi-structured format. At UNH I instituted this second practice as a monthly (non-compulsory) "Dissertation Seminar" – serving free pizza and supplying a doctoral faculty moderator. In addition, I encouraged "dissertation buddies" whenever feasible. On my last count, our Ph.D. program showed over a ninety percent graduation rate among candidates who had participated regularly in at least one of these structures.

But I am, again, getting ahead of my story. When I first arrived at UNH, following brief temporary positions at Wellesley College and at Lowell State, the Ph.D. program was not even on the horizon; all eyes were on the new Five-Year Teacher Education Program.

BECOMING A TEACHER OF TEACHERS

I took up my post as a beginning Assistant Professor just as the University of New Hampshire was about to launch a Five-year Teacher Education Program, one of the first in the country. The Director of Teacher Education, and major author of the program, Professor Michael D. Andrew held philosophy of education in high esteem and had made it a program cornerstone before I arrived. In fact, throughout my tenure at the university, Michael Andrew championed philosophy of education and showed genuine interest in my research. I, as the one and only full-time philosopher of education on campus, was given a free rein to create our core courses for the philosophy of education requirement.

In my second year at UNH, I threw myself with pedagogical fervor into teaching the courses I had designed. Thus began my journey of learning how to teach teachers – both pre-service and experienced. I soon discovered, somewhat to my dismay, that a substantial number of students, graduates as well as undergraduates, carried a fear of philosophy. I later wrote about learning how to work with this discovery in the *Philosophy of Education Newsletter* (May 1992), where I describe my initial surprise when one courageous student admitted out loud (while others nodded in silent agreement) that the very word 'philosophy' brought forth in her feelings of dread and incompetence. This discovery sent me back to Alfred North Whitehead and his learning cycles of Romance, Precision, and Utilization.

I realized that, in contrast to my own personal history, many of my students had missed, and now badly needed to experience, the stage of Romance with respect to philosophy. In addition to Whitehead, I relied heavily on John Dewey as a theoretical guide and pedagogical resource. I incorporated Dewey's insights on 'social control' into classroom structures and methods; and I followed his 'scientific method' as I observed, recorded, reflected upon, and modified my approaches to teaching.

Even as I became a more skillful teacher of teachers, I continued to face new torpedo fish experiences. For instance, listening to my students self-reports about their learning showed me how little I knew about what counted as 'success.' Two contrasting student responses stand out in my memory. Although my methods varied considerably, I always required students to study John Dewey's philosophy. After a class when I had taken pains to explicate Dewey's concepts of educative, non-educative, and mis-educative, one of my teaching interns came up to me in tears. I was worried at first that this might be a new form of resistance to studying Dewey, but her tears turned out to be tears of relief as she told me how, during my lecture, she had suddenly seen the applicability of Dewey's concepts to what was happening with her class of frustrating high school students. Subsequent conversations confirmed the depth of her understanding; and she reported increasing success in her teaching.

In apparent contrast to this intern, another student sat as far back in the corner as he could, often on top of a radiator, visibly, and occasionally vocally, resistant. About five years later he showed up one day at my office for an unexpected visit. Now a parent and a high school teacher in Vermont, he told me of his stint, after graduation, as an Air Force Pilot; he spoke quietly of the grief he and his wife had experienced over the loss of their first child from IDS. Then, as the conversation shifted to his current teaching position, an unmistakable eagerness came into his voice. He wanted me to know that he now "got" Dewey, he now understood what I had been "getting at" five years ago. He pulled out his dog-eared copy of Dewey's book and engaged me in an animated conversation. On the spot I realized, yet again: I did not know what I thought I knew – in this case, whether my teaching had or had not been successful.

While undergraduates presented a bewildering range of pedagogical challenges, most graduate students came as experienced teachers, thoughtful and ready to deepen their understanding of educational philosophy. My work with these able mature teachers was one factor that led to the creation of our Ph.D. in Education program, the first of its kind north of Boston. By this time I was no longer the one and only philosopher of education on campus. During our brief 'golden age' we could boast of four philosophers of education in our relatively small department: Susan Douglas Franzosa, Scott Fletcher, Barbara Houston, and me. Unfortunately for us, Susan and Scott proved to be outstanding administrators and were whisked away to become college deans elsewhere. Although maintaining a doctoral program placed heavy demands on our faculty, working with advanced and eager students also contributed an upsurge of contagious energy. Even with the extra hours and administrative bothers, I remember my almost two decades as doctoral program coordinator as fruitful enjoyable labor; and I am delighted by the accomplishments of our graduates.

RESEARCH AND POLITICS: TWO MORE BIG TORPEDO FISH

The subtitle for our book *The Gender Question in Education*, co-authored with Kathryn Morgan, Barbara Houston and Maryann Ayim, is: Theory, Pedagogy, & Politics.[4] This explicit combination of Theory, Pedagogy, & Politics names a crucial, indeed I believe inevitable, conjunction that characterizes the very nature of Philosophy of Education. In contrast to certain branches of philosophy (sometimes designated as "pure"), the study of educational theory entails the domains of pedagogy and politics; these constitute the basic stuff of our studies, perhaps doubly so for feminists. As a feminist philosopher of education I find myself excited and frustrated, inspired and disheartened, as my focus shifts from theoretical discussions to pedagogical applications and political complexities. I also notice how grounding theoretical constructs in examples of practice helps to "keep me honest."

A brief caveat: while I remain convinced of the inseparability of research and politics, I am now about to distinguish them, for the purposes of discussion, in the next section.

POLITICS

Almost as soon as I landed at the University of New Hampshire, I saw I could not avoid the realm of gender-sensitive politics. Women faculty were such a rarity that we could all fit into one woman's living room. Our numbers hovered between fifteen percent and a high of eighteen percent of tenure-track faculty university-wide. Eventually a concerted conscious effort did manage to address this imbalance and break the eighteen percent ceiling. Meanwhile, those committed to gender-sensitive academic practices and policies were small in numbers. I joined the effort to create a Women's Studies Program; and, soon after its inception, I served on the first W. S. Advisory Board.

Somehow, as a junior faculty member, I became the prime mover for instituting strong new gender-sensitive policies and radical democratic voting procedures for selecting promotion and tenure panels in our College of Liberal Arts (the administrative unit for the education department). After persistent and, at times, delicate, political labor, we succeeded in instituting a gender-balance requirement for every single promotion and tenure panel in our college. Thereafter, no panel could be without at least one woman member. These new policies had an immediate positive effect both on the procedures and also on the morale among women faculty.

Thereafter, it was not surprising, although a bit daunting, to find myself repeatedly re-elected to college promotion and tenure committees. Although the labor entailed was time-consuming and fraught with complex conundrums, the level of conscientious careful commitment I witnessed among the members of these elected faculty committees was heartening; and it increased my respect for colleagues across a wide range of academic disciplines. Also, after receiving tenure and promotion, I served for a number of years on the Dean's Council and briefly as a Faculty Fellow working in the Dean's office. Encouraged by my peers to consider full-time academic administration, I flirted with this idea for a while before deciding against it. I do not regret that decision. I was ready to shift my attention back to research; and I soon became excited by my work on *The Gender Question in Education*.

THE GENDER QUESTION IN EDUCATION: ROOTS AND TENDRILS

The earliest roots for *The Gender Question in Education: Theory, Pedagogy, & Politics* trace back to the days when we were first addressing women's issues, and initiating the Commission on the Status of Women (COSW), in the Philosophy of Education Society. All four of us continued these conversations in various ways. In the mid-1980s Barbara Houston and I labored over a coauthored essay entitled "Trusting Ourselves to Care"[5] as part of our ongoing effort to address controversies among feminists. Then, what was probably a major catalyst for setting the book project in motion occurred one summer at an NWSA (National Women's Studies Association) conference in Ohio. That summer's meeting overflowed with exuberant feminist energy – a perpetual celebration of women's liberation heightened by evening gatherings with live readings by some of the best women writers and poets of the day: Margaret Atwood, Ester Bronner, Nicki Giovanni, Paule Marshall, Marge Piercy, Adrienne Rich, among others. In that wonderfully charged atmosphere, Kathryn Morgan, Barbara Houston, and I presented one of our early public dialogues on: "The Perils and Paradoxes of the Bearded Mothers." Our "Bearded Mothers" presentation received such an enthusiastic reception that it inspired a boost of book-planning energy. After Kathryn Morgan initiated work with the helpful staff at Westview Press, *The Gender Question in Education* was on its way. Over the course of the next five years, working jointly and separately, we moved ever closer to the final draft. And I experienced both the joys and tribulations of being the editor for our co-authored book.

Occasionally something I write takes on a life of its own as it flows back and forth between theory and practice. Sometimes the flow stays contained, close to home, in my own classrooms, along with those of graduate teaching assistants and departmental faculty. For instance, my essay on "The Ethical Education of Self-Talk"[6] has been widely used in my own department as a source of guidelines for student 'self-observation' projects. At other times the theory-practice flow keeps expanding (now, of course, increasingly true, indeed commonplace, with the internet). This expanding flow happened with two of my chapters in *The Gender Question*.

Both expansion and creative evolution occurred with chapter ten: "Is Rapprochement Possible Between Educational Criticism and Nurturance?" Much of the impetus for this essay arose from my difficulties with assigning 'fair' grades to my students and from my agonizing over how best to critique their work. After the essay became available to philosophers of education, it had the good fortune to be taken up by Professor Susan Laird. She invented creative applications such as arranging for students to function as 'Friendly Critics' for each other's rough drafts on important written assignments. I then incorporated Susan Laird's innovations into work with my own students which enhanced their sense of collegial support and alleviated many of my original perplexities. Since then, colleagues and former doctoral students have continued to create their own variations on these practices of 'critical nurturance.'

Turning to one other favorite chapter (chapter twelve in *The Gender Question*), I note my continued delight in the potent combination of co-exploring and co-enjoyment. If I were to revise this chapter today, I would keep the key themes but expand the framework to reach beyond an ethics of care – not because they are out of alignment but rather to avoid confining these endeavors within any single ethical theory. I believe that almost any ethic can, and probably already does (de facto), benefit from extensive co-exploring along with as much concomitant co-enjoyment as participants can muster. I also would not place co-enjoyment last in my list.

When I arrived at UNH soon after completing my dissertation I had no inkling that I would spend my next four decades as a professor in Durham, NH. Part of what kept me happily ensconced, in addition to tenure, was the congenial and vibrant community of scholars and teachers. Before the onslaught of devastating budget cuts, the university provided financial and collegial encouragement for diverse lines of inquiry, research, and teaching. Indeed, before the advent of 'outsourcing' our university community gave supportive recognition not only to faculty, students, and staff, but also to grounds crews, technical workers, and housekeepers. University administrators at all levels made themselves accessible to faculty, kept abreast of campus happenings, and showed genuine concern for persons and for principles.

I found this sense of community enhanced in our department of education where open inquiry and ongoing support constituted norms for most members. It was no accident that when four of us responded to a request for an essay about our program, it was "communities of inquiry and support" that emerged as "critically important."[7] I felt supported by all the teacher education faculty, and especially by

Michael Andrew an indefatigable empirical researcher, by Ellen Corcoran a most perceptive internship supervisor and site coordinator, and by Carl Menge a deservedly popular professor of educational psychology. In Morrill Hall, the old brick edifice that housed our department, everyone seemed welcome – students of all ages, "school-people" (public school teachers, staff, and leaders) as well as young children and friendly animals, for whom the secretaries kept not-very-hidden stashes of candies and generous supplies of dog biscuits. Co-enjoyment mingled with co-exploring.

My own experience, after years as a politically active faculty member, showed me how much the power of co-exploring joined with co-enjoyment can contribute to improved political situations. I would now recommend attending to co-enjoyment, possibly even as a prerequisite, for generating and maintaining cooperation, for facilitating co-exploring, and for providing safer co-existence. And I would change the title of chapter twelve – to something like: "The Power of Co-Exploring & Co-Enjoyment."

A GLANCE BACKWARDS: MY QUEST FOR FREEDOM AND THE SEARCH FOR WISE LOVE IN EDUCATION

Reflecting back on personal patterns and persistent threads, I discern certain prevailing impulses and favored themes. For instance, my penchant for 'co-exploring' coupled with 'co-enjoyment' has led me to pursue opportunities for dialogue and embodied Socratic exchanges. Thus, the annual PES meetings offer one ideal setting for this pursuit, with generous time allotments for session papers, followed by formal responses and open discussion. I have participated in PES meetings as often as possible, presenting my own work and responding to that of others. Given this pattern, a number of the questions addressed in my writing have come and gone in response to the time and context. I do, nonetheless, remain fond of certain short responses such as the discourse on "Wow! Experiences."[8] Other lines of inquiry have persisted, re-emerging in various guises, sometimes after lying dormant for years.

One example of a stubbornly persistent line of inquiry, whose origins remain obscure (perhaps generated during the days of my childhood peripatetic philosophy), kept me immersed, early on, in western philosophy's literature on freedom vs. determinism. A heavy bout of intensive study would halt at some temporary oasis that afforded a partial resolution. During my graduate studies, William James's philosophy provided one such oasis. Sooner or later, however, I would resume my search for more satisfactory resolutions.

Eventually, during my study of eastern wisdom traditions, Buddhism in particular, I began to grasp the significance of "staying in the gap." This 'gap' occurs between (a) some external, potentially triggering, event and (b) one's internal automatic impulse to react, or "get triggered." Recent neuroscience provides scientific explanations, as well as validation, for this ancient Buddhist conception with its emphasis on learning to "stay in the gap." A brief published discussion of this recent resting place can now be found in my PES response to Paul Taylor's Kneller lecture.[9]

Setting aside ruminations over human freedom and determinism, the central themes, subtexts, and personal inspiration for my work often arise out of a respect and concern for teachers and the labors of teaching. Persistent topics reflect my own wrestling with what I perceive as critical matters of educational theory and practice. In fact, appreciation, concern, and wrestling all show up in my very first presentation to PES: "How Strong Is the Case Against Teaching?"[10] Decades later when I sit down to write "The Search for Wise Love in Education" I now hold the hypothesis that our best teachers embody "wise love" – these teachers bring lovingkindness, compassion, sympathetic joy, and equanimity to their teaching and to their students, not in any self-conscious formulaic fashion, just simply as a way of being (without discounting acquired skills and substantial knowledge).[11]

My own experiences of teaching at my best feel as if they too come from a place of wise love. And, I suspect that my best work in Philosophy of Education emerges out of, and draws upon, the resources of wise love. In any case, my work in this field has turned out to be a way for me to contribute to and honor a lineage of teachers and teaching that I deeply value.

FAVORITE WORKS

Favorites Written by Others/Influential Works by Others

de Beauvoir, S. (1962). *The prime of life.*
Dewey, J. (1938). *Experience and education.*
James, W. *Passim.*
Martin, J. R. (1985). *Reclaiming a conversation.*
Nhat Hanh, T. (1988). *The sun my heart.*
Packer, T. (1990). *The work of this moment.*
Plato, *Apology, Meno, Republic.*
Rousseau, J. J. *Émile.*
Whitehead, A. N. (1929). *The aims of education and other essays.*

Personal Favorites

Book

Diller, A. (1996). *The gender question in education: Theory, pedagogy, & politics.*

Essays

Diller, A. (1973). *How strong is the case against teaching?*
Diller, A. (1978). *On a conception of moral teaching.*
Diller, A. (1987). *Trusting ourselves to care.* With Barbara Houston.
Diller, A. (1997). *The importance of Wow! experiences.*
Diller, A. (1998). *Facing the torpedo fish: Becoming a philosopher of one's own education.*
Diller, A. (1999). *The ethical education of self-talk.*

Diller, A. (2004). *The search for wise love in education: What can we learn from the Brahmaviharas?*
Diller, A. (2009). *Uncovering racialized perceptions: Obstacles and antidotes.*

NOTES

[1] "Facing the Torpedo Fish: Becoming a Philosopher of One's Own Education." *Philosophy of Education 1998*. Edited by Steve Tozer. Normal, IL: Philosophy of Education Society, 1999.

[2] "In Praise of Objective-Subjectivity: Teaching the Pursuit of Precision." *Studies in Philosophy of Education: An International Quarterly*, 16, 73-87, 1997. Reprinted in *Reason and Education: Essays in Honor of Israel Scheffler*. Edited by H. Siegel. Dordrecht: Kluwer Academic Publishers, 1997, pp. 73-87.

[3] *Growing Up with Philosophy*, edited by Matthew Lipman and Ann Sharp. Philadelphia, PA: Temple University Press 1978, pp. 326-338.

[4] Diller, A., B. Houston, K. P. Morgan, and M. Ayim. *The Gender Question in Education: Theory, Pedagogy and Politics*. Boulder, CO: Westview Press, 1996.

[5] Barbara Houston and Ann Diller, "Trusting Ourselves to Care." *Resources for Feminist Research*, 16(3), 35-38, 1987.

[6] *Justice and Care in Education*, edited by M. Katz, N. Noddings, and K. Strike. NY: Teachers College Press, 1999, chapter five.

[7] Sharon Nodie Oja, Ann Diller, Ellen Corcoran, and Michael D. Andrew, "Communities of Inquiry, Communities of Support: The Five-Year Teacher Education Program at the University of New Hampshire." *How Teachers Learn*. Ed. by Michael D. Andrew & James R. Jelmberg. NY: Peter Lang, 2010, pp. 11-32. First published in *Reflective Teacher Education Programs: Case Studies and Critiques*. Albany, NY: SUNY Press, 1992, pp. 93-112.

[8] "Expanding Identities: The Importance of Wow! Experiences." *Philosophy of Education*, 1997. Edited by Susan Laird. Urbana, IL: Philosophy of Education Society, 1998, pp. 71-74.

[9] Diller, A. "Uncovering Racialized Perceptions: Obstacles and Antidotes." *Philosophy of Education 2009*. Edited by Deborah Kerdeman. Urbana, IL: Philosophy of Education Society, 2009, pp. 43-47.

[10] Diller, A. "How Strong Is the Case against Teaching?" *Philosophy of Education 1973*. Edited by Brian Crittenden. Edwardsville, IL: Philosophy of Education Society, 1973, pp. 266-272.

[11] Diller, A. "The Search for Wise Love in Education: What Can We Learn from the Brahmaviharas?" *Teaching, Learning and Loving*. Edited by Daniel Liston and Jim Garrison. NY: Routledge Falmer, 2004, chapter ten.

PENNY ENSLIN

LIBERALISM AND EDUCATION

Between Diversity and Universalism

GROWING UP SOUTH AFRICAN

If our interests as philosophers of education are determined by the contexts in which we grow up, a South African childhood undoubtedly shaped mine. I was born three years after the National Party came to power and embarked on its plan for so-called separate development of South Africa's people, more notoriously known as apartheid. White children lived in a bubble: in segregated and more prosperous suburbs where they attended far more generously resourced but nonetheless authoritarian schools, reserved for those registered as white at birth. In childhood and youth one hardly ever encountered those classified as black on equal, everyday terms. An only child, I loved books, but finding enough to read was usually difficult, as small town libraries had limited collections and restricted the number of items borrowers were allowed to take out at a time. While school provided friends, it was rarely edifying; instead I found it stern, narrow-minded and censorious. An early memory is of being smacked repeatedly for failing to write the letter 'b' in the prescribed way (still resisted with a transgressive sense of satisfaction many years later). Rote learning was common.

I can date my awareness that something was strange about our society to the compulsory celebration of South Africa's departure from the Commonwealth and the creation of a Republic in 1961. As part of the festivities white schoolchildren were given a flag and a commemorative coin with bogus gold coating that quickly wore off to expose the cheap metal underneath. Subsequent decades saw increasing resistance and unrest, accompanied by state efforts to convince the white population that they were threatened by communist forces without, rather than a political and economic system that could not be justified or maintained. The education system was a weapon in this strategy.

A more systematic political sensitivity was to emerge later as an undergraduate, but my secondary schooling passed in Anglican girls' schools that were ethnically homogeneous and afforded some opportunities for educative learning – limited mainly to English literature, creative writing and music – and especially to the enjoyment of debating, of crafting an argument of one's own. These activities aside, my last school was quite anti-intellectual, with pressure to conform to a peer culture that was hostile to bookish pupils, and a requirement to accept irksome exercises of authority that made little sense. Compulsory attendance at weekly church services and daily prayers failed to instil any religious spirituality in me.

After school, the University of Natal was liberating, a place to enjoy ideas for their own sake. My majors in History and Political Science set in place some abiding intellectual interests and commitments. The prevalent liberal interpretation of South African history, studied through reading original documents in the history of South Africa, opened my way to later analysis of education policy documents. A turning point followed my decision to try a philosophy course. We began with Plato's Republic, and I was hooked for life. Involvement in student politics affirmed my opinion that apartheid was an injustice detrimental to all South Africans. Liberal student politics took as foundational the principles of university autonomy and academic freedom – both under constant threat from the state. Harmless student protest was monitored by the security police, and a member of the students' representative council on which I served was later exposed as a police spy. The self-consciously separate and more radical black consciousness movement had begun to challenge the prevalent liberal stance in white student politics, as black nationalism and Marxism were bound to do in the subsequent decades that led to the inevitable overthrow of apartheid. The country's political extremes became more evident in the year I spent completing an honours degree in Political Philosophy at the University of Stellenbosch. This Afrikaans-medium university was the intellectual home of the Afrikaner elite, the alma mater of all but one of the National Party Prime Ministers. Yet in its Department of Political Philosophy Johan Degenaar and Andre du Toit's courses offered opportunities to develop critical thinking and to study democratic theory, pluralism, aesthetics and linguistic philosophy. In contrast to these educational benefits, the hegemony of Afrikaner nationalism was strongly apparent in the wider university and beyond – in a dour, humourless authoritarianism, whose brutality became more and more pronounced in the years that followed. The country became increasingly militarised, as most of my male peers and relations were subject to conscription to protect the apartheid regime and its allies in the surrounding territories that were destabilised by being drawn into the conflict. Little though I realised it at the time, my flatmate's textbooks on a subject oddly named Fundamental Pedagogics were to provoke a major research interest within a few years of moving on from Stellenbosch to a career in teaching and postgraduate research in education.

Having left school vowing not to become a teacher, I found myself in need of a career. Undertaking a postgraduate diploma in education brought me into contact with one of several teachers who had a strong influence on my thinking; Wally Morrow taught philosophy of education at the University of the Witwatersrand, Johannesburg. His classes in philosophy of education, which he in turn had studied at the University of London Institute of Education before bringing the 'London School' to South Africa, opened up new directions in both themes in education and in the analytical approach. Conceptual analysis provided a sharp tool to critique the prevailing educational discourse in South Africa, initially the Calvinist ideology of Christian National Education, and later Fundamental Pegadogics.

Four years as a teacher of secondary school history, mostly at a traditional boy's school, presented me with an opportunity to experience segregated white education from the classroom chalk face and to consolidate my views on both South African history and the corrupting effects of segregation and apartheid ideology on white South African youth. Gender discrimination was also crudely obvious; women teachers were tolerated in this rugby-obsessed boys' school as an unavoidable necessity in a profession without enough men, but we were mercifully excused duty in the weekly drilling of khaki-clad military cadets. It would have been hard not to notice that my women colleagues were as capable as the men, and often more conscientious and effective as teachers. When the Soweto uprising erupted in June 1976, many of my pupils were outraged that their ungrateful black counterparts were burning schools that 'we' had provided for them. Given high levels of censorship and crude state propaganda, this perception was not surprising. The school's culture was quite brutish, with an atmosphere of oppressive and homophobic masculinity. Yet even with a history syllabus constructed from a very specifically white perspective and textbooks ranging from the overtly indoctrinatory to those that tried to present a more balanced interpretation of our divided country's history, there were opportunities to foster critical thinking about history as a subject open to interpretation. Learning through teaching demanded consolidation of my historical knowledge, but a low point came in a term teaching in a girls' secondary school where being required to teach South African constitutional history to fifteen year-old girls waiting impatiently to leave school prompted hard questions about the aims and purposes of schooling.

Looking back on these early professional and educational experiences, I find they undoubtedly put in place the issues and intellectual commitments that occupied me in later years: broadly put, a liberal response to injustice, nationalism, gender inequality and ideological hegemony. Holding these interests together has been the theme of diversity, so corruptly and destructively interpreted by the apartheid regime. Difference was a pretext for segregation, for the systematic enforcement of inequality and restricted freedom for all in its defence. Ascribed identities were imposed on all, leaving me permanently sceptical about demands in South Africa and abroad for the recognition of diversity as a principle to underpin policy in education, directing me instead to defend a universalist stance. Emphasis on the associated notions of culture and community also prompted ongoing questions for me about whose interests are served by calls for respect for difference, as does the idea of the nation. Arbitrary exercises of authority, even through petty rules and regulations far from peculiar to apartheid South Africa, later made deliberative democracy so attractive to me. Prohibitions on dissent continued to rile, in the requirement for political correctness in academia, an inclination to expect conformity to intellectual fashions that proscribe deviant intellectual tendencies while requiring prescribed forms of solidarity, reflexiveness and confessions of positionality. Liberal universalism has from time to time been a ready target for such scolding, yet I have found in it a natural intellectual home, with its fundamental commitment to individual autonomy as a central aim of education and to the freedom, equality and universal human rights all too modishly dismissed from the comfort of a European or North American background. This does not constitute a wholesale dismissal of considerations of diversity; the issue is rather one of how to reconcile competing tensions between diversity and universality (Enslin, 1999b), especially as cultural recognition has tended to trump the redistribution of goods that include educational resources (Enslin & Tjiattas, 2009).

PHILOSOPHY AND THEORY OF EDUCATION

Having come to philosophy via history and political science, I took two masters degrees by dissertation, on complementary topics. First, with Wally Morrow I tackled Fundamental Pedagogics, which was the dominant doctrine in educational theory for several decades in the Afrikaans-medium universities and, through their influence, in the segregated black universities and colleges of education. My critique of the treatment of science and values in Fundamental Pedagogics (Enslin, 1986/1987, 1991) argued that its claim to be scientific was based on a controversial notion of science and served as a distraction from its central purpose of endorsing the ideology of Christian National Education (CNE).

Protected from critique by its very constitution, this peculiar interpretation of phenomenology was used to justify apartheid ideology in education, including the segregated provision of inferior schooling for black South Africans. Imported by scholars who had studied in Holland, and cast as the epistemological grounding for theory of education, this science was supposedly free of ideology, metaphysics or dogma. Relying more often on etymology rather than on critical scrutiny of concepts and arguments, it was claimed that the pedagogician as a scientist bracketed off her life- and world-view during the process of scientific reflection on education. Life- and world-views would play a role, instead, in the pre-scientific and post-scientific moments of the research process. Depicting culture as given, internally homogeneous, distinct, unchanging and uncontested, Fundamental Pedagogics proffered a form of universal validity by shielding the particular from the possibility of critique. In doing so it endorsed a Christian National Educational doctrine that depicted the child as helpless and dependant, ignorant and inclined by nature towards sin, in need of guidance towards adulthood within the norms of a given culture. Crudely in service of justification of an authoritarian segregated and unequal educational system, CNE's creationist justification for segregation depicted black South Africans in a state of cultural infancy, needing white trusteeship. Its myth of the child was distinctly at odds with the role of youth in resisting apartheid (Enslin, 1992a).

Fundamental Pedagogics was expressed in a pretentious terminology compared with the clarity of analytical philosophy at its best. Its 'own language' was supposed to grant it some kind of independent credibility as a science, but it played its part in fostering academic isolation that did lasting damage. The effects of this self-imposed isolation, not helped by the academic boycott, will linger long in what remains a very divided society. Its treatment of culture has left me sceptical ever since about claims to cultural particularity and arguments about education that make much of diversity. Whose interests, whose power, do such arguments serve to protect? While I was to make my mark in a series of papers that exposed the bizarreness and significance of Fundamental Pedagogics (Enslin, 1986/1987, 1991, 1992a), this work also prompted questions about how theory and philosophy of education ought to be understood.

With the opportunity to study abroad I chose Cambridge where Paul Hirst supervised my dissertation on the nature and purpose of theory of education. This widened my perspectives in several ways. One was the opportunity to develop the skills, rigour and clarity that typified the analytical approach. While I was later to find conceptual analysis too confining because its focus on ordinary use of concepts tends to endorse traditional understandings and to be insufficiently normative, John Wilson's *Thinking with Concepts* (1970) was hugely instructive at the time and the clarity of analytical philosophy of education has remained a powerful influence. Another opportunity was simply the chance to view South Africa's strangeness from the outside, to place it in a global perspective – though all countries are strange in their own ways. Attending a meeting of the Philosophy of Education Society of Great Britain was my first contact with a community of philosophers of education where I felt at home and which provided contacts and friendships that grew thereafter, as has occurred in the International Network of Philosophers of Education. I also discovered feminist writings, becoming a regular reader of Spare Rib and of authors like Betty Friedan and Germaine Greer.

LIBERALISM AND THE AIMS OF EDUCATION

After Cambridge I returned to South Africa, taking up a lectureship in Education at the University of the Witwatersrand, where I was to remain for 27 years. South African educational problems demanded urgent philosophical attention and I embarked on a PhD, again with Wally Morrow as supervisor. My defence of liberal theory of education, and of individual autonomy as a central aim of education, consolidated my earlier interests and outlook, and developed a theoretical stance that became a platform for later work. By now I was sure that applying normative political philosophy to problems in education was my quest. Taking as its starting point a response to the current Marxist critique of liberal philosophy of education in the 1980s, both in South Africa and abroad, and referring mainly to the works of John Locke and John Stuart Mill, my thesis argued that historically the central distinguishing feature of liberalism is its defence of the principle of freedom, although individual expressions of this core idea vary according to context. There is no simple and timeless statement of the liberal position (Enslin, 1984). Not only was the brand of theory of education denounced as liberal in the South African context not really liberal at all (Enslin, 1985a); I also suggested that in some respects the work of Richard Peters and Paul Hirst could be interpreted as more inclined towards conservatism than liberalism (Enslin, 1985b). The liberalism of John White (1982) offered a more unambiguous example of a liberal account of the aims of education. I argued that Marxism and a genuinely liberal account of education show significant features in common, although some aspects of a

Marxist account lacked coherence (Enslin, 1987). Yet I have remained impressed by Marxism's criticisms of capitalism, which I hold is not a necessary feature of liberalism, and is a threat to educative schooling. While Marxist theory was later sidelined by poststructuralism, its insights about the workings of capitalism and its educational consequences now look urgently prescient. One of my papers on the ideology of teacher education in South Africa under apartheid (Enslin, 1986/1987) was written from an Althusserian perspective, and I resist the notion that one must choose one theoretical stance from which to speak. A Foucauldian perspective has also been instructive for me in analysing teacher education under apartheid (Enslin, 1991).

My liberal trajectory was soon to be complemented and enriched by an ongoing engagement with the work of John Rawls, the magisterial presence in political philosophy since the 1960s. It is tempting to retrospectively impose greater coherence on one's work than there might have been, but as issues to address and arguments to make presented themselves, I was set on a clear path, with forays into topics that ranged across nationalism, feminism, democratic theory and citizenship, higher education, as well as peace education and values education. All have been framed by a commitment to liberalism whilst being appreciative of its internal diversity, and to engagement with its rival theories. Feminist writers' work has been taken up on a range of issues, forcing moments of conceptual alteration, especially in recasting long-held assumptions about citizenship (Enslin, 2000a), multiculturalism (2001) and the public-private distinction (Enslin, 1992, 1997a).

LIBERALISM AND EDUCATION IN THE ERA OF JOHN RAWLS

Rawls' *A Theory of Justice* (1971) has had clear implications for the distribution of educational goods and these have been widely explored. Obviously, the very idea of formulating principles that would be agreed on by participants behind a veil of ignorance, in an original position in which they would have no knowledge of their own situation in society, was ripe for application to the injustices of the South African political and educational order. His two principles of justice, of equal rights to basic liberties for all and that any inequalities be to the benefit of those least advantaged but with opportunities and positions open to all, have opened the way to analysis and critique of educational policies in many contexts. But other aspects of Rawls' interpretation of the liberal tradition have been more generative for me and some co-authors in applying them to education and also in refocusing them, especially in feminist terms.

It was Rawls' *Political Liberalism* (1993) that particularly caught my attention. Still concerned with principles that could be agreed to by free and equal citizens through reasoned discussion, and focused on achieving stability in a well ordered society through the basic structure of a constitutional order, *Political Liberalism* made the key distinction between a political conception of justice and a comprehensive religious, philosophical or moral doctrine about justice. Asking how to ensure justice over time in a society in which citizens hold different and even incompatible though still reasonable doctrines, Rawls' idea of an overlapping consensus of such doctrines is strikingly relevant to contexts like post-apartheid South Africa. But, especially in writing about citizenship education (Enslin, 1997b, 1997c), I have found his articulation of a conception of a constitutional democracy that does not have to invoke either Kantian autonomy or Millian individuality as values in a comprehensive doctrine too restrictive. So, for all the illumination that *Political Liberalism* offers, applying the later Rawls to substantive issues, some of its features are inadequate to problems in politics and education. Yet methodologically and in some of its hallmark devices like the veil of ignorance, Rawls' work and the vast body of engagement it has generated have set much of the agenda for political theory and philosophy of education. This has been especially so in relation to gender justice, to deliberative democracy and citizenship education, to an ongoing defence of liberal theory in the context of South African education, and to a preference for cosmopolitan conceptions of both justice and of democracy.

Rival theories have proposed more agonistic conceptions of deliberation that eschew Rawls' insistence on confining public reason to matters on which all participants could potentially agree in spite of differences in their comprehensive doctrines, thus avoiding contentious disputes between doctrines. Despite the attraction of averting potentially violent disagreement, this narrowing of the agenda could leave most issues requiring deliberation off the agenda. Citizenship education, I have argued, with Pendlebury and Tjiattas (2001), drawing on the work of Seyla Benhabib (1996) and Iris Marion Young (1996, 1997), can and should address diversity by allowing more robust versions of deliberation, encouraging a wider range of topics and forms of expression. This suggests a more demanding conception of citizenship, but still one that can accommodate and draw on diversity. So, inclining also toward a cosmopolitan form of citizenship (Enslin & Tjiattas, 2004) we have favoured accounts of deliberation that draw in all affected and include questioning what is on the agenda and the rules of discourse, while still holding to a Kantian tradition of respect for persons as equal and autonomous. We recognise, as does Benhabib (1996), that deliberative democracy, as practical reason, is the heritage of many cultures and traditions. In citizenship education, learning democracy is about talk and about learning to listen, across difference. Elsewhere, with Patricia White (2003), I have taken up the implications of a deliberative theory of democracy for reconceptualising the idea of citizenship, so that it acknowledges the traditional restriction of women to the private, domestic sphere and addresses the related assumption that active citizenship takes place through participation in the public. Deliberative citizenship, through a variety of associations and contexts, some of which may cross borders, opens the way to more complex forms of participation and representation (Dieltiens & Enslin, 2002).

Debates about Rawlsian liberalism and its critical alternatives, especially those presented from the perspectives of liberal feminism and cosmopolitanism, remain pertinent to education in South Africa. That liberalism remains widely derided there is unfortunate and ironic, with a post-apartheid constitution based on liberal principles of equal rights, human dignity, freedom of belief and opinion, assembly, association and expression, and also of tolerance, the separation of powers and the rule of law. As I argue in addressing civic education since the transition to democracy in 1994 (Enslin, 1997b), the new constitution affirms a distinctly liberal conception of the citizen. Educational policy since 1994 has reflected a liberal conception of education, in its emphasis on freedom from discrimination in the provision of education through a unified system with quality education for all, equal access and a strong commitment to development of critical thinking (1999a). The accompanying principles – constitutional and educational – of respect for diverse languages, traditions and cultures are potentially in tension with promoting critical thinking. At the very least, the problems that arise in Rawls' attempt to reconcile diversity and equality through his contentious notion of political liberalism illuminate the tensions in trying to reconcile the challenges of promoting both respect for cultural diversity and fostering critical thinking though education (Appiah, 2005).

My work has supported versions of liberalism more likely to prompt critical reflection on one's own way of life, in part because gender equality requires this. Internationally, deference to culture is problematic for women, with implications for the 'private' domain of the family (Enslin, 1997a) and for access to schooling. So Susan Moller Okin's response to calls in western multicultural societies for recognition of traditions of cultural minorities (1998, 1999) has been especially open to educational application. Her observation that at the heart of most cultures is the control of women and the evocative notion of cultural alteration have inspired me in exploring the role of education in creating a 'just world without gender' (Enslin & Tjiattas, 2006). I have also found congenial Martha Nussbaum's critical but sympathetic engagement with Rawls' theory of justice and the educational dimension of the Capabilities Approach, with its rejection of cultural relativism exemplary in articulating a liberal feminism with possibilities for universal application that nonetheless remains sensitive to diversity (Nussbaum, 2001, 2006). So too, Kwame Anthony Appiah's (2005) sympathetic treatment of identity politics which accommodates both identity as a source of value and universalist moral concerns (Appiah, 2005). Along with Iris Marion Young, Okin, Nussbaum and Appiah count among philosophers whose work I have most admired.

NATION BUILDING AND AFRICAN PHILOSOPHY OF EDUCATION

From a liberal point of view, was it conceivable that after apartheid a revised conception of the nation could help to address the challenges of diversity and reconstruction? This recurrent interest was the subject of my inaugural lecture as Professor of Education at the University of the Witwatersrand (Enslin, 1994, 1999b). Despite sympathetic treatment of national identity by some liberal theorists, and while recognising that nation building would inevitably be considered to have a potential role in unifying a fractured society like South Africa, I have argued against the idea that fostering national identity has a legitimate place among the aims of education. This stance rests firstly on the conviction that addressing diversity through nation-building was likely to undermine autonomy as a central aim of education. In the absence of a shared mass culture and myths, and with a history of expropriation, oppression and exploitation, some considerable retrospective myth-making – the stuff of nationalism – would have been required, and we already had a history of that. Fostering citizenship through the teaching of myths would have been a threat to the development of the critical thinking at the heart of the post apartheid vision for education. Uniquely, South Africa's Truth and Reconciliation Commission offered another way of thinking about citizenship education (Enslin, 2000b).

There were also feminist reasons for this opposition to nation building (Enslin, 1998). The nation is a gendered notion, usually a celebration of masculine exploits, commonly expressed in military terms. Likely to foster militaristic values and hierarchical authority structures, rather than individual autonomy and reasoned debate, the nation of Afrikaner nationalism and, in a different way, of the black nationalist struggle, excluded women from images of citizenship. Schools have traditionally seen the inculcation of ascribed identities as their prerogative. These have included gendered identities, often homophobic and fixing roles and prospects for life. Instead of nation building, I have thus defended citizenship education as a matter of exploring and understanding alternative identities in a diverse society, with opportunities for choosing new ones, for self-definition as well as respect for the identities of others (Enslin, 2000c).

Not unconnected with nationalism, with the end of apartheid African philosophy emerged as a focus for philosophy of education in South Africa. Reflecting on accounts of African culture and values, African philosophy of education has placed a central emphasis on the idea of ubuntu as shared humanity, relatedness, connectedness, an expression of community and communalism. Often depicted as uniquely African and more appropriate to context than western alternatives, ubuntu has been variously put forward as an ontology, an ethic, a basis for citizenship education and even an approach to research. With Kai Horsthemke (Horsthemke & Enslin, 2005, 2009; Enslin & Horsthemke, 2004) I have argued against the idea that education in South Africa should be underpinned by reviving the assumption that human beings comprise distinct cultures and values, each with its own unifying worldview and matching theoretical orientation, to be applied to various issues – political and educational. We have been particularly dismayed by some similar tendencies to Fundamental Pedagogics in defences of ubuntu, depicting it as unfalsifiable by definition, impervious to critique, with only those inside the doctrine qualified to speak (Horsthemke & Enslin, 2009). Such devices, created to deflect criticism, threaten to keep philosophy of education in South Africa outside the international mainstream of the discipline of philosophy of education.

In contrast to those expressions of philosophy of education that take diversity in a particularist direction, whether in favour of national identity or of Africanism, my own stance can be described as a qualified form of liberal universalism. It is important to distinguish what this says from what it does not. For example, it is not necessarily inclined to endorse atomistic individualism, or to dismiss the benefits of community. To defend liberalism as globally relevant (not restricting it as Rawls does to one country) is not to attempt to impose a solely western construction of education on others, across the globe (Enslin, 1999). Liberal ideas are not peculiar to western countries (Appiah, 1997), though western liberal constitutions should not, of course, be imposed on non-western countries. Yet as soon as one insists that members of any society should be allowed to choose their own political and educational systems, and to decide themselves whether to practise or reform any elements of their cultural traditions, the very conditions of choice imply some kind of democratic decision-making, which in turn requires institutions like a free press, multiple political parties, and that individual members be allowed to acquire the capacity to exercise choice, that is to exert a degree of individual autonomy. Exercising choice too, is not a one-off event, but implies becoming accustomed to doing so regularly, participating on an ongoing basis in some form of democratic decision-making, whether participatory or representative, with opportunities for deliberation. These prequisites happen to be features of democracy as articulated from a liberal standpoint. Global integration makes it harder, in my view, to pretend that the preconditions of choice, and of learning to exercise choice, are the possession of any particular part of the globe and thus irrelevant and inappropriate to other contexts. Cosmopolitanism thus becomes ever more viable as a reasoned response to diversity that reflects elements of both descriptive and normative universalism.

COSMOPOLITAN JUSTICE, COSMOPOLITAN DEMOCRACY: PUTTING COSMOPOLITANISM INTO PRACTICE

Although cosmopolitan justice and democracy emerged as themes in our co-authored work while we taught and wrote together in South Africa (Enslin & Tjiattas, 2004), Mary Tjiattas and I have continued to write about cosmopolitan justice and democracy since we both put cosmopolitanism into practice by moving abroad, to the USA and to Scotland respectively. I came to writing with colleagues after many years of single authored publication and have in the latter half of my academic career enjoyed the friendship that goes with collaborative writing. In a most productive collaboration, Mary Tjiattas and I have addressed the educational implications of the burgeoning literature on globalisation and cosmopolitanism, doing so electronically through the ICTs that we note as a feature of those globalisation processes demanding a transnational frame for thinking about justice in education.

Accelerated global integration in recent decades has put pressure on long-held ethico-political concepts – of the state and of justice and democracy (Enslin & Tjiattas, 2009, 2012). The interrelated concepts of justice and democracy need conceptual adjustment to match a world transformed by globalisation, which has accelerated economic and cultural interconnectedness across the borders of nation states. While global integration is visible in international institutions, agreements and norms, political and educational debates remain constrained by the abiding assumption that the globe comprises separate sovereign territorially-defined nations. But nation states are no longer bounded territories whose borders neatly demarcate the domestic as the sphere of citizen rights and duties and of distribution of goods like education, from the foreign. Global integration is as obvious in education as it is in other spheres, as there is now some shared transnational regulation and common policy objectives as seen in the campaign for universal primary education. Notions of justice and democracy, about who gets what (justice) and how this is decided (democracy) are being prised loose from the constraints of the Westphalian doctrine of the sovereign nation state. The now extensive literature on cosmopolitan justice can take common humanity and human rights as a starting point, or it can work from the principle of association that recognises that globalisation brings us into relations of justice with distant others. If duties of justice are owed to all, not just to fellow nationals, cosmopolitan justice demands a more equal transnational distribution of funding for educational opportunities. Conceptual alteration is also required in our interpretation of the concept of democracy, though transnational theories of democracy are not yet as advanced of those of global justice. This stance does not, however, require one to endorse the idea of world government, and I acknowledge that the nation state remains the primary means of both ensuring liberties and distributing educational goods. But the requisite changes in a conception of the nation state in relation to democracy suggest that for the global distribution and organisation of education to be more just than it is, global decision making will need to be more democratic, if northern prosperity is not to trump the interests and the agency of the less prosperous global south.

These cosmopolitan themes, now examined from Scotland – from inside Europe and outside Africa (Enslin, 2008) – demand ongoing reflection. I view them from within a Scotland with a growing nationalist agenda, as holder of a Chair in Education at the University of Glasgow, an institution older than the first European settlement at the Cape of Good Hope. Relocation to Scotland is in itself a move to cosmopolitanism, a form of border-crossing that embraces homelessness, bringing one closer to international networks in philosophy of education. But it also prompts ongoing demands to reflect on global justice and citizenship in education from within the borders of a former colonial power, prompting questions like: is it just for universities in western countries like the United Kingdom to profit as much as they do from the differential fees charged to international students from developing countries? (Enslin & Hedge, 2008); and what does it mean to educate Scottish students to be global citizens? (Enslin & Hedge, 2009). Educational contexts as different as South Africa and Scotland are both particular in their diversity and strikingly similar, facing universal educational challenges in an increasingly integrated world.

FAVORITE WORKS

Own Favorites

Enslin, P. (1986/1987). Apartheid ideology in South African education. *Philosophical Forum, Special Issue: Apartheid*, XVIII, 105-114.

Enslin, P. (1998). Education for nation-building: a feminist critique. In P. Hirst & P. White (Eds.), *Philosophy of education: The analytic tradition, Vol. III: Society and education* (pp. 363-375). London: Routledge.

Enslin, P., Pendlebury, S., & Tjiattas, M. (2001). Deliberative democracy, diversity and the challenges of citizenship education. *Journal of Philosophy of Education, 35*(1), 115-130.

Enslin, P., & White, P. (2003). Democratic citizenship. In N. Blake, P. Smeyers, R. Smith, & P. Standish (Eds.), *The Blackwell guide to the philosophy of education* (pp. 110-125). Oxford: Blackwell.

Enslin, P., & Tjiattas, M. (2009). Philosophy of education and the gigantic affront of universalism. *Journal of Philosophy of Education, 43*(1), 2-17.

Others' Work That Has Influenced and Inspired Me

Mill, J. S. (1859). *On Liberty*. London: Everyman (1962).

Nussbaum, M. (2001). *Women and human development: The capabilities approach*. Cambridge: Cambridge University Press.

Okin, S. M. (1999). Is multiculturalism bad for women? In J. Cohen, M. Howard, & M. Nussbaum (Eds.), *Is multiculturalism bad for women?* (pp. 7-24). Princeton, NJ: Princeton University Press.

Rawls, J. (1971). *A theory of justice*. Cambridge, MA: Harvard University Press.

Rawls, J (1993). *Political liberalism*. New York: Columbia University Press.

Young, I. M. (1996). Communication and the other: Beyond deliberative democracy. In S. Benhabib (Ed.), *Democracy and difference: Contesting the boundaries of the political* (pp. 120-136). Princeton: Princeton University Press.

REFERENCES

Appiah, K. A. (1997). Liberalism and the plurality of identity. In *Seminar on curriculum responses to a changing national and global environment in an African context* (pp. 12-21). Johannesburg: Centre for Higher Education Transformation.

Appiah, K. A. (2005). *The ethics of identity*. Princeton NJ: Princeton University Press.

Benhabib, S. (1996). Toward a deliberative model of democratic legitimacy. In S. Benhabib (Ed.), *Democracy and difference: Contesting the boundaries of the political* (pp. 67-94). Princeton: Princeton University Press.

Dieltiens, V., & Enslin, P. (2002). Democracy in education or education for democracy: The limits of participation in South African School governance. *Journal of Education, 28*, 5-24.

Enslin, P. (1984). The liberal point of view. *Educational Philosophy and Theory, 16*(2), 1-8.

Enslin, P. (1985a). Is the dominant tradition in studies of education in South Africa a liberal one? *Perspectives in Education, 8*(3), 129-153.

Enslin, P. (1985b). Are Hirst and Peters liberal philosophers of education? *Journal of Philosophy of Education, 19*(2), 211-222.

Enslin, P. (1986/1987). Apartheid ideology in South African education. *Philosophical Forum. Special Issue: Apartheid, XVIII*, 105-114.

Enslin, P. (1987). Can Marxism offer a coherent notion of education? *Journal of Philosophy of Education, 21*(1), 59-74.

Enslin, P. (1991). Science and doctrine: theoretical discourse in South African teacher education. In M. Nkomo (Ed.), *Pedagogy of domination: Toward a democratic education in South Africa* (pp. 77-92). Trenton NJ: Africa World Press.

Enslin, P. (1992a). The political mythology of childhood in South African teacher education. *Discourse, 13*(1), 36-48.

Enslin, P. (1992b). Private schools and public schools: A critical response to the privatisation debate *South African Journal of Philosophy, 11*(3), 62-67.

Enslin, P. (1994). Should nation building be an aim of education? *Journal of Education*, 19(1), 23-36.

Enslin, P. (1997a). The family and the private in education for democratic citizenship. In D. Bridges (Ed.), *Education, autonomy and democratic citizenship in a changing world* (pp. 225-236). London: Routledge.

Enslin, P. (1997b). Contemporary liberalism and civic education in South Africa. *Current Writing, Special Issue: The New Liberalism*, 9(2), 77-90.

Enslin, P. (1997c). Education and the limits of political liberalism. *Theoria, Special Issue: The Scope and Limits of Public Reason*, 90, 65-76.

Enslin, P. (1998). Education for nation-building: A feminist critique. In P. Hirst & P. White (Eds.), *Philosophy of education: The analytic tradition, Vol. III: Society and Education* (pp. 363-375). London: Routledge.

Enslin, P. (1999a). Education for liberal democracy: universalising a western construct. *Journal of Philosophy of Education*, 33(2), 175-186.

Enslin, P. (1999b). The place of national identity in the aims of education. In R. Marples (Ed.), *The aims of education* (pp. 100-111). London: Routledge.

Enslin, P. (2000a). Defining a civic agenda: Citizenship and gender equality in post-apartheid education. In M. Arnot & J. Dillabough (Eds.), *Gender, education and citizenship: An international feminist reader* (pp. 297-311). London: Routledge.

Enslin, P. (2000b). Citizenship, identity and myth: Educational implications of South Africa's Truth and Reconciliation Commission. *Change: Transformations in Education, Special Issue: Citizenship and Education*, 3(1), 80-90.

Enslin, P. (2000c). Education and democratic citizenship: in defence of cosmopolitanism. In M. Leicester, S. Modgil, & C. Modgil (Eds.), *Values, education and cultural diversity, Vol. 1: Political education citizenship and cultural diversity* (pp. 149-156). London: Falmer.

Enslin, P. (2001). Multiculturalism, gender and social justice: Liberal feminist misgivings International *Journal of Educational Research*, 35, 281-292.

Enslin, P. (2008). Between Europe and Africa: Against regionalism in citizenship education. In M. Peters, A. Britton, & H. Blee (Eds.), *Global citizenship education: Philosophy, theory and pedagogy* (pp. 491-501). Rotterdam and Taipei: Sense.

Enslin, P., & Hedge, N. (2008). International students, export earnings and the demands of global justice. *Ethics and Education*, 3(2), 105-117.

Enslin, P., & Hedge, N. (2009). A good global neighbour? Scotland, Malawi and global citizenship. *Citizenship Teaching and learning*, 6(1), 91-105.

Enslin, P., & Horsthemke, K. (2004). Can ubuntu provide a model for citizenship education in African democracies? *Comparative Education*, 40(4), 548-558.

Enslin, P., Pendlebury, S., & Tjiattas, M. (2001). Deliberative democracy, diversity and the challenges of citizenship education. *Journal of Philosophy of Education*, 35(1), 115-130.

Enslin, P., & Tjiattas, M. (2004). Cosmopolitan justice: education and global citizenship. *Theoria: A Journal of Social and Political Theory*, 104, 150-168.

Enslin, P., & Tjiattas, M. (2006). Educating for a just world without gender. *Theory and Research in Education*, 4(1), 41-68.

Enslin, P., & Tjiattas, M. (2009). Philosophy of education and the gigantic affront of universalism. *Journal of Philosophy of Education*, 43(1), 2-17.

Enslin, P., & Tjiattas, M. (2012). Democratic inclusion and lifelong learning in a globalising world. In D. Aspin et al. (Eds.), *International Handbook of Lifelong Learning*, 2nd ed. (pp. 77-90). Dordrecht: Springer.

Enslin, P., & White, P. (2003). Democratic citizenship. In N. Blake, P. Smeyers, R. Smith, & P. Standish (Eds.), *The Blackwell Guide to the Philosophy of Education* (pp. 110-125). Oxford: Blackwell.

Horsthemke, K., & Enslin, P. (2005). Is there a distinctly and uniquely African philosophy of education? In Y. Waghid (Ed.), *African(a) philosophy and education: Reconstructions and deconstructions* (pp. 54-75). Stellenbosch: University Stellenbosch University Press.

Horsthemke, K., & Enslin, P. (2009). African philosophy of education: The price of unchallengeability. *Studies in Philosophy and Education, 28*(3), 209-222.
Okin, S. M. (1998). Feminism and multiculturalism: Some tensions. *Ethics, 105*, 23-43.
Okin, S. M. (1999). Is multiculturalism bad for women? in J. Cohen, M. Howard, & M. Nussbaum (Eds.), *Is multiculturalism bad for women?* (pp. 7-24). Princeton, NJ: Princeton University Press.
Nussbaum, M. (2001). *Women and human development: The capabilities approach.* Cambridge: Cambridge University Press.
Nussbaum, M. (2006). *Frontiers of justice: Disability, nationality, species membership.* Cambridge, MA: Harvard University Press.
Rawls, J. (1971). *A theory of justice.* Cambridge MA: Harvard University Press.
Rawls, J. (1993). *Political liberalism.* New York: Columbia University Press.
White, J. (1982). *The aims of education restated.* London: Routledge & Kegan Paul.
Wilson, J. (1970). *Thinking with concepts.* Cambridge: Cambridge University Press.
Young, I. M. (1996). Communication and the other: Beyond deliberative democracy. In S. Benhabib (Ed.), *Democracy and difference: Contesting the boundaries of the political* (pp. 120-136). Princeton: Princeton University Press.
Young, I. M. (1997). Difference as a resource for democratic communication. In J. Bohman & W. Rehg (Eds.), *Democracy: Essays on reason and politics* (pp. 383-406). Cambridge MA: MIT Press.

MORWENNA GRIFFITHS

MY LIFE AS A VIXEN

INTRODUCTION

Isaiah Berlin's influential essay, 'The Hedgehog and the Fox' suggests that there are two categories of thinkers (Berlin, 1969). Using an ancient Greek poetic fragment ('The fox knows many things, but the hedgehog knows one big thing'), he suggests they can be divided into hedgehogs who view the world through the lens of a single defining idea and foxes, who draw on a wide variety of experiences and for whom the world cannot be boiled down to a single idea. I am a fox – in fact, a vixen (perhaps not something that would have occurred to Berlin whose references are uniformly to males). Looking back on my intellectual history, I see that it is one in which my ideas have changed and emerged as I moved from one social context to another, collaborated with other people, taught in a range of institutions, and relished the challenge of coming to grips with unfamiliar ideas. I have never stopped learning from the very beginning of my career as an educator, when I was an untrained volunteer in a socially disadvantaged primary school, to my current position as a professor of education at Edinburgh University. The longer I continue in education, the more I realise the need to go on developing my practices and my understanding. I still wonder what to do for the best. I keep on making mistakes (new ones!), and I keep on learning from them. I think I understand more than I did. But I am still puzzled and perplexed by the ideas I encounter and am still thinking hard about how to deal with them.

I had wondered how to tell the story of coming to my present understanding of what we educators do and should do. I did not want to write a linear, chronological autobiography in which it would be hard to avoid the familiar, fairy-tale genre of the narrator as hero (or tragic hero). That genre tells the story of the hero's journey towards a worthwhile goal, how obstacles are overcome (or not) through determination, goodness and cleverness, usually with the help of a wise guide. On the other hand I did not want to go to the other extreme of denying my agency altogether, with a story of my being merely a kind of witness of my own life, as I blundered about from one context and social structure to another. Moreover, my ideas have not developed in a neat linear progression but rather in a series of interweaving spirals from the changing circumstances of my life.

I am particularly conscious of the complexities of autobiographical writing. I have written a lot about personal narrative, and have used personal narrative in a range of my work, philosophical and other. I find it theoretically unsatisfactory just to use a straightforward, linear, biographical approach. In what follows, I have constructed a mix of narrative approaches. There are some – sometimes parallel – chronological descriptions. These are punctuated by examples of particular issues that have engaged my attention. Each one has been connected to one example of the circumstances in which these issues have developed. That is, the examples demonstrate a mixture of agency and structure. The issues that have come to matter to me are behind the agency exercised in continuing to address them. The issues I focus on are (in no particular order) (1) social justice, (2) feminism, (3) relational selves and (4) reflective practice through personal narrative. The circumstances in which they arise are one aspect of the structures which have constrained, facilitated and constructed my approach to and understanding of those issues. The ones I present as particularly significant are (again, in no particular order) (a) migrations, (b) openness to happenstance, (c) dialogue of various kinds, and (d) teaching. Other versions – and other examples – of my autobiography in relation to ideas can be found in Griffiths (1995, 1998b, 1999, 2012a, 2013).

FIRST CHRONOLOGICAL DESCRIPTION: A LIFE ON THE MOVE

I was born in Tanganyika, now part of Tanzania. I lived there until I was ten. My father was a colonial administrator, so every two years he had a 'long leave' when we would visit South Africa and the UK for some months, after which he would be moved to a new posting, and we would all move house. The UK was a foreign country. My two brothers and I had all been born in Tanzania, my parents were both born in South Africa, and one grandparent was born in India because my great-grandfather was a soldier in the British army. Most of our closer family of grandparents, aunts, uncles, and cousins lived half a continent away in South Africa. However my parents did not want to return to apartheid South Africa so when my father retired aged 50, we went to England where I had some great aunts and uncles. My father found work there, and so did my mother who had been a physics teacher before she married. They ended up living in Kent for about six years and then my father got a job in Botswana, where my parents spent nearly a decade, before finally retiring to Oxford. By that time I was in my late twenties and had long left home.

I come from a family of migrating teachers, ministers of religion and administrators. My own generation has continued to move. My two brothers live in Australia and we have first cousins in the USA and Botswana as well as in South Africa and the UK. In Tanganyika we all went to boarding schools from seven years old. The children of colonial administrators and of other expatriates had their own schools, separate from the local ones and boarding schools were the only option. Home was a happy place for me so boarding school may sound like a hardship. Seven seems so young to me now! But I loved going to boarding school in the primary years. I liked the school work and I liked having so many other children to play with.

All my own immediate family has been scientifically educated with the exception of my anthropologically trained father. I was hopeless at languages or anything requiring deft handiwork but equally at home with the arts and the sciences. In the last couple of years at school we were required to specialise in one area of the curriculum. I hated dropping any of my favourite subjects. My scientific and book-loving mother explained that I could continue enjoying literature and history more easily than I could keep up physics or mathematics. That made sense to me. I was already, perhaps, developing as a 'vixen.' I took physics and mathematics at A level and went on to get a physics degree at university in Bristol. Before plunging from a school immersion in science into a university one I took a break of a year, something that was fairly unusual at the time. I spent a few months as a volunteer teacher of six year olds in inner city Leicester, followed by a couple of months in Israel on a kibbutz and working in an old people's home in Jerusalem, before having to leave when the 1967 war broke out. I joined a UN work camp in Northern Greece, and stayed there for the rest of that year, working and travelling.

After my first degree I stayed at Bristol University, gaining my PGCE. (I was about to get married to a man living in Bristol.) Initially I had enrolled on the course with a view to becoming a secondary school physics teacher, but the programme began with a week observing in a primary school. From this and from memories of Leicester, it became clear to me that primary teaching was more to my liking. For one thing, I could be less of a subject specialist. The university did not offer a Primary PGCE programme but they allowed me to continue under the guidance of the only primary specialist on the staff, Philip Gammage, who tutored me individually, with the help of his contacts in schools.

Changes of direction and occupation have continued ever since. I got a job in a local primary school in Bristol, but wanted to teach somewhere less suburban. So I transferred to an inner-city school. At that point my marriage fell apart so I handed in my notice and took the opportunity to go travelling. Further changes followed. I ended up in Isfahan in Iran for two years where I taught English as a Foreign Language, first at an air-force school and then at Isfahan University. On my return, I was fortunate, in those better funded days, to get an SSRC grant to study full time for an M.Ed. specialising in philosophy and language. This was followed up by another SSRC grant which enabled me to continue on to a Ph.D. in Philosophy of Education. My career has continued to be punctuated by moves of institution and focus. (I am lucky that my economist husband was employed as an international consultant, and so able to base his home in places that suited my job.) I was employed at Christ Church College of Higher Education in Canterbury for two years as a lecturer in philosophy of education and primary education, then at Oxford Polytechnic for four years as an education lecturer in schools and in Higher Education. That was followed by six years in Nottingham University as a lecturer in Equal Opportunities and Social Justice, ten years at Nottingham Trent University as a Professor of Educational Research, and now for the past seven years at Edinburgh University as Chair of Classroom Learning.

FIRST EXAMPLE: THE ISSUE OF SOCIAL JUSTICE IN THE CONTEXT OF MIGRATIONS

I use the term 'migration' to mean physical, social and intellectual movements. It is an adaptation of what Maria Lugones (1989) calls '"World"-traveling.' Lugones explains that by 'world' she does not mean anything imaginary. Rather it is a material and social association in which it is possible to dwell. However her '"world"-traveling' is between worlds which are all present at the same time, in contrast to my 'migrations' which include not only travel between different existing 'worlds' but also travel to 'worlds' from which steps cannot be re-traced. Migrating has required me to adjust and then re-adjust my understanding of myself, of norms of conduct and of the world at large: in short to adjust my lived theories of identity, ethics, ontology and epistemology. The 'world' may have since disappeared for everyone: Tanganyika is still there as part of Tanzania, but not the British-governed Tanganyika of my childhood. Equally it may be that a new 'world' can make the old one disappear for ever for some people while it continues to exist for others. In my case, a pre-feminist understanding of gender relations is no longer a 'world' I can ever inhabit again.

Migration has been hugely fruitful in my understanding of social justice. I focus on just one way in which migration has influenced my thinking in this regard: the significance of self-identity for self-esteem and for social justice. This only became apparent to me gradually. My understanding of it began, I think, as I reflected on my developing responses to feminism and feminist theory. It was apparent to me that I did not quite fit with mainstream feminist theory of the time, any more than I fitted with mainstream philosophical theory. I explored some of this perception with a feminist philosopher colleague, Anne Seller, in a theoretical paper about the politics of identity (Griffiths & Seller, 1992). We discussed the ways that belonging to one social group and its associated norms of conduct could clash with belonging to another one – and explored the ways in which we both wanted and did not want to belong to various groups. I talked about having a liking for science at a time when much orthodox feminist theory was deeply suspicious of the largely male 'world' of scientists. We discussed the largely male 'world' of philosophy and its norms of conduct.

At the time self-esteem was emerging as a significant concept in education. I reappraised earlier experiences. My increased understanding of what it was to migrate between 'worlds' meant that I did not take at face value a simplistic connection between individual self-esteem and achievement. The correlation existed, in differential academic achievement by different social groups. But the reasons for it might not be the simple causative one that was put forward. I argued that the discomfort of not being able to meet several incoherent social norms simultaneously was a factor in self-esteem. Therefore teachers could promote higher self-esteem in their pupils through implementing inclusive practices for the class as a whole. Focusing on pupils' individual self-esteem and individual achievement dealt with the symptoms rather than causes of the problem. I continued exploring self-identity and self-esteem in relation to social justice in education in my book on identity (1995) and again in my collaborative books on social justice in education (Griffiths & Davies, 1995; Griffiths, 2003) as well as in a number of articles.

SECOND CHRONOLOGICAL DESCRIPTION: GETTING ACQUAINTED WITH PHILOSOPHY AND PHILOSOPHY OF EDUCATION

What starts an interest in philosophy? Indeed why is it that some children find enjoyment in something that other children find uninteresting or worse? Whatever the reason, I seem always to have been interested in logical argument, in abstractions and in the big questions about human lives. That said, as I look back now, and tell an autobiographical story in this article, I am reminded how unreliable memory is, and how, as a life unfolds, different incidents are told and retold with new interpretations and to new audiences. So I can tell of some occasions that seem to have been indicative and significant but I remain uncertain about their accuracy or importance.

Like many very young children I was fascinated by abstractions (pace Piaget!): the logic behind numbers as well as the kinds of ideas presented to us by preachers. In my secondary school I liked all the classes which encouraged speculative or ethical thinking (Religious Education, mathematics, history, English). I joined the debating club but gave it up as it became clear to me that formal debates were all about competitive glory, a kind of jousting for prizes, with which I did not want to be associated. I loved the extra-curriculum discussions organised by the head teacher based on a radio programme about ideas. I was disappointed at university to discover that undergraduate physics seemed to be more about having enough understanding to predict events rather than reaching a more holistic understanding of the world. Or, more accurately, I saw that only the very best physicists were able to understand the world more holistically, and I would never be that good. At best I would become one who could work out the mathematics – but without knowing what it meant. I was one of the very few among the PGCE students who took an option in Philosophy of Education, and struggled to understand Paul Hirst's transcendental argument about curriculum. As a young teacher I attended evening classes run by the Philosophy Department of the University. Probably the first book in philosophy that I tried to read and study was Kant's *Critique of Pure Reason*. Inevitably I struggled, but I loved the struggle and the discussions that the lecturer encouraged. Later, in the months waiting to begin the M.Ed., I attended evening classes run by Stefan Körner who introduced me to his theories of categorial frameworks and the philosophy of mathematics (Körner, 1970). I also avidly followed a television series of the time 'Men of Ideas,' which featured 15 interviews with prominent philosophers who included just one woman, Iris Murdoch (Magee, 1978).

I began my formal education in philosophy and philosophy of education on the M.Ed. My tutor, Gordon Reddiford, encouraged his students to read original works like Hume's *Treatise*, Ryle's *Concept of Mind*, Wittgenstein's *Philosophical Investigations* and Kenny's *Action, Emotion and Will* – as well as what was then orthodox Philosophy of Education, for instance, Hirst on knowledge, Peters on the education of the emotions, and Scheffler on reason. At the point that I had to choose a topic for doctoral studies in order to apply for funding to the SSRC I happened to be writing an essay on the education of emotions, and was finding it complex, difficult and interesting. So I chose that. Gordon helped me fill in the application form. I was puzzled about what to put under 'methodology': he wrote in for me, 'Thinking.' My doctoral studies kept me thinking, as I read, discussed, puzzled, and listened. I audited undergraduate classes in philosophy and attended education graduate seminars in the education department and philosophy graduate seminars in the philosophy department.

SECOND EXAMPLE: THE ISSUE OF FEMINISM IN THE CONTEXT OF BEING OPEN TO HAPPENSTANCE

As with so many of my intellectual developments in philosophy and practice, my understanding of feminism has benefitted hugely from what feels like mere serendipity but which must also be attributed to an openness to happenstance: to treating happenstance as an encouragement to change direction, rather than as a hurdle to be negotiated within an already decided path. Feminist theory and philosophy have been central to my own development as a philosopher of education. My engagement with both has been influenced by such openness. As I have described, my early engagement with both philosophy and philosophy of education was not related to feminist ideas. That changed just as I was completing my doctoral thesis. My philosophical investigation of emotion had been largely based within mainstream philosophy. As I was nearing completion, the question of how I might re-think the education of emotion became more and more relevant. I had seen that one possibility would be to focus on issues of delinquency and deviance. That would have been enough. However at the same time some of my close friends from outside the academy were arguing about feminism in relation to their own lives. I was dismissive about the project of feminism. Wanting some evidence for my attitude I started to read further first in pyschology, and then in other subjects. I read, among others, Archer and Lloyd (1982) and Sayers (1982) on biology and gender, Spender (1980) on language, and Stanworth (1983) on pedagogy – and found, to my consternation, that the arguments for a feminist approach were not as I had assumed. I had, it seemed, been wrong. Involved as I was at the time with constructing philosophical, educational theory, I was set, irrevocably, on a path towards feminist philosophy. Gender became salient in the final chapters of the thesis and appeared not long after in publications about computers (e.g. Griffiths, 1988). However, even more significantly, I had been introduced to a number of other feminists interested in philosophy or, to put it another way, to philosophers interested in feminism. I was fortunate therefore to be there when feminist ideas were discussed, new books were mentioned, and a range of philosophical approaches explored (see next section).

Just as fortunately, I found myself in a position a year or so later to become a co-editor of a book on feminist philosophy. A reading group for women in philosophy across England had been arranged in what was then a typically feminist way of doing things. It met irregularly for a day or two at the weekend. One of our number would agree to host it. Once it was Judith Hughes with Mary Midgely in Newcastle. Another time it was Margaret Whitford with Caroline Bailey in London. I organised some day events in London, with the help of Anne Seller and Alison Assiter. Somebody would suggest a theme, a reading or a discussion of work in progress. It might be a small informal discussion or part of a larger event. Sometimes we stayed overnight somewhere. On one Saturday the weather had been particularly awful, and transport links had been difficult. Margaret Whitford and I were the only two to turn up. We duly discussed the reading. Then one of us suggested that our small group should put together an edited collection of essays, and so we did (Griffiths & Whitford, 1988). Margaret and I drew on very different traditions of philosophy; I had been introduced to the analytic tradition and was using it to investigate emotion, while she drew more on the French theory, and was currently studying Luce Irigaray. The happenstance of this encounter presented the opportunity for me to engage with a set of completely new, unfamiliar and destabilizing ideas. I read Genevieve Lloyd's *The Man of Reason* and re-thought my ideas about rationality. Jean Bethke Elshtain's *Public Man, Private Woman* introduced me to gender assumptions underlying mainstream political theory. Anne Seller explored the philosophical implications of arguments surrounding the women's camp protesting about cruise missiles at Greenham Common (Seller, 1985). Irigaray's *This Sex which is Not One* introduced me to new ways of engaging with psychoanalytic theory. I addressed these ideas in discussions with the rest of the group, radically changing the direction of my own thinking as I did so. Some of this appears for instance, in the dialogue I constructed with Richard Smith on dependence, independence and interdependence in educational practices (Griffiths & Smith, 1989). It can also be seen in my (1988) article 'Strong feelings about computers.'

THIRD CHRONOLOGICAL DESCRIPTION: IDEAS INFLUENCED BY RELATIONS IN PHILOSOPHICAL AND PROFESSIONAL SOCIETIES

Very shortly after I finished my Ph.D., I met Joanna Hodge, a feminist and philosopher, who had just finished her own thesis on Heidegger. We thought it would be good to have a meeting for women in philosophy, but there were very few indeed that we could think of. I remember standing in a university library scanning the title pages of philosophy journals, trying to find any women's names among the authors. (This was a time before Google!) Finally we identified a dozen women working in philosophy, and invited them to an informal meeting in Joanna's college, St Catherine's. Some of us formed the core of a group which began a series of semi-formal weekend meetings where we presented work in progress or discussed books, as explained in the previous section, in connection with Margaret Whitford's and my collection, *Feminist Perspectives in Philosophy*. Over some years the group gained members, some of them highly active, like Christine Battersby and Soren Reader, and it morphed into the Society for Women in Philosophy (SWIP). The group also gave me a reference group of philosophers, mostly based in philosophy departments but also in adult education, French, and women's studies. We have continued to meet, discuss books, argue and occasionally publish collaboratively ever since. In this group I was introduced to Irigaray, Heidegger, Arendt, Kierkegaard and other thinkers who supplemented my original grounding in Anglo-Saxon traditions of philosophy. My reading in feminist theory was given an impetus, especially within the newly forming field of feminist philosophy. The collection, *Discovering Reality*, by Harding and Hintikka (1983) was inspiring for us, for instance, as were Donna Haraway's (1985) article, 'A Manifesto for Cyborgs' and Carole Pateman's book, (1988) *The Sexual Contract*. We read and discussed Judith Butler's *Gender Trouble* when it first came out, and heard Christine Battersby present early versions of what would become chapters in *The Phenomenal Woman*.

In my first year of teaching in Canterbury I went to my first Philosophy of Education Society of Great Britain (PESGB) annual conference where I found myself making new philosophical connections with other philosophers of education and their ideas. I was excited to find myself sitting over breakfast with the authors of the books and papers I had read. Even more exciting was the chance to discuss the presentations with them and to hear what they were working on. As a result I began to respond to some of them in academic papers as well as in discussion. I strongly disagreed with Robin Barrow's position on skills and wrote a response to his paper. A talk with Richard Smith about autonomy led to our paper on dependence. Wilf Carr was in the process of elaborating his theories of action research in relation to philosophy. Michael Fielding introduced me to the double edge of the concept of empowerment. All these, and other discussions, have influenced the direction and manner of my approach to philosophy of education.

The membership elected me to the Executive committee several times, which gave me the opportunity to engage closely with mainstream philosophy of education, responding to the concerns of others in ways which then influenced how I developed ideas from other sources. Sometimes I am invited to contribute to seminar series which include philosophy of education. The directions of my thinking have been influenced by the formal exchanges in these seminars, but even more by the informal face-to-face discussions which they stimulate. Most recently, with the support of PESGB, I have organised a series of three annual seminars for women in philosophy of education at Edinburgh University. Again, the encounters have been personally very fruitful in the development of my own ideas in relation to those of others.

Throughout my career I have sporadically carried out empirical enquiries of various kinds. When I moved to Oxford I was introduced to a very lively group of staff, led by Sarah Tann, Kate Ashcroft and John Isaac, who were designing and implementing a teacher education programme founded on reflective practice. Through them I began to attend the British Educational Research Association (BERA) and to make links with the Collaborative (then Classroom) Action Research Network (CARN). As with PESGB, through BERA (and through election to its Executive committee) I was invited to collaborative enterprises, and got the opportunity for many fruitful face-to-face discussions. While I was at Nottingham University, Jack Whitehead, who I had met through BERA and CARN, invited me to submit a paper to the first Self-Study in Teacher Education Practices (S-STEP) conference. Not knowing what 'self-study' was, but liking the look of the conference venue in Herstmonceux Castle in Sussex, I improvised a short paper on the theme of 'know thyself.' It was a happy decision. Over the following decade, the Castle Conference, as it is known, gave me the chance to interact with a group of people developing lively and creative approaches to understanding ourselves as educators. As a result, I expanded my empirical repertoire to include visual methods and investigations of collaboration. All of these fed back into my theoretical and abstract enquiries, integrating research methodologies and practices with philosophical perspectives and approaches (e.g. Griffiths, 1998a).

THIRD EXAMPLE: THE ISSUE OF RELATIONAL SELVES IN THE CONTEXT OF DIALOGUES

By the term, 'dialogues' I refer to conversations and discussions preferably face-to-face but sometimes also by phone or informal emails when all parties are on-line simultaneously. A dialogue may be backed up by written communications but these are only secondary. Entering into dialogue with others is risky. There is plenty of room for mutual misunderstanding and suspicion. There is also the likelihood that there are significant differences about what the different participants expect to gain. On the other hand, dialogues can lead to exciting and productive new perspectives on old approaches, both theoretically and in educational practice. Belonging, as I did, to a range of philosophical, empirical and professional education circles, I had the opportunity to have conversations and discussions with colleagues who did not share my perspectives and starting points. I found my assumptions and conclusions challenged and changed by these encounters. This has been energising and stimulating. As a result, perhaps, I have increasingly welcomed the chance to be part of collaborative enterprises even when I think they do not fit my plans for future directions.

One recent collaborative enterprise that did not seem to fit my plans has been helpful in furthering my understanding of the significance of understanding selves as relational. I had not expected this when I accepted an invitation from David Bridges to participate in two linked philosophy of education seminars funded by the Teaching and Learning Research Programme (TLRP) on epistemological perspectives on different educational research methods for policy; and then a year later, to be part of a Keynote Symposium at BERA on the relevance of philosophy of education for teaching, research and policy, in which I was asked to focus on policy. The common themes here were policy and the impact of educational research, including philosophical research on policy. Up until then I had paid little attention to policy as an academic focus of interest. I was far more interested in classroom and school-level education. However I found focus on policy and impact fruitful in extending ideas I had been working on since writing *Feminisms and the Self* in 1995.

A number of dialogues were set in train. I worked closely with Gale Macleod, a colleague at Edinburgh to produce a contribution to the TLRP seminar. We talked for hours in the local coffee bars exploring our different perspectives on research, policy and narrative research. The seminars encouraged the ebb and flow of discussion which led to what Leslie Saunders describes as (2008, p. 3):

> The power of the encounter: the dialogic way in which knowledge and understanding are created and developed, and become common property through principled debate.

After the keynote symposium, Gale and I continued our discussions about how philosophy might have an impact on policy. We began to look for opportunities to have conversations with philosophers who reported that they had made an impact and with policy makers who might have felt such an impact. As a result of all these conversations I wrote an article which argued for the significance of understanding the self as relational in determining how impact might be achieved (Griffiths, 2012b). The selves of philosophers and policy makers have been constructed in relation to their social and political positioning and this affects how they can and will relate to the other. I followed this article with another one which examined the issue from the other side, investigating the significance of the policy context for selves of philosophers working within the policy contexts in which impact is so important (Griffiths, 2012c). I argue that the positionality of philosophers of education (their relation to) the policy context constrains who they can then become.

FOURTH CHRONOLOGICAL DESCRIPTION: IDEAS INFLUENCED BY A WORKING, TEACHING LIFE

Every time I have moved jobs, I have had to adjust to a new context of teaching – which is both practically and intellectually difficult. However, these difficulties have been a pleasure for my vixen-like self. My career has taken me from a suburban primary classroom to an inner-city problem school (contexts in which I first began to understand some of the complexities of pedagogical relations). My next moves into teaching English as a foreign language took me into a range of contexts: Iranian air-force cadets, Iranian serving teachers, summer schools for various ages, students in college in England needing to improve their English, and individual tuition (contexts in which I developed an increased appreciation of the many ways of negotiating tensions arising from cultural and social difference). Then I began three decades in British Higher Education, as a lecturer in teacher education and in non-vocational education degrees, in both low and high status establishments, and as part of all that, occasionally teaching in various primary schools (contexts in which I was able to explore some of the intricacies to be found in reflective practices – whether termed 'self-study,' 'action research,' or 'reflective teaching').

Another pleasure for my vixen-like self has been the requirement to teach subjects about which I had not thought myself very knowledgeable, let alone expert. I have found myself learning (very quickly sometimes!) about a range of new areas. Even at the beginning of my career in primary schools, I was expected to teach crafts and games, in both of which I am no more than barely competent. Even when I have been given the – sadly rare – opportunity to teach courses in philosophy of education, it has more often than not been in areas which I had not previously investigated. Moreover, I regularly find that my students' interests provoke me into investigating new areas. It was undergraduate students who encouraged me two decades ago to think more deeply about self-esteem. Knowing many things, as vixens do, means that connections can be made between them. Throughout my career, I have found that philosophy of education and educational theory and practice are in a productive tension, so that each changes iteratively as a result of its relation to the other.

FOURTH EXAMPLE: THE ISSUE OF REFLECTIVE PRACTICE THROUGH PERSONAL NARRATIVE, IN THE CONTEXT OF TEACHING STUDENTS

Reflective practice is a phrase which is much bandied about in teacher education and within policy statements about the continuing professional development of teachers. It is made up of two words which any English speaker would understand, so perhaps it is not surprising that many people think it needs no explanation. However it is a technical term and there has been a great deal of intellectual effort expended in defining what it is and what it ought to be. I first encountered the idea in 1986 at Oxford Polytechnic, as I mentioned earlier, in a team keen to implement reflection. Our work drew on Dewey, Zeichner, Schön and Kemmis; we encouraged students to relate their personal experience to wider theories within the educational literature. We became interested in what it meant to articulate personal experience through narratives, metaphors and visual images. I began to encourage students to use autobiography in their assignments.

The iterative process of moving from teaching to theorising and back to teaching was significant in how I constructed my book on identity, *Feminisms and the Self* in which I drew on the autobiographies of people from a range of 'worlds' to interrogate orthodox theories of the self. The process of researching and writing the book fuelled my interest in personal narratives and how they could be used to re-think orthodox theories within social and political philosophy and theory. Drawing on Lyotard's (1984) concept of 'little stories' in relation to 'grand narratives,' I tentatively named this process 'practical philosophy' as it put the 'little stories' of a particular life with the abstractions associated with philosophy into tension with each other. More recently I theorised personal narrative in terms of an epistemology of the unique and particular (Griffiths & Macleod, 2008). This re-theorisation continues to inform my teaching. I encourage students to use 'little stories' and personal experience in their philosophical arguments. Teaching continues to inform my theorising as I have had to sharpen my own understanding in order to be very clear about the difference between personal experience used as a 'little story' and personal experience used as anecdote, journalism, advertising or rhetorical flourish.

CONCLUDING THOUGHTS

A vixen never reaches a stopping point. There are always so many interesting things to explore and to learn. I am still thinking, still puzzled – and still making mistakes. Dialogues continue serendipitously as ever and, it seems, I am still open to happenstance. My interest in social justice and feminism remains strong, especially in relation to education and philosophy. I continue to investigate them through personal narrative, always alert to how my relational self, the 'I,' is made up of many kinds of 'we.' Meanwhile I look forward to seeing what will come of my next migration into the new world of semi-retirement, and to the opportunities it affords for other forms of happenstance, to new dialogues while retaining the chance to teach new cohorts of education students.

FAVORITE WORKS

Favorites from My Work

Griffiths, M. (1995). *Feminisms and the self: The web of identity.* Routledge.
Griffiths, M. (1995). Making a difference: Feminism, postmodernism and the methodology of educational research. *British Educational Research Journal, 21*(2).
Griffiths, M. (1999). Patchwork and embroidered stories, Playing at/as being authentic. In J. Swift (Ed.), *Art education discourses: Leaf and seed.* Birmingham: ARTicle Press and at http://edinburgh.academia.edu/morwennagriffiths
Griffiths, M. (2003). *Action for social justice in education.* Buckingham: Open University Press.
Griffiths, M. (with J. Berry, A. Holt, J. Naylor, & P. Weekes). (2006). Learning to be in public spaces: In from the margins with dancers, sculptors, painters and musicians. *British Journal of Educational Studies* (Special Issue on Social Justice), *54*(3).
Griffiths, M. (with G. Macleod). (2008). Personal narratives and policy: Never the twain? *Journal of Philosophy of Education, 42*(1).
Griffiths, M. (2012). Social justice and educational delights. *Journal of Education Policy* (Special Issue on Social Justice), *27*(5).

Favorites from Others

Cavarero, A. (1995). *In spite of Plato: A feminist rewriting of ancient philosophy.* Cambridge: Polity
Hannah Arendt's collected works but if I have to choose one:
Arendt, H. (1958). *The human condition.* University of Chicago Press.
Foucault's collected works but if I have to choose one:
Foucault, M. (1978). *The history of sexuality, Volume 1* (Trans. Robert Hurley). London: Penguin.
Martin, J. R. (1985). *Reclaiming a conversation: The ideal of an educated woman.* New Haven and London: Yale University Press.
Richardson, R. (1990). *Daring to be a teacher.* Stoke-on-Trent: Trentham
Ryle, G. (2009). *Collected essays 1929-1968.* Abingdon, Oxford: Routledge
Charles Taylor's collected works but if I have to choose one, I'll cheat a bit by choosing:
Taylor, C. (1985). *Philosophical papers.* Cambridge: Cambridge University Press.

REFERENCES

Archer, J., & Lloyd, B. (1982). *Sex and gender.* Harmondsworth: Penguin.
Battersby, C. (1998). *The phenomenal woman: Feminist metaphysics and the patterns of identity.* London and New York: Routledge.
Berlin, I. (1969). *Four essays on liberty.* Oxford and New York: Oxford University Press.
Butler, J. (1999). *Gender trouble: Feminism and the subversion of identity.* New York and London: Routledge.
Elshtain, J. B. (1981). *Public man, private woman.* Princeton: Princeton University Press.
Griffiths, M. (1988). Strong feelings about computers. *Women's Studies International Forum, 11*(2).
Griffiths, M. (1995). *Feminisms and the self: The web of identity.* London and New York: Routledge
Griffiths, M. (1998a). *Educational research for social justice: Getting off the fence.* Open University Press.
Griffiths, M. (1998b). *Being naughty: A play for justice?* Inaugural Lecture, Nottingham Trent University, Nottingham, Available at http://www.morwennagriffiths.pwp.blueyonder.co.uk/social_justice.htm (Accessed 24 April 2013).
Griffiths, M. (1999). Patchwork and embroidered stories, Playing at/as being authentic. In J. Swift (Ed.), *Art education discourses: Leaf and seed.* Birmingham: ARTicle Press and at http://edinburgh.academia.edu/morwennagriffiths
Griffiths, M. (2003). *Action for social justice in education.* Buckingham: Open University.
Griffiths, M. (2012a). Social justice and educational delights. *Journal of Education Policy* (Special Issue: B. Francis & M. Mills, Eds., What would a socially just education system look like?), *27*(5).
Griffiths, M. (2012b). Re-thinking the relevance of philosophy of education for educational policy making. *Educational Philosophy and Theory,* DOI: 10.1080/00131857.2012.753371.
Griffiths, M. (2012c). Is it possible to live a philosophical, educational life in education, nowadays? *Journal of Philosophy of Education, 46*(3).
Griffiths, M. (2013 in press). Social justice in education: Joy in education and education for joy. In I. Bogotch & C. Shields (Eds.), *International handbook on social (in)justice and educational leadership.* Springer.
Griffiths, M., & Davies, C. (1995). *In fairness to children: Working for social justice in the primary school.* David Fulton.
Griffiths, M., & Macleod, G. (2008). Personal narratives and policy: Never the twain? In D. Bridges, P. Smeyers, & R. Smith (Eds.), *Evidence-based education policy: What evidence? What basis? Whose policy?* Oxford: Wiley Blackwell.
Griffiths, M., & Seller, A. (1992). The politics of identity, the politics of the self. *Women: A Cultural Review* (Special Issue: Gendering philosophy), *3*(2).
Griffiths, M., & Smith, R. (1989). Standing alone: Dependence, independence and interdependence. *Journal of Philosophy of Education, 23*(2).
Griffiths, M., & Whitford, M. (Eds.). (1988). *Feminist perspectives in philosophy.* Macmillan and Indiana University Press.
Haraway, D. (1991 [1985]). A cyborg manifesto: Science, technology and socialist feminism in the late twentieth century. In *Simians, cyborgs, and women: The reinvention of nature.* London: Free Association Books.
Harding, S., & Hintikka, M. B. (1983). *Discovering reality: Feminist perspectives on epistemology, metaphysics, methodology, and philosophy of science.* Dordrecht: D. Reidel.
Hume, D. (1962). *A treatise of human nature.* Glasgow: Collins/Fontana.
Irigaray, L. (1985). *This sex which is not one* (Trans. Catherine Porter with Carolyn Burke). Ithaca, NY: Cornell University Press.
Kant, I. (1933). *Critique of pure reason* (Trans. Norman Kemp Smith). London: Macmillan Education.
Kenny, A. (1963). *Action, emotion and will.* London: Routledge and Kegan Paul.
Körner, S. (1970). *Categorial frameworks.* Oxford: Basil Blackwell.

Lloyd, G. (1984). *The man of reason: 'Male' and 'female' in western philosophy*. London: Methuen and Co. Ltd.
Lugones, M. (1989). Playfulness, "world"-traveling, and loving perception. In Ann Garry & Marilyn Pearsall (Eds.), *Women knowledge and reality: Explorations in feminist philosophy*. Boston: Unwin Hyman.
Lyotard, J.-F. (1984). *The postmodern condition: A report on knowledge* (Trans. Geoff Bennington & Brian Massumi). Manchester: Manchester University Press
Magee, B. (1978). *Men of ideas*. www.imdb.com/title/tt1046679/epcast (Accessed 15 April 2013).
Pateman, C. (1988). *The sexual contract*. Cambridge: Polity Press.
Saunders, L. (2008). Preface. In D. Bridges, P. Smeyers, & R. Smith (Eds.), *Evidence-based education policy: What evidence? What basis? Whose policy?* Oxford: Wiley Blackwell.
Sayers, J. (1982). *Biological politics. Feminist and anti-feminist perspectives*. London and New York: Tavistock.
Seller, A. (1985). Greenham: A concrete reality. *Journal of Applied Philosophy*, 2(1) 133-141.
Spender, D. (1980). *Man made language*. London: Routledge and Kegan Paul.
Stanworth, M. (1981). *Gender and schooling. A study of sexual divisions in the classroom*. London: Hutchinson.
Ryle, G. (1949). *Concept of mind*. London: Hutchinson.
Wittgenstein, L. (1958). *Philosophical investigations* (Trans. Elizabeth Anscombe). Oxford: Basil Blackwell.

DAVID T. HANSEN

ON WONDER

One of Teachers College's finest presidents, Lawrence Cremin, used to emphasize the difference between education and institutions such as schools and universities. The latter are vital for learning, he argued, but they do not operate in a formative vacuum. Students do not come to them as empty vessels. A superb historian, Cremin documented the educational impact of life in the home, on the street, at the shop, and elsewhere. In this spirit, an intellectual autobiography can mean something other than an institutional or disciplinary account. In my own case, I know my ways of thinking about philosophy and education bear the imprint of people, places, books, and experiences that were not part of my formal university tuition. I will describe some of them here, alongside references to what I've learned in the academy. If I had to single out a core lesson from all this, it would be how invaluable it has been to regard the work of philosophy and education as constituting an art of living – an attempt, never wholly successful, to integrate teaching, reading, researching, presenting, writing, advising, mentoring, and administrating into an edifying whole that, hopefully, adds some good to the world however modest or local the scale.

PHILOSOPHICAL WONDER

John Dewey argued that what he called "the immediate quality of experience" decisively influences a person's sensibility and orientation toward the world. He had in mind a person's pre-cognitive aesthetic, emotional and tactile response in particular environments to being alive. These responses can evoke a sense of enduring wonder. One day in 1958, my family and I were at a beach not far from our home in Karachi, Pakistan. The beach was uncrowded and vast, or at least seemed so when I was six years old. At one point I found myself wading and crawling on all fours through warm eddies of water left by the tide, near where the sand met the sea. I stopped and grasped a handful of sand below the water surface. Out of my balled fist tumbled large grains of sand – purple, brown, yellow, multicolored, translucent. Each grain sparkled as it caught the sun, just as the now gently rippled water surface glistened almost blindingly.

Out in the light, and taking in the light; sensing the warmth of the sun-heated water, and the granular sand shift in my hand: it felt enchanting, but mostly it just "felt," the feeling of feeling, of living, of being. Though I cannot be certain about it, this experience and others like it from childhood seem to have permanently shaped my perception of things in the world including education. I have had the same unanticipated feeling of wonder while observing in classrooms, listening to one of my students work out an idea, or watching words emerge on the computer screen in front of my nose. The same feeling occasionally happens while riding on the subway, walking through a forest, sitting on a rooftop, or watching a film: unexpected, spontaneous, momentary, and yet recurrent wonder at the "is-ness" of things. Everything I have said or written about education feels undergirded by wonder, if not amazement, at what people can do within the space and time we inhabit. More than that, the very selection of topics and questions I have studied seems guided by this same sense of wonder at the primordial facts of our being and becoming.

As a doctoral student and then assistant professor in the early 1990s, I participated in a longitudinal study that examined the moral dimensions of life in classrooms and schools. The study was directed by Philip W. Jackson at the University of Chicago. The research team included Robert Boostrom, now at the University of Southern Indiana, and me. I learned how complex, many-layered, and significant are the meanings that saturate the interaction between teachers and students. This interest in the moral has continued through the present. It led to another long-term study in the 1990s of several accomplished teachers' philosophies of education. On the basis of extended observations and interviews, I argued that the teachers illuminate why teaching can be a profound calling, as opposed to merely a job or occupation. During and since that time I have worked my way through the complicated, sometimes contradictory philosophies of education of figures such as Plato, Rousseau, and Dewey. That experience has been an education in the very idea of a "philosophy of education." Since moving to Teachers College in 2001, my work has focused increasingly on the idea of cosmopolitanism and its educational meanings – a study animated, again, by wonder, in this case at the astonishingly diverse ways in which people not only communicate with different others but learn from them and let their lives be influenced by them. I am fascinated and moved by this kind of cultural creativity.

The wonder to which I refer is not at what people do in a behavioral sense, though that is mesmerizing enough. Watching people at play or at work can mirror witnessing a spider weave its web, a robin hop along the lawn to find its worm, or a floating leaf bob and weave its way to the ground. It is incredible that all of this *is*. Nor is it wonder, leaving the behavioral surface behind, at what people do at the level of intent and purpose, though that is even more remarkable. Rather it is wonder at movement within the light of the Good, to deploy a motif from Plato. The effect on me of the sun, sand, and sea as a boy was *good*: it was generous, generative, and embracing. There is a line between that moment and the sense of being moved today while observing in a classroom: to be a witness, for example, to the non-self-conscious expression of generosity and hope embodied in a suddenly noticed act of the teacher or of a student. Where *does* that generosity and hope come from? From where does the fact of goodness spring? What manner of world is this that has a place for such things, and for the very possibility of what we call education? In retrospect, I became an educator and later a scholar of education in order to better understand these moral facts of the cosmos, and to support and expand their place in human life.

On the other side of wonder is despair and outrage. My questions about the moral dimensions of teaching, about teachers' philosophies of education, about cosmopolitan cultural creativity, about the educational perspectives of Montaigne, Kant, Wittgenstein and many other thinkers, also emerge from awareness of the power of injustice. That power is so great at times that it all but shatters notions of the benign, the good, and the generous. There is also a line between childhood scenes of instruction and the demoralizing, sometimes unmanageable awareness of injustice that can all but sunder a person's sense of agency. As a boy I saw a child being brutally beaten by a man on a public road. I lay in a hospital bed with severe diarrhea in a large, sparsely lit room filled with sick and sometimes screaming adults. I was a mute witness to stupefying poverty day after day. I saw people literally torn apart on the news and in war films and other media. Such scenes can mark a sensibility. The appalling reality of cruelty, avarice, and indifference in the world teaches me how someone can end up disgusted by humanity and irredeemably cynical about its future prospect. "One need not be an enemy of virtue," wrote Kant, "but only a cool observer who does not confuse even the liveliest aspiration for the good with its actuality, to be sometimes doubtful whether true virtue can really be found anywhere in the world" (1990, p. 23).

To "widen the skirts of light," as the novelist and moralist George Eliot put it in her *Middlemarch*, people need to study violence and injustice rather than recoil from them. They need to bear witness to these things if they are to develop sound responses. In Pakistan and then Nigeria, where we moved when I was eight years old, my father had colleagues from different parts of the world (all of whom worked as advisers to the newly established government). I remember times when I would stand near their outdoor table where they often gathered socially on a weekend day, listening intently to their talk of surviving World War II, at that time a mere fifteen years in the past. My father served in the navy in the Pacific theater on an anti-aircraft gun, and I recall him recounting how in one battle he and his crew were ordered to fire at a particular patch of the sky rather than target specific planes. The fleet he was part of wanted to saturate the sky with fire to shoot down as many Japanese planes as possible. My father described the excruciating and terrifying experience of seeing planes zooming all over the place overhead but not being able to turn and fire at them. His German colleague Wolfgang was an officer in the Afrika Korps, and shared comparable harrowing tales about fighting in North Africa up to the point where he and his men surrendered to the Allies in 1943. His English colleague John was in the first wave at Sword Beach in Normandy on June 6, 1944, and he too had things to say that overwhelmed my childhood capacity to understand.

From those days forward I have never ceased trying to grasp the terrible fact of war, exemplifying as it does all that is dreadful about the human condition. I entered my final year at the University of Chicago not long after the close of the American war in Vietnam, for me as for many others a deeply confusing, morally vertiginous event. That year I chose to write my required Bachelor's Degree thesis on the Stockholm Conference of 1917. The conference was an attempt by representatives of socialist and labor parties from both sides of World War I, then three years old, to create a mechanism for peace. Ultimately, government authorities on both sides refused to grant passports to the representatives, and the conference failed to materialize. As background for this project, I read intensively writings by Eduard Bernstein, Rosa Luxembourg, and numerous other activist thinkers, building on my earlier course work on Marx, Engels, and the convulsive intellectual ferment surrounding the First and Second Internationals of 1864 and 1889. I read many histories of World War I, and also novels and poetry that emerged from it. Upon graduation I devoted six summer weeks to hitch-hiking, walking, and taking trains down the entire Western Front, from Zeebrugge in Belgium to the border of Switzerland. I toured the vast battlefields of Verdun with two American army officers who picked me up along a local road where I was hitchhiking, and who seemed as stunned as me by the somber sights. I wandered alone through the frontlines in the Meuse-Argonne region, where my maternal grandfather had served as an army doctor. I felt driven to see the places I had read about and to try to grasp the sheer fact of the war, its immense scale, its horrific slaughter of so many young men my age that culminated in the attempt to bring peace in 1917. It was a strange pilgrimage, to pay homage to people of another time and place.

Since that summer odyssey I have visited countless battlefields and military cemeteries the world over, and have continued to read novels as well as historical and philosophical accounts of war and peace. I can't say that I've made much progress in understanding the fact of war. Perhaps it's simply not comprehensible, a terrible "immediate quality of experience" that defies cognition and that is rooted in the same mysterious source as are the facts of truth, goodness, and beauty. I do know that educational work must be peace-oriented, if not labeled in so many terms. Every admirable conception of education of which I'm aware, and every argument I have myself sought to put forward, presumes that it is good to communicate seriously and well with others, to work cooperatively and collaboratively with them, to understand their ideals and hopes, and to learn both from and with them. Conflict may be inevitable, but I agree with those who argue that education can and should help people handle it in better rather than worse ways.

WONDER AND BOOKS

Philosophical wonder springs from books, too, which can be as much a part of reality as people and places. However, the influence of books, like that of our fellow human beings, is not always benign. Books can lead to trouble if they undermine a sense of reality, as Gustave Flaubert's Madame Bovary discovered. Taking a book in hand remains a risky prospect since the reader never really knows what will result from the encounter. Will the book clarify or occlude vision? Will it strengthen or debilitate an ethical outlook? Will it inform or distort understanding? In this light, the first books of childhood can feel decisive since we may be tempted to say they shape a sensibility forever after. Happily, parents and primary school teachers needn't panic since it seems people's reading habits can and do change, and sometimes often, over the course of a life. To echo a perspective from Aristotle, a reader can in time come to grips with the effects books have and can develop a mature, critical relationship with them.

Still, childhood readings can feel like the voice of the gods themselves, dropping from the sky through some sort of magic. It was my mother's mother who gave me *Bulfinch's Mythology* when I was seven or eight years old. I'm not sure I have ever been as mesmerized by a book. Holding the big hardback tome in my lap, or leaning over it in bed while resting my head in my hand, I found the tales and accompanying pictures, mostly of paintings from the European tradition, absorbing to an acute degree. I remember rereading the myths again and again, and with an urgent curiosity (or so it feels like today) about human psychology, although I certainly had no clue about that concept. The stories of lovers, warriors, old people and children; of kings and queens and seamen and wanderers; all exerted a hypnotic power on my still-forming sensibility. I found the very words "me" and "you" uttered by the classical characters quite incredible. I would stare at those little words on the page – among the shortest in the English language – and stare some more, almost wanting to climb inside them, it seems, or perhaps metabolize them, or be metabolized by them. Sometimes I would touch them with my finger. "Me." "You." "You." "Me." *Oh, what are they – WHAT ARE THEY? "Me." "You." And what is their relation? Why do they occur together?*

I read continuously through the years of primary and secondary school. I never ceased to be transfixed by pronouns (I still am), wondering how they can embody as well as represent the human. But above all was a fascination with psyche understood as soul or spirit in their existential, humanist sense. "If you look into her soul" – "His spirit is infectious" – "What a soulful singer" – "Nothing could break her spirit" – these and other familiar usages point to an encompassing image of a person's character, their very being-in-the-world. Psychology: *logos* or words about *psyche* or soul. Psyche was the name of a Greek mortal whose beauty was so great it eventually led to her marrying the god Eros and enjoying everlasting life. Philosophy has generated words, *logoi*, about the very idea of what it means to be a person, a being marked by yearning, longing, and hope. In a spirit I can't adequately describe, I would immerse myself after school or during summer break in novels such as Boris Pasternak's *Doctor Zhivago*, James Joyce's *A Portrait of the Artist as a Young Man*, Chinua Achebe's *Things Fall Apart* (the basis of my senior year thesis in high school), Emily Bronte's *Wuthering Heights*, Mark Twain's *Huckleberry Finn*, Jane Austen's *Pride and Prejudice*, Charles Dickens' *Hard Times*, Fyodor Dostoyevsky's *Crime and Punishment*, Mikhail Sholokhov's *And Quiet Flows the Don*, and numerous others. I read them all with wonder at their portraits of what it means to be a human being and how human beings can vary so much, as well as how people become who and what they are.

I discovered philosophy in college. The idea of philosophy as the art of living had an instant appeal given the particular experiences and questions I brought to it. From the very first time I read Plato, I was taken by philosophy's long-standing attempt to address questions of wonder, of soul, of meaning, and more. I also began to appreciate philosophy as theory – its long-standing quest to grasp and clarify concepts such as knowledge, belief, morality, justice, and beauty. I began to get a sense of the history of ideas, that they have enduring effects on the world as well as on subsequent thought. But it has been philosophy as the art of living that has gripped my imagination and guided my scholarship, since I see it as so deeply bound up with the idea of education. In college I could not read enough Plato, Emerson, Nietzsche, Sartre, Camus, and many others. I also took a year-long course in South Asian civilization in which we read deeply in the Upanishads, among other philosophical texts, an experience which triggered an enduring interest in comparative philosophy including when viewed as the art of living.

After graduating from college, I taught at several levels and earned a master's degree, then enrolled in a doctoral program in education at my alma mater. My initial plan was to study comparative education. I had had some experience teaching abroad, had visited schools in several countries, and as mentioned was interested in thinking about the underlying philosophies of education that can be found in different cultural and national settings. I had an image that this trajectory might put me in contact with thinkers and educators in different parts of the globe, which I thought would be fascinating. However, I quickly realized I was indeed interested in the *philosophical* rather than the policy or programmatic side of matters. Hence, I shifted to formal work in philosophy of education. I studied with Sophie Haroutunian-Gordon and Philip W. Jackson, as well as others including Hugh Sockett who was a visiting professor at Chicago for a time. I took a wide array of courses elsewhere on campus ranging from Kant's Ethics, to Cultural Conceptions of the Self, to American Autobiographies. My dissertation committee included the anthropologist Richard Shweder and the ethicist Robin Lovin.

I had read Plato while an undergraduate, but as a doctoral student I met him on a new plateau. I now brought some years of teaching experience to my reading – and during those years I continued to read widely in philosophy and literature – and thus was closer to being mature enough to keep up with him. The old adage that all philosophy is a footnote to Plato is not true. But it is true that his work remains a footnote to nobody's. The originality of his mode of philosophizing, the range of topics he investigates, the power of his artistic writing style, and the many-sided sense of humanity in his vision constituted a learning I cherish beyond words, and a learning which continues every time I take one of his dialogues in hand. Part of his enduring appeal is that he inaugurates the idea that philosophy and education move hand in hand, as witnessed in the famous opening line of the *Meno* with the latter's question about whether virtue can be taught, which instantly launches an inquiry into both virtue and teaching. Plato also captures the idea that a key task of philosophy, one running parallel to its theoretical aims, is to help people lead their lives in moral and ethical fashion. In dialogues such as *Alcibiades* and *Gorgias*, Socrates underscores the importance of self-cultivation – understood as an ethics of the self – if a person is to develop the strength and sensitivity to treat others justly no matter who they are or what our relation with them may be.

Jean-Jacques Rousseau's *Emile* was a revelation. When I took it in hand as a doctoral student, I thought I knew what it meant to be serious about education. Rousseau taught me what a novice I was. The philosophical sophistication of this magnificent writer, his powerful understanding of what is at stake in education for the individual and society, and – as with Plato – the artfulness of his writing, were overwhelming my first time through the book. At times I found myself literally rising out of my chair, holding the book tightly and staring at what I had just read. It was (and remains) hard to picture fully, much less understand, the book's kaleidoscopic range of insights about teaching and learning. With tongue in cheek, I'm tempted to say the book eclipses the entire industry of educational psychology, so nuanced and brilliant it is in portraying the development of a human being in relation to society, and so in touch as it is with the primordial idea of soul. I don't agree with everything the book says, but then I'm not sure I agree with anything it says; somehow, "agreement" is not what matters most here, at least for me. Instead, it is ascending to a new platform for perceiving, interpreting, and judging educational significances.

While Rousseau has a feeling for the beautiful aspects of romance and marriage that is rare among philosophers, I find the book's treatment of the education of Sophie quite problematic. I appreciate the critiques of commentators such as Rousseau's near contemporary Mary Wollstonecraft (*A Vindication of the Rights of Women*) and our contemporary Jane Roland Martin (*Reclaiming a Conversation*). At the same time, Rousseau's gift as a thinker is to compel readers to become thinkers themselves, or at least aspire to be. To me, his over-arching philosophy of education, like Plato's, has not aged but rather awaits us. Both philosophers' conceptions still belong to the present and future.

The same can be said of John Dewey's philosophy, which I also studied in depth as a doctoral student. My initial encounter with his work was unmemorable. I read *Democracy and Education* right after reading *Emile*, and the former seemed not only badly written but philosophically obscure. I was wrong on both counts, in time appreciating Dewey's distinctive style, and also realizing he had rich and suggestive insights about education, not to mention philosophy, art, politics, and other topics. Since then I have never stopped reading and drawing upon Dewey's work. It has helped me in studies of teaching, teacher education, curriculum, moral education, and most recently, cosmopolitanism. Dewey fuses sharp-eyed intelligence and faith in human possibility in a way few writers in any genre have managed.

Since becoming a professor in 1990, I have taught Plato, Rousseau, and Dewey many times, in courses for doctoral students and for men and women preparing to become teachers. The cliché that to learn a book you need to teach it contains a deep truth. What I find most remarkable about teaching their work is how fresh it feels on each occasion, almost as if I had never read them before. Their books have become a mirror in which I can see the changes in my own soul, and through which I can discern the soul in my students and what fuels their deepest interest, curiosity, and commitment about education, including (and sometimes especially) when they most resist the texts. Plato, Rousseau, and Dewey share, I think, the hope that their work will provoke the kind of response that transforms itself into fruitful, humane, and just action.

Michel de Montaigne, one of the shrewdest and most insightful readers of books I have ever come upon, once complained that the reading world groans under the weight of ever-proliferating criticisms of the same authors and texts. "The hundredth commentator," he remonstrated, "dispatches [the text] to his successor prickling with more difficulties than the first commentator of all had ever found in it. Do we ever agree among ourselves that 'this book already has enough glosses: from now on there is no more to be said on it?'" (1991, p. 1210). "It is more of a business to interpret the interpretations," he protested elsewhere, "than to interpret the texts, and there are more books on books than on any other subject: all we do is gloss each other. All is a-swarm with commentators: of authors there is a dearth" (p. 1212). To judge from Montaigne's own glosses (!) on Plato, he regarded the latter as an *author*. The same can be said of Rousseau and Dewey. And because their oeuvre embodies the philosophical strength and future-based vision to invite as well as withstand endless criticism, it will have a vibrant place as long as people care about philosophy and education.

PRACTICES (1): WRITING

I had some good teachers in secondary school and university who inspired me to cultivate the arts of scholarship, which I would characterize as follows: how to conceive a significant question that has not already been exhaustively addressed, how to find and study pertinent resources, how to take useful notes and organize them for the task of writing, and ultimately how to write a coherent and interesting paper. I first experienced the distinctive satisfaction to be had from these arts with my afore-mentioned Bachelor's Degree thesis. It would be nearer the mark to say this paper wrote me rather than the other way around. I was absorbed for months on end with note-taking and then writing. The thesis mushroomed into seventy-three double-spaced pages. I would spend hours in the library perusing original sources (this was in the days before the internet). I remember several Friday evenings in a row when I stayed in the library until closing, reading the proceedings of the English House of Commons from 1917, during which time the members were debating the prospect of the Stockholm Conference and whether to issue passports to members of their socialist and labor parties. After these late evening travels back in time, I would head off to Jimmy's (a renowned local watering hole) and swap stories with friends, many of whom were engaged in their own thesis projects. My first draft was in long-hand, double-spaced, on 8x14 yellow, lined paper. I would festoon the table I worked at with 3x5 note-cards containing relevant material so that I could have it ready at hand. I had piles of such cards, a numbered set from each source I had consulted. The table looked like a strange jigsaw puzzle, or the scene of a bizarre card game, but I knew the secret of what was written where.

As a doctoral student I wrote two papers that further clinched for me how meaningful research and writing could be. The first was on the literary qualities and cultural reception of René Maran's novel *Batouala*, a tale of village life in what is today called the Central African Republic. Maran based the story on his work there in the French colonial service. He received the prestigious Prix Goncourt for his novel at ceremonies in Paris in 1921; he was the first non-European to be so honored (Maran, who was black, was born in Martinique). The award was controversial, since some critics thought the novel both too naturalistic and too condemnatory of French colonialism (it led to a parliamentary investigation into the abuses Maran recounted in the book). At the same time, Maran was something of an assimilationist, admiring aspects of the French 'civilizing mission' which he felt had been betrayed by corrupt colonial administrators. For this reason he had uneasy relations with more critical Caribbean and African writers in the French-speaking world, including those who like him resided in France after World War I.

I was drawn to the events surrounding the novel because they opened a window to the emergence of the literary, philosophical, and political movement known as *négritude*. Sparked by writers such as Aimé Césaire and Léopold Sédar Senghor (who later became the first President of Senegal), *négritude* pivoted around what today might be called post-colonial ideas about identity, voice, authenticity, and justice. Its participants accomplished something other than a simplistic (and ultimately chimerical) cutting of the cord with the culture in whose language they wrote. Rather they sought to move beyond stereotypes – all stereotypes, whatever their origin – and to portray their experience, values, ideas, and aspirations in a clear-eyed, artful manner. I read widely in their writings. To complete the paper, I ventured to the Moorland-Spingarn Research Center at Howard University, which among other collections houses Alain Locke's papers. I spent an absorbing day in a quiet, empty room reading the correspondence between Locke, Maran, and other figures surrounding the publication and reception of *Batouala*. There was a sacral quality to opening one folder after another and finding their actual letters. The feeling resembled some of the emotions I felt making my post-college trek down the Western Front.

If I had to pinpoint the origins of my current research on cosmopolitanism and education, they would include my inquiry into the movement called *négritude* triggered, in part, by the publication of Maran's provocative oeuvre. I understand the movement as an attempt, among other things, to fuse a serious-minded openness to generative ideas from anywhere in the world – including the so-called West – with a dedicated spirit of reflective, critical loyalty to local values and identities, in this case emanating from the African diaspora. In studying the movement, I learned that while Alain Locke was corresponding with Maran, he was playing a major role in making known to his French-speaking confreres the ideas, ideals, and activities of the Harlem Renaissance. Of special note here is that Locke was also writing about cosmopolitanism in a way that anticipates today's strong interest in the concept across the academy.

For example, Locke conceived a cosmopolitan-minded analysis of cultural relativism. His essays illuminate differences between relativism and being relativistic: the former can denote a serious regard for cultural distinctiveness, while the latter simply undermines any meaningful form of judgment including of one's own roots. Locke argues, on the one hand, against an "all-inclusive orthodoxy of human values" which would smother local and transactional values. On the other hand, he argues against holding cherished values and cultural symbols irrationally, as if the application of reason and criticism is at all times acidic rather than potentially substantiating. To think matters through – including one's bedrock values – can help lead, in Locke's view, to "a safer and saner approach to the objectives of practical unity" amongst people (1989, p. 71). A recurrent theme in cosmopolitan philosophizing today is how to fuse reasoned, self-critical judgment with a thoughtful regard for differences and similarities in belief and form of life. Locke captures this theme in emphasizing the difference between what he calls "practical" unity and "theoretical" unity. He suggests it is useful to imagine the latter: to conjure the content and expression that universal values might take. But in life as lived, theory takes a back seat to practice. Practical unity constitutes a working relation based on a willingness to communicate. It is a unity without uniformity. It does not presume agreement on values, beliefs, or purposes. Practical unity denotes a commitment to keep communication open and moving rather than slamming doors shut in the face of conflict, disagreement, or confusion.

I have learned much about how to think about cultural and moral cosmopolitanism from Locke and other public-minded writers near or of his generation, such as Rabindranath Tagore, José Enrique Rodó, and Stefan Zweig. I continue to learn from contemporary thinkers such as Kwame Antony Appiah and Martha Nussbaum, who analyze cosmopolitanism and how the orientation can help people respect shared human values while adhering to revered local ones. I seek in my research to elucidate the educational meanings immanent in cultural and moral cosmopolitanism, and have come to understand cosmopolitanism as a way of dwelling educationally in the world. I have greatly benefitted from the growing number of colleagues in philosophy of education, including the editor of this volume, who have addressed the topic (for references, see Hansen, 2011).

The other highly formative manuscript I wrote while a doctoral student – and I can recall the sounds, smells, and quality of light in Regenstein Library where I penned it – was a Qualifying Paper required of all Ph.D. students as a final step before moving to their dissertation proposals. My paper came out of several courses taught by Philip Jackson and Sophie Haroutunian-Gordon where Plato figured prominently. I read the *Theaetetus* for the first time in one of these courses and, like countless readers, was taken with Socrates' self-description as the "midwife" of others' ideas. I was more taken by what I saw as tensions barely below the surface regarding Socrates' uncertain attempts to teach the youthful and talented Theaetetus (the dialogue pivots around questions concerning the nature of knowledge). The familiar ambiguities surrounding Socrates' 'method(s)' became even more ambiguous to me. It was a marvelous experience to spend months on the dialogue, working through the entire text line by line, and attending especially to passages saturated with pedagogical tension. Each day I would reopen the dialogue, notebook ready at hand, and be lost within seconds in the prose. I ended up writing a nearly seventy-page-long paper which, after some major surgery in light of criticism it received, became my first published article. It was entitled "Was Socrates a 'Socratic Teacher'?" I am still not sure whether he was. But his practices have fueled my career-long absorption with the art of teaching.

Since those undergraduate and graduate student days I have continued to relish scholarly writing. For me, writing constitutes an always new and peculiar combination of solving a puzzle, engaging in a dialogue with other writers and commentators, playing with words and phrases in their endless permutations, and trying (as the fine cliché has it) to say what I mean and mean what I say. I have had my share of successes and failures. It still stings when reviewers and editors point out the failures, but I like to think I always learn from them. And it still triggers a feeling of accomplishment when people report that a piece has 'worked.' I have kept the two-page letter that Ralph Page, then editor of *Educational Theory*, wrote to me regarding my afore-mentioned article on Socrates (published in 1988). He stated that it was very rare for him as editor to tell an author 'We are happy to publish your manuscript exactly as is.' He then proceeded to tell me just that. I was equally moved by the fact that he added an extended commentary on the manuscript. He recommended I consider the modest suggestions for revision the reviewers offered, but emphasized in his conclusion that the decision whether to do so was entirely mine. I now appreciate how rare this experience is in publishing!

PRACTICES (2): TEACHING AND COMMUNICATING

Before matriculating in a doctoral program, I did some teaching at the middle and secondary school level. Among many memories, I recall as vividly as if it transpired this morning an interaction I had with one 12-year-old boy in a class I was teaching on economics and agricultural science; I was working at the time in Sierra Leone. I had drawn on the board several agricultural implements and we were discussing their origins and uses (a topic I found had intriguing philosophical dimensions). The boy raised his hand to offer an interpretation, but then became stuck and confused. I found myself walking down the aisle between the rows of wooden desks until I was standing right by him. I squatted down until I was eye level with him. He was staring at the figures on the board, and I was staring at him staring – and suddenly knew, for the first time as a teacher, that I was witnessing a mind at work. I don't recall saying anything to the boy, save perhaps a word or two of encouragement, but he managed to come out with a sensible idea and was satisfied. I was elated, not because I had 'taught' him – I'm not sure I did – but because I *felt* like a teacher. He had made a genuine intellectual move, and it had taken place in my classroom.

My initiation into teaching in higher education came while I was a doctoral student. I was an adjunct instructor at DePaul University in Chicago in a number of introductory courses on politics, economics, and society. I also taught a course in philosophy and literature in my institution's Continuing Education program for adults. In the introductory courses I learned a great deal about the craft of lecturing, in which I drew heavily on what I had learned about the arts of scholarship touched on previously in this essay. I remember sitting in the adjuncts' quiet office rehearsing my lectures for hours so I could deliver them in as polished a manner as possible. I also used these part-time positions to test out various approaches to discussion. I learned a lot the hard way. I recall a session of my Continuing Education course at the end of which students complained vociferously about the reading selection (I believe it was Plato!). I was really thrown by their criticism; I thought the course had been going well. Happily, I received some good advice from my doctoral colleagues back on campus. The advice boiled down to stating honestly to the class, at the start of the next meeting, that I felt the previous session had gone badly and that I would try to provide a bit more background and scaffolding to our readings. I was quite nervous about how the class would respond. To my relief and delight, they seemed to appreciate my frankness and plunged into our new reading in an energetic spirit.

Successes and failures have continued in my teaching life, not unlike the ups and downs of scholarly writing. But a key difference between the two realms is that teaching involves face-to-face interaction with persons, and thus involves an ever-unpredictable possibility of immediate, mutual influence. Among what feels like a million moments that attest to these truths, let me mention two from my first year as a full-time teacher in higher education; this was at the University of Illinois at Chicago. I taught an undergraduate course on curriculum and teaching at the secondary level. One of my students, Audra, was a first-generation college student currently in her second year. She struggled in the course. Her writing was weak, at the start, and she had a hard time speaking up in class, even though she wanted to. She truly aspired to become an English teacher, but was also terrified at the prospect. One day after class I suggested she drop by my office to talk through these various issues. We had a good discussion, at the end of which she said my recommendation to come talk was the first time in her life a teacher had suggested such a thing to her. With the help of other colleagues, and peers she got to know, Audra graduated and became a high school English teacher.

Also in that first year in the academy, I taught a graduate level course on the history of curriculum thought. One day about half way through the term, I arrived as usual in class shortly before the starting time. After sorting out my materials I found myself getting up and going down the hall to the washroom. I arrived there feeling panic-stricken and nauseous. I propped myself up on the sink and frantically questioned what was going on as I looked at my face in the mirror. I realized I had stage fright. Like Audra, I was suddenly terrified by the idea of being a teacher. Who was I to take on such a role? What did I have to offer these graduate students? Was I a person who could do this, or who should be doing this? I don't quite recall how, but I did make my way back to class and got through it – in part because the students were actively engaged (how little they knew what I was feeling!), and in part because we were studying Dewey's ever-provocative *Democracy and Education*. The questions I felt that afternoon, alone in the bathroom, still spring themselves on me from time to time. The stage fright has mostly disappeared.

One upshot of these and other experiences is a strong sense of sympathy with the teacher's world. My professional work with schoolteachers and school administrators spans over thirty years, and has deeply influenced my sense of the meanings in education. Before matriculating in a doctoral program, I spent several years working for The Great Books Foundation, based in Chicago. The foundation makes available to teachers and schools a discussion-based program intended to cultivate reading comprehension and critical thinking. I traveled to many states in the nation while employed with them. I met for several days at a time in training seminars with groups of between twenty and forty teachers and adult volunteers; I sometimes made return trips for continued seminars. I left almost every seminar impressed with the number of teachers who cared deeply about their students and who sought to enrich their own knowledge and their ability to teach. I also met enough inadequately prepared, dispirited, or indifferent teachers to confirm just how demanding the practice of teaching is, and how vital are opportunities for continued learning and renewal.

As a doctoral student I participated in a three-year-long study called the Moral Life of Schools Project, to which I referred at the start of this essay. There were eighteen teachers involved in the endeavor, including nine middle-school and high school teachers whose practices and views became the focus of my research. I observed over 400 classes they taught, and conversed with them innumerable times in both formal and informal circumstances. This project, coming as it did on the heels of my previous years of teaching and working extensively with teachers, proved to be career-shaping. It triggered lines of inquiry I have pursued to the present. It taught me more than I can describe not only about how to talk with teachers (to echo a famous lecture title by William James), but why such talk buoys my very reasons for being as a scholar. Since then I have given many seminars, workshops, and presentations in schools and in district centers.

These varied exchanges have been formative because, in retrospect, I now see that many of us in them were engaged in philosophy as the art of living – not in so many words, to be sure, but in actual practice. *We were thinking and valuing together.* We were not just giving reports about our past thinking. It was moral thinking: that is, it was thought tied to questions of efficacy but above all to matters of goodness, rightness, and fittingness for students and whoever else was of concern. It was ethical thinking because we ourselves were implicated in our work: what we said for the sake of others was for our sake, too, in our condition as (hopefully) growing educators. We sought to *think well*, to listen, to imagine, and to change our views of ourselves and of others, indeed of education itself, when compelled by the direction the work took. On many occasions, as I now look back, I see how engaging in philosophy as the art of living paved the way for excurses into philosophy as theory. Teachers and I would find ourselves willingly turning to various texts, ideas, and conceptions about education in order to test our evolving thought against them, and in order to satisfy a newly vibrant hunger to study and understand.

* * *

In thinking about the many teachers I know, the research and writing I've undertaken, and the administrative work I've pursued, I can hardly help but return to the sense of wonder with which this essay began. Wonder at being, at becoming, and at dwelling in the world. What was it that the elderly officer said at the magnificent dinner Isak Dinesen conjured in her short story, "Babette's Feast"? – "We tremble before making our choice in life, and after having made it tremble again in fear of having chosen wrong." I have trembled in making various decisions in writing, teaching, advising, and administrating, and there are times when I still do. But somehow that's never been the case about participating in the vocation of philosophy and education.

SOME INFLUENTIAL WORKS NOT MENTIONED IN THE CHAPTER

Cather, W. (1990). *The professor's house*. New York: Vintage. (Original work published 1925.)

Emerson, R. W. (1983). *Emerson: Essays and lectures*. New York: Library of America. (Original work published 1841-1876.)

Foucault, M. (2005). *The hermeneutics of the subject: Lectures at the Collège de France 1981-82* (Ed. F. Gros, trans. G. Burchell). New York: Picador. (Original work published 2001.)

Gadamer, H.-G. (1996). *Truth and method* (second rev. edition, trans. J. Weinsheimer & D. G. Marshall). New York: Continuum. (Original work published 1960.)

Heidegger, M. (2004). *What is called thinking?* (Trans. J. G. Gray). New York: Perennial. (Original work published 1954.)

Hillesum, E. (1996). *An Interrupted Life & Letters from Westerbork* (Trans. A. J. Pomerans). New York: Henry Holt. (Original work written 1941-1943.)

Lear, J. (2006). *Radical hope: Ethics in the face of cultural devastation*. Cambridge, MA: Harvard University Press.

Murdoch, I. (1970). *The sovereignty of good*. London: Routledge & Kegan Paul.

Rilke, R. M. (1989). *The selected poetry of Rainer Maria Rilke* (Ed. & trans. S. Mitchell). New York: Vintage. (Original work published 1905-1923.)

Sebald, W. G. (1998). *The rings of Saturn* (Trans. M. Hulse). New York: New Directions. (Original work published 1995 with a subtitle: *An English pilgrimage*.)

Taylor, C. (1989). *Sources of the self*. Cambridge, MA: Harvard University Press.

SOME CORE PUBLICATIONS

Jackson, P. W., Boostrom, R. E., & Hansen, D. T. (1993). *The moral life of schools*. San Francisco: Jossey-Bass.

Hansen, D. T. (1995). *The call to teach*. New York: Teachers College Press.

Hansen, D. T. (2001). *Exploring the moral heart of teaching: Toward a teacher's creed*. New York: Teachers College Press.

Hansen, D. T. (2002). Well-formed, not well-filled: Montaigne and the paths of personhood. *Educational Theory, 52*, 127-154.

Hansen, D. T. (2004). John Dewey's call for meaning. *Education and Culture, 20*, 7-24.

Hansen, D. T. (2004). A poetics of teaching. *Educational Theory, 54*, 119-142.

Hansen, D. T. (2011). *The teacher and the world: A study of cosmopolitanism as education*. London: Routledge.

REFERENCES

Kant, I. (1990). *Foundations of the metaphysics of morals* (second edition, trans. L. W. Beck). Englewood Cliffs, NJ: Prentice Hall. (Original work published 1785.)

Locke, A. (1989). Cultural relativism and ideological peace. In L. Harris (Ed.), *The philosophy of Alain Locke: Harlem renaissance and beyond* (pp. 69-78). Philadelphia: Temple University Press. (Original work published 1944.)

Montaigne, M. (1991). *The essays of Michel de Montaigne* (Trans. M. A. Screech). London: Penguin. (Original work published in 1592.)

KENNETH R. HOWE

AN UNLIKELY PHILOSOPHER?

LEARNING TO LABOR

When I landed in a faculty position in philosophy of education I took it upon myself to learn a good deal of social science, something I hadn't felt the need to do when I spent all of my time in a philosophy department. One of social science works I looked at was Paul Willis' *Learning to Labor*,[1] in which he documents how a group of working class boys in a town in the West Midlands of England – the "lads" – developed an oppositional stance toward schooling that, ironically, served to prepare them for work on the shop floor. It was highly unlikely that any of the lads would wind up being an academic philosopher. And so it was with me.

I went to public school in the industrial city of Flint, Michigan. I did very well until the 8th grade, when the lad in me began to emerge. I regularly challenged the teachers to the point of calling one stupid. For this I received a ferocious paddling from the dean of boys. There came a time when I defied the school authorities by refusing to submit to being paddled again. When the school called my mother to get some help in dealing with me, she, a single working mother on the night shift, let them know that when I was in school I was their problem, not hers. My grades began to decline (I had gotten straight As the year before) and my English teacher, Mr. Pincum, assured me that once I had gone into such a tailspin there was no pulling out of it.

This pattern persisted throughout my high school years. I did graduate, though, in 1967, and on time. I finished with a gpa around 2.5, in about the middle of the pack. Notwithstanding, I had taken a college preparatory curriculum and had even been placed in an advanced math track. (I dropped out of the track in my junior year because, as the only lad, I felt like an alien being in the courses.) My grades exhibited a bi-modal distribution: As and Bs in math, science, and economics; and Ds and Fs in English, History, and typing. Oh, and an A+ in driver training.

I probably would have settled for becoming a "shop rat" in one the many General Motors factories in Flint like so many of my lad friends, but I didn't want to have to marry and begin having children in order to avoid being drafted and sent to Viet Nam. So, I avoided the draft by signing up for classes at the local junior college. Here I immediately met another inspiring educator, reminiscent of Mr. Pincum. It was the admissions counselor, who suggested that I begin in a non-credit, remedial track because of my overall poor grades in high school. I refused, pointing to, among other things, my more that respectable scores on the ACT. He went along but warned me that skid row is lined with people with high test-scores. Thus began my higher education.

FLINT J.C.: GOD EXISTS!

I enrolled in Flint Junior College (F.J.C.) in January of 1968. The previous summer and fall semester I had been working in several General Motors factories, which I continued to do throughout most of my time in F.J.C. I initially had some vague interest in becoming an engineer, but was soon turned off by what I surmised life as an engineer might be like based on my observations as a janitor in the Buick Motor Co. engineering plant. I thus decided to major in math. I did not get off to a good start at F.J.C.: in my first year I earned a 2.0 gpa in introductory writing courses, calculus, and other distribution requirements.

I married my high school sweetheart in February of 1969, at the beginning of my second year at F.J.C. At the ripe old age of 19 ¾, I was one of the last of the lads to marry. My academic performance turned around dramatically in that year. I earned a 4.0 gpa on my way to finishing the requirements for an Associates degree. (Ha! Mr. Pincum.) I had become a little more forward-looking and responsible by this time. The key, however, was that I had discovered philosophy. Here was a place where disagreeing with the readings and, indeed, the teacher, was actually welcomed! So maybe I wasn't an unlikely philosopher after all. Maybe it was just that up to this point in my education I had not encountered the kinds of question and instructional tacks that suited my disputatious, "smart mouth" style. ("Kenneth has a very smart mouth" was one of my first-grade teacher's remarks on my report card.)

My first philosophy course was Introductory Logic, which was devoted to propositional logic and informal fallacies. I soon took to the manipulation of symbols that represented things other than numbers and the snob appeal associated with those highfalutin Latin terms, *Petitio Principii, Ignoratio Elenchi, post hoc ergo propter hoc,* and the like. I also soon came to appreciate the limits of symbolic logic when, in my second philosophy course at F.J.C., General Philosophy, I attempted to symbolize the sentences in the *Meno* so that I might determine the validity of its argument(s). It was also in that course that I was coerced by the power of argument to accept God's existence. Descartes had proved it – and in several ways. This astonished me. What power these philosophers wielded with their arguments! I had had no religious training to implant belief in God in me and, in response to the death of my father when I was eight, I had long since rejected belief based on my rudimentary formulation of the problem of evil.

But my belief in God was short lived. I found the counter-arguments offered by the instructor, Eli Labiner, who had much impressed me by this time, more compelling than Descartes' positive arguments for God's existence. How had I ever fallen for the Ontological Argument? And, yes, there was the matter of the problem of evil, now available to me in more sophisticated and precise form. I had come full circle on the issue in just a couple of days. I left F.J.C. "infected" with philosophy.

OFF TO STATE U AND TAKING UP "BUBBLE GUM PHILOSOPHY"

My dramatic second-year turn around put me in the group of students graduating from F.J.C. who were being recruited by four-year institutions to complete their baccalaureate degrees. I chose Michigan State University (MSU) from among the pool that recruited me. By this time, I had decided to major in philosophy, so I was looking for a major university. The only other possible choice for me would have been the University of Michigan (though I don't recall being recruited by them). Going out of state or to a private institution was not in the cards.

I went to MSU aspiring to earn my BA and MA degrees and then become an instructor at a junior college. As I said, Eli Labiner had much impressed me. As I began my studies "infected" with philosophy, I put other concerns aside. I simply wanted to study and converse about philosophy. I quickly began to take upper level undergraduate philosophy courses that also enrolled graduate students, particularly courses classified as history of philosophy, for example, continental rationalism, British empiricism, Kant, and 19th century idealism. Though a philosophical neophyte, to be sure, I wasn't much intimidated by the graduate students. One exception was Lester Schick, who was *old* (looking back, I'd say all of 27 when I first encountered him) and the spitting image of Karl Marx. Of course, as an undergraduate I also had to satisfy general requires for the BA. What I remember most was the German language (interesting but too much emphasis on spelling and getting the genders right), intellectual history (turned out the famous professor's riveting lectures were borderline plagiarism), and psychology (a professor, impressed with my insights to the point of recruiting me to pursue the graduate study in psychology, was truly aghast – "Philosophy?!" – to learn that I was committed to graduate study in philosophy).

My all consuming infection with philosophy resolved during my graduate school career. This transpired in two ways. First, after interacting with my philosophy professors at MSU, I was no longer quite so star struck with Eli Labiner. His intellectual style and argumentative "moves" had become more familiar to me. Beyond that, my professors at MSU were not just undergraduate teachers; they also wrote articles and books as well as worked with graduate students. I came to see their way of life as one I wanted to have and consequently set my sights for a career several notches higher. Not only did I want to be a professor rather than a junior college instructor, I wanted to be a professor at a research university. That meant earning a PhD.

Second, coming later and pushing in the opposite direction, the job market for philosophy professors had become bleak – very bleak. My fellow Ph.D. students had begun taking jobs as insurance agents, legislative analysts, and faculty members at tiny institutions with heavy teaching loads. None of that was for me. I coincidentally had grown weary of philosophy, which I had come to see as arcane and out of touch, and I effectively dropped out of graduate school. During a period of several years in the mid 1970s, I taught the same courses at F.J.C. that I had previously taken there as a student and ran a house painting business. I completed an elementary teacher preparation program in which I experienced something akin to "mental whiplash" as I moved from practice teaching elementary school children the 3Rs in the daytime to teaching philosophy to adults in the evening. My son, Paul, was also born during this period, in 1976. This was a very busy and chaotic time.

After receiving my teaching certification, I had about a half dozen interviews for elementary school teacher positions but failed to get any offers. I shielded my ego by telling myself that elementary school principals were just intimidated by the idea of having a Socrates around to torpedo them. In any case, I soon returned to graduate school with a new philosophical interest in moral education that had been sparked by my brief excursion into elementary education. I wrote an MA paper that provided a sustained critique of the approach to moral education called "values-clarification." Having finished my MA, in 1978, but still groping for direction, the MSU Philosophy Department chair, knowing of my interest in education, advised me to talk to folks in the MSU College of Education to explore arranging a joint degree. I followed his advice and began taking education courses. One of my fellow philosophy graduate students, who remained seriously "infected" with philosophy, sneered at my move into what he called "bubble gum philosophy." This just confirmed his suspicions about me that had been prompted by my budding interest in John Dewey and pragmatism more generally.

By the time I had recruited Bob Floden to be my advisor and had put together a formal joint degree plan in philosophy and education, I had taken considerable coursework in philosophy and passed comprehensive examinations is value theory and logic/philosophy of science. I had also taken considerable coursework in program evaluation, measurement, statistics, and qualitative methods. Because of the unique blend of knowledge and skills I had acquired, I was hired by the Medical Humanities Program in MSU's College of Human Medicine to lead the evaluation of a National Endowment for the Humanities medical ethics curriculum development grant. Program evaluation thinking at the time (and it may not have progressed much since) posed two philosophical-cum-methodological obstacles to the evaluation of ethics teaching: the fact/value dogma and the quantitative/qualitative dogma.

The fact/value dogma renders the very idea of evaluating medical ethics teaching suspect, if not incoherent, for it relegates ethics to a non-cognitive epistemic domain, not subject to reason, argument, and evidence. The quantitative/qualitative dogma limits the investigation of program effects to quantitative methods; qualitative methods, which are clearly valuable in evaluating the nuances of ethics teaching, are only suitable for exploration and as a source of conjectures to be investigated by quantitative methods. My dissertation sought to overcome these obstacles and determine whether the methods and content of the medical ethics curriculum I was evaluating were, indeed, effective. Upon completion of my dissertation, in 1985, I was appointed assistant professor in the Medical Humanities Program. My duties included teaching medical ethics and producing scholarship in medical ethics as well as medical education.

CARD CARRYING PHILOSOPHER OF EDUCATION

Soon after my appointment in the Medical Humanities Program I resolved to gain experience and visibility in the field of education so that I might be qualified for a position in philosophy of education and exit the medical school scene. I took an adjunct position in MSU's College of Education, teaching social foundations in the teacher education program and philosophy of education in the graduate program. In 1985, I published the "Two Dogmas of Educational Research," in *Educational Researcher*[2] and, in 1986, "A Basis for Ethics in Teacher Education" in the *Journal of Teacher Education*.[3] Both of these journals have relatively large readerships in education. In 1987 I landed a philosophy of education position in the School of Education at the University of Colorado Boulder. Although I have gotten restless a few times, I have remained in that position to this day.

As I geared up for my full transition from medical education/ethics to philosophy of education in my first year at Boulder, I was invited by Jim Nickel of the philosophy department to give a talk to the Center for Values and Policy based on my chapter "Why Mandatory Screening for AIDS is a Very Bad Idea" (1988).[4] I mention this apparently minor event because although my topic clearly fell with the domain of medical ethics, much of the Center audience didn't see what was philosophical about this kind of work: it depended more on Bayes' Theorem and the statistical properties of medical tests than on things like Rawls' theory of justice (which one graduate student tried to work into the conversation). I realized early on that I had drifted quite some distance from *mainstream* philosophy and that my relationship with faculty in the philosophy department would not be very strong. Jim was an exception to this (as political philosophers Claudia Mills and Alison Jaggar have also proven to be).

At the time, I was searching for a topic for an internal University of Colorado summer grant. This was soon after Amy Gutmann's *Democratic Education*[5] had come on the scene, which incorporated her *threshold* principle of equal educational opportunity. Jim suggested I might take on the issue of measuring equal educational opportunity. Although I abandoned that project in rather short order, I did apply for and win a summer grant for a related project entitled "Equal Educational Opportunity: Will the Threshold Principle Work?" Equal educational opportunity thus joined my previous work in professional ethics and philosophical issues in education research to make up the third primary strand of scholarship I have pursued throughout my career.

Professional Ethics

My experience in professional ethics began with my work as a graduate assistant in an undergraduate medical ethics course with my favorite philosophy professor, Martin Benjamin. I subsequently did considerable work in Michigan State's Medical Humanities Program, also in medical ethics.

My first foray into education ethics was the piece referred to above: "A Basis for Ethics in Teacher Education." An important element of my thinking was that the case study method of ethics teaching, which at this time was widely embraced, should be based on real cases from the field, not cases fabricated to illustrate this or that ethical theory or principle. I had gained experience with this approach in the Medical Humanities Program and it fueled my growing doubts about *applied* ethics, in which general ethical systems developed in the abstract – utilitarianism and Kantianism being the most prominent – are used to analyze and make recommendations about concrete cases. These doubts about applied ethics foreshadowed my later doubts about *ideal* ethical theory, a current interest of mine about which I will have more to say later.

In Boulder, I pursued education ethics on two fronts. First, I obtained a small grant from the University to work with elementary school teachers on ethics in their schools, including gathering cases from them. For a short time, I also edited a section in the School of Education's modest journal in which university faculty and practicing public school teachers commented on ethically problematic cases from the field. Because of the press of other concerns to which beginning assistant professors must turn their attention if they are to survive, both of these projects were short lived.

An interesting by-product of my small grant, however, was what ensued from a minor brouhaha that arose between the University's IRB and me. I had identified a school in which to pursue my project and began meeting with teachers, assuming it would be "exempt" from full IRB review per the exemption for education research in the regulations. I soon received a rather shrill cease and desist order, apparently because I was talking to teachers about what the IRB perceived to be a dangerous subject. (I doubt that I would have gotten the same response if I had been talking with them about problems in teaching science.) My less than politic suggestion to the IRB, that they didn't understand how to apply the regulations to education, prompted a somewhat surprising response: they extended an invitation to me to join the IRB and have my voice heard. I accepted (perhaps I was just a rube who got tricked into doing committee work). During my tenure on the committee I was given a small grant to help formulate the principles regulating education research vis a vis the protection of humans subjects.[6] I subsequently investigated the full scope of research ethics in education with my former student and now colleague, Michele Moses, adding an analysis of research misconduct to that of the protection of human subjects.[7]

The second front on which I pursued the cases from the field approach was special education. I came to Boulder in the same year that the Partners in Education (PIE) program was inaugurated. This program brought highly skilled and experienced public school teachers to campus on a part-time basis to collaborate with the faculty, teach courses to teachers-to-be, and mentor select first-year teachers in the field. Among these "clinical professors," as they are called, was my current wife, Tonda Potts, who worked in special education as an itinerant speech and language therapist. In short order, my conversations with Tonda led me to see her wealth of practical wisdom and commitment to doing the right thing on behalf of children with disabilities. (This is a big part of what attracted me to Tonda, though not the only thing, of course.) Tonda caught on quickly to what I was getting at in asking her to describe ethically problematic cases, of which she provided several very interesting ones. She also agreed to help me (who by this time she'd nicknamed "blue collar philosopher") identify others involved in special education to talk to in order to collect additional cases. Meanwhile, I had developed a relationship with a faculty member who had special education among her specialties, Ofelia Miramontes. She, too, had ethically problematic cases from the field, and agreed to collaborate with me on my first book in 1992: *The Ethics of Special Education.*[8]

I have continued to teach ethics, on and off, including a Ph.D. level course in the last several years, and recently served on the American Educational Research Association's inaugural standing ethics committee. Otherwise, professional ethics has receded as an area of my scholarship, partly absorbed into my other scholarly endeavors.

Philosophical Issues in Education Research

The job talk I gave at Boulder in 1987 was subsequently published in 1988 with the title "Against the Quantitative-Qualitative Incompatibility Thesis (or Dogmas Die Hard)."[9] I joined philosophers of education such as D.C. Phillips[10] and James Garrison[11] in the effort to communicate to the larger education research community a more sophisticated understanding of positivism and its legacy than was in circulation. I aimed to refute the all too common view that quantitative methods and qualitative methods mapped on to positivism and interpretivism, respectively, and were thus incompatible with one another. My general tack was to argue that pragmatists such as Dewey,[12] Quine,[13] Rorty,[14] and Putnam,[15] had thoroughly undermined positivist epistemology and the associated technocratic approach to social science and politics and, as a consequence, *no* research methods should be mapped on to it. The differences that exist between quantitative and qualitative methods, then, have to be characterized in a way that doesn't appeal to positivism. In my case, quantitative and qualitative methods work together within a general pragmatic framework. I published several more articles extending the argument in various ways. Two were co-authored by my close colleague Margaret Eisenhart, an anthropologist of education, in which we set down general criteria for evaluating the validity of education research, not specific to quantitative or qualitative methods.[16]

Under the impression that the quantitative-qualitative dogma had finally been relegated to the dustbin, I moved on to a new methodological fault line that had developed in educational research between two general post-positivist views associated with the "interpretive turn" in philosophy of social science: "transformationism" and "postmodernism."[17] In very broad strokes, I identified transformationism with a commitment to continuing the Enlightenment project of emancipation, but with the kind of tentativeness and appreciation of the role of contingency of self and social arrangements associated with post-positivist, non-foundationalist epistemology.[18] I identified postmodernism with the view that the Enlightenment project of emancipation had "exhausted itself"[19] and that all that is left to do is unmask oppressive power relationships. I argued that this view is untenable where radically relativist; or is inconsistent with the project widely shared by postmodern theorists in education of fostering more just (less oppressive) educational arrangements. [20] That the predominant variant of postmodernist research in education seeks to promote social justice entails that, at bottom, it is transformationist itself. Thus, it need not be at loggerheads with other transformationist views in education research, for it differs primarily in being more leery and tentative about identifying and implementing effective means for pursuing social justice.

This marked an important development in my thinking, for it drew together research methodology and politics more closely than my previous work had. This theme was further developed and refined in a book I co-authored in 1999 with my close colleague Ernie House entitled *Values in Evaluation and Social Research*.[21] Ernie and I had become fast friends when I came to Boulder, and he was to become best man at my wedding with Tonda. Ernie is a leading figure in the field of program evaluation and has a good understanding of and interest in the intersection between social research methodology and political theory. Our shared interest here (and in hoisting a few beers) made for a fruitful collaboration.

Values in Evaluation and Social Research consisted of a two-part argument. First, we endeavored to defeat the *radical undecidability thesis* regarding value claims – the notion that value claims cannot be cognitively investigated or warranted – in its various manifestations, from the positivist fact-value dogma to the excesses of constructivism and postmodernism. Second, from here we went on to develop a deliberative democratic political-cum-methodological framework for the conduct of social research. Consistent with the defeat of radical undecidability thesis, we insisted that no approach to social research could avoid some stance toward democratic politics and that, upon analysis, the deliberative approach proved best. Our primary foil was the "emotive theory of democracy" (more widely known as "aggregative democracy"), which reduces democracy to the strategic pursuit of group preferences.

I synthesized and extended the work described so far in this section in a book entitled *Closing Methodological Divides: Toward Democratic Education Research* in 2003.[22] While this book was in press a rather major methodological shift was underway toward a fixation on *scientific* education research, spurred in large part by external forces. The U.S. Congress in particular, which, borrowing from a certain (erroneous) conception of medical research, clamored for *evidence-based* research in education. It eventually took on the grating descriptor *scientifically-based* research. There were enough willing accomplices within the education research community to form the *new orthodoxy* that turned the clock back toward the heyday of the two dogmas, prompting in me a distinct feeling of *déjà vu*.

My response was to pointedly criticize this retrograde development by reformulating some of my previous syntheses of methodology and politics under the label *political methodology*, playing on the concept of *political economy* and what motivated it.[23] I also challenged what I called the *third dogma* of education research, which drew a sharp dividing line between the humanities and the *empirical* social sciences that was no more defensible than that positivist dividing line between the purely conceptual (or "analytic") and the purely empirical (or "synthetic").[24] I thus challenged the grounds for isolating *education science* from humanities oriented scholarship in education, including in my contribution to the AERA task force on Standards zz Humanities-oriented research.[25] Finally, and related to this, I drew on work in the rhetoric of science to complement more long standing pragmatist arguments against the idea that the meaning and function of "elevator" or "sublime" concepts,[26] including "science," can be determined independent of the interests and purposes they serve.[27] This doesn't mean that anything goes. But because whoever gains the ability to don the moniker of science gains prestige, credibility and financial support for their research, the consequences of excluding philosophy, history, and a host of other approaches in education research from the alleged paragon of knowledge should have been approached much more carefully and with considerably more nuance than it was in the most influential formulations.[28]

Equal Educational Opportunity, Democracy, and Social Justice

Early in my thinking about equal educational opportunity I concluded that there was something to James Coleman's[29] suggestion that the principle had evolved to the point where it became outcomes-based. My reading of Amy Gutmann[30] indicated that she, too, embraced an outcomes-based conception, at least implicitly.

I advanced my ideas in a 1989 piece entitled "In defense of outcomes-based conceptions of equal educational opportunity."[31] By "outcomes-based," I didn't mean a simple equating of opportunities and outcomes such that "outcomes" can be substituted for "opportunities" in "equal educational opportunities." I meant that opportunities and outcomes had become too thoroughly entangled to be identified with exclusive principles of equality. My argument, stripped to the bone, was that *formal* conceptions of equal educational opportunity, whether they focus on equal access or equal resources, are inadequate because different children will interact with these features in different ways. Thus, a more adequate conception requires schooling to provide *effective*[32] inputs – *real* opportunities – that can only be judged effective, can only count as opportunities, if they regularly produce desired outcomes. To further complicate matters, what is initially an opportunity is subsequently an outcome in an *opportunity chain*. For example, children who have not realized the fruits of the opportunity to learn to read, acquiring the ability to read, have no opportunity to master the huge part of the curriculum that can be accessed only through reading. How far to go in equalizing educational outcomes through means that intervene in family life, for instance, is a political question, not a question that turns on the kind of *rigid conceptualism*[33] that would divorce equality of opportunity from equality of outcomes on the basis of linguistic (or metaphysical) tradition.

The position I advanced did not receive an enthusiastic greeting from philosophers of education. Most visibly, I engaged in an exchange with Nick Burbules in print[34] about his concerns about what he perceived to be the authoritarian and coercive dimensions of my concept of education as a *mandatory opportunity* – an opportunity that the state must provide and that children must take up to produce desired education outcomes. On the more amusing side was Fran Shrag's response. This came when I was first introduced to Fran at an impromptu dinner gathering at an annual meeting of the American Educational Research Association. Our initial exchange went something like this: FS: "So, you're Ken Howe." KH: "Yes." FS: "You wrote the piece in Ed Theory using the concept of a *mandatory opportunity*"? KH: "Yes." I then waited to hear how interesting it was, or, if he disagreed, something along the lines of how novel or provocative it was. But this is what I got instead, FS: "I thought it was preposterous." Here I was, a beginning assistant professor being put upon by one of the established senior scholars in the field. But I was used to the ways of philosophers. After a fruitful back-and-forth at dinner, in which I explained how I had modeled the concept of a mandatory opportunity on the concept of a *mandatory right*, developed by prominent philosopher of law Joel Fineberg, Fran became more receptive to my view, not to say convinced.

As my familiarity with the terrain of education policy grew, I became interested in the role of the principle of equal educational opportunity across different arenas. I initially believed it changed meanings from one arena to another. For example, in puzzling through what equal educational opportunity requires, "separate but equal" is not legitimate for race but seems quite legitimate for women's athletics. But how about special education and bilingual education? Here the principle of separate but equal seems to vacillate between situations in which it looks more like race and those in which it looks more like women's athletics. This led me to the conclusion that the principle of equal educational opportunity has "many faces" and that a proper understanding requires a explicating each of them. I applied for and won a National Academy of Education/Spencer Foundation post-doctoral fellowship to pursue this general line.

The culmination of this line of thinking was *Understanding Equal Educational Opportunity: Social Justice, Democracy, and Schooling*, published in 1997,[35] several years after the completion of my fellowship. By this time I had abandoned the idea of many faces, in favor of a single principle that required educational opportunities to be equally *worth wanting*.[36] In terms of my previous examples, the opportunity for African Americans to attend an integrated (not to be conflated with "desegregated") school system better meets this standard than the opportunity to attend school in a *de jure* segregated system. On the other hand, the opportunity to compete against other women in a segregated collegiate basketball system better meets this standard than the opportunity to compete against men. In general, the question of what the principle of equal educational opportunity requires will turn on the particulars that determine what opportunities are most worth wanting.

The need to make the determination of what educational opportunities are worth wanting – and for whom – leads rather straightforwardly to the issue of democratic participation. Consider curricular controversies over what and who to include in the curriculum and controversies over policies such as talent tracking and school choice. These are not matters that can be settled by curricular content and policy specialists. Legitimate resolutions require defensible forms of democratic negotiation. Consequently, a central thrust of my thinking about equal education opportunity was that it needed to be reframed not only regarding the issue of outcomes. It also needs to be reframed in terms of a conception of social justice that incorporates the democratic requirements of *inclusion* and *recognition* in addition to (not instead of) the traditional emphasis on *distribution*.[37]

My thinking retained an element of the many faces idea insofar as I applied my general participatory democratic principle across the education policy arenas of gender equity, talent tracking, standards and testing regimes, multicultural education, and school choice. I did a modicum of additional work in several of these areas,[38] including, most recently, a critique of the "accountability regime" exemplified by the No Child Left Behind law.[39] My work on school choice, however, has been the most extensive.[40] I joined other egalitarians in challenging the promise of school choice to promote equality, particularly school choice policy based on free market principles. But I also parted ways with egalitarians, particularly Harry Brighouse, who, although not embracing market-based choice, argued that school choice had not been shown to exacerbate inequality and that it has promise to improve upon the *status quo ante*.[41] I countered that the preponderance of the empirical evidence established that, overall, existing school choice policies exacerbated inequality. And, overall, traditional public schools have a better track record than choice schools, and that the focus on choice as the solution just diverts attention from the real remedies for educational inequality. This work included several collaborative pieces on the effects of school choice on special education with my colleague, Kevin Welner.[42] (A noteworthy aside here is that I was instrumental in recruiting Kevin to Boulder as an education policy analyst and to help me establish the Education in the Public Interest Center, which has done significant work on school choice, among other education policy issues. The Center has since grown significantly since Kevin assumed leadership and has been renamed National Education Policy Center.)

My work on school choice also included an empirical study of the Boulder Valley School District's "open enrollment" system,[43] which came about because of my experience in program evaluation and the recommendation of my close colleague and dean, Lorrie Shepard. My findings corroborated the mounting evidence that school choice exacerbates inequality. But my participation in such a study did more than simply produce findings on how Boulder Valley's particular choice system exacerbated inequality. It also provided me the opportunity to put the deliberative democratic model of evaluation and social research Ernie House and I had developed to the test with respect to the issue of equal educational opportunity, bridging these two major strands of my scholarship. Not surprisingly, the model only loosely fit with the real world of education policy context. In general, the participants were too suspicious of the researchers, and sometimes of one another, to engage in the kind of good faith give-and-take to which deliberative democracy aspires. This required an adaptation of the deliberative democratic ideal,[44] and illustrated well the melding of the methodological and the political in real world democratic policy forums.[45]

PRAGMATISM, NON-IDEAL THEORY, AND SOCRATES' LEGACY

Blurring the boundaries between philosophy and empirical social science and then putting them in constructive tension with one another has been a fundamental element of my approach to the philosophy of education. This is a feature of my deep-seated pragmatist impulse to critically engage the world of educational research and policy analysis as we find it.

I am now in the process of writing two books in this general vein. Each traces and critically analyzes the philosophical stances, typically implicit, suffusing the history of education research and policy analysis. One of the volumes will provide a general analysis of education research and policy analysis, framed in terms of the "liberal," "conservative," and "deliberative democratic" *paradigms*.[46] The other volume will focus more specifically on the evaluation of schools.[47]

Rooted in the same pragmatist impulse, I have recently become interested in an issue that has always been lurking: the methodological (or meta-philosophical) issue of *ideal* v. *non-ideal* theory. This, as it turns out, was prompted by my renewed interest in the concept of equal educational opportunity.

Philosophers since Plato have unapologetically employed the concept of natural talent to justify inequality. In *ideal* liberal political theory, Rawls' *A Theory of Justice* being the most celebrated and influential exemplar, natural talent plays a central role in conceiving "fair equality of opportunity:"[48] persons with the same natural talents ("endowments") and willingness to apply them should have the same chance of success in the competition for benefits, independent of features of the social position into which they are born, such as race and class. This framework has been picked up and applied to educational opportunity by contemporary philosophers beginning with Kenneth Strike[49] and extending, most recently, to Harry Brighouse.[50]

The concept of natural talent is itself *ideal* in the following sense: when we leave the realm of ideal theory for the real world, we are unable to cull natural, or *latent*, talent from the social and cultural influences that go into producing *manifest* or *developed* talent. At best, we can infer natural talent as something latent in individuals that helps explain observed differences in developed talents within collectives. But this provides no guidance whatsoever in allocating educational opportunities to individuals. Worse, allocating educational opportunities on the supposition they are being awarded on the basis of natural talent, as typically measured by academic tests, serves to perpetuate and mask injustice.[51] For the underlying basis of such allocations is developed talent, which significantly tracks race and class.

My thinking on how to better conceive of equal educational opportunity, minus the reliance on natural talents, is inchoate at this stage. I am attracted to the kind of *fundamental non-ideal* theory[52] that begins the project of developing a theory of justice with the felt difficulties we experience and have experienced in the world as it is and has been. This approach may be contrasted with non-ideal theory that amounts to *applied ideal theory*, which brings ethical theory developed under ideal circumstances to bear on non-ideal circumstances.[53]

The fundamental non-ideal approach jettisons the competitive conception of justice for a relational conception, which gives a much more central place to democracy. At the same time, it retains the fundamentally Rawlsian premise that differences in human capacities are not something individuals can claim to have created for themselves. They are products of social arrangements influenced by human actions. Accordingly, education policies and institutions should be designed so as to recognize differences in human capacities that are brought to, and produced by, education and employ these differences for the benefit of all.[54]

The issue of ideal versus non-ideal theory and its role in understanding equal education opportunity has captured my attention in a way that brings back the feeling of being "infected" with philosophy: though it retains a connection to the real world – indeed, understanding the connection is part of its motivation – in doing this work I'm not much affected by the "felt difficulty" of how to change that world in an immediate or direct way. My audience is philosophers of education.

As one who has spent his career as a philosopher of education devoting at least as much time and effort engaging the wider education community as those specializing in philosophy of education, however, I am never content for long being a *stargazer*.[55] Such philosophers, off in their own worlds, are *harmless* because their concerns are irrelevant to the pressing concerns of the polity and its institutions. They are therefore to be excluded from serious conversation about these matters. Many philosophers of education today, if not most, reject the role of stargazer and willingly grapple with the philosophical quandaries that take as their point of departure the vocabularies and frameworks of existent education policy and practice and what empirical social science has to say about them. One might expect these philosophers to be welcomed for having turned their talents from stargazing to illuminating the conversation of the wider education community. But more common for these philosophers of education, I fear, is to be viewed as *subversive*, irritating to the powers-that-be in the same way as Socrates. They are labeled irrelevant not because of their concerns are detached from real issues of concern, but because their suggestions are so *impractical*. These philosophers are also to be excluded from serious conversation but for a quite different reason.

If I have this right, philosophers of education are not going to have much influence on the wider arenas of education policy and practice any time soon. But they still have each other as well as a not insignificant number of other fellow travelers with whom to engage and strategize. For my part, the urge to be suspicious of and challenge authority is the lad in me that remains irrepressible. Philosophy has taken me a long way past its generalized and unruly form to a much deeper penetration of the way things are and ought to be. Or so I would like to believe.

NOTES

[1] Willis, P. (1977). *Learning to labor: How working class kids get working class jobs.* Farnborough, U.K.: Saxon House.

[2] Howe, K. (1985). Two dogmas of educational research. *Educational Researcher*, *14*(8), 10-18.
[3] Howe, K. (1986). A conceptual basis for ethics in teacher education. *Journal of Teacher Education*, *37*(3), 5-12.
[4] Howe, K. (1988). Why mandatory screening for AIDS is a very bad idea. D. VanDeVeer & C. Pierce (Eds.), *AIDS: Ethics and public policy*, Wadsworth, pp. 140-149.
[5] Gutmann, A. (1987). *Democratic education*. Princeton, NJ: Princeton University Press.
[6] Howe, K. & Dougherty, K. (1993). Ethics, IRB's, and the changing face of educational research. *Educational Researcher*, *22*(9), 16-21.
[7] Howe, K. & Moses, M. (1999). Ethics in educational research. In A. Iran-Nejad & P. D. Pearson (Eds.), *The Review of Research in Education*, Vol. 24, pp. 21-60. Washington, D.C.: American Educational Research Association.
[8] Howe, K. & Miramontes, O. (1992). *The ethics of special education*. New York: Teachers College Press.
[9] Howe, K. (1988). Against the quantitative-qualitative incompatibility thesis (or dogmas die hard). *Educational Researcher*, *17*(8), 10-16.
[10] Phillips, D.C. (1983). After the wake: Postpositivistic education thought. *Educational Researcher*, *12*(5), 4-12.
[11] Garrison, J. (1986). Some principles of postpositivistic philosophy of science. *Educational Researcher*, *15*(9), 12-16.
[12] Most pertinent here are Dewey, J. (1922). *Human nature and conduct: An introduction to social psychology*; Dewey, J. (1927). *The public and its problems*. London: George Allen and Unwin; and Dewey, J. (1938). *Logic: The theory of inquiry*. New York: Holt Rinehart and Winston.
[13] Most pertinent here are Quine, W. V. O. (1970). Two dogmas of empiricism. In J. Harris & R. Severens (Eds.), *Analyticity* (pp. 23-53). Chicago: Quadrangle Books; Quine, W. V. O., & Ullian, J. S. (1978). *The web of belief* (2nd ed.). NewYork: McGraw Hill.
[14] Most pertinent here are Rorty, R. (1982). *Consequences of pragmatism*. Minneapolis: University of Minnesota Press.
[15] Putnam, H. (1990). *Realism with a human face*. Cambridge, MA: Harvard University Press; Putnam, H. (2002). *The collapse of the fact/value dichotomy*. Cambridge, MA: Harvard University Press.
[16] Howe, K. and Eisenhart, M. (1990). Standards in qualitative (and quantitative) research: a prolegomenon. *Educational Researcher*, *9*(4), 2-9. And Eisenhart, M. and Howe, K. (1992). Validity in educational research. In M. LeCompte, W. Millroy, & J. Preissle (Eds.), *Handbook of qualitative research in education*. San Diego: Academic Press, pp. 642-680.
[17] Howe, K. (1998). The interpretive turn and the new debate in education. *Educational Researcher*, *27*(8), 13-21.
[18] Charles Taylor and John Searle are strong influences on my thinking here. Taylor, C. (1964). *The explanation of behaviour*. New York: The Humanities Press; Taylor, C. (1987). Interpretation and the sciences of man. In P. Rabinow & W. Sullivan (Eds.), *Interpretive social science: A second look* (pp. 33-81). Los Angeles: University of California Press; Taylor, C. (1994). The politics of recognition. In A. Gutmann (Ed.), *Multicul- turalism: Examining the politics of recognition* (pp. 25-74). Princeton, NJ: Princeton University Press; Taylor, C. (1995a). Explanation and practical reason. In *Philosophical arguments* (pp. 34-60). Cambridge, MA: Harvard University Press. Taylor, C. (1995) Overcoming epistemology. In *Philosophical arguments* (pp. 1–19). Cambridge, MA: Harvard University Press; Searle, J. (1986). *Minds, brains, and science*. Cambridge, MA: Harvard University Press; and Searle, J. (1995). *The construction of social reality*. New York: The Free Press.
[19] Lyons, D. (1999). *Postmodernity*. Minneapolis: University of Minnesota Press.
[20] Aronowitz, S., & Giroux, H. (1991). *Postmodern education: Politics, culture, and social criticism*. Minneapolis: University of Minnesota Press.
[21] House, E. & Howe, K. (1999). *Values in evaluation and social research*. Thousand Oaks, CA: Sage.

22 Howe, K. (2003). *Closing methodological divides: Toward democratic educational research.* Dordrecht, the Netherlands: Kluwer.
23 Howe, K. (2004). A critique of experimentalism. *Qualitative Inquiry, 10*(4), 42-61.Howe, K. (2005); The question of education science: *Experiment*ism versus *experimentali*sm. *Educational Theory, 55*(3), 307-322; Howe, K. (2005). The education science question: A symposium. *Educational Theory, 55*(3), 235-244
24 Howe, K. (2009). Isolating science from the humanities: The third dogma of educational research. *Qualitative Inquiry, 15,* 766-784.
25 Standards for Reporting on Humanities-Oriented Research in AERA Publications: American Educational Research Association (2009). *Educational Researcher, 38,* 48.
26 Ian Hacking and Ludwig Wittgenstein use these terms, respectively. Hacking, I. (1999). *The social construction of what?* Cambridge, MA: Harvard University Press; Wittgenstein, L. (1958). *Philosophical investigations* (3rd ed.). New York: Macmillan.
27 Howe, K. (2009). Positivist dogmas, rhetoric, and the education science question. *Educational Researcher,* 38, 428-440.
28 National Research Council. (2002). *Scientific research in education.*Washington, DC: National Academy Press. National Research Council. (2004). *Advancing scientific research in education.* Washington, DC: National Academy Press.
29 Coleman, J. (1968). The concept of equal educational opportunity. *Harvard Educational Review, 38*(1), 7-22.
30 Gutmann (1987). *Democratic education.*
31 Howe, K. (1989). In defense of outcomes-based conceptions of equal educational opportunity. *Educational Theory, 39*(4), 317-336.
32 Coleman (1968). The concept of equal educational opportunity.
33 Dewey, J. (1958). Philosophy of education: (problems of men). Ames, IA: Littlefield Adams.
34 Burbules, N. (1990). Equal opportunity or equal education? *Educational Theory, 40*(2), 221-226; Howe, K. (1990). Equal opportunity *is* equal education (within limits). *Educational Theory, 40*(2), 227-230.
35 Howe, K. (1997). *Understanding equal educational opportunity: Social justice, democracy and schooling.* New York: Teachers College Press.
36 I adapted the idea of opportunities worth wanting from Daniel Dennett's idea of "free will worth wanting." Dennett, D. (1984). *Elbow room: The varieties of free will worth wanting.* Cambridge, MA: MIT Press.
37 Among important influences here are Taylor, C. (1994). The politics of recognition; Young, I. M. (1990). Polity and group difference: A critique of the ideal of universal citizenship. In C. Sunstein (Ed.), *Feminism and political theory* (pp. 117–142). Chicago: The University of Chicago Press; and Fraser, N. & Honneth, A. (2003). Redistribution or recognition: a political-philosophical exchange. New York: Verso.
38 Examples include: Howe, K. (1992). Liberal democracy, equal educational opportunity and the challenge of multiculturalism. *American Educational Research Journal, 29*(3), 455-470; Howe, K. (1994). Standards, assessment, and equality of educational opportunity. *Educational Researcher, 23*(8), 27-33; Howe, K. (1995). Setting standards for standards: wrong solution, wrong problem. *Educational Leadership, 52*(6), 22-23; Howe, K. (1996). Validity, bias, and justice in educational testing: The limits of the consequentialist conception. In A. Neiman, Ed., *Philosophy of education 1995.* Normal, ILL: Philosophy of Education Society, pp. 295-302; Howe, K. (1996). Educational ethics, social justice, and children with disabilities. In C. Christensen and F. Rizvi (Eds.), *Disability and the dilemmas of education and justice,* pp. 46-62. Open University Press; and Howe, K. (1997). Liberalism, ethics and special education. In J. Paul & M. Churton (Eds.), *Foundations of special education: Some of the knowledge informing research practice in special education,* pp. 215-228. Pacific Grove, CA: Brooks/Cole.

[39] Howe, K. & Meens, D. (2012). *Democracy Left Behind: How Recent Education Reforms Undermine Local School Governance and Democratic Education.* Boulder, CO: National Education Policy Center. Retrieved 1-31-13 from http://nepc.colorado.edu/publications/democracy-left-behind

[40] Howe, K., Eisenhart, M. & Betebenner, D. (2001). School choice crucible: A case study of Boulder Valley. *Phi Delta Kappan, 83*(2), 137-146; Howe, K., Eisenhart, M. & Betebenner, D. (2002). The price of public school choice. *Educational Leadership, 59*(7), 20-24; Howe, K. & Welner, K. (2002). School choice and the pressure to perform: Déjà vu for children with disabilities? Journal of Remedial and Special Education, 23(4), 212-221; Welner, K. & Howe, K. (2005). Steering toward separation: The evidence and implications of special education students' exclusion from choice schools. In J. Scott (Ed.), *School choice and diversity*, 93-111. New York: Teachers College Press; Betebenner, D. W., Howe, K. R., & Foster, S. S. (2005). On school choice and test-based accountability. *Education Policy Analysis Archives, 13*(4) (Available: http://epaa.asu.edu/epaa/v13/n40); Howe K. & Ashcraft, C. (2005). Deliberative democratic evaluation: Successes and limitations of an evaluation of school choice. *Teachers College Record, 7*(10), 2274-2297; Howe, K. (2007). On the (In)Feasibility of school choice for social justice. *Philosophy of Education 2006.* Normal, IL: Philosophy of Education Society, pp. 259-267; and Howe, K. (2008). Evidence, the conservative paradigm, and school choice. In W. Feinberg & C. Lubienski (Eds.). *School choice policies and outcomes: Philosophical and empirical perspectives on limits to choice in liberal democracies.* Albany, NY: SUNY Press, pp. 61-78.

[41] Brighouse, H. (2000). *School choice and social justice.* New York: Oxford University Press; Brighouse, H. (2002). A modest defense of school choice. *Journal of philosophy of education, 36*(4), 653-659.

[42] Howe and Welner (2002) and Welner and Howe (2005).

[43] Howe, Eisenhart, and Betebenner (2001).

[44] Howe and Ashcraft (2005).

[45] Howe, K. & MacGillivray, H. (2008). Social research attuned to deliberative democracy. In *Sage Handbook of Social Science Ethics.* Los Angeles: Sage, pp. 565-579.

[46] This volume is co-authored by Nick Burbules, has the tentative title *Liberalism and education research,* and is to be published by Rowman-Littlefield.

[47] This volume is co-authored by Tracey Steffes, has the tentative title *the History and philosophy of school evaluation,* and is to be published by University of Chicago Press.

[48] Rawls, J. (1971). *A theory of justice.* Cambridge, MA: Belknap Press.

[49] Strike, K. (1982). *Education policy and the just society.* Champaign, IL: University of Illinois Press.

[50] Brighouse, H. (2010). Educational equality and school reform. In Brighouse, H., Tooley, J., & Howe, K. *Educational equality.* New York: Continuum; Brighouse, H. & Swift, A. (2009). Educational equality versus educational adequacy: A critique of Anderson and Satz, *Journal of Applied Philosophy, 26*(2), 117-128.

[51] Bell, D. (2004). *Silent covenants: Brown v. board of education and the unfulfilled hopes for racial reform.* New York: Oxford University Press.

[52] Non-ideal theoretical works (not always explicitly so) addressing educational equality include Walzer, M. (1983). *Spheres of justice: a defense of pluralism and equality.* Basic Books; Gutmann, A. (1987) *Democratic education.* Satz, D. (2007). Equality, adequacy, and education for citizenship. *Ethics 117,* 623-648. Anderson, E. (2007). Fair opportunity in education: a democratic equality approach, *Ethics 117,* 595-622. Anderson, E. (2010). *The imperative of integration.* Princeton: Princeton University Press.

[53] John Rawls, of course, is the most celebrated theorist in this tradition.

[54] Anderson, Fair opportunity in education: a democratic equality approach.

[55] The model here of the detached philosopher is Thales. He is said to have tumbled down a well as a result of being unable to avert his eyes from the night sky as he was walking along.

PERSONAL FAVORITES

Books

Howe, K. (2003). *Closing methodological divides: Toward democratic educational research.* Dordrecht, the Netherlands: Kluwer.

House, E. & Howe, K. (1999). *Values in evaluation and social research.* Thousand Oaks, CA: Sage. (Translated 2001, Valores en evaluacion e investigation social. Madrid: Morata.)

Howe, K. (1997). *Understanding equal educational opportunity: Social justice, democracy and schooling.* New York: Teachers College Press (Translated 2005 into Japanese zz further info needed).

Howe, K. & Miramontes, O. (1992). *The ethics of special education.* New York: Teachers College Press. (Translated 2001, La etica de La educacion especial. Barcelona: Idea Books.)

Articles & Chapters

Howe, K. & Meens, D. (2012). *Democracy left behind: How recent education reforms undermine local school governance and democratic education.* Boulder, CO: National Education Policy Center. Retrieved 1-31-13 from http://nepc.colorado.edu/publications/democracy-left-behind

Howe, K. (2010). Educational equality in the shadow of the Reagan era. Part II. Iin Hayden, G. (Ed.), *Equality and Education* (pp. 71-95). New York: Continuum.

Howe, K. (2009). Positivist dogmas, rhetoric, and the education science question. *Educational Researcher, 38,* 428-440.

Howe, K. (2008). Evidence, the conservative paradigm, and school choice. In Feinberg, W., & Lubienski, C. (Eds.). *School choice policies and outcomes: Philosophical and empirical perspectives on limits to choice in liberal democracies.* Albany, NY: SUNY Press, pp. 61-78.

Howe, K. (2004). A critique of experimentalism. *Qualitative Inquiry, 10*(4), 42-61. (Reprinted 2007 in V. Plano Clark & J. Creswell (Eds.), *Mixed methods reader.* Sage.)

Howe, K., Eisenhart, M. & Betebenner, D. (2001). School choice crucible: A case study of Boulder Valley. *Phi Delta Kappan, 83*(2), 137-146. (Condensed and reprinted, 2002, under the title Research scotches school choice. *Education Digest, 67*(5), 10-17. Reprinted, 2002, in A. Kohn & P. Shannon (Eds.), *Education Inc.: Turning learning into a business,* pp. 146-166. Portsmith, NH: Heinemann.)

Howe, K. & Moses, M. (1999). Ethics in educational research. In A. Iran-Nejad & P. D. Pearson (Eds.), *The review of research in education,* Vol. 24, pp. 21-60. Washington, D.C.: American Educational Research Association.

Howe, K. (1998). What (epistemic) benefit inclusion? In S. Laird (Ed.), *Philosophy of Education 1997.* Normal, IL: Philosophy of Education Society, pp. 89-96.

Howe, K. (1993). Equality of educational opportunity and the criterion of equal educational worth. *Studies in Philosophy and Education, 11,* 329-337.

Howe, K. and Eisenhart, M. (1990). Standards in qualitative (and quantitative) research: a prolegomenon. *Educational Researcher, 9*(4), 2-9. (Translated and reprinted (1993, Abril) *Revista De Educacion,* 173-190).

Howe, K. (1989). In defense of outcomes-based conceptions of equal educational opportunity. *Educational Theory, 39*(4), 317-336.

Howe, K. (1988). Against the quantitative-qualitative incompatibility thesis (or dogmas die hard). *Educational Researcher, 17*(8), 10-16.

Howe, K. (1985). Two dogmas of educational research. *Educational Researcher, 14*(8), 10-18.

MOST INFLUENTIAL REFERENCES

Dewey, J. (1922). *Human nature and conduct*. New York: Henry Holt and Company.
Dewey, J. (1927/1954). *The public and its problems*. Chicago: Swallow Press.
Dewey, J. (1938). *Experience and education*. New York: Macmillan Publishing Company.
Gutmann, A. (1987). *Democratic education*. Princeton, NJ: Princeton University Press.
Kymlicka, W. (1991). *Liberalism, community and culture*. New York: Oxford University Press.
Putnam, H. (1990). *Realism with a human face*. Cambridge, MA: Harvard University Press.
Quine, W.V.O. (1970). Two dogmas of empiricism. In J. Harris & R. Severens (Eds.), *Analyticity*. Chicago: Quadrangle Books.
Rorty, R. (1982c). *Consequences of pragmatism*. Minneapolis: University of Minnesota Press.
Searle, J. (1995). *The construction of social reality*. New York: The Free Press.
Taylor, C. (1995). *Philosophical arguments*. Cambridge, MA: Harvard University Press.
Taylor, C. (1987). Interpretation and the sciences of man. In P. Rabinow & W. Sullivan (Eds.), *Interpretive social science: A second look* (pp. 33-81). Los Angeles: University of California Press.
Young, I. M. (1990). *Justice and the politics of group difference*. Princeton, NJ: Princeton University Press.
Wittgenstein, L. (1958). *Philosophical investigations* (3rd ed.). New York: Macmillan.
Wittgenstein, L. (1969). *On certainty*. New York: Harper and Row.

DONNA H. KERR

TACKING TOWARD THE SUBJECTIVE

Request of my audience. How you listen to what I have to say matters deeply to my telling of this story. I need you to listen not just as the scholar you are, but as the whole person you are – as the one who conducts your scholarly work in the context of living your larger life. Indeed, to trust that you will hear what I have to say to you, I need to allow myself to imagine you as a capacious person, who happens also to have a professional life as a scholar. If as the curtain goes up, you are present in this way, then I can tell you of my struggle to bring myself into my work, which has been and remains my central narrative.

With the license of an autobiographical essay, I offer not an argument, but my professional life's case for expanding how we think of education to include a most central educative aim: developing a robust self-awareness and our related capacities as creatures formed in and thriving through relationships. Contrary to the permission that the fairly recent use of narratives in academic work may seem to offer, I continue to believe that saying something about one's own story is risky. As I do so, I risk feeling vulnerable. So much is humanly at stake in redrawing the boundaries of the educative responsibility that we bear for one another.

Today I am deeply content and enjoy a profound sense of equanimity born, I believe, of self-awareness. To me, this being present to myself and to others supports living at its best. This is not some sort of end state, but a way of being. It remains a life's work, however long that may be. With it, I am launching a career into another form of education – a kind that succeeds only in measure that educators are present to themselves and others. On entering my career as a philosopher especially interested in education, I did not set out with the aim in mind of becoming present to myself. No, I could not even have comprehended the idea. I do, though, have some understanding of how I came to live this way.

EDUCATION WITH MINIMAL SELF-AWARENESS

I began my university studies excited to pursue a career in nuclear physics and mathematics. Fortunately in my view, a program of liberal studies intervened – studies in which I learned that a way of inquiring called analytic philosophy asked fascinating questions about disciplined ways of thinking, such as what is the nature of historical narrative, of scientific fact, of legal reasoning and the like. During the years that the intervened between physics and philosophy, I studied the Russian language, literature and history; Slavic and Soviet area studies; and the French language and culture. Throughout these adventures, the lure of philosophy dangled as a shiny object, especially as I experienced two long Alaskan winters of reading philosophy. On returning to the "lower 48," it was with great relish that I treated myself to those intense years of doctoral study in philosophy and education at Columbia University. Jonas Soltis pulled together challenging texts for seminars. The brilliant and dear Ernest Nagel lectured with unparalleled clarity and was notably respectful of his students' work, including mine on the uses of theoretical models. Arthur Danto dazzled me with his novel work, such as his distinction between basic and mediated action. Sidney Morgenbesser, with his legendary analytic mind, could spot seventeen senses of a word pervading a single brief philosophical paper. It was he who inspired me to write what still I regard as my best analytic work ever, "Six Senses of Certainty in C. I. Lewis's *Mind and the World Order*."[1] To me, this was education at its best.

Moving from studying physics and mathematics into doing analytic philosophy flowed so easily and took me exactly where I wanted to be. Indeed, I experienced coming up with multiple senses of certainty embedded in Lewis's work with utter delight of a certain familiar sort. Now I am going to say something quite strange to account for the ease of that disciplinary shift: I did not take myself into my study of philosophy and education. I "did" philosophy much as one might do mathematics, all while thinking of myself as a point in space at the intersection of skills, capacities, abilities, and particular interests that I'd acquired. I myself did not have a story to tell or at least shunned such an activity, so told none; instead, I could tell you how well an argument was made or whether the concepts employed were adequate to the task. It is in that mode that I wrote both *Analysis of Educational Policy*[2] and *Barriers to Integrity*.[3] While I enjoyed writing them and still believe each to be a useful book in its own way, they do not represent taking myself into my work in a way that would reflect substantial self-awareness. I was not present in my academic work, but absent from it, even though I thereby enjoyed certain satisfactions.

STUMBLING ONTO EDUCATIONAL PRACTICE THAT GROWS A SENSE OF THE *SELF AS OTHER*

I set out as a young professor to educate in the fashion at which I excelled as a student. My approach fit well in the academy. However, stirred to attention by an abusive, but common classroom practice, I came to make a major adjustment. At Columbia I had noticed some fellow doctoral students and now some of my own students doing something that severely limited their relationships both to the authors of course readings and to their peers. They demonstrated their "prowess" as critical thinkers by first saying everything they believed to be wrong with the text under consideration and then blamed that which they did not understand on purported repetitiveness or obscurity in the text. It did not take these "critical thinkers" long to trash any and all texts – texts I had chosen for us to discuss because I believed them to be of value. The stunning result was that by practicing critical thinking, so conceived, these students failed even to perceive the author, but referred instead to the text as "it" or "they." These texts might as well have consisted of pages of randomly generated numbers.

Based on this experience, I introduced the practice of *reading generously*, which responds to questions that treat the text as a human artifact: What is the author trying to do in writing this text and how is he or she doing it? Only after carefully constructing answers to these questions from the evidence in the text could we then move to a third question: what modifications might this person make to enable *him* or *her* to better accomplish what he or she is attempting? After some initial grumblings about how this way of reading demands so much more of us as readers, we settled into satisfying discussions about texts. Happily and, to me, unexpectedly, students who had previously found writing to be even painful reported that generous reading changed their writing experience for the better, enabling them to write without fears born in anticipation of imagined "critical thinking." No longer did they discard draft after draft as they stumbled over their disabling fears. The questions to themselves as writers became "what am I trying to do," "how am I trying to do it?" and "how could I do it better?" That is, by honoring text as another person's effort to do something, students seemed more accepting of their own efforts in writing a paper – something that could be safely put in front of those whom they trusted to hear them out rather than risking a hostile response. That is, the practice of generously reading another's text led to a greater generosity toward oneself as a writer, *as an other* to be honored. This shift was powerful in ways I would only later come to understand.

THE PEDAGOGIC FAILURE OF NOT TAKING MYSELF INTO MY WORK

And then one day, something happened that made me both stop taking on graduate students and cease classroom teaching. Yes, it was that big. In a meeting with her doctoral supervisory committee to discuss the scope of Sharon's general exams, one committee member outside of her "specialization," a senior faculty member, declared that Sharon would need to be responsible for reading the basic texts in his field and likely change her topic. That sent Sharon packing. As the chair of her committee, I was stumped. She was passionate about her topic and a strong student as measured by her GRE and MAT scores, by her writing, and by her performance in classes. Moreover she was highly personable. I blamed myself for not standing up to a senior colleague. Further there seemed to be something terribly wrong with a set-up that would not allow a student to pursue that about which she was so passionate, providing that she could do so in an academically solid way. A couple of trusted colleagues opined in confidence that they saw no action by which I could help her continue her studies, at least not short of persuading her to acquiesce to this committee member's demands. Perhaps as viewed by others, I gave up teaching seamlessly, without any hint of my dismay. The sleight of hand was easy, for I increasingly immersed myself in my expanding administrative and leadership roles, which I found enormously engaging and satisfying. And yet, what happened to Sharon haunted me. I wanted eventually to return to the classroom and again mentor graduate students, but I knew that if I were to do that, I would have to bring myself into my work. Only then could I know how to help Sharon be there with her passions and interests. I only vaguely understood my words "bring myself into my scholarly work." All I knew was that I needed to learn something to get "there" – for me, a powerful possibility that would not wane, though it had to wait.

Some years passed as I served as the University's academic vice provost and then as the dean to lead the development of two new campuses, from "need studies" through garnering public support and legislative approval, and on through program development and the hiring of faculty. Even during those times when my reading consisted of little beyond executive summaries, I still wondered how I might one day return to the classroom. Minimally, I imagined that I would need to give myself permission to "follow my nose" – to read on issues that *moved* me. An invitation from the Center for Advanced Study in the Behavioral Sciences nudged me to decline offers of new leadership challenges at other institutions and make the shift back to teaching, even though I could not figure out a way to take advantage of the Center's attractive offer. Hoping for clarity, I opted for a sabbatical year in the context of a yet longer self-imposed moratorium on publishing. I needed to create space to figure out a new way forward.

I read around, fueling my fires. I succeeded in following my passions in my own studies. Then in the crucible of graduate seminars, there evolved a pedagogy that both honors students' passions and develops the student's capacity to enter conversations of scholars. This became my signature approach both to mentoring my own doctoral students and in my "mega," intensive seminars, for which students would register with enough credits to be able to stay focused. My intent was to offer a safe, significant opportunity for students to bring themselves into their graduate studies and, at the same time, enable them to enter the scholarly conversations of the careers toward which they were navigating.

ENABLING STUDENTS TO BRING THEMSELVES INTO THEIR STUDIES AND CAREERS

I do not know how broadly the practice I am about to describe can be applied. Whatever its applicability, the approach has successfully helped mid-career adults bring themselves into their work, something of which I had no clue until the last twenty years of my own academic career. For me, it represents more than a pedagogic achievement. It ushered in a personal transformation.

Rather than recounting the specifics of how this pedagogic practice for doctoral studies evolved, I begin in the middle, by describing its full-blown version in two contexts. (Here I use the present tense to represent how I hold it in mind; indeed, if I were to step back into the academy, this remains exactly the practice I would continue to refine.) The first context regards how I mentor or coach my doctoral advisees. With a wink, I package it here as a recipe. Step One: on first meeting, ask the student to tell the story that has her in its grips – the story that motivates her to undertake doctoral studies in philosophy of education or cultural studies of education. Step Two: ask the student to give that story a title, as if it were to become the topic of her dissertation, and then to jot down her dissertation's five chapter titles. Step Three: encourage the student to select courses and a supervisory committee that she believes will help her learn to write that dissertation. Those three steps take about an hour total; the rest of the time of, say, four years, consists in the student's acting on her plan. Of course the student modifies the story and along the way rethinks the tasks she needs to address, but one fact remains: the student thereby brings herself into her work; her passion supports not just the dissertation, but subsequently her career.

These three steps are repeated in the context of the mega-seminars, populated by more than just the graduate students whose studies I supervise. Students supervised by others in the College of Education and elsewhere in the University join us. Here the steps are descriptively more revealing. I structure these seminars to provide an "umbrella" under which students can bring their interests in education. While I never repeat a course and the readings are almost always new, the rubric regards asymmetrical and symmetrical human relationships as contexts for human formation, for better or worse: domination and acquiescence and the alternative of equality or mutuality. Sometimes the course texts on the book store shelf draw students to the seminar; other times, a one-page handout provides the hook. But after a few such seminars, students come mostly by word of mouth. I interview all students who are interested in registering, so that I can signal that our work begins with the stories they initially bring in truncated form. Hence, students walk in the door with the expectation and commitment to bring themselves into their work with others.

When we meet, Step One consists in the students getting to know their own and each other's stories – stories that arrive inchoate. The first assignment is to produce a one-paragraph version of the story and to share it in a small group. Subsequently, the students retell their stories in more powerful forms. It is not surprising that even with the initial version eyes well up in the telling and listening, for students bring what matters most to them, whether it is a story they live (or lived) or one they witness: the man who feels a deep tension between being a black male and literate: a woman's touched by her aunt's unsuccessful attempt to get her child into an educational program; a school psychologist who was touched by the homeless child who became honored as the class poet; the teacher who challenges his school's argumentative students to join his after-school debate team; the father who catches himself bullying his own son; and so on. Sometimes these narratives feature *mis*education rather than education. Either way, *these stories move us.*

Before hearing one another's narratives, we talk about how to listen and respond to one another. We need to be attentive, to respond in respectful ways, and to let the teller know its impact on us. All of this attention to each other's stories comes before we begin reading the course texts. Or, I should say, that the stories become the focal texts, which we come to view through the lenses of the course texts. By telling one another our stories about which we are passionate, we seminar participants come to matter to one another as persons, as evidenced by our voluntarily meeting in pairs or small groups outside of class sessions.

Now familiar with one another's stories, we are ready for Step Two: giving each assigned text a generous read, responding to the questions noted above: what is the author (*for example*, Michel Foucault, Danielle Allen, Mikhail Bakhtin, Michael Oakeshoot, Richard Wollheim, Amy Gutmann, Elisabeth Young-Bruehl, Martha Nussbaum, Toni Morrison,[4] Alan Roland, John Dewey, Ramon Guitierrez, Jessica Benjamin, or Michelle Alexander) trying to do?; how is he or she doing that?; and what, if anything, would help him or her strengthen the text? With regard to the latter, hard as we try, we rarely come up with much of a suggestion. Mainly, we think and think and think **about** the texts, until together we construct the most generous reads we can. Of course, we are never of a single mind.

Then and only then do we progress to Step Three: thinking **with** the text *about* our stories, treating the text as a lens through which to regard our stories or to invite the text's author to listen to our stories and tell us what he or she hears or notices. We even role play the text authors. Step Three seems no less than magical. Playing a course author to hear one's own story almost always provides a welcome relief from being inside the story to being outside with a fresh perspective, a way of making new sense of the power of the story. In Step One, we hear our colleagues listen empathically; that feels good and helps us care about one another. In Step Two, we together practice reading generously, so that we can together better appreciate the text. That provides its own reward and sense of achievement. Then in Step Three, as we "become" the authors of the course texts, we acquire the capacity to look back at ourselves as a respected other, to visit our stories anew. We do so as if among friends, so in safety. And we read for one another, thinking of each other's stories, thereby attending to one another in ever richer ways.

The "academic products" of this disciplined work appear as course papers that grow into conference presentations or published papers, into dissertations or, as has happened in a number of instances, into books. From the outside, the process can be described as a recipe or formula: Bring something to the table about which you care deeply, consider it through the lenses of works of mostly scholarly conversations, and share your insights in scholarly conversations, whether in-person or in-print. The semblance of being formulaic disappears when we add the layers of refinement with which the stories are told and when we see the methodological shifts made in gravitating to what feels most profoundly insightful.

That is the story of how I learned to bring myself into the classroom. I gave myself permission both to follow my interests by reading across disciplines and to forebear publishing for several years. What resulted pedagogically was my fierce insistence on providing graduate students who study with me a context and process whereby they might bring themselves into their studies – a context where I imagine that Sharon, too, would have flourished. Together we come to appreciate ever more fully the human and educational import of honoring one another's stories, the discipline of reading generously so that we ourselves can assume generous readers of our own writing, and the power of regarding ourselves from the outside -- providing welcoming interior space for the insights of others. As I witness my students so bringing themselves into their work, I myself learn to do so.

Now I could stop here with the observation that this is an effective educational approach to helping students contribute to academic conversations in cogent and important ways about what matter to them. But ending with this claim, although I believe it true, would lose track of the central thread of my story. Yes, this approach enables students to do excellent academic work that matters deeply to them. And it allows me to produce what I regard as some excellent academic work addressing issues of profound import to me, such as is represented in the capstone to my career as a scholar, "Cruelty to Compassion: The Poetry of Teaching Transformation."[5] Ending the story here would stop with only a hint of importance of the subjective work embedded in excellent, humanly powerful academic work as measured with "objective" yardsticks.

To appreciate what comes next, my turn to purely subjective education, it is helpful to highlight the highly subjective sources of power in my beloved form of graduate studies. Something very exciting happens when students tell their stories, read generously rich texts, and then revisit their stories again and again from the perspectives of the texts they've studied so closely. They *link their passions with their studies*. This is not just another form of education made "relevant" by linking "it" to what students enjoy doing, such tying a science lesson to a fifth grader's joy of building model airplanes. Instead, it is a matter of mature adults learning to tap the profoundly felt narrative wellsprings of their pursuit of advanced studies, to practice "getting outside of themselves" (i.e., thinking about their own narratives from other perspectives – perspectives that differ from their own), so as to enrich their own narratives, to write them anew, and to express what matters deeply to them in the conversations of scholarly conferences and publications. Hence, the aim of this form of graduate studies is hybrid, intentionally tapping the power of one's own subjectivity and grounding one's work in "objective" scholarly conversations.

UPPING THE ANTE FOR THE SELF: SUBJECTIVE EDUCATION

As was my wont, I exercised prudence in planning for my retirement from the University of Washington. I had other interests, in which for years I'd already been engaging "on the side." In particular, I longed to have more time to study languages, compose photographs, and do improvisational theatre. Logistically speaking, I was ready. But when retirement came, the wildly unexpected happened. These familiar longings did not, as I'd anticipated, motivate me, even though the longings remain, as is the case to this day. (Being a human is so very interesting! As it turns out, I enjoy them not as my main focus, but as "get-aways.") Instead, again I needed to follow my heart, as I had done two decades earlier. So I took myself into new terrain, exploring without a clue where I'd land. Unsurprisingly in retrospect, this exploration has led me to a new, yet ever so old, form of subjective education.

Historically, the first case of such subjection education I know of appears as a kind of coaching that Mencius (fourth century B.C.E) provides King Hsuan of Chi', the point of which is to encourage the King to "follow his heart" in his actions as king, so as to become the better leader he wants to be.[6] On passing through the courtyard, King Hsuan had gazed into the eyes of the ox that was being prepared for a ceremonial sacrifice and felt empathy; King Hsuan's people are upset because he sacrificed but a sheep instead of an ox. The King is anguished, so seeks Mencius' help. King Hsuan does not need further "objective" education, say (in a fit of anachronistic playfulness), advanced studies in strategies of wielding power in kingdoms. No, he already knows the ropes. Instead, he is struggling with his experience of acting out of good intentions and yet, in doing so, annoying his subjects, whose views matter to him. He is shaken. His concern is not how to manage some kingdom, but how he can serve as a good king in both his own eyes and those of his people. That is, he seeks an education not in an *objective*, but a *subjective* sense, so that *he himself* can to choose to be the king he wants to be. He approaches Mencius because by himself he cannot see a way forward; he is stopped in his tracks. For Mencius to help King Hsuan build this capacity, he has to focus precisely on King Hsuan's interior life, his immediate circumstances, and relationships in which he finds himself.

What sort of educative help does Mencius provide? What sort of educative responsibility does he bear for King Hsuan? Here I take license to map language of the last couple of centuries back onto this ancient encounter. Clearly his educative task is not to introduce the King to an opus of academic literature and the disciplinary bases that guide its production. Instead, it is to be present as another human being who can stand alongside him in a way that will help the King follow his heart. My attention rivets on the fact that Mencius can coach the King in this way *if and only if* he Mencius takes himself into it what he is doing – a presence without which he cannot help the King build the needed self-awareness.

Mencius' coaching King Hsuan of Chi' beckons me. Such education bears no resemblance to my relationship with my own doctoral studies and my early writing and teaching. I can learn to do what Mencius does (here it comes again!) *if and only if I take myself into my work*. Mencius raises the bar. Such presence of one human being to another is not just nice, but necessary to the enterprise.

Today's "kings" are similarly persons in leadership roles: CEOs, department heads, mayors, heads of schools and universities, community or other political leaders, and others for whom the stresses of demands for ever higher productivity with dwindling resources and long work hours commonly exact anguishing tolls in severely diminished personal lives, career burnout, problematic working relationships, and the like. For others, the challenges that bring them to today's Mencius arise at times of transition, such as upon the loss of a job, a divorce or the death of life partner, deep disenchantment with one's work, or a serious illness. In the first case, Mencius' work is called "executive coaching" and in the second, "transition coaching." Whichever the label, the point is to not to "fix" the client. No, Mencius is not there to "correct" the King. Nor is it to *heal* the King. He is mentally healthy. Instead, the aim is *educative*, i.e. to help the King *acquire the capacity to chose to a different way of being* – a way that enables him to both follow his heart and to be a better king.

Years ago, when Sharon left the doctoral program, I had no idea of how to structure graduate studies so as to enable her to bring her passions into her work and find support, precisely because I did not know how to do it for myself. Subsequently, in figuring out how to structure my work so that students could bring themselves into theirs, I myself learned to do so. At least I developed a way for students (and me) to honor the stories that move us in how we enter and participate in academic conversations. Now Mencius ups the ante. How can I help another person develop the capacity to choose another way of being, this time without the course texts to help shed light?

What if I have only myself and not a stack of course readings to bring to the table? Whatever am I to *do*? What does education consist of when one aims to help another person to build the capacity to be in the world in a different way? Yes, what if my pedagogy consists in using myself as the educative instrument – myself out there and visible, with no course texts to hide behind? Clearly, I as a person with self-awareness I must show up present to my client. My aim is educative: to help my client acquire the capacity to develop a new way of being with himself and others. That capacity consists of self-awareness: a *clarity* about what is at stake in one's actions and a *commitment* to do the work of developing new practices or patterns of acting that support and express the desired new way of being. However, just saying that the coach's self-awareness and presence constitute the chief pedagogic instrument and noting the educative aim does not tell us what any coach *does*. For that, we need to consider, at least in a general way, the general coaching moves that constitute this form of subjective education, viz. helping the client acquire the needed capacity.

Not surprisingly, coaching's "doing" is not singular, but complex. *The focal points* of the educator coach's attention contrast sharply with the educator's focus in traditional or objective education, where typically one is thought to attend in some objective way to subject matter and students, little if any note is made of the teacher's self-awareness, and the focal pedagogic outcomes are named in advance of any educative efforts and evaluated by similarly external measures. To show the stark contrast with objective education, I offer the three focal points to which I attend and note the *subjectively educative* action.

What I am experiencing, while I am with my client.

Only if I show up self-aware and present can I hear and respond to my client as distinct from me. That is, I can enact the subjective curriculum if and only if I have the capacity to use myself as an instrument. The action required of me is a constant, ever deepening practice of being present to myself and to my client.

How the client would like to live.

As a coach, I derive my subjective educative aim from the passions and hopes of the client. I solicit and, where needed, assist my client in helping her learn to refine the way she articulates that aim as she develops self-awareness.

Building the client's capacity to choose the new way of being.

I offer the "process curriculum" (the client provides the content) based on the educative need for the client to develop self-awareness that enables the choice and practices to constitute the new way of being. I call my client to self-notice, to see her own subjective (emotional, cognitive, somatic) patterns, and to locate and consider her own resistance or reluctance and other obstacles to her living in the way she desires.

With that overview, you have caught up with my narrative, a story that continues. Now practicing being present to myself and learning my way into a practice of such subjective education, I am able to see and say that of which I was incapable when I stepped into my academic career four decades ago. Having arrived at this point, I utter my findings as the whole person I am as I continue to conduct my professional life. In doing so, I will be measured in my words, as befits my professional persona. For a moment, I set that aside to say that I love my new career as a subjective educator and feel so fortunate to have the opportunity to keep learning my way along. I am not just present, but dancing, alive to life.

CONCLUDING NOTE: MY FINDINGS

The subjective education for which King Hsuan approaches Mencius cannot substitute for the objective education that introduces him to what the knowledge disciplines have to offer. I believe that is well and widely understood. What goes largely unnoticed, however, is that such objective education cannot substitute for subjective education -- the kind that attends to the formation of the psyche and individuals' patterns of interacting with others. So common is the belief that within the traditional curriculum and methods of our educational institutions we can educate for responsible citizenship in a democracy within or educate for other subjectively rooted capacities. Yet we know that the curriculum of objective education alone does not help Lisa, a small child, understand that her isolating bossiness derives from her jealousy of those who have friends.[7] Nor does it help ourselves as today's King Hsuans acquire the self-awareness that will enable to us to become better versions of ourselves. In a general sense we hope that "objective" doctoral education, perhaps especially when the general topic is education, can help us learn how to better live our lives, yet unless we are prepared to structure doctoral education to invite students to bring their lived stories into their academic work, such is but pie in the sky.

I offer my career-long quest to bring myself into my work as a plea to reconsider the aims and practices of objective education specifically alongside the character and power of subjective education. I applaud the *Harvard Business Review* for publishing papers and blogs on the role of self-awareness in successful leadership and those writing about the theory and practice of leadership and transition coaching.[8] Let us, as philosophers of education, rethink our educative responsibilities for one another as persons. Studies of leadership and various psychological theories are pertinent to my plea, but they alone cannot be expected to provide the broader understandings of *subjective education as an essential part of acquiring the capacity to develop livable, moral lives* – understandings without which many graduate-student Sharons will be sent packing or (worse) become subservient to others' passions, without which we will continue to define basic education mistakenly and anemically as solely objective education, and without which we ourselves as King Hsuans will founder, isolated in our anguish.

I invite your company in redrawing the boundaries of educative responsibility that we bear for one another.[9]

WORKS THAT HAVE INFLUENCED ME

During the last twenty years of my academic career, I focused on relationships of domination and acquiescence and their alternatives. I have come to believe that the key moral and educational question is what sort of asymmetrical relationship might not only avoid the ravages of domination, but also grow psyches capable of participating responsibly in relations of mutual respect – a necessity for the practice of democracy in its deeper sense. Or, cast within the project of this self-portrait, the point would be to grow a psyche and community that would support persons bringing themselves into the way they live their lives. In my view, that is a matter of life and death of sorts. Here I list books by a half dozen contemporary writers whom I've found especially helpful as I've mapped and remapped this terrain. Each calls me in a different way to see what is humanly at stake in how we are with one another. OF course, there are scores more, from Mencius to Albert Memmi and Elisabeth Young-Bruehl, to whom I am indebted.

Toni Morrison
A Mercy
Beloved
Bluest Eye
Home
Jazz
Paradise
Playing in the Dark

Mikhail Bakhtin
Problems of Dostoyevsky's Poetics
Rabelais and His World
The Dialogic Imagination

Jonathan Lear
Love and its Place in Nature
Open-minded
Happiness, Death, and the Remainder of Life
Radical Hope

Richard Wollheim
The Mind and its Depths
On the Emotions
Thread of Life

Vivian Paley
The Boy Who Would Be a Helicopter
You Can't Say You Can't Play

The Girl with the Brown Crayon
In Mrs. Tully's Room

Martha Nussbaum
Upheavals of Thought
Therapy of Desire
Love's Knowledge
The Fragility of Goodness
Poetic Justice

NOTES

[1] Unpublished manuscript, 1972.
[2] Donna H. Kerr, *Analysis of Educational Policy: Analysis, Structure, and Justification* (New York: David McKay Company, Inc., 1976).
[3] Donna H. Kerr, *Barriers to Integrity: Modern Modes of Knowledge Utilization* (Boulder, CO: Westview Press, 1984).
[4] Fairly frequently I include a novel by Toni Morrison, who powerfully portrays lived asymmetirical relationships and their human costs.
[5] Delivered at Oxford University to the Philosophy of Education Society of Great Britain, and subsequently published in *Studies in Philosophy and Education* (2011) 30: 574-574.
[6] See Donna H. Kerr and Margret Buchmann, "On Avoiding Domination in Philosophical Counseling," *Journal of Chinese Philosophy* 23 (1996): 341-351.
[7] See Vivian Paley, *You Can't Say You Can't Play* (Cambridge: Harvard University Press, 1992).
[8] Two such works that I find helpful as overviews are Pamela McLean, *The Completely Revised Handbook of Coaching* (San Francisco: Jossey-Bass, 2012), and Doug Silsbee, *Presence-Based Coaching* (San Francisco: Jossey-Bass, 2008). Pamela McLean co-founded and heads the Hudson Institute of Coaching, where I am studying. I've have the good fortune to have Doug Silsbee serve as my coaching coach.
[9] For related invitation, see my "Cruelty to Compassion: The Poetry of Teaching Transformation," *Studies in Philosophy of Education*, as cited above.

SUSAN LAIRD

HUNGRY FOR INSUBORDINATE EDUCATIONAL WISDOM

I came of age to womanhood in a hopeful, angry generation for whose social challenges, moral controversy, and iconoclastic artistry many war-weary, loving parents and teachers were utterly unprepared. Within that painful intergenerational predicament, from early girlhood onward, I have encountered repeatedly the ethical necessity of my own and others' insubordination – which has posed complex questions about its possible enactment with wisdom. Those questions – and wondrous encounters suggesting various possible constructive answers to them – have made philosophy of education vital for me. Confronting the postmillennial market society's demoralizing effects, both ecological and educational, makes insubordinate educational wisdom more urgent now than ever. My intellectual self-portrait consists of three brief narratives about my hunger for insubordinate educational wisdom and how I have fed it: in my initial choice of professional path, in my early education, and in my philosophical-educational inquiry itself.

CHOOSING PHILOSOPHY OF EDUCATION

Blue-eyed, cross-eyed daughter of southern New Jersey's Jim Crow culture, I was born and grew up on the Delaware Bay's Quaker-colonized eastern shore, once the peaceful Lenni Lenape's tribal territory, three years before Brown v. Board of Education. I graduated from elementary school one year after the Civil Rights Act of 1964; graduated from high school one year after Martin Luther King, Jr.'s assassination; and graduated from college one year after President Nixon's signature on Title IX of the Education Amendments of 1972 – also one year after proposal of the Equal Rights Amendment to the U.S. Constitution, still not ratified in 2013.

Title IX states simply, No person in the United States shall, on the basis of sex, be excluded from participation in, be denied the benefits of, or be subjected to discrimination under any education program or activity receiving Federal financial assistance. Before the Ford and Carter administrations had finished translating that legislation into federal policy, I entered architecture school with very few other women students. I encountered only one African American classmate, not one woman-professor, not even one woman in the history of architecture curriculum. By the end of my fifth loan-financed semester, I let go of my developing gifts and intense hunger for design, dropping out in utter disgust at pervasive sexual harassment, a practice that did not yet even have a name. My recent critical plea for educators' theoretical attention to learning environments harks back to my architectural learning, itself an undeniable intellectual watershed for me. But chastened by that profession's hostility to women, I took up pink-collar wage-labor in 1976 – becoming a secretary for several African American women who were administering the government-assisted Educational Opportunity Programs at mostly white Ithaca College.

Learning much from my bosses' instructive advocacy and mentoring and from our experiences together serving the belated education of smart, hard-working, high-achieving African American and Hispanic American undergraduates whose talents New York's urban public schools had neglected, abused, and squandered, I became involved also as a volunteer in teaching English to evening GED students. While contemplating what I could and would do with my post-architectural work-life, I learned much about other struggles against political-economic injustice from Spanish, Mexican, and Latin American graduate-student friends as I began reading romantic white public intellectuals' polemics about education's needed radical transformation – Kozol, Ashton-Warner, Illich, Postman and Weingartner, Goodman, Silberman, Holt, Wigginton, Kohl, et al. Finally I decided to devote my own privileged learning to a life's work in public education for social justice. Still smarting from my architecture-school wounds, I started on that path by joining what Catherine Beecher had named "woman's true profession," school-teaching.

I found my "methods" courses (required for Cornell's Master of Arts in Teaching English) shallow and stupid. Therefore, a half-decade before Donald Schon's *The Reflective Practitioner* inspired constructivist teacher education reformers with its case studies of architectural and other professional practices, I designed my own professional preparation within that MAT program to resemble my abandoned architectural design curriculum's constant, dialectically fluid learning interactions between theory and practice – then a distinctive feature of architectural studio education at Cornell. Previously, as an undergraduate at Vassar College, I had double-majored in English and Art, minoring in Classical Greek, and had also studied philosophy of art and aesthetics, so I had necessary conceptual tools for making that logical curricular translation from one artful profession to another. Intent upon theorizing metaphorically my own concept of teaching and locating my own teacher-preparation's academic curricular core in philosophy of education electives, I applied those studies of Dewey's moral and aesthetic thought, and of related literary theory, to close reflection upon my student-teaching field experiences in public junior and senior high-school settings – including what may be the longest-enduring public progressive-alternative school in the U.S. Oddly, however, no course introduced me to either Maxine Greene's *Landscapes of Learning* or Israel Scheffler's *Reason and Teaching*, although I learned years later that both classics spoke directly and usefully to what I was then attempting.

When I graduated and became a certified Secondary English teacher in 1979, already considering future doctoral study, I remained in Ithaca to teach high school. I "did" philosophy of education, on my own, just as I had learned, in order to design and critique my own classroom curriculum and teaching practice, which I conceived as an art form. I began reading feminist theory and racially diverse women's literature also, while educating myself more specifically about African American literature and culture in order to desegregate the school's English curriculum racially. But I found that literature I was reading and teaching often expressed and provoked educational thought of a differently useful sort; for it spoke critically to emotions and imagination as well as reason, to hearts and bodies as well as minds, to characters, events, and settings as well as language and ideas, and to aesthetic complexities of reader-response whose significance for education of moral imagination in contexts of cultural diversity both Deanne Bogdan and Martha Nussbaum would later theorize so brilliantly. Even now, I cannot understand why the educational foundations field's self-definition excludes mention of literature as one of its core liberal disciplines, using literary artifacts as mere auxiliary resources (interpreted only mimetically) to inform philosophical, historical, anthropological, or sociological studies of education. This is one theoretical issue that remains nagging on my life-work agenda.

I met weekly after school with several teaching colleagues, librarians, aides, and parents from across the school district to discuss popular books about sexism in schooling. With encouragement from an African American woman administrator in 1982, we organized the Ithaca Feminist Education Coalition, a school-district Title IX Committee, and the PreK-12 Caucus of the National Women's Studies Association – at whose conference I heard an unforgettable standing-room-only philosophical symposium presented by Ann Diller, Maryann Ayim, Kathryn Pauly Morgan, and Barbara Houston, which cast new, conceptually clarifying light upon our after-school discussions: "Should Public Education Be Gender-Free?" Earlier that year, a friend had shared with me Jane Roland Martin's 1982 *Harvard Educational Review* article, "Excluding Women from the Educational Realm," whose insubordinate questions about the conceptual meanings of both teaching and coeducation I thought about often while on my daily cafeteria duty at IHS.

After earning tenure there, one year after the Equal Rights Amendment's unexpected defeat, I went back up the hill to Cornell for doctoral study in philosophy of education, literature, and gender. However, my doctoral adviser had encouraged no expectation whatsoever of future employment in the Education professoriate, because he said university faculty positions in philosophy of education were then scarce, and many women with PhDs found themselves in clerical jobs instead, which I knew to be true.

LEARNING LOVE, DISSONANCE, AND DOUBT

My parents discouraged my doctoral study. But the foundational structure of their objections seemed so fraught with significant contradictions that I chose to rely gratefully on strengths they had taught me while staying my course without their further support. Recovering from world-war traumas and grief together, they had settled on a ramshackle old farmstead near their own families' homes and there had two children. They kept mostly to themselves, living quietly as they repaired our house; built a good family library; fed me much poetry and many women's biographies; taught my little brother and me to value their own parents' wisdom;

shared with us their love for animals and the natural world; and enjoyed mind-challenging games, crafts, and conversations with us. Thus they taught us deliberately and joyfully everyday at home – my mother as an artful modern blend of Rousseau's Sophie, Pestalozzi's Gertrude, Alcott's "Marmee," and Girl Scouts; my father as a modern self-styled sort of Epictetus. If philosophy for children had yet appeared on the U.S. educational landscape, he might have wanted it included in his children's schooling. His only career guidance came as a dinner-table confession that he'd rather have become a philosophy or history professor, or perhaps an architect, than an engineer, the profession his own father had chosen for him – so he promised never to dictate such a choice to us.

While educating us at home, instead of sustaining both their families' strong traditions of musicianship which I hungered intensely to learn, my parents sent us to the local Christian day school, where we suffered daily bullying – perhaps because on our applications for admission, asked if he believed in the Bible, my father had responded simply that he believed in God. But my parents and grandparents collaborated to contradict our school-days' abusiveness with loving lessons in rational self-respect and mutual sibling care, as they got together with our family's Episcopal parish and some extremely prosperous friends to found a new day school with a loving ethos and a classical curriculum in 1959, as war began in Viet Nam. Within two years, the Church developed sufficient anti-racist conscience to withdraw diocesan support from this all-white school, which continued to grow independently and, somewhat later, welcomed children of color. Committed to gender equality, the school never even sex-segregated its playground activities – offering tumbling and judo to all children in response to boys' pleas for football. But during my last two years, much to my parents' chagrin, I tried to trivialize my own intelligence in school lest it might make me an unattractive girl.

So they sent me away at age thirteen to an Episcopal diocesan convent school for girls in long flowing chapel veils, with a classical curriculum, on a remote northern New Jersey hilltop. Its "High-Church" (Anglo-Catholic) rituals and disciplines were so intensely ascetic that my "Low-Church" (evangelical) father could only counsel Spartan forbearance, with stories of his own army experiences while my mother wrote her love daily. The following year, my parents transferred me to a "Broad-Church" (liberal) Episcopal diocesan school for girls in Maryland, run by egalitarian progressives, explicitly grounded in "situation ethics" and existentialist theology, the core of its college-preparatory curriculum – about which I suspect my conservative parents had no clue. That is where, as philosophers say, I fell in love with wisdom.

Arriving there fresh from the convent school's doctrinaire rigors, I titled my first week's tenth-grade English composition "Logic, Not Faith," which (much to my surprise) teachers circulated among one another, applauding my skepticism. That first year, I argued often with the Lutheran priest who was my New Testament teacher and loved composing geometric proofs. The following two years' theology classes (whose pedagogy anticipated Maxine Greene's *Teacher as Stranger* by more than a half-decade) shocked us with Holocaust documentaries and offered my first heady tastes of philosophy – Kierkegaard, Sartre, Camus, Tillich, and philosophical interpretation of fiction as well as basic conceptual analysis and radically free-thinking but careful construction of our own sexual ethics. This racially desegregated, but still mostly white school proved to be a loving, joyful, democratic, faith-and-doubt community of girls led by girls. I graduated one year before the Kent State Massacre, already pacifist and egalitarian, inwardly baffled by my entire family's social and political values, which seemed so obviously to contradict compassion and love that they and our church had taught me.

Thus I left school, church, and home in 1969, clueless about my future, but eager in my deep quiet puzzlement at age 17 to study philosophy, literature, and other arts in college, among other women who dared to claim intellectual vitality, without fear of denigration for breaching feminine propriety. When I opened my letter of acceptance to Vassar, my father joked memorably that I would finish by becoming a suburban mother of four and drive a station wagon. I did not yet realize that my unusually religious, conservative early education had posed so many contradictory challenges for me that I would feel compelled to think hard about education for the rest of my life.

At Vassar I never went to chapel – except for poetry readings and lectures, some of the most important events in my education: Muriel Rukeyser, Denise Levertov, Mary McCarthy, the Berrigan brothers, Herbert Marcuse, Angela Davis. But my first philosophy course disappointed me so deeply that I took no more courses offered by that department until my senior year. Although that first course did engage arguments about God that I had been eager to study, it was conducted as if no cultural events outside the text and its logical forms were noteworthy in the least, as if early modern arguments were irrelevant to late modern problems. By contrast, even my courses in Classics addressed our contemporary cultural surround with strong critical comparisons, and my freshman orientation began memorably with student-led seminars on ancient and American philosophical classics in searching dialogue with Eldridge Cleaver's *Soul On Ice*. As the year began, Black Panthers were occupying Main Hall to support African American students' demands for a Black Studies program and for a separatist residence hall.

My first English course at Vassar, taught by a Johns Hopkins doctoral candidate who had experienced the 1968 Paris student revolts, posed provocative ontological, ethical, political, and aesthetic questions – insubordinate questions – about gender and race, segregation and desegregation, equality and freedom, war and peace through studies in twentieth-century literature. Thus I encountered my first major reading in educational thought, Virginia Woolf's *Three Guineas*, and through my senior seminar on English Romantic Poetry I met my second reading in educational thought, Mary Wollstonecraft's *A Vindication of the Rights of Woman*. I did not choose to take philosophy of education at Vassar, so I did not recognize these two landmark texts from my undergraduate experience as educational theory until I met them again as a doctoral student. However, they prodded my thinking about social justice as well as my own education and life-choices.

My first year at Vassar, the first U.S. women's college, was its last year as a women's college, which many (like me) had chosen precisely for that reason. Gradually it became more coeducational over the following three years, allowing students to choose between sex-segregated and sex-desegregated residence halls, while admitting veterans and other anti-war men as well as gay and transgender students. In my second year, the intellectual tone of classroom discourse became abruptly more informal with men's arrival (as exchange students from men's colleges). This sex-desegregation process's challenges and consequences provoked my first comparative reflections about my experiences in girls' schools and my quite different experiences of variously configured coeducation both in elementary school and at home. Later, the entirely different process of sex-desegregation in architecture school and my encounter with a more taken-for-granted coeducational configuration in the public high school where I taught English would complicate those comparisons even more – especially when I amended them with thought about racial segregation, desegregation, and separatism.

THINKING ABOUT COEDUCATION

In 1983 I began doctoral study deeply concerned that feminist pedagogy and the women's studies movement had focused (as women's colleges had) almost exclusively on undergraduate women's learning in higher education and, within that limited context, almost exclusively on liberal education, as if no other kind of education were valuable or necessary, as if boys' and men's learning were of no consequence to girls and women. Urgent concerns about girls' learning, about boys' and men's brutal miseducation, about racism and public schooling, about professional education, about domestic education and childrearing, including sexuality education, all seemed to be off the women's studies radar no less than they were off the education profession's radar. Therefore I intended to answer Martin's 1982 call to conceptualize coeducation with my own dissertation.

My adviser Bob Gowin had expressed enthusiasm about my research interest in philosophy of education, literature, and gender, and taught inspiring courses on Dewey, Rorty, conceptual analysis, and modern movements in educational thought, welcoming my eagerness to engage the arts campus culture's exhilarating conversations with and about Barthes, DeSaussure, Derrida, Foucault, Habermas, Adorno, and others. With his guidance I assembled my doctoral committee to include a pioneer scholar of children's literature, Alison Lurie, and a pioneer scholar of African American literary theory, Henry Louis Gates, Jr., for I wanted to continue my studies in African American literature and culture and integrate them into my research, if I could do so credibly. As I embarked upon my dissertation prospectus, I met Jane Martin, who encouraged my plan warmly. But soon thereafter my adviser surprised me by rejecting it on grounds that coeducation was "not a concept." Since coeducation meant nothing more than sex-desegregation, he explained, it was not a specifically educational concept.

I had experienced so many different configurations of coeducation myself, with such vastly different consequences for teaching, learning, and curriculum that I thought him mistaken. I argued that coeducation was not yet a concept only because no one had yet bothered to formulate it in terms of the "commonplaces" of educating that he had theorized. In retrospect, perhaps I did not persuade him because (following the analytic tradition) he understood the meaning of a philosophical concept to be a generalization that formulates a standard sense of common regularities to be found in experiences, events, activities, and objects bearing a particular name. The only such regularity about a-theoretical coeducation seemed to be both sexes' presence in a particular setting, so he was plainly right about the concept's thinness in educational discourse.

I did not then attempt to make my own insubordinate argument by citing the different meaning of "concept" that I had learned in architecture school, which had shaped my thinking on this subject. Even though educators often claim to be engaged in curriculum "design" and instructional "design" as "constructivists," I had never heard any of them engage the theoretical language and logic of design that I had studied with architects, nor (oddly, I thought) had I ever read any philosophy of educational design. I was wandering into some kind of philosophical wilderness with this line of thinking from another artful profession. The various cases of coeducation (and sex-segregated schooling) that had convinced me it was worthy of conceptual study reflected no standard pattern, so they suggested to me a problem for which there might be better and worse concepts – since my design education had taught me to form concepts as statements of or solutions for problems. (Architects have theorized this notion of "concept" too extensively and subtly to explain here.) Different configurations of coeducation that I had experienced were mostly not by thought or design, but by mere happenstance of different locations, times, demographics, policies, prejudices, or economic conditions. Those different configurations did not necessarily reflect coherent ideas of coeducation, because often little or no thought about gendered learning aims, or consequences of those configurations, seems to have been exerted in their formulation. Concerned about harms done by educators' obliviousness to such thoughtless configurations, I wanted to identify and analyze concepts of coeducation that might stimulate coeducational imagination pragmatically and critically astute about gender – not to formulate a standard sense of coeducation that might yield a correct, best, standard, or systematic gender practice. This approach's logical appropriateness seemed clear to me in view of the variously gendered conceptual foundations for public schooling that Ayim, Morgan, and Houston had theorized in Diller's NWSA symposium. Thus I came to draw up my plan to analyze distinctive concepts of coeducation evident in writings of Wollstonecraft, Alcott, Dewey School teachers, and Adrienne Rich. Upon that plan's rejection, I had to go back to my drawing board to design my dissertation, but I did compile some of my abortive doctoral research into a paper that won the John Dewey Society's essay contest, "Women and Gender in John Dewey's Philosophy of Education." Meanwhile mentored by Jane Martin, I developed a dissertation prospectus that my adviser approved: a conceptual analysis of "maternal teaching" in its achievement sense, indebted to Audre Lorde's essay, "Man Child" and represented in Louisa Mary Alcott's Little Women and Ntozake Shange's Betsey Brown, which also enacted it textually for girl readers and their mothers. My work on the former source drew also upon particular advising by Lurie; the second, upon particular advising by Gates. Both Jane and Bob advised me I might focus only on Little Women, but I insisted on studying Betsey Brown too – not only to racially desegregate and historicize my own educational thought, but also to show that, although both texts instantiated my proposed achievement sense of maternal teaching, each author narrated a substantially different interpretation of educational problems standing in that aim's way and therefore differently interpreted the maternal curriculum and the teaching activities it required. This conceptual inquiry constructed a useful foundation for other insubordinate thinking I undertook: about the analytic standard sense of teaching that grounded the teaching reform movement, about feminist pedagogy in that context, about in *loco parentis* teaching, about the curriculum of childrearing, about ideals of the educated teacher (much as Martin had theorized ideals of the educated woman in *Reclaiming a Conversation*), and eventually also about coeducational teaching and the coeducational childrearing possibilities of school lunch.

But my doctoral program itself had no design concept beyond completion of coursework and dissertation. My various graduate assistantships and campus jobs offered no opportunity for substantial experience educating pre-service schoolteachers philosophically, which might strengthen my candidacy for the Education professoriate. Therefore, in 1987, after I had completed my dissertation draft, I took my philosophical inquiries on teaching westward across the Mississippi River, into collaboration with Landon Beyer, a generous new curriculum-theorist mentor with whom I discovered profound common ground in aesthetics, on design of a "foundational" teacher education program for an undergraduate liberal arts college, much like the secondary teacher education I had designed for myself at Cornell the previous decade, albeit more fully developed for elementary teacher education also. After completing my Ph.D., I moved into a tenure-track assistant professorship in philosophy and history of education, serving the professional preparation of teachers, counselors, and leaders at the University of Maine. While there, my philosophical education continued through monthly participation in a Boston group of feminist philosophers who offered one another a helpfully critical audience for their writing in progress, "PHAEDRA," which at that time regularly included Jane Martin, Ann Diller, Susan Franzosa, Barbara Houston, Beatrice Nelson, Jennifer Radden, and sometimes Janet Farrell Smith. Four years later I moved into an associate professorship for which the University of Oklahoma targeted me with an explicit charge to develop a doctoral program in philosophy of education. I have regarded that charge as a design problem also, a challenge to formulate my own concept of doctoral education. My collaborations with Susan Franzosa, Lucy Townsend, and my advisees to found the Society for Educating Women have been pragmatically integral to that thinking. In my scholarly writing, however, I have focused on the research program that I had wanted to pursue as a doctoral student.

Writing various encyclopedia, handbook, and otherwise expository articles about coeducation, women's and girls' education, domestic education, Mary Wollstonecraft, Louisa May Alcott, and Jane Roland Martin has proven to be useful preliminary work for that research, and new reading of African American educational thought and of feminist philosophy and theory that I have undertaken both to teach courses and to prepare response essays for conferences have broadened and deepened my study of coeducation. Autobiographical reflection upon my educational experiences has taken my inquiry on coeducation in directions it might never otherwise have taken, as well. But I came to particular new clarity when Jim Garrison invited me to respond to critics of my first gender critique of Dewey, a project through which I studied closely Bob Gowin's objections to my initial doctoral proposal. With reference to a racially diverse variety of philosophical, literary, and historical sources on coeducation, I analyzed the concept's imprecision as a framework for examining particular conceptual understandings of coeducation that grounded Dewey's high modern defenses of the practice and Rich's late modern critique of it: its relativity to setting; its vagueness with regard to learning, teaching, and curriculum; and its ambiguity with regard to ends and means. Thus, in "Rethinking Coeducation," I raised theoretical questions about its political-economic foundations, about spatial manipulations' consequences for its changing meaning, about its logical relationship to changing conceptions of family, and about its possible pragmatic dependence upon the educational value of friendships in order to avoid pitfalls occasioned by those problems.

That latter point prompted my own practical inquiry on possible strategic responses to a-theoretical coeducation's most stubbornly pervasive, harmful problems, in a context of misogynist backlash against feminism. I embarked upon a service project – Girl Scouting for undergraduate students as well as for racially, sexually diverse teenagers coming of age in severe poverty – which informed my construction of a new concept I named "Befriending Girls as an Educational Life-Practice," that later I made more broadly inclusive. My own experience of this practice, like that of maternal teaching, included encounters with girls' eating disorders and their gatherings around food whose leftovers went home to hungry families. Thus I was inspired to undertake research that became my presidential address to the Philosophy of Education Society, "Food for Coeducational Thought."

That effort also took shape within the context of my writing a volume on Mary Wollstonecraft's educational thought, based on my philosophical reading of multi-disciplinary research that 1989 publication of her complete works in seven volumes had prompted, not yet available to Jane Martin when she wrote "Wollstonecraft's Daughters" in *Reclaiming a Conversation*. Here I discovered that Wollstonecraft had developed her thought as a Philosophical Mother of Coeducation by writing in multiple genres: recounting experiences in letters, composing her reflections upon experience and its educational possibilities into fiction, and finally also theorizing in philosophical treatises. I also found that, although her thought on coeducation has often been reduced to mere advocacy of gender-blind sex-desegregation, it does begin to formulate a more complex concept of coeducation in a sense whose understanding of gender was more deeply critical than blind. For she constructed her concept through critical analysis of what I named "monarchist miseducation," advancing five propositions that composed her sense of "republican" coeducation's definitive purposes and challenges – several of whose structural elements my research had already begun to theorize.

As an architecture student I had learned to generate a design concept by looking at other past solutions to similar problems and then subjecting those solutions to transformations determined or suggested by the problem's particular contextual and relational demands – its site, its people, and so on. Thus I began to see the Girl Scout idea of educating girls and women as a kind of sex-segregated coeducation, insofar as it has pursued Wollstonecraft's coeducational purposes despite Baden-Powell's exclusion of girls from Scouting. In similar fashion, feminists after Wollstonecraft have transformed her conception of coeducation variously – Alcott, Dewey, Woolf, and Martin, as well as the African American feminist orator Anna Julia Cooper and the American Association of University Women. In these several concepts of coeducation we may read diversely imagined ways that its practice might resist coeducation's presently misleading and harmful character and at the same time provide new foundations from which to critique and reconstruct policies for compliance with Title IX and UN-CEDAW. Two particular gaps in Wollstonecraft's theory require urgent attention: her failure to theorize coeducation for childrearing and her failure to theorize aesthetic coeducation. This is my current work: breaching those gaps while responding to global-corporatist miseducation just as Wollstonecraft responded to monarchist miseducation. As we confront challenging climate changes, we need concepts of intercultural coeducation for social justice that can re-educate our ways feeding, sheltering, transporting, nurturing, and healing ourselves no less than future generations.

FAVORITE WORKS

Personal Favorites

Book

Mary Wollstonecraft: Philosophical Mother of Coeducation (2008).

Essays and Articles

Women and Gender in John Dewey's Philosophy of Education (1988).
The Concept of Teaching: *Betsey Brown* vs. Philosophy of Education? (1988).
Learning from Marmee's Teaching: Alcott's Response to Girls' Miseducation (1998).
Befriending Girls as an Educational Life-Practice (2002).
Food for Coeducational Thought (2007).
Aesthetics and Education (2012).

Influential Works by Others

Deanne Bogdan, *Re-Educating the Imagination* (1992).
Lorraine Code, *What Can She Know?* (1992).
Anna Julia Haywood Cooper, "The Higher Education of Woman" (1902).

John Dewey, *Art As Experience* and *A Common Faith* (1934).
Ann Diller, Barbara Houston, Kathryn Pauly Morgan, Maryann Ayim, *The Gender Question in Education* (1995).
Maxine Greene, *Landscapes of Learning* (1978) and *Teacher as Stranger* (1973).
Audre Lorde, *Sister Outsider* (1984).
Jane Roland Martin, *Reclaiming a Conversation* (1985) and *Cultural Miseducation* (2002).
Adrienne Rich, *On Lies, Secrets, and Silence* (1979) and *Blood, Bread, and Poetry* (1984).
Virginia Woolf, *Three Guineas* (1938).

LARS LØVLIE

THE FREEDOM OF PARADOX

CHILDHOOD AND TEENS

I still remember the joy of reading my first book. It was as if the words and the sentences promised a world of endless surprises – and that I had unlocked the door to freedom. The next book I fondly remember was – of all things – a dictionary of foreign terms. It came in a blue hardcover published by Gyldendal, literally the golden valley, the name a pleasure on the tongue. The pages had a nice shiny touch to them and the paper an agreeable smell, what more could I want? The book turned out to be a treasure chest of secret meanings – and it released my parents from my persistent questions of word meanings that increasingly went beyond their ready answers. The taste for grasping what words promised to reveal came to good use when many years later I took a university course in Latin, and got as far as to appreciate the brisk syntax of Caesar's de Belle Gallico. In my primary school days I read whatever came my way after the literary attrition of the Second World War. I went from some traditional cartoons to translations of *Reader's Digest* and to books for boys and girls: But a five-volume leather-bound *History of Nations* was my first guide to the world at large. It set me on a journey of wonderment at the beauty and brutality of history, and it introduced me to cultures that kindled my imagination. So I persisted in a pursuit that came to enrich my life beyond mere curiosity and ambition. I didn't yet know the enduring joy of getting to know contemporary life through the raster of history. And I didn't see that my fascination with history was about finding my place in it.

In my teens – we are now in the 1950s – I discovered the Pelican Books blue series, sold from a tiny bookshop in downtown Oslo. I took a special interest in the academic readings: the social sciences, psychology in particular, which went along with reading popular books and the texts on the natural sciences and technology that came my way. The Norwegian classics were my constant companions; I got them from my grandfather's library. But it was Arthur Koestler's books that caused my intellectual awakening and gave it direction – or so I liked to think. Koestler was a Hungarian who fled from the Nazis, became a British citizen and began writing in English. He rose to a star intellectual on the European scene after the war, his fame comparable to Sartre's. I was particularly taken with his autobiography *An Arrow in the Blue* (1952) and his novel *Darkness at Noon*, originally written in German (1940). *An Arrow* was a text deeply inspired by psychoanalysis. I admired it as a blueprint for coming to terms with my teenage confusion. It provided me with a method in the wide sense of a road to be taken; and it gave direction to my reading by offering no less that the promised land of knowledge and self-understanding. Or am I deceived? Leafing through the book now doesn't support what I seemed to remember. Apart from the fact that Koestler, as a young student of engineering in Vienna, spent a semester in the local library furiously reading Freud, he explicitly refers to psychoanalysis as unscientific, much the way Karl Popper and other critics did. And there is precious little in the tale of a young man and budding journalist in Palestine and Paris that reminds us of Freud. So my interest in psychology must have originated elsewhere, from reading Neo-Freudians like Erich Fromm and from what I imbibed from my immediate surroundings – psychoanalysis had enthusiastic followers in Norway between the wars and the effect lingered on in the decades after 1945. My bookish life had taken shape.

If *An Arrow* introduced me to the personal and subjective, *Darkness* opened my eyes to world politics, to the weird rationality of Stalin's and Hitler's minds, and to the state terror they unleashed upon Europe. The book describes Stalin's purges in the late 1930s of political enemies across the board – from high up in the cadres of the Communist Party, to the military hierarchy and to the secret police. The so-called Moscow show trials presented the most improbable confessions of anti-Communist conspiracy by people whom Koestler, as a member of the German Communist Party from 1931 till 1938, had met during his travels in the USSR. Koestler tried to explain the strange fact that defendants confessed to trumped-up charges that they knew would lead to their certain execution. His answer was that they were compelled by their dedication to the cause and by an utterly confused revolutionary logic. What drove them to false testimony was not Stalin, the torture in the prisons or even the wish to spare their families from persecution, but the belief that their sacrifice and death would save Communism for the future. I like to think that *Darkness* forever inoculated me against revolutionary rhetoric, whatever its guise. More important, it directed my interest to the political history of the 20th century and to the twisted logic of revolutionary movements both on the left and the right. So it came as no surprise that I chose history as my first subject when I entered the University of Oslo in the early 1960s.

STUDENT YEARS

My early intellectual inspirations came from books rather than from persons. My teachers in primary school were admirably tolerant and reasonably firm towards a restless boy of occasional mischief. I can't remember any teacher who infringed or humiliated me or my peers. We were probably helped by the fact that the rules of conduct were few and well defined and that a breach of rules had mild material consequences – there was no psychological fuss about it. In upper secondary school, or Gymnasium, two of my teachers had Ph.D.s, not unusual in those days because teaching in the Gymnasium was a step towards a university position. They impressed me with their knowledge and wisdom, but I can't remember that I ever discussed my extracurricular readings with them. It didn't occur to me that

Koestler could be of any interest to them, and even less so my intellectual flutterings – my fascination with psychology was an utterly personal thing. Neither can I remember that they asked about my intellectual predilections. Other teachers I remember more for their enthusiasm in teaching and for their dedication to us, their students. They left me to the fancies of my own growing universe of experience while I followed the routines of school life. Later, at the university, I didn't have any sustained supervision, and felt all the better for it. I may have needed the personal authority of a teacher both at school and in the university, but for better or worse studying was for me a personal and even idiosyncratic quest. My days in the Departments of History, English and Education were rather uneventful. I was eager to learn, and critique came after I had left my Alma Mater. When I had finished history, I opted for English, and became an Anglophile. I felt uncultured because I did not take to Dickens, and Thackerey's *Vanity Fair* did not win my young heart. But I still thank God for English poetry and for giving us Shakespeare's plays and the Scottish philosophers!

For all my newly acquired knowledge I left the university with a feeling that I really knew nothing. But in my youthful confidence I had already decided that psychology – my initial intellectual inspiration – did not answer the deeper questions of existence. So I turned to philosophy and caught a passing interest in theosophy. I tried religion but was repelled by the doctrines, the pressure to believe, and the personal whims of those who represented both the Protestant and Catholic faith. I realized that I was a secular person in a secular country. Later I learnt that Kant had similar reactions to the emotional practices in Collegium Friedericianum, his Pietist grade school in Königsberg. But I didn't have any qualms reading religiously inclined philosophers and I found "existentialist" philosophers like Gabriel Marcel and Karl Jaspers particularly interesting. I had in fact already knocked on the door to existential philosophy after having submitted my final thesis on existentialism and education.

I tried "pure" philosophy while I was teaching full time at Sagene Lærerskole, a teachers college in Oslo, and visited university seminars in philosophy in the spring of 1969. It was a sobering experience – I could hardly breath in that rarefied air. I blamed myself for it but even more the dogmatism of Neo-Marxist students and the aggressiveness that dimmed the discussions – it was decidedly not the place for pondering existential questions. I was indeed grievously disappointed and decided that my practical interest in questions of truth, freedom and existence would not be satisfied in philosophy departments. Neither did departments of education give me much comfort – they did not teach philosophy of education. I had to seek other pastures. One had already emerged – I became engaged in the so-called "critique of positivism." I found my first intellectual home in a growing group of like-minded philosophers, sociologists and educationists. But I became an absentee member. I had a family and landed a job at a teachers college in Bodø located 1200 kilometers north of Oslo by car. We didn't have any car and travel by air was too expensive. We stayed there for two years. I became enchanted by the incredible beauty of North Norway nature with its call to outdoor life – and I enjoyed teaching in the faint glow of the Paris riots of 1968.

THE CRITIQUE OF POSITIVISM

The critique of positivism started as a discussion or Auseinandersetzung between Theodor W. Adorno and Karl Popper at a conference for sociologists in Tübingen in 1961, and later grew into a more general conflict between the young philosopher Jürgen Habermas, a defender of "Critical Theory" in the tradition of The Frankfurt School, and Hans Albert, a defender of Popper's "Rational Empiricism." The Streit or quarrel turned on the political role of the social sciences. Popper, a Viennese fugitive from the Nazis, had already in his exile in New Zealand during the war written a searing critique of Hegel and Marx in *The Open Society and Its Enemies*. Popper wanted to build modern democratic society on the pillars of the empirical sciences, and gave his critique an interesting, or should I say: colloquial twist. Theories were hatched not only in science departments, but could be collected from nearly every source, myth, literature and art. Theory should be tested against the facts yet truth was not a property of facts but of the logic of science. To top it all, no theory, not even that of evolution could be finalized as true because in principle there was always the possibility that it could be falsified. This view, which was based on his argument against induction, released me from the idea that facts are all there is to science. I took great pleasure in Popper's two tenets of freedom: that we can learn from our mistakes and that we should try to kill our theories – both aspects of his "fallibilism." With his brisk no-nonsense prose he became to me the embodiment of a common sense intellectual who never minced words and put philosophy and science into a practical setting in the service of democracy. There was, however, a hitch: Popper was an epistemologist who saw things in terms of a rational method modeled on the natural sciences. I felt that his concept of rationality could not fully answer my pedagogical questions. Still I would not call him a "positivist," for his philosophy was open-ended, practical, and politically informed. As for method, dialectics held a more promising future for pedagogy – or so it now seemed to me.

In 1959 Hans Skjervheim, a young Norwegian student of philosophy, published his first book: *Objectivism and the Study of Man*. During a subsequent three-year stay in Munich he acquired a firsthand knowledge of the new generation of German philosophers, particularly Karl-Otto Apel and Jürgen Habermas. Skjervheim was an independent practical thinker who used philosophy to address problems in politics and in the academic professions, particularly sociology. Around 1970 he also published several essays that turned out to be a philosophical critique of pedagogy and of educational policy in general. Thus he became the spiritual father of Norwegian philosophy of education, which until then had existed as a history of ideas without the critical bite that was inspired by The Frankfurt School and later by the May 1968 student riots in Paris. In other words, the 1960s had already prepared the intellectual scene for those of us who found professional pedagogy wanting. I did not become a political activist, that is to say, part of the more or less militant and politically active generation of 1968. I was a few years too old and the radicals, to my mild consternation and amusement, chided me for having written a thesis on existentialism. That was deemed a bourgeois pursuit and I was a political laggard. That set me free from wasting my radical mettle in Marxist circles, and I could devote myself to a critique of the existing pedagogy the way Skjervheim had marked it out as a critique of positivism.

What shape did the critique of positivism take in pedagogy? First of all, it was a critique of the experimental psychology that came to dominate education after the war. Before 1940 Norwegian educationists looked to German psychology and sociology, and to its Reformpedagogik. After 1945 educational studies were progressively covered by American empirical psychology, and around 1970 behaviorism became en vogue. B. F. Skinner's method of operant conditioning was used in the construction of learning machines and practiced in the treatment of severely handicapped people. There were a few scandals when such treatment escalated into severe physical punishment. Skinner himself had warned against punishment because it only taught young people to revolt or protest or drop out of school, so he was not to blame on that count. On the other hand, his political utopia in Walden Two seemed to be a society where everyone was set to reinforce the behavior of everyone else, a good example of how the best of intentions may lead down the road to fascism. The anti-positivist critique pointed out that the connection between a behaviorist theoretical scheme and its practical regime issued in objectivism, that is to say, in a third person perspective that missed the educative relation between adult and child. The critique was not directed at scientific inquiry, but at the unmediated transfer of experimental knowledge into the classroom, and at a vocabulary that described the child as a repository of drives, motives, and capabilities that could be utilized for educational purposes. This particular view was labeled "instrumentalism." Skjervheim put Dewey squarely into the instrumentalist camp. That was unfair. After all, Dewey was true to his Hegelian past when he rejected "the spectator theory of knowledge," and he gave pedagogy a much wider scope than experimental behaviorism could ever do.

But there was still the wider problem that bothered the critics: the idea of a value-free social science seemed to insinuate itself into social and political life. Some scientists acted as if the scientific facts described the world as it truly was. It was for politicians, social workers, and teachers to transfer scientific findings into practical measures, and that included ethical education. In the 1970s Habermas described this as the system's colonization of the life world. This was more than a professional squabble; it grew into a cultural war in which a Continental hermeneutic tradition was pitted against an Anglophone scientistic one. I felt the debris of that war many years later, when lecturing on the possibilities of the Internet. My optimistic views were countered by anti-technological arguments. I took that to be a mistake. The classical critique of instrumentalism was directed at education as forms of manipulation. Today instrumentalism finds its way into systems of tools for testing and behaviour modification that aims at improving education. I hope that later generations will see this line of thinking as one of the less successful fads and follies of the early 21st century. The critique of the early 1970s was more than a passing fashion. It drew on Kant and Hegel and the aftermath, which included Heidegger and Gadamer's hermeneutics and the phenomenology of Merleau-Ponty. But it was Hegel that made a lasting impression on me.

A WINDFALL

At the same time a windfall came my way, a surprising invitation to say the least. In 1970 I was asked to apply for a position as a Lecturer at a Regional College that was to be located in Lillehammer – and still on the drawing board! In other words the heady future of joining a group of like-minded colleagues and start a brand new institution, unhampered by a settled culture, fell into my lap. The conservative political establishment would allow us to test our brand of the educational critique as part of its higher education policies! My guess is that this could only happen in a country of less than four million people, a land tucked away on the very edge of Europe, ethnically homogeneous and with a long national tradition of fighting itself free from foreign dominance: from Denmark (1814), Sweden (1905), and German occupation (1945). The background was this: the Parliament had decided that new colleges be erected in 12 regions across Norway. They should offer one- and two-year vocational courses preferably adapted to the local needs of the region. At Lillehammer a one-year study in general education, soon followed by two others in history and political science, could hardly be said to be vocational in the narrow sense, all the more since the teachers were a select group of young and able people just out of university departments of the social sciences and the humanities. Since I left for the University of Oslo in 1990, Lillehammer University College has grown to today's full-fledged academic institution of 4000 students. But I am ahead of myself.

In the fall of 1971 our teaching careers at Lillehammer began, and we went along struck with a zest for change. During the first semester we worked out the regulations and exam procedures in cooperation with the students, most of them teachers who wanted to add another year to their former vocational training. We belonged roughly to the same age group, there were no senior professors and authority in matters theoretical and practical was spread among teachers and students and depended on negotiation and argument. The 1970s gave us unique experiences with serious students eager to learn as well as the stray opportunist and the power-seeker. It was the closest we could get to Dewey's idea of school as a society in miniature. I look back upon that decade of professor bashing and student power with joy and gratitude, both for what we did – and did not – accomplish. At the end of the decade revolutionary Marxism had exposed its futility, Popper had already prepared me for killing darling theories, and German philosophers marked out the path ahead.

THE HEGELIAN INSPIRATION

My first flash of enthusiasm for Hegel came after reading Habermas' early article, titled "Arbeit und Interaction" ("Work and Interaction"), an interpretation of

Hegel's so-called Jena Lectures. I came across it in a Norwegian translation in 1969, and did not at that time know what had struck me. Only later did I see that it was dialectics: the to and fro between opposites that were deeply related. I did not really go into Hegel till 1973, and this is a fact, because I have scribbled that year down on the first page of my Suhrkamp edition of Hegel's Collected Works. There was a quite rational – and it also turned out: naïve – motive that made me buy the work. I wanted to know more about dialectics, and he apparently was the original source. The word dialectics was at that time bandied about by orthodox Marxists and rejected by critics like Popper who thought that Hegel's dialectics was a high-flying sham. They both missed the point, I felt. The Marxists went on with their revolutionary predictions till history itself shattered their dreams. Popper's rejection of dialectics I didn't take seriously because he seemed to repeat the bygone critique of Hegel's idea of reason's march through history, and he missed out what was the gist of dialectics: the force of ironies and paradoxes that worked from within practical life. The basic opposition in this cultural war between positivists and their adversaries was one of logic, that between an epistemology of testing causal relations and a hermeneutics mindful of practical or performative paradoxes between what you intend and what you say; and between what you say and what you do. Hegel's *Phenomenology of Spirit*, shorn of its metaphysics, appeared to hold a treasure of formative and future-directed oppositions.

It was Hegel's dialectics that set me on the course towards the pedagogical paradox and its importance in pedagogical thinking. I will get back to that. I first presented Hegel as a pedagogical thinker in a book titled *Dialektikk og pedagogikk* (Dialectics and Education), published as a monograph at Lillehammer Regional College in 1979. The book grew out of the need for putting my initial fascination to paper. I had already embarked on a study of John Dewey, and had spent much time reading him and the other great American Pragmatists. On the face of it the written results were puny, two articles on Dewey and one on William James to this day. I saw Dewey as a good social democrat, but he didn't excite me, and I realized that I now had Hegel and not Dewey on my mind. What they had in common, though, was a relational view of the world, apparent in Dewey's description of mind as not confined to the brain but rather as "a course of action," or if you will: a distributed intelligence expressed in bodily movement and interaction. I returned to Dewey in several later essays. He had left a "permanent deposit" in my thinking, to use his words about Hegel's influence on his own philosophy. My trouble with Dewey, as with Popper, was their "methodolatry," the idea that problems of politics and education could be solved by a method of inquiry.

Why this fascination with Hegel? For me it was the mystery of the *Phenomenology*, a book I have read almost to tatters. It held the promise of getting to know culture or Bildung in its radical expression, as we shall soon see. The movement – Bewegung – of dialectics kept my philosophical fire aflame during the 1970s, for me a time of intellectual exile from a formalist philosophy that had untied itself from lived life. Only later I translated the force of dialectics into pedagogy with the pedagogical paradox as its particular term. I made the first step in *Det pedagogiske argument* (The Pedagogical Argument), published in 1984. On the face of it the book was based on Habermas' theory of communication, and was a frontal critique of what I felt was a Neo-Traditionalist backlash in Norway of the 1980s, a badly argued back-to-basics call in teaching and in moral education.

To forward a bit, in an article published in 1995: "On the Educative Reading of Hegel's 'Phenomenology of Spirit,'" I scaled the Phenomenology down to the interplay between three figures that appear in the book: the implicit author, the implicit reader, and the protagonist, "natural consciousness." In other words I went literary and saw the book as a unique Bildungsroman, the story of the formation of the Western mind till the dawn of constitutional democracy. I also suggested that the apotheosis of the book, called "absolute knowing," was just another word for the mutual transparency and reconciliation between these characters engaged in self-formation. By following their story I, the present reader, would repeat the educative process of the Western mind till about 1807, when the book came off the press. Hegel also presented a surprising intellectual gap. The man who gave us the *Phenomenology* also offered up a disastrous idea of pedagogical psychology. Not only was he on all accounts a dull teacher in his years as Rector at the Neo-Humanist Gymnasium in Nuremberg, he also embraced a contemporary trope, the distinction between the child's "first" and "second" nature, and proceeded to say that we have to root out the first, animal one in order to make way for the second, cultural one.

What surprised me was that John McDowell, as late as in the 1990s, could restate the dichotomy without batting an eye. It was undialectical, and it also ignored Kant's liberal reception of Rousseau. I would not criticize Hegel for rejecting the Romantic child, but for disregarding dialectics in matters educational. So I left Rector Hegel behind and decided to carve out pedagogy from his general dialectical philosophy. For this was Hegel's radical observation: dialectics arises when social and political institutions take on historical shapes or Gestalten that generate their own internal stresses and strains. A theory, an institution, or a habit, produce contradictions that lead to their disintegration from within, as witnessed in the demise of feudalism, described by Hegel in the famous struggle for recognition between master and slave. Recent examples are the crumbling of the European welfare system that takes place when solidarity is replaced by ego-related entitlement; or pursuing democratic aims of participation by turning schools into boot camps for efficient learning.

The *Phenomenology* as the story of civilization repeated in memory, also made me abandon perfectionism, the idea of the perfectibility of man as the apotheosis of life and the goal of Bildung. Perfectionism was a household idea among contemporary intellectuals and deeply connected with the idea of a call or vocation to live a Christian life. My move may seem implausible, for on the face of it the *Phenomenology* supports a linear view of history and biography, and thus a version of perfectionism. But as already mentioned, in my 1995 article I had decided to pass over Reason's march through history, and see the text as a story about our Bildung, with the title *Phenomenology of Spirit* on the front page. This literary turn revealed a Bildungsroman that actually presented life in a circular fashion: real history repeated and grasped in interpretation or "thought." Add the fact that the present reader recollects his or her biography by melting it into the history of culture as such, and you have an interesting theory of Bildung. Education is partly cultural anamnesis and a person's *ex post facto* self-creation as a historical individual. This effort traces in general features what is forgotten in our common history and hidden in the reader's biography. I came to think that Freud's psychoanalysis around 1900 was just another version of Hegel's dialectics of culture. In a 1999 article "Hegels dannelsesbegrep – noen synspunkter" ("Aspects of Hegel's Concept of Bildung"), I pursued the idea of education as formation as bound to include a retrospective reflection on the cultural past realized in the here and now of a person's life. I still hold the *Phenomenology* to be a breathtaking feat by the author of a highly idiosyncratic book.

IN GRATITUDE

In 1982 I went as a Visiting Scholar to Cambridge in the spring semester. Paul Hirst had wished me welcome to the Institute of Education at Trumpington Street. There I met Terry McLaughlin and a few weeks later, Joe Dunne. They became my friends. Terry introduced me to his students and to colleagues at Homerton College, at that time an independent teachers college, and aided my further integration into the network of Anglophone educationists. I enjoyed their blend of ordinary language approach and taste for rationality, and my stay in Cambridge did much to inspire *The Pedagogical Argument*. I was on my way towards a more explicit pedagogical point of view. In the spring of 1989 I spent a semester in the Department of Psychology at the University of Aarhus, invited by a colleague of mine, Steinar Kvale. I was asked to give seminars on education, particularly on Habermas' theory of communication. But Kvale, with his intellectual curiosity, was already well into "postmodernism." I remember we both greatly enjoyed Jean Baudrillard's *America* – the book ran like a road movie by a latter-day Tocqueville. I pursued my reading of French philosophers, in particular Jacques Derrida. It came as a relief. I had tired of the relentless rationality of Habermas' diction – my pedagogical imagination had come to a standstill. Kvale edited a book in 1992, *Psychology and Postmodernism*, in which I had a piece titled "Postmodernism and Subjectivity."

In 2001 I was called to Örebro University as a Visiting Professor. Tomas Englund and his students had established a milieu of scholars on curriculum theory and education for democracy. My article "Education and Democracy" (2007) grew out of this setting and confirmed my belief that educational critique had to start with the nitty-gritty details of educational policy and its effects on the daily life of teachers and students in our schools. From the middle of the 1990s on I regularly met with German colleagues, a result of my philosophical inclinations – after all, I read British philosophers but studied the German ones. In the Institute for Educational Research in Oslo I ran yearly courses in what we dubbed the Educational Classics. "We" included Stefan Hopmann and Christopher Lüth, two scholars who blended the German scholarly tradition with independent thinking. The seminars turned into intellectual happenings to deep satisfaction both for us and for our students – if I may talk on behalf of us all. Throughout these years research societies, the NERA in the Nordic countries, the PESGB in Oxford, the INPE internationally, and the DGfE in Germany among them, acted as key venues for professional learning and exchange. The trusted backdrop for these excursions was my benefactors and colleagues abroad, in the Institute, and elsewhere in Norway. In 2002 my colleague Tone Kvernbekk and I had the pleasure of hosting the biennial INPE conference in Oslo. Over the past decades several of our fellow philosophers of education have given lectures and seminars in the Institute, from 2007 home to the Humanities Studies in Education research group. Throughout these years my students contributed greatly to academic life. – At the end of the day I wouldn't trade that life for any other.

JOYRIDES

During the 2000s I went from interpretation of classical texts to writing imaginative essays. Imaginative here means something like the joy and fun in making forays into the future and putting the ideas that came my way to paper. In the "Promise of Bildung" (2002) I saw education in terms of the image rather than of the text. The essay came out of my fascination with the representative arts and photography: look at a photograph and you have a prime case of history abbreviated in the now – here the influence of Walter Benjamin and Roland Barthes' *Camera Lucida* made its appearance. My conclusion that Wilhelm von Humboldt's idea of freedom in interplay might unfold on the Internet was, and now is even more, a bit over the top. In any case, Sherry Turkle's seminal book Life on the Screen (1995) suggested that the Internet could spawn new concepts of self and interaction, just what I was looking for. In another article, "Teknokulturell danning" ("Technocultural Education") (2003), I introduced two concepts, the cyborg and the interface, the first inspired by Donna Haraway, as part of a different description of man and machine, mind and nature. In a piece with the title "Is There Any Body in Cyberspace? Or the Idea of a Cyberbildung" (2008), I suggested that the distinction between virtual and real didn't hold because the computer is not a machine but rather an extension of our mind, with its interfaces modelled on the situated body as described by Edmund Husserl and Maurice Merleau-Ponty. These and other essays in the same genre were joyrides partly inspired by two fellow Internet enthusiasts, Morten Søby and Winfried Marotzki. If in "The Promise" I tried to refashion classical Bildung by introducing the image, I now tried to move further into the age of the Internet. For me the metaphors "interface" and "cyborg" did away with the age-worn dichotomy between man and machine, and between the sciences and the humanities. It was therapeutic: I had finally put the dated struggle about positivism behind. More important yet was that I now saw how the the old dichotomy between naturalism and humanism could be shelved; it was as if I could strike an arc from the moral beauty of nature (Kant) to neuroscience! That goes with two caveats, though: don't think we can explain mind by brain, or poetry by the firing of synapses: and beware of the wave of brain-training programmes that will soon inundate our schools!

SUBJECTIVITY REVISITED

Derrida's texts first struck me as extremely imaginative and often far-fetched; I approached them in bits and pieces. I saw that his "deconstruction" offered up a new take on Hegelian dialectics. I hardly overstate my case if I say that reading his texts persuaded me that paradox was an indispensable part of pedagogical freedom. Which freedom? What immediately comes to mind are the *aporias* that contrary to expectation may bring you out of deadening intellectual and practical routines, or the dead-ends that ironically promises freedom from the petrified ideas and habits that are part of our academic institutions. Add the freedom of pondering intangible and indefinable first-order values like justice and human dignity, and you get an idea of what I was at. For me this transcendental effort morphes naturally into the image of the open-eyed imagination and anticipation you can often find in a child's face. It was Derrida, not surprisingly for some readers, who also brought me back to Kant and to the force of transcendental thinking. The influence of Kant is obvious in Derrida's juxtaposition of justice and the law. Justice is evasive and mysterious, and rightly so. It is more than just a fact in the sense of statutory laws or regulations that positively determines what is or is not a breach of the rules. When can we say of the law that it is unjust? We can when justice is untied from established institutions, practices, and habits by the transcendental gesture. Justice in the untied sense, as "pure" principled justice, give us the freedom to question what is usually taken for granted, it points to alternative interactions and standards of critique. This freedom exists and comes into existence by analysis and interpretation, imagination and reflection. Derrida's intellectual independence added new features to my idea of dialectics. It also reminded me that Kant, as the author of anthropological descriptions of humans in their common social settings, could set me free from the communitarian Hegel. That meant another look at subjectivity, autonomy, and critique.

I still think that Hegel got it basically right 200 years ago when he said that in the course of experience or Erfahrung, both the object observed and the standards used by the observer undergo a change. This relation or "identity" between thing and thought I hold to be the essence of a concept of Bildung or culture as transformative. But it turns radical only when you realize that identities or historical forms of life break up owing to their self-engendered contradictions. The discrepancy between our conceptions of the world and the world as it actually turns out to be makes a form of life tremble and dissolve from within, like an organism from its own autoimmunity. I tried to translate this insight into pedagogy, and gradually the pedagogical paradox came into clearer view. I don't think of it as a theory of education that should replace other theories or even a method that should surpass other methods in education. I think of it rather as an "existential" that pertains to pedagogy because it is essentially a practice based on the asymmetric relation between child and adult. As for the school as an institution, the paradox works more like the ironic gaze that unties the knots that old habits and schemes have tightened. So what is the pedagogical paradox and what is the practice that goes with it when it is neither a theory nor a method? The preliminary answer was: In the beginning was Rousseau.

REREADING ROUSSEAU AND KANT

In the middle of the 1990s I sat down once again to read Rousseau's *Emile* in order to see what I had missed in my earlier readings of that marvelous book. I then wrote a paper for the *Norwegian Journal of Pedagogy* in 1997 on the well-known fact that Rousseau pronounces the freedom of his charge to make authentic choices, and then immediately adds that he, the teacher, will decide on the boy's behalf. That Emile should freely choose Sophie for his wife, but that his teacher should actually make the choice for him, I saw as a particularly bad case of the pedagogical paradox. I took it for granted that the author was to blame for not seeing the contradiction that shattered his idea of a pedagogy of freedom. But my conclusion lingered uncomfortably in my mind. I felt there was something amiss in my reading, and I could not leave it behind and put my doubt to rest. I first tried to explain the flawed logic – after all one of the greatest minds of his generation just doesn't make such simple practical mistakes! Since *Emile* was a so-called Bildungsroman, could the paradox be part of the plot, a teaser directed at the reader? Or did the author regard himself as a godly representative of the new science of man? Some of his compatriots had already written tracts on naturalistic man. Or could it be that the teacher regarded himself a friend of Emile, and that the paradox was just the good counsel given within the bounds of a growing friendship between teacher and student? Or did it result from his view of a person who should act both according to his ability and to another's counsel and care, in itself a great advance in educational thinking? Apart from the last question, which Rousseau obviously answers in the positive, my questions were skewed, and I realized that I went down the wrong path. So I returned to Rousseau around 2000 and made another try in an article first published in connection with his 300 years anniversary in 2012.

My question now was this: Can we take Rousseau's embrace of paternalism as native to education? If answered in the affirmative his gentle paternalism states our essential duty to educate the child according to our best intentions and adjusted to the child's ability to fashion its own life. This view meshes with quite reasonable ideas of ordinary adult responsibility and care for the young. Why not, then, stop beating about the bush and admit that the paradox simply describes the necessary business of pedagogy, and that even to call it a paradox is to conjure up a ghost that disappears with the dawn of day? But I persisted: Rousseau's paternalism was paradoxical, and the irony of the paradox did exist. That consideration made me pick out the significant differences between Rousseau, Kant, and Hegel on education. My answer goes something like this: Rousseau sidesteps the paradox by making it into a mere dilemma and so setting the scene for what later generations of the Romantic bent came to defend as child centeredness in its fierce opposition to traditionalism. Hegel seemed to split his allegiances: he opted for a straightforward paternalism in pedagogy, yet the dialectics of the *Phenomenology* gave us the actualization of selfhood in a series of paradoxes. Kant, on the other hand, saw the paradox as immanent to pedagogy and – this was his great contribution – profoundly related to subjectivity and personal autonomy. In his *Lectures on Education* he first states the obvious: that we are bound to educate our children. Then he reminds us that we cannot instruct children to be moral persons because morality depends on the independent or autonomous judgement of the child. I took up this theme in "Does Paradox Count in Education?," first presented at the PESGB conference in Oxford in 2008, and later in "Kant's Invitation to Educational Thinking," in 2012. This double take on pedagogy: that you must and yet cannot teach children to be independent persons, came as more than a mild satisfaction – I was on my way to a better appreciation of pedagogy as an open-ended and infinite relation between subjects in their struggle for autonomy. Hegel for his part fell short of Kant's insight by underrating subjective independence. I still wonder what may have happened if Hegel, the philosopher who breathed life into Kant's formalism, had made the paradox the linchpin of a dialectical pedagogy! To sum up, to me it seemed that Rousseau brought us to see the pedagogical paradox as existing for pedagogy; that Kant took a decisive step further by his concept of autonomous judgement; and that Hegel in his concept of mutual recognition retained the social dynamic of the paradox. My next step was to reintroduce the Kantian subject within Hegel's social dialectics.

In hindsight the pedagogical paradox depends on the subject-object distinction that was common in the Norwegian critique of positivism in the 1970s. I felt that Kant's idea of subjective freedom make us appreciate the significance of the paradox. In order to get there I went beyond Kant's transcendental philosophy to embrace his "anthropology," of which pedagogy is a part. With the distinction he draws between the intelligible and the empirical, mind and world, I was now better able to define the boundaries of the self and the place of selfhood in ethical and social life. Words like violate, insult, offend, and hurt all point to this selfhood and its boundaries, and to the emotional universals that form human experiences. We know that there are psychological limits to intervention in children's lives, but Kant is particularly clear about the limits of a pedagogy that has moral education as its aim. Kant's' acute sensitivity for protecting the child's integrity from the best intentions of adults is expressed in his concept of dignity. Dignity is not an individual capability or even a character trait; it is something he ascribes to human beings as such, and it cannot, like knowledge and skills, be defined and determined. Dignity is a dialectical concept, that is to say, it is the other of infringement or humiliation. Dignity comes to mind when personal boundaries are threatened by injustice and disrespect, be it by bullies or patronising adults. It's relational, as witnessed in personal conflicts and legal disputes, and it yields to social or relational descriptions. The bottom line is, however, that dignity is ascribed to children and adults universally as members of humanity. Dignity is proper to a person in the sense of property or *proprium*, his or her selfhood and integrity. Despite the fact that I am deeply intertwined with others, I cannot be your self and you cannot live my life without forfeiting your subjectivity.

There is another aspect to be considered. If we hold on the idea of dignity as intrinsic to humanity, we can also appreciate it as non-developmental. Educators will at first sight see this proposal as wrongheaded: since children and adults grow and change, often at a fast pace, pedagogy is and must be based on the idea of human development. I agree, but let me try the following argument. If for a moment we let development aside, we also do away with perfectionism, for without the idea of development there will be no idea of perfection of man's capabilities. Philosophers generally take rationality as a pure intellectual capacity and as the sign and standard of perfection, the final goal or "finality" of education – they are perfectionists to the hilt. I have already suggested that a circular reading of Hegel's *Phenomenology* disproves rationality as perfection. I would now suggest that the Kantian ascription of good will and dignity to all humans performs the same trick: it presents an alternative to rationality as the end product and criterion of human development. The alternative may be called distributed rationality: rationality as the ability to cope with the world at any and every stage of a child's development. It is to see the child as perfectly rational according to his or her – at times astounding – capacities for relating to other persons and the world. Children are citizens of the same world with adults. In order to come to its own, pedagogy needs to avoid the fallacy of perfectionism as it figures in contemporary philosophy. What I would call the philosophy of place is a step in that direction – more about that below.

Hegel pursued a social logic, the idea that contradictions were resolved historically in a step-like fashion. The Kantian approach, on the other hand, suggests that dignity is "outside of history" and thus constitutive of humanity. To put it crudely: dignity is ascribed to man, irrespective of time and place; we even respect the newborn's boundaries, less out of principle than of sensing its extreme vulnerability as a human being. Mutual recognition, though, seems to appear only in modern history and marks the achievement of enlightened thinking around 1800. But a closer look makes us see that they are deeply connected. Dignity and humiliation refers to us humans in general, albeit under different historical and social conditions; the struggle for recognition carries the passion for solidarity: the "'I' that is 'We' and 'We' that is 'I,'" as Hegel had it. If mutual recognition is a force in life, dignity is an intrinsic feature of that life. It is on par with other existentials, like friendship, trust, or love. I like to think of the pedagogical paradox as an existential, a product both of modern 1800th century subjectivity and of the intrinsic difference between self and other. A paradox that is pedagogical too, depends on subjectivity and the boundaries of the self, but comes to its own in the discrepancy between what we say and what we do. From the point of view of socialisation it may puzzle you that there is freedom in the limits between self and other. But within the social self there is an "I" who, as George Herbert Mead had it, reacts towards the social "me." The "I" is always beyond our intellectual and social grasp; it is the personal presence that dwells within the heart, in Rousseau's famous metaphor. It was Rousseau's radical idea that freedom is first expesseed as a feeling in the voice of the heart.

THE POLITICS OF PARADOX

It was time to free the play of contradiction from the restraints of the Hegelian logic. I went to literary theory to bolster my case. The genres of irony, parody, and satire gave me a lead, enriched by the new rhetoric of writers like Paul de Man and Stanley Fish. Without my literary studies I would hardly be able to fathom the depths of paradox and find a place for it within pedagogy. My penchant for paradox began as a wild card, but I thought it was worth pursuing until I was beaten by the game. Now to describe the "I" and personal dignity as undefined and a matter of the heart seem to make them phantasms that belong more to the psychiatry ward than to reality. I think not. Even to say that the factual is negated or undone by the undefined or abstract is more than lofty talk. Just to take some relevant examples from political life. Civil disobedience began when a general idea of human rights challenged the discrimination of blacks in America of the 1960s. In Norway the UN Child Convention was recently used to confront the Government's handling of child asylum seekers threatened by forced return to their country of origin, a country in which many of them had not even set foot. The ubiquity and force of the abstract as the most practical is all around us, for example in children's role-play. Children show an early acquaintance with the abstract – they are indeed masters of make-believe and counterfactual thinking, and that mastery makes a difference in life.

Tradition would have it that children are either noble savages or barbarians outside the citadel of reason. But the distinction is a *non sequitur* – neither view can be resolved as true or false, and the stale opposition has indeed worked as a trap for reasonable thinking in pedagogy. If children are the future of nations, we should take a look at future's freedom, and freedom is not found in the either-or categories. Dewey's idea of inquiry took care of future's freedom, but that's old hat. Now our current educational institutions anticipate the future of their students by tight goal-related learning schedules in a competitive society. In the Neo-Liberal society there is a freedom of choice between different preferences and courses of life, under the general anticipation that the young ones should find their slot in the workforce. This way of thinking eclipses the indefinable, replaces it by habits and puts the future in chains. What Hegel once used to call the "infinite" is not the trajectory of endless infinity. It is rather the twin of the finite, or to put it like this: without the infinite ideas of humanity, dignity and hope we become hostages of mere habit. If the infinite is an anticipation only of things to be achieved, we pre-empt the future by steering towards fixed goals. The governed perfectionism of today's education is oblivious of its roots in a moral figure of thought, and reduces education to management. The deep paradox of contemporary schooling is the growing chasm between the aims of moral education and the tools that are used to bring it about.

What does this interplay between the finite and the infinite tell us? To begin with, they show us as a contrast to dialectics that whenever you see this and other relations as dilemmas, you end up with the tiring conflict between entrenched positions and the endless turf wars that make the freedom of one party the unfreedom of the other. For me the alternative turned out to be the twisted road that took me from Popper's conjectures and refutations over the Unruhe or restlessness of Hegel's dialectics and to Derrida's idea of the "messianic." That is to say, to experiences without origin and finalities. Derrida's messianic struck me as Romantic beyond Romanticism. It made me mindful of experiences that simply happen to people, of things that comes into being by surprise, and of insights that may occur without forewarning. This became for me the most uncompromising description of freedom in pedagogy, particularly in the life of children. Children are living instances of the messianic; the young ones live without origins and finalities – that is the strength of their vulnerability, and that's where their creativity lies.

Why the pedagogical paradox? To sum up, the paradox is embedded in the Enlightenment idea of subjectivity and the later idea of a democracy based on rights, common values and interaction. In that general sense the paradox is historical. Yet I would say that the paradox is inherent in a pedagogy that builds on the ideas of moral autonomy and authenticity in upbringing. And I would even say that in one sense it is constitutive of pedagogy. To put it this way: as long as there is the asymmetry between adults and children there is also the pedagogical paradox. Second, the paradox is not a tool or a method, but the expression of an uneasy and troubled freedom in pedagogy. It's brought into play by an experience of frustration and disappointment, of being stopped in your steps, of being caught in mental dead ends. The irony lies in the fact that dead ends may morph into new experiences and alternative avenues of action. The paradox shakes off the authority of paternalism, and that's practical freedom. What to do with the pedagogical paradox? Well, it may give you a good laugh at your own follies. Or you may turn to inquiry and discussion. Or you may put your judgement on hold, wait out the situation and let it come to its fruition. After all, the paradox only points to relational knots that may be untied. With children this last option offers itself as a gift to pedagogy. If you are given to wonderment, children are great companions.

CRITICAL PEDAGOGY

This description of the pedagogical paradox is theoretical in the sense of being discussed in academic seminars. I was keenly aware of the need for a political perspective and the view from the classroom. The ground – literally – of pedagogy I found in Heidegger's philosophy of place. I toyed with the idea of topos in some essays in the 2000s and tried to sum up my position in "The Pedagogy of Place," a NERA conference keynote given in 2006 in Örebro, Sweden. The conviction that experience and pedagogy originates in place rather than in someone's mind was neither new nor radical. For me it agreed nicely with my own observations of children, with recent children's psychology, and with the fact that experiences unfold from situations. Pedagogy starts in medias res, it sets out from the here and now and grows, as Dewey emphasised, out of situated experiences. It seemed that I now had the outline of a critical education: a notion of freedom, a place for it in everyday life, and the idea of paradox that would get pedagogy moving along paths of experience. To marry philosophical thinking with contemporary pedagogy was, as with so many of my colleagues, a task I had set myself before I wrote *The Pedagogical Argument* back in the early 1980s. The question was how to meddle in the politics of schooling.

The answer turned out to be a series of critical observation about present educational reforms in Norway from the middle of the 1990s, even before the PISA-shock of 2001. My views have been published in Scandinavian journals and the stray newspaper article, in talks to teachers, interviews and blog contributions, preferably in the polemic genre, but I believe sufficiently parsed with philosophical argument. In 1998 I highlighted three related paradoxes in the preamble to the new Education Act of 1997, in an essay with the title "The Paradoxes of Educational Reforms: The Case of Norway in the 1990s" The first was the be-independent-on-my-authority paradox that urges teachers to be bold, enthusiastic and independent – on the premises of the then wilful and patronising Minister of Education. The second was to hail thick moral values and portray teachers in terms of their performance in the new "competitive democracy" – teachers as their "own best tools." The third and more serious paradox was that teachers were expected to represent and present the national moral tradition without being given the independent professional voice to go with it – the Minister fought the teachers unions much like a true Thatcherite. The paradoxes pointed as far as I could see to a growing paternalism in a public school system that still caters for around 95 percent of the more than 600 000 students in Norway's primary and lower secondary education.

In later pieces I criticised the authorities for imposing a system of tests on children who are not eager to compete for excellence in the first place – actually an exclusion of children who are interested in making friendships and relate to teachers rather than to fill out tests. The PISA impacted education by making it a race for more screening and knowledge tests. I found it futile to speak in general terms. For me the hand-on criticism of national public policy, as found it in the Official Norwegian Reports, the Education Act, the National Frameworks for teacher education, and the public debates, was important. Now – and this is 2013 – the Ministry of Education has, in cahoots with the market, introduced behavioural programmes for 6-year-olds in order to prepare them for schooling. In the article titled "Verktøyskolen" ("The Tool Kit School"), I argue that the Ministry engage in a power play that violates the general aims of the Education Act and parental rights. This is an example of the new instrumentalism as based on the misuse of bureaucratic governance and the market. It disregards formative learning, elementary children's psychology and the basic aims of democracy.

WRITING THE SELF

In 1998 I wrote an essay, "The Internet and the Rewriting of the Self," a sweeping tour of self-presentations, starting with Leonardo da Vinci's painting in the Uffizi, the Adoration of the Magi, and ending with research on Internet-made personalities. Ten years later I penned another essay: "Dannelse og profesjonell tenkning" ("Education and Professional Thinking"). There I suggested – among other things – that the education of the self is best expressed in the autobiography, in this case John Stuart Mill's *Autobiography*. Wilhelm Dilthey had long ago persuaded me that autobiography performs a beautiful dialectics: by one stroke it both inscribes the biographee into history and lets the author – literally the individual auctor and augmenter – appear as a character in his or her own right. The autobiography as a genre realizes the two basic aspects of education: culture and selfhood. Biography on the other hand lacks this intimacy. A biography is quite literally a description of a person's life, often reflected on the title page of such books, usually the name of the biographee followed by A Life. Biographies are at best research works by independent scholars subject to the strict rules of professional fact-finding and interpretation. Autobiographies belong to a different genre, for here the author is also the protagonist of the story. The difference between the two genres can be indicated by the words truth and truthfulness: the biographer is responsible to truth, the autobiographical writer to truthfulness. We criticize the former for falling short of truth, and we reproach the latter for being dishonest. Autobiography is subjective and ethical rather than objective, is part of everyday life of the civil society where everyone has a say. We all relate to the genre. Writing diaries, memoirs or telling stories to family members, even browsing through an album, takes part in the genre. And then there are the invisibles: the "I" that cannot be pinned down, the imagination that cannot be harnessed, the impressions that cannot be determined. And don't forget the poetry. About 20 years after he began writing his autobiography, *Dichtung und Wahrheit*, Goethe commented on the title to a friend. He had found that truth belonged to the facts of his life, to persons that had a name and events that had a date. Poetry on the other hand belonged to the author's imagination, his ways with the language, and to the art of story-telling. – I like to think of Goethe's autobiography as a "thick" personal retake on Hegel's *Phenomenology of Spirit*.

THE TASKS AHEAD

What are the tasks ahead? First, education needs to take back and renew a children's psychology based on relational thinking, scientific research and the accumulated knowledge of children's needs in their interactions with adults. Education is more than getting children to learn. We should give teachers the chance to practise moral imagination by asking themselves in their encounters with children: Who are you? Where are you coming from? What do you think about me? How do you feel about being here with us? Moral imagination connects to what is now called empathy or mentalisation; it is to sense and to make sense of the other – the child – in its particular world, a world that aligns itself with the adult's universe without copying it. Second, pedagogy should take its historical roots seriously, not only in order to learn from its mistakes, but also because history circumscribes our pedagogical concepts: like it or not, their genealogy also plays significantly into their future success. When history is reduced to the local history of the teacher profession, the loss of vision endangers the profession itself. Third, pedagogy should be brought back to where it belongs, to the practice of organized cooperation. The so-called academic drift and the idea that professional teaching should rely almost exclusively on evidence-based research, disregards the sense of place that goes with reflective pedagogy. What is needed is a radical overhaul of the relationship between theory and practice, radical in the literal sense of going to the root of pedagogy. Last but not least, philosophers of education should, as quite a number of them actually do, regard themselves as citizens with a special expertise and obligation to bring pedagogy into the broad public discussion – free discussion is not a given, but has to be won every day.

FAVORITE WORKS

Favorites by Other Authors

Dewey, J. (1916). *Democracy and education*. New York: Free Press.
Habermas, J. (1968). *Erkenntnis und Interesse*. Frankfurt a. M.: Suhrkamp.
Hegel, G. F. W. (1977). *The phenomenology of spirit*, trans. A. V. Miller. Oxford: Clarendon Press.
Kant, I. (1951). *Critique of judgement*. New York: Hafner Press.
Popper, K. R. (1972). *Objective knowledge*. Oxford: Clarendon Press.
Rousseau, J.-J. (1991). *Emile or On education*. Harmondsworth: Penguin Classics.
Skjervheim, H. (1959). *Objectivism and the study of man*. Oslo: Universitetsforlaget.

Personal Favorites

Løvlie, L. (1984). *Det pedagogiske argument*. Oslo: Cappelen.
Løvlie, L. (1992). Postmodernism and subjectivity. In Steinar Kvale (Ed.), *Psychology and postmodernism* (pp. 119-135). London: Sage.
Løvlie, L. (1995). On the educative reading of Hegel's phenomenology of spirit. *Scandinavian Journal of Educational Research, 39*(4), 277-295.
Løvlie, L. (1993). Of rules, skills, and examples in moral education. *Nordisk Pedagogikk, 2*, 76-91. Reprinted (1997) as: The uses of example in moral education. *Journal of Philosophy of Education, 31*(3), 409-427.
Løvlie, L. (2000). The Internet and the rewriting of the self. In M. Sandbothe & W. Marotzki (Eds.), *Subjektivität und Öffentlichkeit. Kulturwissenschaftliche Grundlagenprobleme virtueller Welten*. Köln: Herbert von Halem Verlag.
Løvlie, L. (2002). The promise of Bildung. *Journal of Philosophy of Education* (Special issue on "Educating humanity: Bildung in postmodernity," L. Løvlie, K. P. Mortensen, & S. E. Nordenbo, Eds.), *36*(3), Autumn.
Løvlie, L. (2003). Teknokulturell danning. In R. Slagstad, O. Korsgaard, & L. Løvlie (Eds.), *Dannelsens forvandlinger* (pp. 347-373). Oslo: Pax Forlag.
Løvlie, L. (2007). Does paradox count in education? *Utbildning & Demokrati, 16*(3), 9-25.
Løvlie, L. (2007). Education for deliberative democracy. In Ilan Gur Ze'ev & Klas Roth (Eds.), *Critical issues in education in a global world* (pp. 123-147). Springer.
Løvlie, L. (2012). Kant's invitation to educational thinking. In Klas Roth & Chris Surprenant, *Kant and education: Interpretations and commentary* (pp. 107-124). Routledge Studies in Contemporary Philosophy. New York: Routledge.

REFERENCES

Bostad, I., & Løvlie, L. (2013). Deliberative democracy and moral disturbance. In *Reimagining democratic societies. A new era of personal and social responsibility* (pp. 89-109). Council of Europe Publishing: Strasbourg.
Dewey, J. (1916). *Democracy and education*. New York: Free Press.
Von Goethe, J. W. (1988). Dichtung und Wahrheit. In *Johann Wolfgang von Goethe Werke*, Hamburger Ausgabe, Band 9. München: Deutscher Taschenbuch Verlag.
Habermas, J. (1969). Arbeid og interaksjon (Work and interaction). In J. Habermas, *Vitenskap som ideologi* (trans. Thomas Krogh and Helge Vold) (pp. 84-109). Gyldendal Forlag: Oslo. In German (1968), *Technik und Wissenschaft als "Ideologie."* Frankfurt a. M.: Suhrkamp.
Hegel, G. F. W. (1977). *The phenomenology of spirit* (Trans. A. V. Miller). Oxford: Clarendon Press.
Kant, I. (2007). Lectures on pedagogy. In P. Guyer & A. W. Wood (Eds.), *Anthropology, history, and education, The Cambridge edition of Immanuel Kant* (pp. 434-486). Cambridge: Cambridge University Press. Swedish trans. (2008) *Om pedagogik*. Göteborg: Daidalos.
Løvlie, L. (1979). *Dialektikk og pedagogik*. Oppland Distriktshøgskole, Skrifter nr. 22. Write pedagogikk.
Løvlie, L. (1984). *Det pedagogiske argument*. Oslo: Cappelen.
Løvlie, L. (1992). Postmodernism and subjectivity. In Steinar Kvale (Ed.), *Psychology and postmodernism* (pp. 119-135). London: Sage.
Løvlie, L. (1995). On the educative reading of Hegel's *Phenomenology of Spirit*. *Scandinavian Journal of Educational Research*, *39*(4), 277-295.
Løvlie, L. (1998). Paradoxes of educational reform: The case of Norway in the 1990s. In B. B. Gundem & S. Hopmann (Eds.), *Didaktik and/or curriculum. An international dialogue*. New York: Peter Lang. Norwegian version (1997) Utdanningsreformens paradokser. *Norsk Pedagogisk Tidsskrift*, *6*, 350-362; and in Ebbestad, J. E. (Ed.) (2001), *Norsk tro og tanke 1940-2000* (pp. 893-903). Oslo: Universitetsforlaget.
Løvlie, L. (1993). Of rules, skills, and examples in moral education. *Nordisk Pedagogikk*, *2*, 76-91. Reprinted as (1997) The uses of example in moral education. *Journal of Philosophy of Education*, *31*(3), 409-427.
Løvlie, L. (1997a). Rousseau og den paradoksale oppdragelsen. Første del. *Norsk Pedagogisk Tidsskrift*, *3*, 115-122.
Løvlie, L. (1997b). Rousseau og den paradoksale oppdragelsen. Andre del. *Norsk Pedagogisk Tidsskrift*, *4*, 195-203.
Løvlie, L. (1999). Hegels dannelsesbegrep – noen synspunkter (Aspects of Hegel's concept of Bildung). In Ø. Andersen (Ed.), *Dannelse, humanitas, paideia* (pp. 43-63). Oslo: Sypress Forlag.
Løvlie, L. (2000). The internet and the rewriting of the self. In M. Sandbothe & W. Marotzki (Eds.), *Subjektivität und Öffentlichkeit. Kulturwissenschaftliche Grundlagenprobleme virtueller Welten*. Köln: Herbert von Halem Verlag.
Løvlie, L. (2002a). The promise of Bildung. *Journal of Philosophy of Education* (Special Issue on *Educating humanity: Bildung in postmodernity*, eds. L. Løvlie, K. P. Mortensen, & S. E. Nordenbo), *36*(3), Autumn. Book reprint by Blackwell Publishing 2003. Swedish trans. "Löftet om bildning" in Jan Bengtsson (Ed.) (2004), *Utmaningar i filosofisk pedagogik*, pp. 89-121. Danish trans. "Løftet i Bildung," in *Udfordringer i filosofisk pædagogik* (pp. 77-103). København: Danmarks Pædagogiske Bibliotek.
Løvlie, L. (2002b). Rousseau's insight. *Studies in Philosophy and Education* (Special Issue on Higher education, democracy and citizenship, T. Englund, ed.), *21*(4-5), July-September.
Løvlie, L. (2003). Teknokulturell danning. In R. Slagstad, O. Korsgaard, & L. Løvlie (Eds.), *Dannelsens forvandlinger* (pp. 347-373). Oslo: Pax Forlag. English trans. (2006) Technocultural education. *Seminar-net – International Journal of Media*, *2*(1), www.seminar.net
Løvlie, L. (2005). Ideologi, politikk og læreplan. *Norsk Pedagogisk Tidsskrift*, *4*, 269-279.

Løvlie, L. (2007a). Does paradox count in education? *Utbildning & Demokrati*, *16*(3), 9-25. Danish trans. in L. E. D. Knudsen & M. Andersson (Eds.), *Har det pædagogiske paradox nogen betydning i uddannelse?* (pp. 13-31). København: Skab dig. Pædagogisk filosofi, Forlaget Unge Pædagoger.

Løvlie, L. (2007b). The pedagogy of place. Keynote at the 2006 NERA Örebro Congress. *Nordisk Pedagogik*, *1* (Special Issue), 32-38.

Løvlie, L. (2007c). Education for deliberative democracy. In I. Gur Ze'ev & K. Roth (Eds.), *Critical issues in education in a global world* (pp. 123-147). Springer. Swedish trans. (2007), Utbildning for deliberativ demokrati. In *Utbildning som kommunikation. Deliberativa samtal som möjlighet* (pp. 273-311). Göteborg: Daidalos.

Løvlie, L. (2008). Is there any body in cyberspace? Or the idea of a cyberbildung. In F. von Gross, W. Marotzki, & U. Sander (Eds.), *Internet – Bildung – Gemeinschaft* (pp. 31-45). Wiesbaden: Medienbildung und Gesellschaft, Vs Verlag für Sozialwissenschaften.

Løvlie, L. (2012a). Kant's invitation to educational thinking. In K. Roth & C. Surprenant, *Kant and education: Interpretations and commentary* (pp. 107-124). Routledge Studies in Contemporary Philosophy. New York: Routledge.

Løvlie, L. (2012b). Dannelse og profesjonell tenkning. In B. Hagtvet & G. Ognjenovic (Eds.), *Dannelse. Tenkning, modning, refleksjon. Nordiske perspektiver på allmenndannelsens nødvendighet i høyere utdanning og forskning* (pp. 735-754). Oslo: Dreiers Forlag.

Løvlie, L. (2012c). Rousseau i våre hjerter. *Studier i Pædagogisk Filosofi*, *1*(2), Online journal, http://ojs.statsbiblioteket.dk/index.php/spf/index

Løvlie, L. (2013). Verktøyskolen. *Norsk Pedagogisk Tidsskrift*, *97*(3), 185-199.

Mead, G. H. (1962). *Mind, self, and society*. Chicago: University of Chicago Press.

Mill, J. S. (1989). *Autobiography*. London: Penguin.

Rousseau, J.-J. (1991). *Emile or on education*, trans. Harold Bloom. Harmondsworth: Penguin Classics. Norwegian trans. (2010), *Emile – eller om oppdragelse*. Oslo: Vidarforlaget.

Skjervheim, H. (1959). *Objectivism and the study of man*. Oslo: Universitetsforlaget. Norwegian trans. (1974), *Objektivismen og studiet av mennesket*. Oslo: Gyldendal Norsk Forlag.

Turkle, S. (1995). *Life on the screen, identity in the age of the internet*. New York: Simon & Schuster.

JAN MASSCHELEIN

PEDAGOGUE AND/OR PHILOSOPHER?

Some Comments on Attending, Walking, Talking, Writing and ... Caving

For Myriam, Marthe and Sam

LABORATORY FOR EDUCATION AND SOCIETY

The man has been teaching educational philosophy and philosophy of/as education at the university for a rather long time. Now, at his pleasant surprise, he has been invited to write an 'intellectual self-portrait.' He accepted the invitation, as he mostly accepts them, but he knows it would be an illusion to conceive of this labor as a recollection of his past. As if the words he heard, read and wrote and now intends to recall maintained their meaning, as if the desires which affected him still pointed in the same direction, as if the ideas which came to him retained still the same logic, as if the encounters he experienced simply conserved their effect. As if the man who is writing about what happened to him then is the same as the one to whom it happened. Besides, there is no final coherence to be discovered, but rather a fiction to be invented. The hundreds of (lost) events, places, encounters, moves, chances, errors and misjudgements which made appear what he values and inscribed themselves on the surface of his body, in the form of his hands, the style of his writing, the tone of his voice, the gaze of his eyes, the connections in his mind cannot be synthesized or traced back to their origin.

Nevertheless, the invitation is an occasion, he considers, to confront his memory. However, not as an exercise of recollection but as an attempt to think his past, his own history, which is crucially and essentially a shared history, and to explore to what extent this can help him, perhaps, to open his gaze for future perspectives. It is an occasion to re-construct the encounters and events, re-read the texts, re-watch the images, not in order to find out, confirm or explain who he was or is, not to reflect (on) himself, but rather in order to get himself at a certain distance from himself and his present. Maybe in that way, this writing of a self-portrait could become in itself an exercise in philosophy of/as education i.e. an exercise bringing he himself as a writer into play – a non-specular self-portrait – and at once an invitation to others to meet in the exercise and cross his thoughts. Another man, Michel Foucault, had said much earlier that today that practice which we call philosophy is only to be understood as an 'askesis': "an exercise of oneself in the activity of thought" (1985, pp. 8-9). Which echoes the words of this amazing woman, Hannah Arendt, calling her famous essay on 'The crisis of education' also 'an exercise of thought.' And he strangely recalls that both of them – whose work he has been rereading time and again – at several occasions emphasized that they were no (professional) philosophers, both refusing the ambition to build systems of thought, refusing the critical judgemental attitude, the tendency to tell others where their truth is and how to find it, all of which they associated with philosophy. Both also claiming that their work was rather that of 'an experimenter' being a way to think and live the present otherwise. And yes, he tends to agree, and even wants to add that their work is maybe rather one of (self-)education.

So he decided to write a kind of selective 'pragma-graphy.' However, not in the form of a linear succession of sequences, but aiming at an approximate description of some events that actually happened to him and of what they brought about. These events were not spectacular, they were essentially invitations and/as occasions, but they made him move, they displaced him, not only his body but also his gaze and mind. They pushed him away from where he was and how he thought and lived. Not in one sudden big move (a sudden fulguration or an abrupt opening that sparks a profoundly reorienting conversion), but slowly from step to step they made him engage in particular practices, brought him to particular places and inspired thoughts he never could have imagined before. It was, thus, not that he had a great plan, some strong ambition, a clear ideal or big dream. In fact, he can't remember anything important in his life that happened because he was aiming at it or looking for it. It was that he felt always again that he had to accept the invitation, seize the opportunity, engage in the occasion and that he had to move away from where he was, from what he thought (and taught), that it was not so important to try to remain the same.

ATTENDING UNIVERSITY LECTURES, SEMINARS AND ... CINEMAS

One of the decisive moves the man made, was to leave his small hometown and go to the university. Another man had sung that there is only one good thing about a small town: you know that you want to get out. However, the move he made might not have been so exceptional, and had very little of a conscious choice. He in fact joined the fast growing number of young people out of the rising middle class that, at least partly due to the strong economic development, were offered the opportunity to access higher education and started to populate the 'mass' universities at the end of the sixties and beginning of the seventies. His move was, thus, a very common one, but it nevertheless remained a decisive one, not only regarding climbing the social ladder, but primarily because it opened up a whole new world. Even if it was a world that precisely at that moment was also shaken into its very foundations. It were the beginning of the seventies and the May'68 revolt was still very much alive: long student strikes, occupations of university buildings for months, demonstrations, student pickets at factory's, student councils, endless discussions, anarchist, Marxist, Maoist groups calling for the revolution, fights with the police. The unrest shook the foundations of cities and states, and the academic apparatus was itself one of its targets. At stake: democratization of higher education, solidarity between workers and students, solidarity with the oppressed in the 'third world,' the Vietnam War, struggles for independence and against oppression around the world, inventing new ways of living together (communes, community houses, etc.) and very central: the anti-authoritarian movement in all domains of society (family, church, education, state and the work place). All of these in the 'air' (radio, television, newspapers) but also very present within the buildings and surroundings of his university.

The man started to study educational sciences at the Leuven university, the university where he is still teaching today. It was a four year program strongly inspired by the German tradition of 'Pädagogik.' It was just recently created but already very popular. As popular as political sciences and mainly for the same reasons: it was seen by many students as a way to engage in the struggle for a better, just world. Indeed, education was not exclusively seen as a means for individual development and self-realization, but was regarded also as the road to collective emancipation and to a better common world. In his mother tongue, masters in educational sciences are also called 'pedagogues' and what he studied was called in fact, literally translated: 'pedagogical sciences.' He must confess that at the time he had not a very clear idea of what 'pedagogue' meant, but he associated it, like most of his fellow students, with emancipation and liberation and that was enough to attract him. In Leuven, as it was then the case in many continental universities, it was evident that multiple courses in philosophy were an obligatory part of the education of 'pedagogues.' So he attended lecture courses on 'philosophical anthropology,' 'philosophy of science,' 'ethics,' 'metaphysics,' 'epistemology and logic,' 'philosophical foundations of education.' He was thus introduced into the work of Plato, Aristotle, Kant, Husserl, Levinas, Foucault, Derrida, and especially Heidegger and Sartre. Additionally his courses in education offered an insight into the rich tradition of educational thought and practice (from Plato over Rousseau, Herbart and Schleiermacher to Langeveld and Flitner), reconstructing that tradition mainly as one of enlightenment, progress and emancipation. Rogers' *Freedom to Learn* had been around since the late sixties. Freire's *Pedagogy of the Oppressed* and Illich's *Deschooling Society* together with Marcuse's *One-dimensional Man* were becoming main references for critical emancipatory pedagogy all over the world and also in Leuven, inspiring even the teaching body to experiment with alternative forms of university education.

It was, he thought, as if in May 68 the awareness of the historicity of every present, to use Gadamers phrasing, manifested itself massively on the public scene accompanied by a lot of noise and tumult. A manifestation in the guise of a contestation of authority and especially also of educational authority i.e. the authority which is related to the relation between the younger and the older generation and concerns the way in which we have to understand a valuable human life. Indeed, not only was the hope for a better and just world connected to education, as was often the case before, but simultaneously, and that was new, the central role of authority in education was attacked. It was attacked both theoretically and practically (he recalls all the experiments of anti-authoritarian education at different levels, all the contestation of himself and his fellow students against their parents, teachers, pastors, politicians).

Mariette Hellemans – who had studied with Eugeen Fink (the disciple of Husserl and close colleague of Heidegger) and was trained in phenomenology – invited him to write his master thesis on the idea of critique in Max Horkheimer's essay 'Critical and Traditional Theory,' considered to be one of the main texts of the early Frankfurt School. In order to engage in this work he enrolled in a special philosophy program and attended a course by J.M. Broeckman, a then famous philosopher of law. It was this event that initiated him into the world of philosophy for good and offered the occasion to meet up with early critical theory. The course was in fact a comment on a footnote out of Horkheimers essay: "Es muss nicht so sein, die Menschen können das Sein ändern, die Umstände dafür sind jetzt vorhanden" (Things must not be as they are, human beings are able to change Being, the conditions for change are actually present). From this course the man learned that it is indeed possible to comment during twelve two-hours sessions on one footnote of a few words, that attending somebody who really thinks in public can transform the listening public into a thinking public even if it is not invited to say a single word, that it is, hence, totally false to create an opposition between the lecturer who would be active and the listener who be just a passive receiver, and of course he would never forget the words anymore. The words resonated with the times, the era of emancipation and liberation, where students en masse enrolled in educational studies in order to be able to play a role in this emancipation and liberation movement. They resonated more particularly with the thoughts and practices of the German critical emancipatory pedagogy of Klaus Mollenhauer and Wolfgang Klafki which Mariette Hellemans started to introduce into the course program of educational sciences and which offered the man a basic educational thought frame that would never leave him anymore.

It is also she who invited the man to become an assistant at the Centre for Foundations of Education and to start a PhD research on Jurgen Habermas' theory of communicative action and on the way it affects foundational ideas about speech and dialogue in education. In the early eighties he starts to delve into the rich history of Critical Theory and of Emancipatory and Critical Pedagogy in Germany. In the summer semester of 1984 the man is in Frankfurt am Main as a student of Habermas. It is the period where Habermas is working and lecturing on his 'Philosophical discourse of Modernity.' At the same time he invites many of his opponents to Frankfurt: Pierre Bourdieu, Jacques Derrida, Stephen Toulmin, K.O. Apel and many others appear in his Monday seminars. On Tuesdays he attends also his seminar on 'Communicative Action and Moral Consciousness.' One year later he will drive in his small car every Monday morning 350km from Leuven to Frankfurt, and 350km back in the evening to attend Habermas and Apels seminars and lectures on communicative ethics. And it happens that later in the week he drives another 300km to Paris, to dwell around in the bookstores but also to attend some seminars of Alain Touraine. All these seminars were at once overwhelming (he felt often totally lost and sometimes paralyzed) and fascinating and inspiring. And of course, he learned a lot. They made him discover in practice and in theory the fundamental role of power, dialogue and speech in educational practices, they confronted him with the challenge how to think and conceive more particularly dialogue and speech in the context of educational relations which always seemed to rest on inequality (the teacher/parent in relation to the pupil/child) and to imply the operation of hidden power structures. These were challenges he would confront in his PhD through a reading of the work of Habermas, Arendt and Buber, in discussing German critical emancipatory education and arguing on Wittgenstein with his then colleague and friend Paul Smeyers. It were the challenges which would bring him through the brilliant teaching of Mariette Hellemans, who he assisted over many years, to Levinas and back again to Buber, before he would go other ways occasioned by his reading of Rancière's *Maître Ignorant* (Ignorant Schoolmaster) with his students in the nineties.

But maybe all this was not the most important. What seems now maybe more important was that he apparently felt in love with the particular practices and places itself (lectures, seminars, conversations), with the way he could be in these places and practices: devoted to and absorbed by an issue, engaged in a common concern. In fact he realizes, that this is related to what Mariette Hellemans taught him through the way she embodied academic life: that the (critical) role the university has to play in society has to be related in the first place to the scene of teaching itself (and not to study as such). And he must confess to himself that he still loves to attend these places and practices, that he still feels a slight thrill and curiosity passing the threshold of the lecture hall or the seminar room, never knowing exactly what is going to happen, feeling exposed. Today, the man would say that this practice of attending lectures and seminars, which were essentially open for everyone interested, has offered him the crucial experience of these particular pedagogical forms of gathering a public and of public thinking where people are turned into students and professors (as in the lecture) or all into students (as in the seminar). And where matter (words, things, practices) becomes public matter, is getting authority and makes us hesitate and slow down in order to have a closer look, develop a better, different or more elaborated look and in order to think about it. Public gatherings, collective experiments that install hesitations, temporally suspend institutional positions and personal opinions, turn things into matter that provokes (public) thinking and discussion. Of course, sometimes during lectures and seminars he was overwhelmed, often also bored and absent, but there were always again those moments where something and some ones seemed to be really at stake.

And there is this other place he attended: the cinema. Indeed, the move away from his small hometown offered him also a sudden and unprecedented easy access to (bookshops and) cinema and the discovery of the movies of Italian neo-realism, the nouvelle vague and the surrealists (Bunuel, Fellini, Pasolini, Rossellini, Antonioni, Visconti, Truffaut, Godard, Rohmer, Rivette, and so on). It is of course a somewhat different place than the one of lectures and seminars, but it seems to him that it at least allowed for an experience which is strongly related to the one in lectures and seminars and which maybe can be called a basic educational experience. The experience which the Belgian filmmakers the Dardenne brothers would much later describe to him as the experience where we forget regular time, where we lose even the company of ourselves and give up our usual vigilance, where we are brought as close as possible to our birth, to the silence of the beginning, where all images and judgments which made up our existence are for a moment suspended, where a different world can become alive, start to speak, where we can become for a moment someone different, someone which we can bring to silence again upon leaving the cinema, but someone which we could also allow to converse with us and with others about the world which was disclosed. And yes, when he thinks about it now, cinema and film altered him and have disclosed him the world, and he is surprised that he even thinks that only that world, the world that appears on the wall, is the real world, or better, the world 'as such.'

WALKING CITY LANDSCAPES: E-DUCATING THE GAZE

Being educated in the tradition of phenomenological existentialism, critical theory and critical emancipatory educational theory, he started to teach at the university at the end of the eighties. He tried to develop an idea of education as a 'responsive communicative action of doing justice' (rather than a productive intentional goal oriented action) and adhered to a longstanding critical tradition which conceives of the practice of philosophy (of education) primarily as a work of judgment (separating between valid/not-valid; right/wrong, etc.) or de-mystification (revealing what is underlying or supposed i.e. denouncing illusions). In a certain way, this tradition defines the public as people that lack enlightenment, that is, the appropriate knowledge (or the appropriate awareness, criteria, virtues, etc.). In that sense, it continues the inaugural gesture that lies at the basis of Plato's cave allegory: making a difference between those in the darkness of the cave and those in the bright light of the sun affirming that those in the cave need the philosopher to lead them towards the light. However, by the end of the nineties this philosophical gesture had become increasingly and patently questioned by so-called post-structuralism and post-foundationalism that seemed to demonstrate that it was impossible to get out of context, history and culture and that power relations reign everywhere. This made that the critical gesture more explicitly turned into a de-constructing and explanatory one, demonstrating exactly that and how we are all captured by language, embedded within cultures and histories, disciplined by omnipresent power structures. It therefore seemed often to lead to a nihilist impotence, bearable through feeling better than the others (who wrongly believed to have foundations or who were not aware of their assumptions).

Being very tired of being a critic and de-constructer and not knowing what exactly to do with his students, the man was invited, early 2002, by his friend, the architect Wim Cuyvers, to join him in a trip to Sarajevo. Almost 40 hours in a bus with a mixed group of students from architecture and educational sciences towards a devastated city to have students walk along arbitrary lines and think about the design of a school. It turned out to be the start of a new practice, constructing a new gaze. Ever since he travelled every year, often with Wim, or his other friend

Jorge Larrosa, with post-graduate students for 10 to 14 days to post-conflict cities (Sarajevo, Belgrade, Tirana, Bucharest, Kinshasa), non-tourist megapoles in China (Shenzhen, Chongqing), small banal cities (St-Claude, Kortrijk) and recently, on invitation, to an iconic city (Rio de Janeiro). Students are asked to walk day and night along arbitrary lines drawn on city maps. Lines starting and leading nowhere particularly, lines without plan, crossing at random neighborhoods, buildings, areas. Along these lines they map their observations and register parameters. He equally walks along these lines and every day, during long talks at night he asks each of them very simple questions: What have you seen? What have you heard? What do you think about it? What do you make of it? At the end of the travel students have to present in the streets somewhere in the city their 'design.'

In September 2003 the man organized a five day seminar in La Bâtie (French Vercors). Jorge Larrosa, Gert Biesta, Norbert Ricken, Ilan Gur Ze'ev, Wim Cuyvers and Maarten Simons participated in an exercise which started from viewing two movies of Rossellini (Europa 51 and Europa Anno Zero) in order to talk about education in the present conditions and in order to explore various educational practices: conversation, studying, recognizing, displacing, responding, and indeed also walking. The intensive talks helped him to clarify and articulate what was at stake in these practices and in the city walks. At first, he had no idea at all of what he was engaging in. He had simply accepted the invitation to go to Sarajevo, to leave the institutional space of the university and try to find other ways to deal with education, with students, with the world at a moment that he was in fact very close to step out of the academic life altogether. Now he thinks that it was the point where he started to deviate, where he got the sense that indeed other practices were possible, where his being enclosed in this dead end of a critical position that does nothing more than judging others and asking others to justify their claims in order to demonstrate that they are in fact unable to do so (since there seem to be no ultimate foundations possible, only historical, social or cultural ones) was getting loosened so that new thoughts could come to his mind and he could start to think differently. Indeed they could come to his mind and not out of his mind because he got exposed (out-of-position) himself. And he realizes that this had nothing to do with his intention to be exposed or 'open,' but that it had to do with the material, social and intellectual conditions that characterized more of less unintentionally the trip to Sarajevo which made him exposed and vulnerable. It were conditions which he reconstructed gradually only later on and then tried to produce more consciously in the subsequent city-walks. He can mention a few and hopes to once be able to write more extensively about it. First of all, he had no idea where they were going. Of course he knew things about the history, the war, etc. But he had never been there and was far from being an expert in the history of the Balkans or the educational policy of Sarajevo. It was thus impossible to take the position of the guide who explains what you encounter and relates it to history, culture or social conditions. Moreover, he had no idea of the kind of design that the students would have to come up with in response to what they encountered and registered during their walks, he could not lead them towards an outcome. In fact, the only thing he did do was offering them a protocol (go along the lines and stay as close as possible to these lines, days and nights, make detailed maps of what you observe, take notes of your encounters) and helping them to keep to the protocol. There was the relative 'seclusion' strengthening the sense of being away: no internet, no google-maps, no mobile phone network available or very expensive. There was nothing really to see, at least from a tourist standpoint, the only more or less 'famous' building being the library which had burned during the war, on the other hand: a lot of devastated buildings, most facades plenty of bullet traces, the war written in stone and even more terrible than the ruins. There was the exhaustion, both of him and the students (40 hours bus drive, walking day and night, talking day and night). There were the poor living conditions which he shared with the students: rooms of 4 or 6, collective shower, no heating (with still snow outside). In fact all this made it that he and his students were more or less in equal position, more or less disarmed. He was surprised that it produced also a way of speaking with the students which was no longer about explanations, arguments and positions, being right or wrong, but, as Jorge Larrosa clarified to him, about regarding and conversing, about finding the right words. And later he learned that it was also interesting to have students or colleagues joining in the walks who spoke no Dutch, so that he had to speak another language, again something that helped to weaken his position. None of these conditions was decisive as such, but they contributed to make him (just as they did to the students) vulnerable and exposed, to be in a different position and relation towards students, towards himself and towards the world. As he mentioned already, it created conditions making it possible that new thoughts could come to his mind, that his intentions and urge to judge were suspended and that he could start to imagine a kind of critical thought that would intensify the possibilities within existence.

EXPLORING CAVES: FROM POSTMODERN ENLIGHTENMENT TO PREHISTORIC DARKNESS

It was during his first years at the university that the man learnt about caves. Plato's famous cave time and again recalled and discussed in his various philosophy and education courses. The caves of the age old wall paintings in southern Europe (Altamira, Lascaux) through the brief texts and films of Marguerite Duras and Georges Bataille discovered more or less by accident. But it was also the time in which he was invited by a student friend to join a caving club and to participate in their weekly cave explorations. In the karstic regions of Belgium at first, but later on throughout Europe. It was the beginning of a passion which has not left him ever since. During many years he spent almost every week at least some hours, more often many hours, underground. He discovered the hostile but fascinating world of caves and underground rivers, the marvels of rock walls, big chambers, deep pitches, small passages and got intrigued by the cave experiments 'out-of-time' of Michel Siffre. Later on, the search to explore caves brought him also to the most spectacular and beautiful landscapes of China and Vietnam, and occasioned a decisive encounter with caver-architect Wim Cuyvers.

The man realizes that his passion for caves has not only brought him to often remote and beautiful places as well as hostile fascinating environments, but that it made him also develop a desire for physical effort, even exhaustion, that it generated a longing for exploration of the unknown, for living and moving in uncomfortable conditions, that it formed the way he goes about things, also in his research and teaching, that it even is shaping the way in which he is travelling and walking with students in cities all over the world.

And although caves and caving have, thus, been very present throughout his life, it is only within the last years that it came clearly to his mind that, even if being strongly attracted by philosophy and by this movement of enlightening and liberation as ascending that is so powerful imagined in Plato's cave allegory, he has always looked for the opposite movement: to enter caves, longing to wander around in them even if they are, indeed, inhabitable and rather hostile. Exploring them in the light of a small lamp and relying only on the force of his body, the power of his senses and the company of his fellow cavers. And in fact, it was another man, Maarten Simons, a man who earlier had made him know Foucault as an unexpected great 'friend,' and who became in fact himself a friend, who now also helped him to discover that exactly this movement might be related to his other passion, the passion for the university and the school itself as particular places of education. Both strongly related to the adventure of humankind and the exploration and disclosure of worlds.

Philosophy had, thus, something with caves. Indeed philosophy and philosophy of education seemed to find in Plato's cave allegory their common inaugurating story, founding their own necessity and especially the necessity of the presence of a master. The story, as he knew, offers a scene of impotence: (wo)men chained in darkness, trapped in sheer appearances, who at the hand of the philosopher, who breaks their chains, have to turn around and ascend to the light, leaving the cave behind and going to a world beyond. The turn being in fact a return to the world out of which (wo)men had fallen into the final darkness of a disastrous condition. This philosophical story is basically a story to maintain the sovereignty of Being and especially also of the master as the one who is needed to lead the human being from the darkness to the light.

Foucault – in the lectures he had been given on the hermeneutics of the subject at the Collège de France, which the man heard from the tapes, and which he considers to be one of the greatest lectures on/of philosophy of/as education, to which he returns time and again – had taught him already that this conversion of the immortal soul ('epistrophé') towards the 'true world' of ideas as the source of light and being, was to be contrasted to the conversion of the immortal soul towards God in Christianity ('metanoia'). A conversion which is equally based on a distinction between two worlds: the bright reign of God and the dark reign of the devil. And, more crucially, for it opened up a different way to approach philosophy of/as education, Foucault had taught him about a third form of conversion: the conversion of the mortal soul to herself in the ancient form of 'care for the self' or self-education ('epimeleia') – a conversion which is based on a distinction between what is not depending upon us and what is depending upon us. This care for the self didn't imply the withdrawal of oneself from the world but required precisely an acceptance of that world and a focusing on one's relation to the present world (rather than on the attempt to escape or get delivered from it). It didn't rest on a scene of impotence or transcendence which affirmed the exclusive value of the light or the divine order, but on a belief in the absence of any pre-existing order and any human destination and thus on the recognition of the value of shadow and on the affirmation of the central role of (self-)formation or 'epimeleia' in the undestined adventure of humankind. It was finally Marie José Mondzain who helped him to understand that he could maybe relate this scene to another cave story. A story, or phantasia as Mondzain (2007) calls it, which he would like to call the educational story of the cave, to be distinguished from the philosophical one. The story of the beings that enter the cave to paint on its walls, offering a scene of the education of the human being as a scene of potency and immanence. One that speaks to his own yearlong experience in entering and wandering around in caves. One that is not reducing the caves and the activities within them immediately to symbolic places and symbolic activities. One that starts from a phenomenology of the cave and of the time-space experiences related to entering and dwelling around in them, one that takes the activities of entering and painting first as gestures instead of symbolic actions, one that offers a different scene of the (self-)education of the human being.

Mondzain bases her fiction mainly on the findings related to the rather recent discovery of the Chauvet cave in the French Ardêche region which contains the oldest wall paintings of the world (approximately 32,000 BC), paintings extremely well conserved and of an extraordinary beauty. Paintings made in such an ingenious way, that in the light of torches they become moving images. The cave as the first cinema. Based on these findings Mondzain constructs a 'phantasia' which is not telling the story of a return of 'man' to the light of eternal truth which is shining from behind him. The 'man' of the Chauvet cave enters the cave and produces light with his own hands and to his own hands. It is these enlightened hands which will reveal their power or capacity to make an image, including an image of his hands. The image of a being which becomes at once the spectator of the work of his hands, not simply as an object or tool, but precisely as an image, thereby inaugurating the human gaze on the human being and on the world. Men's eyes were not from the outset destined for contemplation, thinking and regard. It is to these images made by the hand in the cave that we owe it, so Mondzain teaches him, to have eyes that open themselves to the world in an incomparable way. These image-building operations make the world visible in a new way, they make ourselves visible in a new way. To see oneself is always to see oneself at and from a distance, in the cave however this seeing is not seeing oneself from the mirroring water surface or from the reflection in the eye of the other, but from an image on a wall. And Mondzain further tells him: In the cave, the hand is not taking or hewing or carving, not performing the gestures for survival but changes its use and destination, thereby demonstrating a sort of sovereign de-adaptation: it is depositing paint on the wall. The hand marks a distance which it will propose to the eyes and which will also change their use. The hand produces before the eyes the object of the first gaze, it makes visible and this making articulates itself in plain autonomy. It is not about the meaning of an object, but about the sense of the gesture, articulating us as beings who have the task and potency to humanize themselves.

And he thinks that it is a truly fascinating story. The cave as a scene of potency and immanence, neither a prison or hell, nor a temple of the gods, but a limited, particular walled space, where light is made and images are projected on a wall (without horizon and 'out of time'). Images of the hands, but also images of animals and landscapes. The hands no longer objects or tools, no longer submitted to regular use. The animals no longer prey or danger, taken out of the cycle of reproduction and survival, naked and beautiful. Not the idea 'horse,' but an image which is made and contains a profanation and suspension of the 'horse' in its natural or social environment. The images offered for thinking and for exploring different ways to deal with oneself and the world, at a distance. Not from the top of a mountain, offering an overview that inspires phantasies of conquest or offers sights that inspire awe, but a distance at hands. And now the man realizes that here we have not only a truly educational cave story but the origin of a school history, the origin of an experience of potentiality. What is missing to turn the first 'cinema' in a school is not the master that leads out of the cave, but the pedagogue that leads towards the cave and the teacher that not only projects on the wall, but turns the wall also into the surface of a table where the image can become the subject of a conversation, where words are added to the image, not to explain them but to name them, making them into a thing (that starts to 'speak'). The school not offering a mirror or a window, but walls! Walls that shape time and space outside the 'natural' time and the 'natural' environment, walls that offer the world 'at hand' and make an experience of 'being able' possible, of being able to think and to take one's life in one's hands. Which is not the recognition of an 'essence' or a 'destination,' but an experience of the present, 'now' (main-tenant), of the con-tact in the darkness of the cave (within the shadow of the light of the torch). And so, at his surprise, his passion for caves seems to join his passion for the university and the school.

THINKING AND WRITING WITH FRIENDS

Of course many more things could be mentioned that shaped his intellectual life: the circumstance to have been at the crossroad of French, German and Anglosaxon thought and traditions, to have to inhabit, read and write always different languages, to be almost permanently 'in translation.' But there are two things he feels which have to be mentioned more particularly. First, he remembers Heinrich von Kleist's famous statement that thoughts do come to one's mind through talking to others ("l'idée vient en parlant"). For von Kleist these others can be anyone. And from his experience with all kinds of 'publics' or audiences and certainly also from his conversations with students and colleagues, he agrees. But, and that is the second point, there is something more to say about particular others and a particular experience. Indeed, he increasingly came to experience that it is impossible to talk, to think and write alone about the things that are really of interest and really matter. Another, maybe the only name for that experience is friendship. Friendship is not about intimacy or privacy. It is a worldly experience; for friends the world becomes something of a concern, something to think about, something that provokes experimentation and writing. Is a philosophy of education, as far as it faces the world, possible without friendship? And of course, philosophy and friendship have been coupled to each other time and again, and in many very different ways, also in his case and engaging various young and old friends, nearby and around the world. But looking back he notices that in his case this impossibility of philosophy without friendship articulated itself more peculiarly in two kinds of joint exercises. First, through the city walks, as a space and time for friendship, as joint exercises of shared exposition and thought, especially with Wim Cuyvers and Jorge Larrosa. And secondly, maybe even more surprisingly within 'philosophy' – it seems indeed as if only few examples exist, Deleuze et Guattari being maybe the most famous one – through the exercise of joint writing, especially with Maarten Simons. Indeed, his writings have often been shared exercises, not 'his,' or better, not his alone, although it has never been, institutionally, more strongly required to indicate and claim one's own contribution. And he has frequently been asked how it works. But he can only say that it is truly joint writing, that maybe the new technology helps, and repeat that he experiences it as the articulation of a friendship, a time and space for friendship which however risks to be banalized under the changing conditions of academic life. And he liked it when Walter Kohan compared it to the Dardenne brothers, the Coen and Tavianni brothers, maybe again no coincidence: examples out of cinema.

BECOMING A PEDAGOGUE (THROUGH PHILOSOPHY)?

As he recalled before, he got an education as philosopher and pedagogue. And although he has never been really sure about what either of these 'titles' precisely meant, for a long time it sounded more serious to him to be considered as a philosopher (even if one dealing with education and therefore maybe not a 'real' one). However, since the turn of the century this started to shift fundamentally. The walks with students made him re-discover this beautiful meaning of education as e-ducere, taking by the hand and leading out. And the conversations with his colleagues and students, with his old and young friends ('Paul, René et les autres') against this background brought him back to Isocrates, who is commonly known as the founder of the school as a particular place of 'scholè,' and especially also to the original meaning of the pedagogue: the slave who accompanied youngsters to the school as a place and time of study and exercise. And now that he learned how 'school' can be conceived not as an institution (which in fact is mostly a taming of school) but as a form of gathering in a place of 'free time,' out-of-(regular)-time, out of the natural environment, where the world is profanated, dis-closed and can be attended, is at a distance, at hand and an experience of being able is possible, now that he learned that 'school' is a cave, now he can find himself not only in the idea of e-ducere, but, finally, with enthusiasm, in being a pedagogue: leading out of the home into the world i.e. leading to school. And no, pedagogues don't lead youngsters to a particular predefined goal, they don't practice the art of making others into some kind of (ideal) persons, or make them acquire predefined competences, or reach certain levels of development. Pedagogues do not help to 'develop,' they simply lead to a particular e-ducational place and help to make and protect that place, they engage in the art of making 'scholè.' And of course, he knows that there is "the usual passivity and dispassion that prevails in classrooms in schools and especially also in universities around the world." And he concedes that the university "is rarely a place to perpetuate the revolutionary desires of a young generation, that the tenure position can be a sleeping pill of comfortable living, and that the main arguments are now about the protections of the privileges of students and professors" (Kishik, 2012). However, he not only believes that within these institutions (and often despite them) there are still strong moments where lectures and seminars operate as educational spaces, where people are turned into students and matter becomes public matter (and he has to mention the Friday-seminars and the London-Leuven ones). But it became also obvious for him and for his friend, with whom he is writing about these things, that especially today it is worthwhile not just to defend such places, but especially also to try to invent and experiment with new forms of 'scholè,' to find new ways to enter caves and 'make' caves, to invent and experiment with new disciplines of mind and body, with new forms of gatherings and new ways of leading out. It became obvious that philosophy of/as education is in need of laboratories and fieldwork, in need of an academic community as a community of people sharing the exposition towards the present, whose speaking together is no imitation of war with other means, who do not so much share a language, doctrine or method, but have in common an experimental ethos putting themselves to the test. He now tends to declare that it is worthwhile to be a pedagogue, to be devoted to philosophy as education. And he confirms his commitment to the invention of forms of free time for all, and to the belief that there is no (predefined or 'natural') destination, but that the human being can be called with some reason an animal educandum.

FAVORITE WORKS

Favorites from My Own Work

Masschelein, J., & Wimmer, M. (1996). *Alterität, Plularität, Gerechtigkeit. Randgänge der Pädagogik.* Sankt Augustin: Academia.

Masschelein, J., & Simons, M. (2002). An adequate education in a globalised world? A note on immunisation against being-together. *Journal of Philosophy of Education, 36*(4), 589-608.

Simons, M., & Masschelein, J. (2008). From schools to learning environments: The dark side of being exceptional. *Journal of philosophy of education, 42*(3-4), 687-704.

Masschelein, J., & Simons, M. (2009). From active citizenship to world citizenship: A proposal for a world university. *European Educational Research Journal, 8*(2), 236-248.

Masschelein, J., & Simons, M. (2010). *Jenseits der Exzellenz. Eine kleine Morphologie der Welt-Universität.* Regensburg: Diaphanes.

Masschelein, J., & Simons, M. (2010). The hatred of public schooling: The school as the mark of democracy. *Educational Philosophy and Theory, 42*(5-6), 666-682.

Masschelein, J. (2010). The idea of critical E-ducational research-E-ducating the gaze and inviting to go walking. In I. Gur-Ze'ev (Ed.), *The possibility/impossibility of a new critical language in education* (Chapt. 13, pp. 275-292). Rotterdam/Boston/Taipei: Sense Publishers.

Masschelein, J., & Simons, M. (2011). The university: A public issue. In R. Barnett, *The future university: Ideas and possibilities* (Chapt. 13. pp. 165-177). New York: Taylor and Francis.

Masschelein, J. (2011). Experimentum Scholae: The world once more ... But not (yet) finished. *Studies in Philosophy and Education, 30*(5), 529-535.

Masschelein, J. (2012). Inciting an attentive experimental ethos and creating a laboratory setting. *Zeitschrift für Pädagogik, 58*(3), 354-370.

Masschelein, J., & Simons, M. (2013). *In defence of the school. A public issue.* Leuven: E-ducation, Culture & Society Publishers.

Influential Works

Agamben, G. (1993). *Infancy and history. Essays on the destruction of experience.* London: Verso.

Arendt, H. (1958). *The human condition.* Chicago/London: University of Chicago Press

Arendt, H. (1977). *Between past and future. Eight exercises in political thought.* New York: Penguin.

Buber, M. (1925/1962). Über das Erzieherische. In M. Buber, *Werke I. Schriften zur Philosophie* (pp. 787-808). Heidelberg: Lambert Schneider Verlag.

Deligny, F. (2007). *Oeuvres* (Ed. S. Alavarez de Toledo). Paris: L'Arachnéen.

Foucault, M. (1981/2005). *The hermeneutics of the subject: Lectures at the Collège de France 1981-1982* (Ed. Fréderic. Gros, Trans. Graham Burchell). New York: Palgrave Macmillan.

Freire, P. (1970). *Pedagogy of the oppressed.* New York: Herder and Herder.

Habermas, J. (1971). *Knowledge and human interests.* Boston: Beacon Press.

Horkheimer, M. (1937/1977). Kritische und traditionelle Theorie. In A. Schmidt (Ed.), *Max Horkheimer. Kritische Theorie* (pp. 521-575). Frankfurt/M: Fischer.

Mollenhauer, Kl. (1972). *Theorien zum Erziehungsprozess.* München: Juventa.

Rancière, J. (1987/1991). *The ignorant schoolmaster. Five lessons in intellectual emancipation* (Transl. K. Ross). Stanford, CA: Stanford University Press.

Sartre, J. P. (1946). *L'existentialisme est un humanisme.* Paris: Nagel.

REFERENCES

Foucault, M. (1985). *The use of pleasure. The history of sexuality,* Vol. 2. New York: Pantheon.

Kishik, D. (2012). *The power of life: Agamben and the coming politics.* Stanford, CA: Stanford University Press.

Mondzain, M. J. (2007). *Homo spectator.* Paris: Bayard.

PETER ROBERTS

AN ACCIDENT WAITING TO HAPPEN

Reflections on a Philosophical Life in Education

INTRODUCTION

My journey into the field of philosophy of education might be described as an accident waiting to happen. As a university student in the early 1980s I enrolled in two Stage One Education papers not with any well-developed professional plan but because the material sounded interesting and the lectures were at times that worked well with my other courses. I initially had no intention of going on to further study in the subject. By the end of that year, I had formed a clear view that I wanted to major in Education. I subsequently completed courses in sociology of education, history of education, comparative education, and other areas of educational study, but philosophy of education was my main focus. A Masters degree, and later a doctorate, followed and now, decades on, I find myself still seeking the forms of understanding philosophy of education can bring. In one sense, then, this is a story of a chance decision taken more than thirty years ago; a story that might very well never have been told. Yet, with the opportunity for self-reflection afforded here, I can see that the 'accidental' path I've taken is one I was always going to take, in some form or another. As a child, I loved to read and to think; I had questions about the meaning of life that demanded answers; and I was troubled by situations, events and interactions that seemed, to my young mind, to be unfair, inconsistent or unhelpful. Philosophy of education has aided me greatly in the process of searching that started early in my life, but this remains very much an incomplete project. In the discussion that follows I set out to show why this is so.

SCHOOLING AND UNIVERSITY EXPERIENCES

The oldest of four children, I grew up in Auckland, New Zealand in the 1960s and 1970s. My time at primary school was pivotal in shaping my later educational development. The school I attended for most of my primary years was in a small semi-rural, working class town northwest of central Auckland. Several teachers at the school provided pedagogical models that still influence my educational thinking today. One was quiet and caring, demonstrating the distinctive power of gentleness that I would later come to appreciate through reading the *Tao Te Ching* (Lao Tzu, 1963). Another allowed unusual degrees of independence for students, bearing witness to the significance of trust and responsibility in teaching and learning. Such notions, I would discover in due course, were key elements in the pedagogy of Paulo Freire (Freire, 1972, 1998a, 1998b; Freire & Shor, 1987; Horton & Freire, 1990). While not without some periods of difficulty, those years were, overall, the happiest in my schooling life. It was not merely the school teachers I encountered who contributed to my education; equally significant were my family experiences, the friendships I developed, and the myriad activities of boyhood – hut-building, fishing for eels in the river, wandering far and wide, tennis, athletics, and so on – that collectively, and often silently, taught me how to begin trying to make sense of a complex world. My parents were tireless in their service to the wider community, their own example speaking more insistently to we children about our ethical obligations to others than any words could express. From my friends, with their varied backgrounds, I came to see that solidarity, commitment and companionship could be built across class and ethnic lines, even if I could not have articulated our relationships in exactly that way at the time. During these formative years, I also developed a love of literature that continues to the present day. I recall reading some books from our school library multiple times, swept up in the adventures they described and already seeking out other places, other modes of life, in my child's mind.

I was not a 'bookish' child; equally, I was not one of those boys who regarded reading and study as a waste of time, as something for 'sissies.' Whatever I was doing, whether it was reading, writing, running, riding, talking, or listening, I found it hard to stop thinking, pondering, wondering. I wanted to know: Why are we here? What is our purpose in life? Is there a God? What happens to us after we die? How can we strive to be good? How can we best understand ourselves, others and the world? What should we do when we see or experience injustice? I did not formulate such questions in precisely those terms, but my musings were broadly along these lines. Where some of my friends seemed content to let life 'wash over them,' I tended to mull things over at greater length. When I thought I had done something wrong, I would worry about it, sometimes losing sleep over what would now appear to be trivial incidents. I also found myself getting upset when I saw someone else being hurt. The passing of decades can warp recollections of this kind, and there is always a danger of distorting events to make them fit with our current analytical categories. Nevertheless, there are some experiences, some thoughts and feelings, that never leave us, and I can still recall specific events that seemed to show, in a manner comprehensible to a child, just how perplexing and difficult life could be.

If I needed further proof of my vaguely formed convictions about life as a process involving a good deal of searching and struggle, my experience of high school provided it for me. My memories of that period in my educational history are mostly unpleasant, though not without some redeeming features. The journey to and from school each day involved a lengthy bus ride on dusty roads, with a substantial delay before the afternoon departure. In my first year at high school I had a science form class, meaning the school classroom was off-limits before and after school, and during lunchtimes and other breaks. We had to stay outside, regardless of the weather. The physical discomfort created by these realities, while mild compared with the challenges faced by many, was accompanied by other concerns of a more emotional kind. Almost all my friends from primary school had gone elsewhere for their secondary education, making high school a lonely place, and these were difficult years for other personal reasons as well. There were, however, some sincere and dedicated teachers in different classes, and from them I acquired a keener sense of the seriousness of study and pedagogy. Teaching, I could see, involved a total commitment of one's body, soul and mind. Teaching could be exhilarating but it could also be exhausting. If it wasn't hard to see why so many students found high school alienating, it also wasn't too difficult to appreciate the courage that must have been required by some teachers in continuing to turn up to their classes, day after day, year after year. While my sense of well-being improved at the senior secondary school level, there is much I would rather forget from this period of my life. Of course, that too has been an educational lesson: memories may fade, but one can never fully forget. Part of the despair of education, as I have argued elsewhere (Roberts, 2013d, 2013e), lies precisely in this: it does not allow us to go back. We cannot return to a state we have left behind but must learn to live with the new forms of understanding education brings, distressing though this may be.

Existentially, high school was troubling, but in academic terms I was fine, and having gained an A Bursary I was ready to begin the next phase of my formal education at the University of Auckland. It was hardly a promising start, with a first year spent on a degree to which I was manifestly ill-suited (a BCom) and mixed success in my examinations. Thereafter I resolved to take the riskier path, switching to a BA degree, with a suite of courses in English, Geography, Anthropology – and Education. The last of these subjects, as noted in the introduction to this chapter, was selected more by chance than design. One of the two Education courses I took was largely devoted to educational psychology; the other was an introduction to Western educational thought. The latter course would prove pivotal in setting me on the path toward a life committed to philosophy of education. The course was taught by Colin Lankshear and Jim Marshall. My tutor was Michael Peters. It was a course of the kind we seldom see these days: a history of educational ideas, beginning with Plato and ending with Freire, having examined Rousseau, Dewey, R.S. Peters, and others along the way. Fascinated by what I discovered in that Stage One Education course, I made a decision to major in Education, and by the end of my second year in the subject was already beginning to ask how I might make this my life's work. In completing my studies in Education at undergraduate level, I had the good fortune to be taught by a number of excellent scholars from different fields, but philosophical concerns remained to the fore.

Philosophy of education appealed not because it was easy but because it was difficult. Immersion in philosophical work enabled me to challenge some of my hitherto untested assumptions about the social world. I felt uncomfortable yet right at home, as if my life to date – the reading completed, the questions asked, the decisions made, the actions taken, and the relationships formed – had been working towards this moment. I put tremendous effort into my essays for philosophy of education courses, reading, thinking, agonising over what I wanted to say and how I wanted to say it. We learned how to construct and deconstruct an argument, how to unpack educational concepts, and how to compare different theoretical positions. The demands of philosophy of education were exacting but there was, at least in my experience at the University of Auckland, also considerable freedom to explore new ideas. One could be creative but within certain limits, and always with a view to upholding the highest standards of academic rigour.

We were encouraged to read and discuss radical analyses of schooling but also did not ignore liberal and conservative accounts. Works by deschoolers such as Illich (1971) and Marxists such as Harris (1979, 1982) were studied, but due attention was also paid to Peters, Hirst, and others in the analytic tradition of philosophical inquiry (Dearden, Hirst, & Peters, 1972; Hirst, 1974; Peters, 1970, 1973). (For an insightful account of the impact of the analytic revolution in philosophy of education, see Waks, 2008.) Postmodern and post-structuralist currents of critical thought were, in Education at any rate, rather less visible at that stage. A more mature reading of Dewey (1966, 1997), Scheffler (1960), and other influential North American figures would also have to wait until later. There were brief forays into original works by Marx (Marx, 1964, 1976; Marx & Engels, 1972), but these too were unfinished journeys. We ventured beyond philosophy of education to consider a number of thinkers who were better known as psychologists (e.g., Fromm, 1942) and sociologists (e.g., Althusser, 1971; Bourdieu & Passeron, 1977; Bowles & Gintis, 1976; Sharp, 1980; Willis, 1977). Among the teachers with whom I studied there was already a strong commitment to social justice in education, and that was to develop further with new appointments in the 1990s.

While this process of intellectual formation was underway, I was simultaneously gaining other forms of life experience, working in a number of different jobs – as a caster in a pottery factory, shoe making, and house hauling, among others – on a part-time or temporary basis. I sometimes regret that I wasn't able to continue with an existence of that kind, engaging in both manual and mental labour for extended periods of time, the different activities complementing each other. It is easy to romanticise such notions, but there is an important connection, I would argue, between different forms of craftsmanship, where struggle and sweat and tension can co-exist with concentration, skill and careful attention to detail to produce something beautiful – whether this is in the form of a shoe, a piece of pottery, a building, or an academic paper (cf. Roberts & Freeman-Moir, 2013). My experiences on factory floors taught me a good deal about education and the politics of difference; about the links between social class, ethnicity and educational aspirations. Far from resenting the hours I spent pouring liquid clay into plaster moulds, operating leather presses, and preparing houses for removal, I relished the time I devoted to these activities. A less than ideal start to my university studies had turned out to be a blessing in disguise, not only in allowing the 'accident' of finding my way into Education to happen but also in opening up more space for other forms of work, other life experiences outside the academy.

Encouraged by my results in the final year of my undergraduate study, I proceeded directly on to a Masters degree. My courses in the first year of the degree had a sociological and revolutionary flavour as well as an emphasis on the philosophical study of education. One course, unusually for the time (this was the mid-1980s), was entirely devoted to the work of Michel Foucault, with a particular focus on *Discipline and Punish* (Foucault, 1979) and the collection of essays and interviews published under the title *Power/Knowledge* (Foucault, 1980). My Masters thesis addressed Paulo Freire's concept of conscientisation and was supervised by Colin Lankshear, who had inspired me as a teacher from my first contact with him several years earlier. This was the beginning of a research programme of nearly three decades. As it turned out, Freire was then at the cusp of his most productive period as a writer, authoring a series of co-authored dialogical books and multiple sole-authored volumes over the last decade of his life (Freire, 1993, 1994, 1996, 1998a, 1998b, 1998c; Freire & Faundez, 1989; Freire & Shor, 1987; Horton & Freire, 1990). There would be no shortage of material for reflection and critical engagement.

I never regarded myself as a 'follower' of Freire, let alone a 'disciple' of him (see Roberts, 2010). Instead, from the beginning I felt that with Freire I was in the company of a fellow traveller – someone with whom I would not always agree but whom I respected for his educational ideas, his strengths as a teacher, and his political and ethical commitment. In my published work, I have argued that Freire must be read holistically, critically and contextually. Given its enormous influence as a text read not just by educationists but by theorists and practitioners in many other fields, *Pedagogy of the Oppressed* (Freire, 1972a) has been the primary focus for many accounts of Freirean ideas. This classic work of critical educational scholarship, by any fair-minded assessment of 20th century educational thought, stands as a landmark in our understanding of the politics of education. It provides a powerful account of oppression and liberation, a rigorous critique of banking education, and a well developed alternative in problem-posing education. But as Freire himself stressed, there is much more to his corpus of published writings than this one book. When a reading of texts from his earlier and middle writing phases (Freire, 1972a, 1972b, 1976, 1985) is combined with a close examination of the later works cited above, a more rounded, nuanced, complex picture of education and humanization emerges.

In his later publications, Freire stresses the importance of ethical and epistemological virtues such as humility, openness, curiosity, a willingness to listen, an inquiring and investigative frame of mind, care for the students with whom one works, and political commitment (Peters & Roberts, 2011; Roberts, 2010). He addresses aspects of postmodern thought and acknowledges more fully the multi-layered nature of oppression and liberation. He tackles practical questions relating to the process of teaching, language differences, university reading requirements, and the difficulties of bringing about social change. He talks a great deal about the value of questions, the nature of dialogue and critical thought, the challenges he faced in his adult education work, and the need for gritty, 'armed' pedagogical hope. From these later books, a distinctive approach to critical literacy emerges. The publication of two collections of writings that had previously enjoyed only limited circulation, *Pedagogy of Indignation* (Freire, 2004) and *Daring to Dream* (Freire, 2007), has added to ongoing interest in Freire's work. But Freire welcomed constructive criticism, and at the time of his death in 1997 key areas of his work remained underdeveloped. He was just beginning, for example, to pay more extended attention to the world ecological crisis and its educational significance. There are many other omissions, contradictions and tensions that can be identified (see Roberts, 2000, 2010). This is not the place to comment at length on Freire's strengths and weaknesses. The point I want to stress here is that Freire was, in his own terms, an *unfinished* human being: a teacher, husband, father, thinker, and writer who sought to understand himself and the world as deeply as possible, but who realised he could not do this alone and would inevitably fall short in some of his endeavours. In this humble attitude toward his own achievements and struggles, Freire provides a worthy model for other philosophers of education.

ACADEMIC LIFE

In 1987, I noticed an advertisement in a daily newspaper for a Junior Lectureship at the University of Waikato, applied as a complete outsider, and after an interview was delighted to be offered the job. The position would begin early the following year. The University of Waikato was located in Hamilton, about two hours' drive south of Auckland, and I will always be grateful to the Education Department there for providing my first step on the academic ladder. The Head of Department was a little embarrassed to discover that I'd spent the night prior to the interview sleeping in my van in a camping ground, having come to Hamilton a day early to prepare. He explained to his new, rather naïve recruit that the Department's budget could have stretched to a room in a motel or hotel. My doctoral thesis was completed on a part-time basis while I was holding down a full-time academic position. I carried a heavy teaching load for several of my first few years at Waikato, making the process of finishing the doctorate doubly difficult, but I was also gaining experience that would serve me well in later years. Among other responsibilities, I taught on large Stage One courses, initially as a tutor, then as a lecturer, and later as both a lecturer and course coordinator. (I was appointed to a permanent Lectureship at the end of my second year in Hamilton.) My time at Waikato not only helped me learn something about the art of teaching; it also provided a good grounding in institutional politics. In addition, it enabled me to expand my research interests to include work on the philosophy of literacy and the higher education curriculum. This would later bear fruit in a series of publications through the 1990s (e.g., Roberts, 1993, 1995a, 1995b, 1995c, 1997a). My contributions in these areas built on my investigation of Freirean themes, which had deepened and extended considerably in completing my doctorate.

At the beginning of 1995, I moved back to a position at the University of Auckland. Our first child had been born a year earlier and our second would arrive just 18 months later. With strong family ties in Auckland (my wife too had grown up there), and with the Education Department experiencing significant growth, this seemed like the right time to make such a move. The department comprised two main academic groups, one of which was Cultural and Policy Studies in Education (CPSE). It would have been difficult to find a stronger collection of scholars in critical educational studies anywhere in the southern hemisphere. Within the first year or two of my return to Auckland, my CPSE colleagues had included Roger Dale, Jim Marshall, Michael Peters, Linda Smith, Graham Smith, Alison Jones, Megan Boler, and Susan Robertson, to name but a few. Philosophy of education, sociology of education, educational policy studies, and indigenous education were key strengths of the Education Department at that time. In such an environment, I was able to flourish as a researcher.

While I remained a philosopher of education first and foremost, I also started to write in the policy domain, with work on reforms in qualifications, the curriculum, and tertiary education (e.g., Roberts, 1997b, 1998, 2003, 2005; Roberts & Peters, 2008). I continued to publish on Freire, with my sole authored book, *Education, Literacy, and Humanization* (Roberts, 2000) representing the culmination of much that I had done in the previous decade. I completed the book while on sabbatical leave in 1999, also finishing an edited volume on Freire (Roberts, 1999) and a co-authored text on university futures (Peters & Roberts, 1999) in the same year. Freire had much to offer, but he was not enough on his own and over the years I have drawn on the work of a number of other thinkers, including Nietzsche (Roberts, 2001, 2012a), Lyotard (Peters & Roberts, 1999; Roberts, 2013a), Levinas (Roberts, 2013b), and Weil (Roberts, 2011). I am not an expert on any of these philosophers, but have simply tried to work with them in productive ways to address key educational questions and concerns. I found Nietzsche enjoyable to read, seeing in his work (Nietzsche, 1996, 1974, 1976, 1989, 1996, 1997) and his biography an attempt to make philosophy not merely an academic exercise but a way of life (Hadot, 1995; Solomon, 1999). Levinas has been more difficult. As I have said to one or two friends, reading works such as *Totality and Infinity* (Levinas, 1969) and *Otherwise Than Being or Beyond Essence* (Levinas, 1998) gives me a headache. But sometimes pain of this kind is necessary if we are to make philosophical progress. As an aside, I might note that I found Heidegger's *Being and Time* (Heidegger, 1996) equally challenging, and I have thus far mustered the courage to refer to it only briefly in my work. (I was able to make more headway with 'The Question Concerning Technology': Heidegger, 1997.) Simone Weil, a teacher and social activist as well as a remarkable thinker, died at a very young age but left behind a body of work that merits greater recognition from educationists. Like Nietzsche, she was an exemplary exponent of the aphorism as a mode of philosophical expression, and I have revisited some sections of the posthumously published *Gravity and Grace* (Weil, 2001) many times. Lyotard, together with Nietzsche, has enabled me to combine my philosophical and policy interests. His classic work, *The Postmodern Condition* (Lyotard, 1984) offers an especially helpful framework for getting to grips with policy changes in New Zealand.

New Zealand underwent a rapid and dramatic process of neoliberal reform in the 1980s and 1990s, with the sale of state assets, the removal of tariffs and subsidies, reductions in welfare, the introduction of market rates in social housing, and the rise of cultures of accountability and performativity in public institutions. Education, particularly in the tertiary sector, was reconceived as something to be traded in an international marketplace, with private benefits but little value as a public good (Peters & Roberts, 1999). The idea was to enhance choice for students, minimising bureaucracy while maximising competition between tertiary education providers. Underpinning this shift in thinking was a conception of human beings as rational, self-interested, individual consumers (Olssen, 2001; Peters & Marshall, 1996). The move to a modified version of Third Way politics (Giddens, 1998, 2000) in the New Zealand context from 1999 to 2008 rubbed off some of the harsher edges of neoliberalism, with the 'more market' mantra giving way to an emphasis on advancing the country as a knowledge society and economy. An attempt was made to create a 'shared vision' for tertiary education, with greater inclusiveness and support for Maori and Pasifika aspirations (Ministry of Education, 2002). In some respects, however, aspects of the neoliberal reform process – competition within and between institutions, and the commodification of knowledge – have been pushed even further during this period (Roberts & Peters, 2008). This has been particularly evident in the move to a performance-based system for research funding and the growth of 'export education' as an industry. These changes have influenced all academic lives in New Zealand. Philosophers of education can contribute significantly in identifying, explaining and critiquing the ontological, epistemological, and ethical assumptions underpinning neoliberal reforms. There is also much that we can do in setting these policy ideas in their broader intellectual and political contexts. But we must acknowledge that we too have been shaped by neoliberalism; our very survival as academics has often depended on a certain kind of adaptability. We have all been expected to 'perform,' in the narrow sense demanded by managerialist regimes, and this has exacted its toll on us as we have tried to reconcile our ideals with the sometimes brutal realities of institutional politics.

As the years went by, institutional support at the University of Auckland for work in the social, philosophical and historical foundations of education, along with other areas such as adult education, declined. Many who were part of the CPSE group in 1995 and 1996 moved on to other positions within or beyond New Zealand, and most were not replaced. Meanwhile, my research continued to develop in new directions, with an emerging interest in the value of literature for philosophical and educational inquiry. This programme would grow to become a key research area in the years ahead. While there is a substantial body of philosophical work on literature, ethics and the emotions (Barrow, 2004; Carr, 2005; Gribble, 1983; Jollimore & Barrios, 2006; Novitz, 1987; Palmer, 1992; Solomon, 1986), much of this has focused primarily on *theorising* such connections. My principal concern has been to *demonstrate* what literature has to offer by taking selected novels and plays as examples for analysis. This project builds on a tradition of ethical inquiry established by philosophers such as

Cunningham (2001) and Nussbaum (1990, 1995), and educationists such as Katz (1997), Sichel (1992), and Siegel (1997), among others. I have paid particular attention to fictional work by Fyodor Dostoevsky (e.g., Roberts, 2010, 2012b; Roberts & Freeman-Moir, 2013), Hermann Hesse (e.g., Roberts, 2012c), and Albert Camus (Roberts, 2008a, 2008b, 2013b, 2013c). In the case of Dostoevsky, I have concentrated to date on some of his shorter fiction (Dostoevsky, 1997, 2004) but in future work (Roberts & Saeverot, forthcoming) will draw more heavily on *The Brothers Karamazov* and the other great novels of his maturity (Dostoevsky, 1991, 1993, 1994, 2001). In considering what Hesse has to offer educationists, I have thus far focused mainly on his later books, *The Journey to the East* (Hesse, 1956) and *The Glass Bead Game* (Hesse, 2000). With Camus, it has been a combination of novels, a short story, and a play (Camus, 1958, 1991, 1996, 2000). In offering papers on these authors at conferences and other events, I have found lovers of literature in surprising places, with some very stimulating dialogues during and after my presentations.

With literary works having occupied such a special place in my life for so long, I was at first reluctant to treat them in a new 'academic' way. For many years, when time from other duties permitted, I read novels by the above mentioned writers, together with works by Homer, Virgil, Cervantes, Shakespeare, Tolstoy, George Eliot, Virginia Woolf, Franz Kafka, Iris Murdoch, Umberto Eco, Ben Okri, Milan Kundera, and Margaret Atwood, among others, but I did so as a kind of 'private' ethical education. My wife and I would often read the same books and discuss them in the evenings. Reading was an important part of our home life, and 'home' was meant, to some degree, to be separate from 'work.' I was concerned that subjecting the novels I loved to more formal philosophical analysis would destroy my enjoyment of them. These fears proved to be unfounded. I have found myself appreciating these works in new ways. The discipline required to construct a tight, well structured argument in response to a novel or play has sharpened the questions I wanted to ask of texts. It has opened up the range of sources I now include on student reading lists. It has allowed me to draw connections that hitherto had been obscured between different thinkers. It has taught me that the barriers between different genres of writing are not as rigid as we are sometimes led to believe. Indeed, many of the novelists I find most engaging, most helpful when addressing educational and ethical questions, are also fine philosophers. Iris Murdoch is an excellent example of this (see Roberts & Freeman-Moir, 2013), but it is also possible to read Dostoevsky, Camus, and many others in this light, even if they did not claim the label 'philosopher' for themselves (compare, Ford, 2004; Hanna, 1958; Scanlan, 2002).

Research never occurs in a 'pure' space; instead, it often must be conducted under institutional conditions that are complex and draining. Sabbatical leave for a semester in 2004, with visits to colleagues in Canada and the presentation of a number of talks at different universities, provided a brief, partial intellectual oasis. When I returned from leave, however, the CPSE group faced some of its sternest challenges. Some excellent scholars and committed teachers remained but by the middle of the first decade in the new century it had become increasingly difficult to maintain viable programmes of study at undergraduate and Masters levels in key areas. The amalgamation of the University of Auckland and the Auckland College of Education provided something of a boost to this dire state of affairs, with the opportunity, from 2006, to join kindred spirits at what became known as the Epsom Campus. The sociological study of education in particular was considerably strengthened by the merger, and there were also promising signs for philosophical and critical policy work. Interest in the study of philosophy of education at doctoral level was high, despite the paucity of university positions in the field. I had come to realise that this was the part of my job I valued most: the quiet, patient, in-depth work one undertakes in supervising serious research students. With the amalgamation and the relatively senior position I had in my new School I was able to take this commitment further, serving in various research mentoring roles with colleagues. This was just the preparation I needed for my next move.

In April 2008 I relocated to Christchurch to take up a chair at the University of Canterbury. I was appointed to offer research leadership, and I welcomed the opportunity to build on the supervision and mentoring work I'd undertaken in Auckland. My wife and I could also see benefits in giving our children a chance to experience the beauty and splendour of New Zealand's South Island for a few years before they reached adulthood. I settled into my new role quickly, and within 12 months I was chairing the College of Education Research Committee, writing research plans, developing mentoring schemes, organising seminars and symposia, and receiving a steady stream of inquiries about doctoral supervision. For the first six months of 2009 I also served, in an acting capacity, as Associate Dean (Postgraduate) in the College. As it turned out, demand for philosophical and policy research among PhD candidates in Education was as high in Christchurch as it had been in Auckland, and it didn't take long before I found myself in the unfortunate position of having to turn away prospective students. As had been the case in Auckland, limits had to be set on the number of doctoral candidates one could accept, given that most of us also had to teach at undergraduate and Masters levels. For the last dozen years or more, I have typically worked with at least 10 doctoral students (plus Masters thesis students) at any one time. While high by New Zealand university standards, such numbers are not altogether unusual. Thankfully, my undergraduate teaching load at the University of Canterbury has been very reasonable.

Canterbury has also been very good to me in many other ways, providing opportunities to spend time at the University of Oxford (as a Canterbury Fellow based in the Education Department in 2010) and the University of Cambridge (as a Rutherford Visiting Scholar at Trinity College in 2012). I loved the architecture, the sense of history, and the cultures of academic excellence at both of these extraordinary institutions. Invitations to give Keynotes and other academic addresses have taken me to a number of other parts of the globe over the last five years, and the College of Education has been supportive of these contributions. Throughout this time, I have been heavily involved with the Philosophy of Education Society of Australasia (PESA), serving on the Executive and most recently as President. After some difficult years in the late 1990s and early 2000s,

PESA has over the last decade gone from strength to strength. Boosted by the success of the Society's journal, *Educational Philosophy and Theory*, edited by Michael Peters, PESA has provided a welcoming environment for younger and newer scholars as well as 'old hands.' As an organisation, its reach now extends well beyond Australia and New Zealand, with members and conference participants from many different parts of Asia as well as North America and Europe. In my role as President of the Society, I am keen to continue building our links with other philosophy of education groups across the world. Differences must be recognised and respected, but there is also much that we have in common. Struggles to retain positions in our field, and to play an active part in teacher education, are shared by many. Similarly, while there is no one best way of responding to dominant trends in educational thinking – e.g., the obsession with measurement, performance, and accountability (Biesta, 2010; Roberts & Peters, 2008) – such developments are of serious concern to a good number of educational philosophers. Solidarity and support have never been more needed than they are now.

My time at Canterbury has, of course, been shaped significantly by something else we never could have expected when we moved here as a family in early 2008: the devastating earthquakes of September 2010 and February 2011, with literally thousands of aftershocks between and after these events. More than 180 people were killed in the February 2011 quake. Many houses and city buildings were damaged or destroyed. The University of Canterbury is located in an area that fared better than most in the quakes. Still, several key buildings on campus have been put out of action (including a five-storey tower block on the College of Education site, now demolished), and with a decline in student enrolments following the quakes there have been widespread redundancies. Everyone in Christchurch has been affected in one way or another by these events, and there will be years of rebuilding ahead. But the city has proven itself to be remarkably resilient, with businesses relocating and reinventing themselves in novel ways, communities supporting each other, and new programmes of research and teaching on earthquake-related topics and themes emerging in the university. The quakes have shaped the way many at the University of Canterbury think about themselves as academics and as citizens of Christchurch; they have prompted us to ask searching ethical questions of ourselves and to reassess personal priorities.

Partly as a response to these events and their consequences but also for other reasons, I have in recent years found myself writing more directly on the nature of despair and its significance for educationists (Roberts, 2013d, 2013e, forthcoming). Doing so has allowed me to see with greater clarity why and how I work as a philosopher of education. A number of other theorists have addressed questions relating to suffering, despair, and the tragic sense of education (e.g., Arcilla, 1992; Boler, 2004; Burbules, 1997; Chen, 2011; Liston, 2000), and my current work is intended to complement these studies. Drawing on literary figures such as Dostoevsky (1997, 2004), as well as Kierkegaard (1985, 1987, 1988, 1989), Unamuno (1972), Weil (1997, 2001), and other philosophers (e.g., Dienstag, 2006; Schopenhauer, 1969), I have argued that despair need not be conceived as something we must always seek to avoid or overcome. Despair, understood in a certain way, can be seen as a defining feature of human life. Education, in developing our capacity for reflective and critical thought, can enhance our awareness of injustices, intensify our frustrations in not being able to adequately understand and change ourselves and the world, and thereby heighten our sense of despair. But it can also enable us to work with despair in more fruitful ways. Through education, we can come to more deeply understand the suffering experienced by others and place our own troubles in broader perspective. Acknowledging the central role that despair plays in many lives need not mean the abandonment of hope or happiness. To the contrary, it is precisely in situations of despair that hope comes into its own, gaining renewed significance and meaning. Accepting that despair can be part of a well lived human life, without endorsing it or promoting it, can allow one to more deeply appreciate the joy in small things. It can help us to see qualities in ourselves and others that may previously have been obscured. It can permit us to value what we have, while holding on to our dreams, and foster greater openness to the unknown and the unexpected.

CONCLUSION

My own journey as a philosopher of education has taken me into 'unknown and unexpected' territory, and I have as many questions now as I had when growing up in Auckland. There is inevitably much that remains hidden in any account of this kind. A reader will often be left in the dark on many matters of detail relating to family or working life. Inner struggles and tensions can never be fully conveyed through the written word, even if we were inclined to reveal such things. Lives are frequently characterised not by a smooth, upward path of development, with a succession of high points in a glorious career, but by unevenness and messiness. A retrospective examination of a philosophical journey can gloss over, or ignore entirely, traumatic events, sustained periods of difficulty, and chronic pain. It can place before readers the masks we hold up to ourselves, our frailties and burdens too much to bear. These silences notwithstanding, there is also much that can be gained from a deliberate attempt to examine one's work in a more autobiographical manner than is usually warranted. Among other benefits that may accrue from such an exercise is the encouragement it offers in trying to see links between different parts of a life – different research programmes, different activities, different ways of tackling problems. When I look back now on the path I've taken, I can see that despite some detours it has been largely constructed on a set of questions and concerns that troubled me from childhood.

I found my way to Freire not just because Colin Lankshear pointed me there but also because in Freirean theory and practice questions about education, ethics and the meaning of life are to the fore. Freire offers not a perfect recipe or method for educational success but an ethic of humanization that can serve us well in a variety of personal and professional situations. From Freire, Lao Tzu, Simone Weil, and many others we can learn the importance of humility, equanimity, patience, commitment, and care, whether this is in a classroom with 30 students, a meeting with colleagues, or an e-mail discussion. Freire and Weil, together with Unamuno, Kierkegaard, and Nietzsche, may have had their faults, but they faced up more resolutely and honestly than most to the despair, and the joys, of human life. Many of the thinkers to whom I feel most closely connected, and I include here literary figures as well as philosophers and educationists, lived in some way 'on the edge.' They had questions that couldn't be easily answered. They had doubts and uncertainties. They were restless and uncomfortable. They suffered greatly but they were also able to appreciate the beauty and goodness that exists all around us. The destructiveness of neoliberalism as a doctrine for economic and social development also plays its part in creating a sense of despair, and a need for ongoing work in building better worlds. Philosophy of education helps us on our way in addressing these problems. As a field, it is under constant threat of dismissal within teaching programmes, but it has refused to be extinguished. As a profession, it promises neither wealth nor unending happiness. As a mode of being, philosophy of education makes life harder, not easier, but it is all the more important for that. I for one am looking forward to continuing this difficult journey.

INFLUENTIAL WORKS

Camus, A. (1991). *The myth of Sisyphus and other essays* (J. O'Brien, Trans.). New York: Vintage International.
Camus, A. (1996). *The first man* (D. Hapgood, Trans.). London: Penguin.
Dostoevsky, F. (1991). *The brothers Karamazov* (R. Pevear & L. Volokhonsky, Trans.). New York: Vintage.
Dostoevsky, F. (1994). *Demons* (R. Pevear & L. Volokhonsky, Trans.). London: Vintage.
Dostoevsky, F. (2004). *Notes from underground* (R. Pevear & L. Volokhonsky, Trans.). New York: Everyman's Library.
Freire, P. (1972). *Pedagogy of the oppressed*. Harmondsworth: Penguin.
Freire, P. (1998). *Pedagogy of freedom*. Lanham, MD: Rowman and Littlefield.
Freire, P. & Shor, I. (1987). *A pedagogy for liberation*. London: MacMillan.
Hadot, P. (1995). *Philosophy as a way of life* (M. Chase, Trans.). Oxford: Blackwell.
Hesse, H. (1956). *The journey to the east* (H. Rosner, Trans.). New York: The Noonday Press.
Hesse, H. (2000). *Siddhartha* (S.C. Kohn, Trans.). Boston: Shambhala.
Hesse, H. (2000). *The glass bead game* (R. Winston & C. Winston, Trans.). London: Vintage.
Horton, M. & Freire, P. (1990). *We make the road by walking: Conversations on education and social change*. Philadelphia, PA: Temple University Press.
Illich, I. (1971). *Deschooling society*. Harmondsworth: Penguin.
Kierkegaard, S. (1989). *The sickness unto death* (A. Hannay, Trans.). London: Penguin.
Lankshear, C. with Lawler, M. (1987). *Literacy, schooling and revolution*. London: Falmer.
Lao Tzu (1963). *Tao Te Ching* (D.C. Lau, Trans.) London: Penguin.
Lyotard, J.-F. (1984). *The postmodern condition: A report on knowledge* (G. Bennington & B. Massumi, Trans.). Minneapolis: University of Minnesota Press.
Murdoch, I. (1993). *Metaphysics as a guide to morals*. London: Penguin.
Murdoch, I. (1999). *Existentialists and mystics: Writings on philosophy and literature*. London: Penguin.
Nietzsche, F. (1966). *Beyond good and evil* (W. Kaufmann, Trans.). New York: Vintage.
Nietzsche, F. (1996). *Human, all too human* (R.J. Hollingdale, Trans.). Cambridge: Cambridge University Press.

Nussbaum, M. (1990). *Love's knowledge: Essays on philosophy and literature*. New York: Oxford University Press.
Plato (1974). *The Republic* (H.D.P. Lee, Trans.). Harmondsworth: Penguin.
Solomon, R.C. (1999). *The joy of philosophy*. Oxford: Oxford University Press.
Tolstoy, L. (1981). *The death of Ivan Ilyich* (L. Solotaroff, Trans.). New York: Bantam Books.
Tolstoy, L. (1987). *A confession and other religious writings* (J. Kentish, Trans.). London: Penguin.
Tolstoy, L. (2000). *Anna Karenina* (R. Pevear & L. Volokhonsky, Trans.). London: Penguin.
Unamuno, M. de (1972). *The tragic sense of life in men and nations* (A. Kerrigan, Trans.). Princeton, NJ: Princeton University Press.
Weil, S. (1997). *Gravity and grace* (A. Wills, Trans.). Lincoln: Bison Books.

PERSONAL FAVOURITES

Roberts, P. (1996). Structure, direction and rigour in liberating education. *Oxford Review of Education*, *22*(3), 295-316.
Roberts, P. (1996). Defending Freirean intervention. *Educational Theory*, *46*(3), 335-352.
Roberts, P. (1996). Rethinking conscientisation. *Journal of Philosophy of Education*, *30*(2), 179-196.
Roberts, P. (1999). The future of the university: Reflections from New Zealand. *International Review of Education*, *45*(1), 65-85.
Roberts, P. (2000). *Education, literacy and humanization: Exploring the work of Paulo Freire*. Westport, CT: Bergin and Garvey.
Roberts, P. (2006). Performativity, measurement and research: A critique of performance-based research funding in New Zealand. In J. Ozga, T. Popkewitz, & T. Seddon (Eds.) *World yearbook of education 2006: Education research and policy* (pp. 185-199). London: Routledge.
Roberts, P. (2008). From West to East and back again: Faith, doubt and education in Hermann Hesse's later work. *Journal of Philosophy of Education*, *42*(2), 249-268.
Roberts, P. (2008). Life, death and transformation: Education and incompleteness in Hermann Hesse's *The Glass Bead Game*. *Canadian Journal of Education*, *31*(3), 667-696.
Roberts, P. (2008). Teaching, learning and ethical dilemmas: Lessons from Albert Camus. *Cambridge Journal of Education*, *38*(4), 529-542.
Roberts, P. (2010). *Paulo Freire in the twenty-first century: Education, dialogue, and transformation*. Boulder, CO and London, UK: Paradigm Publishers.
Roberts, P. (2011). Attention, asceticism and grace: Simone Weil and higher education. *Arts and Humanities in Higher Education*, *10*(3), 315-328.
Roberts, P. (2012). Education and the limits of reason: Reading Dostoevsky. *Educational Theory*, *62*(2), 203-223.
Roberts, P. (2013). Acceptance, resistance and educational transformation: A Taoist reading of *The First Man*. *Educational Philosophy and Theory*, *45*(11), 1175-1189.
Roberts, P. (2013). Happiness, despair and education. *Studies in Philosophy and Education*, *32*(5), 463-475.
Roberts, P. (2013). Education, faith, and despair: Wrestling with Kierkegaard. *Philosophy of Education Yearbook 2013* (pp. 277-285). Urbana, IL: Philosophy of Education Society.
Roberts, P. & Freeman-Moir, J. (2013). *Better worlds: Education, art, and utopia*. Lanham, MD: Lexington Books.
Roberts, P. & Peters, M.A. (2008). *Neoliberalism, higher education and research*. Rotterdam: Sense Publishers.

REFERENCES

Arcilla, R. V. (1992). Tragic absolutism in education. *Educational Theory*, *42*(4), 473-481.

Althusser, L. (1971). Ideology and ideological state apparatuses. In L. Althusser, *Lenin and philosophy and other essays* (B. Brewster, Trans.). London: New Left Books.
Barrow, R. (2004). Language and character. *Arts and Humanities in Higher Education, 3*, 267-279.
Biesta, G. (2010). *Good education in an age of measurement.* Boulder, CO: Paradigm.
Boler, M. (2004). Teaching for hope: The ethics of shattering world views. In D. Liston & J. Garrison (Eds.), *Teaching, learning, and loving: Reclaiming passion in educational practice.* New York: RoutledgeFalmer.
Bourdieu, P., & Passeron, J. C. (1977). *Reproduction in education, society and culture.* London: Sage.
Bowles, S., & Gintis, H. (1976). *Schooling in capitalist America.* New York: Basic Books.
Burbules, N. C. (1997). Teaching and the tragic sense of education. In N. C. Burbules & D. Hansen (Eds.), *Teaching and its predicaments.* Boulder, CO: Westview Press.
Camus, A. (1958). The misunderstanding. In *Caligula and three other plays* (S. Gilbert, Trans.). New York: Vintage Books.
Camus, A. (1991). The guest. In *Exile and the kingdom* (J. O'Brien, Trans.). New York: Vintage International.
Camus, A. (1996). *The first man* (D. Hapgood, Trans.). London: Penguin.
Camus, A. (2000). *The fall* (J. O'Brien, Trans.). London: Penguin.
Carr, D. (2005). On the contribution of literature and the arts to the educational cultivation of moral virtue, feeling and emotion. *Journal of Moral Education, 34*, 137-151.
Chen, R. H. (2011). Bearing and transcending suffering with nature and the world: A humanistic account. *Journal of Moral Education, 40*(2), 203-216.
Cunningham, A. (2001). *The heart of what matters: The role for literature in moral philosophy.* Berkeley, CA: University of California Press.
Dearden, R. F., Hirst, P. H., & Peters, R. S. (Eds.). (1972). *Education and the development of reason.* London: Routledge and Kegan Paul.
Dewey, J. (1966). *Democracy and education.* New York: Free Press.
Dewey, J. (1997). *Experience and education.* New York: Touchstone.
Dienstag, J. F. (2006). *Pessimism: Philosophy, ethic, spirit.* Princeton, NJ: Princeton University Press.
Dostoevsky, F. (1991). *The brothers Karamazov* (R. Pevear & L. Volokhonsky, Trans.). New York: Vintage.
Dostoevsky, F. (1993). *Crime and punishment* (R. Pevear & L. Volokhonsky, Trans.) London: Vintage.
Dostoevsky, F. (1994). *Demons* (R. Pevear & L. Volokhonsky, Trans.). London: Vintage.
Dostoevsky, F. (1997). The dream of a ridiculous man. In F. Dostoevsky, *The eternal husband and other stories* (R. Pevear & L. Volokhonsky, Trans.) (pp. 296-319). New York: Bantam Books.
Dostoevsky, F. (2001). *The idiot* (R. Pevear & L. Volokhonsky, Trans.). London: Granta.
Dostoevsky, F. (2004). *Notes from underground* (R. Pevear & L. Volokhonsky, Trans.). New York: Everyman's Library.
Ford, R. (2004). Critiquing desire: Philosophy, writing and terror. *Journal of Human Rights, 3*(1), 85-98.
Foucault, M. (1979). *Discipline and punish: The birth of the prison* (A. Sheridan, Trans.). Harmondsworth: Peregrine.
Foucault, M. (1980). *Power/knowledge: Selected interviews and other writings, 1972-1977* (C. Gordon, L. Marshall, J. Mepham, & K. Soper, Trans.; C. Gordon, Ed.). London: Harvester Press.
Freire, P. (1972a). *Pedagogy of the oppressed.* Harmondsworth: Penguin.
Freire, P. (1972b). *Cultural action for freedom.* Harmondsworth: Penguin.
Freire, P. (1976). *Education: The practice of freedom.* London: Writers and Readers.
Freire, P. (1985). *The politics of education.* London: MacMillan.
Freire, P. (1993). *Pedagogy of the city.* New York: Continuum.
Freire, P. (1994). *Pedagogy of hope.* New York: Continuum.
Freire, P. (1996). *Letters to Cristina: Reflections on my life and work.* London: Routledge.
Freire, P. (1997). *Pedagogy of the heart.* New York: Continuum.

Freire, P. (1998a). *Teachers as cultural workers: Letters to those who dare teach*. Boulder, CO: Westview Press.
Freire, P. (1998b). *Pedagogy of freedom*. Lanham, MD: Rowman and Littlefield.
Freire, P. (2004). *Pedagogy of indignation*. Boulder, CO: Paradigm.
Freire, P. (2007). *Daring to dream*. Boulder, CO: Paradigm.
Freire, P., & Faundez, A. (1989). *Learning to question: A pedagogy of liberation*. Geneva: World Council of Churches.
Freire, P., & Macedo, D. (1987). *Literacy: Reading the word and the world*. London: Routledge.
Freire, P., & Shor, I. (1987). *A pedagogy of liberation*. London: MacMillan.
Fromm, E. (1942). *The fear of freedom*. London: Routledge and Kegan Paul.
Giddens, A. (1998). *The Third Way: The renewal of social democracy*. Cambridge: Polity Press.
Giddens, A. (2000). *The Third Way and its critics*. Cambridge: Polity Press.
Gribble, J. (1983). Literature and the education of the emotions. In *Literary education: A revaluation* (pp. 95-113). Cambridge: Cambridge University Press.
Hadot, P. (1995). *Philosophy as a way of life* (M. Chase, Trans.). Oxford: Blackwell.
Hanna, T. (1958). *The thought and art of Albert Camus*. Chicago, IL: Henry Regnery.
Harris, K. (1979). *Education and knowledge*. London: Routledge and Kegan Paul.
Harris, K. (1982). *Teachers and classes*. London: Routledge and Kegan Paul.
Harvey, D. (2005). *A brief history of neoliberalism*. Oxford: Oxford University Press.
Heidegger, M. (1996). *Being and time* (J. Stambaugh, Trans.). Albany: State University of New York Press.
Heidegger, M. (1997). The question concerning technology. In *The question concerning technology and other essays* (W. Lovitt, Trans.). New York: Harper & Row.
Hesse, H. (1956). *The journey to the east* (H. Rosner, Trans.). New York: The Noonday Press.
Hesse, H. (2000). *The glass bead game* (R. Winston & C. Winston, Trans.). London: Vintage.
Hirst, P. H. (1974). *Knowledge and the curriculum*. London: Routledge and Kegan Paul.
Horton, M., & Freire, P. (1990). *We make the road by walking: Conversations on education and social change*. Philadelphia, PA: Temple University Press.
Illich, I. (1971). *Deschooling society*. Harmondsworth: Penguin.
Jollimore, T., & Barrios, S. (2006). Creating cosmopolitans: The case for literature. *Studies in Philosophy and Education, 25*, 263-283.
Katz, M. (1997). On becoming a teacher: May Sarton's *The small room*. *Philosophy of Education 1997*. Normal, IL: Philosophy of Education Society. Retrieved October 29, 2001 from: http://w3.ed.uiuc.edu/EPS/PES-Yearbook/97_docs/katz.html
Kierkegaard, S. (1985). *Philosophical fragments* (H. V. Hong & E. H. Hong, Trans.). Princeton, NJ: Princeton University Press.
Kierkegaard, S. (1987). *Either/or*, 2 vols. (H. V. Hong & E. H. Hong, Trans.). Princeton, NJ: Princeton University Press.
Kierkegaard, S. (1988). *Stages on life's way* (H. V. Hong & E. H. Hong, Trans.). Princeton, NJ: Princeton University Press.
Kierkegaard, S. (1989). *The sickness unto death* (A. Hannay, Trans.). London: Penguin.
Lao Tzu. (1963). *Tao Te Ching* (D. C. Lau, Trans.) London: Penguin.
Levinas, E. (1969). *Totality and infinity* (A. Lingis, Trans.) Pittsburgh, PA: Duquesne University Press.
Levinas, E. (1998). *Otherwise than being or beyond essence* (A. Lingis, Trans.). Pittsburgh, PA: Duquesne University Press.
Liston, D. (2000). Love and despair in teaching, *Educational Theory, 50*(1), 81-102.
Lyotard, J.-F. (1984). *The postmodern condition: A report on knowledge* (G. Bennington & B. Massumi, Trans.). Minneapolis: University of Minnesota Press.
Marx, K. (1964). *Economic and philosophical manuscripts of 1844* (M. Milligan, Trans., D. Struik, Ed.). New York: International Publishers.
Marx, K. (1976). *Capital*, vol.1 (B. Fowkes, Trans., E. Mandel, Ed.). Harmondsworth: Penguin.

Marx, K., & Engels, F. (1972). *The Communist manifesto*. In R. C. Tucker (Ed.), *The Marx-Engels reader*. New York: Norton.

Ministry of Education. (2002). *Tertiary education strategy, 2002/07*. Wellington: Ministry of Education. (Office of the Associate Minister of Education – Tertiary Education.)

Nietzsche, F. (1966). *Beyond good and evil* (W. Kaufmann, Trans.). New York: Vintage Books.

Nietzsche, F. (1974). *The gay science* (W. Kaufmann, Trans.). New York: Vintage Books.

Nietzsche, F. (1976). *Thus spoke Zarathustra*. In W. Kaufmann (Ed.), *The portable Nietzsche* (pp. 103-439). Harmondsworth: Penguin.

Nietzsche, F. (1989). *On the genealogy of morals* and *Ecce homo* (W. Kaufmann, Trans.). New York: Vintage Books.

Nietzsche, F. (1996). *Human, all too human* (R. J. Hollingdale, Trans.). Cambridge: Cambridge University Press.

Nietzsche, F. (1997a). *Daybreak: Thoughts on the prejudices of morality* (R. J. Hollingdale, Trans.; M. Clark & B. Leiter, Eds.). Cambridge: Cambridge University Press.

Nietzsche, F. (1997b). *Untimely meditations* (R. J. Hollingdale, Trans., D. Breazeale, Ed.). Cambridge: Cambridge University Press.

Novitz, D. (1987). *Knowledge, fiction and imagination*. Philadelphia, PA: Temple University Press.

Nussbaum, M. (1990). *Love's knowledge: Essays on philosophy and literature*. New York: Oxford University Press.

Nussbaum, M. (1995). *Poetic justice: The literary imagination and public life*. Boston, MA: Beacon Press.

Olssen, M. (2001). *The neo-liberal appropriation of tertiary education policy in New Zealand: Accountability, research and academic freedom*. 'State-of-the-Art' Monograph No.8. Palmerston North: New Zealand Association for Research in Education.

Palmer, F. (1992). *Literature and moral understanding: A philosophical essay on ethics, aesthetics, education, and culture*. Oxford: Clarendon Press.

Peters, M., & Marshall, J. (1996) *Individualism and community: Education and social policy in the postmodern condition*. London: Falmer Press.

Peters, M., & Roberts, P. (Eds.). (1998). *Virtual technologies and tertiary education*. Palmerston North: Dunmore Press.

Peters, M., & Roberts, P. (1999). *University futures and the politics of reform in New Zealand*. Palmerston North: Dunmore Press.

Peters, M. A., & Roberts, P. (2011). *The virtues of openness: Education, science, and scholarship in the digital age*. Boulder, CO: Paradigm Publishers.

Peters, R. S. (1970). *Ethics and education*. London: Allen and Unwin.

Peters, R. S. (1973). *Authority, responsibility and education*. London: George Allen and Unwin.

Roberts, P. (1993). Philosophy, education and literacy: Some comments on Bloom. *New Zealand Journal of Educational Studies, 28*(2), 165-180.

Roberts, P. (1995a). Defining literacy: Paradise, nightmare or red herring? *British Journal of Educational Studies, 43*(4), 412-432.

Roberts, P. (1995b). Political correctness, great books and the university curriculum. *Sites: The South Pacific Journal of Cultural Studies, 31*, 81-111.

Roberts, P. (1995c). Literacy studies: A review of the literature, with signposts for future research. *New Zealand Journal of Educational Studies, 30*(2), 189-214.

Roberts, P. (1997a). The consequences and value of literacy: A critical reappraisal. *Journal of Educational Thought, 31*(1), 45-67.

Roberts, P. (1997b). A critique of the NZQA policy reforms. In M. Olssen & K. Morris Matthews (Eds.), *Education policy in New Zealand: The 1990s and beyond* (pp. 162-189). Palmerston North: Dunmore Press.

Roberts, P. (1998). The politics of curriculum reform in New Zealand. *Curriculum Studies, 6*(1), 29-46.

Roberts, P. (Ed.). (1999). *Paulo Freire, politics and pedagogy: Reflections from Aotearoa-New Zealand*. Palmerston North: Dunmore Press.

Roberts, P. (2000). *Education, literacy and humanization: Exploring the work of Paulo Freire.* Westport, CT: Bergin and Garvey.
Roberts, P. (2001). Nietzsche and the limits of academic life. In M. Peters, J. Marshall, & P. Smeyers (Eds.), *Nietzsche's legacy for education: Past and present values* (pp. 125-137). Westport, CT: Bergin and Garvey.
Roberts, P. (2003). Contemporary curriculum research in New Zealand. In W. Pinar (Ed.), *The International handbook of curriculum research* (pp. 495-516). Mahwah, NJ: Lawrence Erlbaum.
Roberts, P. (2005). Tertiary education, knowledge and neoliberalism. In J. Codd & K. Sullivan (Eds.), *Education policy directions in Aotearoa New Zealand* (pp. 39-51). Palmerston North: Thomson/Dunmore Press.
Roberts, P. (2008a). Teaching, learning and ethical dilemmas: Lessons from Albert Camus. *Cambridge Journal of Education, 38*(4), 529-542.
Roberts, P. (2008b). Bridging literary and philosophical genres: Judgement, reflection and education in Camus' *The fall. Educational Philosophy and Theory, 40*(7), 873-887.
Roberts, P. (2010). *Paulo Freire in the twenty-first century: Education, dialogue, and transformation.* Boulder, CO and London, UK: Paradigm Publishers.
Roberts, P. (2011). Attention, asceticism and grace: Simone Weil and higher education. *Arts and Humanities in Higher Education, 10*(3), 315-328.
Roberts, P. (2012a). Scholars, philosophers or performers? The politics of research in contemporary universities. In R. Openshaw & J. Clark (Eds.), *Critic and conscience: Essays in memory of John Codd and Roy Nash* (pp. 87-104). Wellington: New Zealand Council for Educational Research.
Roberts, P. (2012b). Education and the limits of reason: Reading Dostoevsky. *Educational Theory, 62*(2), 203-223.
Roberts, P. (2012c). *From west to east and back again: An educational reading of Hermann Hesse's later work.* Rotterdam: Sense Publishers.
Roberts, P. (2013a). Academic dystopia: Knowledge, performativity and tertiary education. *The Review of Education, Pedagogy, and Cultural Studies, 35*(1), 27-43.
Roberts, P. (2013b). Education and the Face of the Other: Levinas, Camus and (mis)understanding. *Educational Philosophy and Theory, 45*(11), 1133-1149.
Roberts, P. (2013c). Acceptance, resistance and educational transformation: A Taoist reading of *The First Man. Educational Philosophy and Theory, 45*(11), 1175-1189.
Roberts, P. (2013d). Happiness, despair and education. *Studies in Philosophy and Education, 32*(5), 463-475.
Roberts, P. (2013e). Education, faith, and despair: Wrestling with Kierkegaard. *Philosophy of Education Yearbook 2013* (pp. 277-285). Urbana, IL: Philosophy of Education Society.
Roberts, P. (forthcoming). *Living on the edge: Educational spaces in the midst of despair.* New York: Peter Lang.
Roberts, P., & Freeman-Moir, J. (2013). *Better worlds: Education, art, and utopia.* Lanham, MD: Lexington Books.
Roberts, P., & Peters, M. A. (2008). *Neoliberalism, higher education and research.* Rotterdam: Sense Publishers.
Roberts, P., & Saeverot, H. (forthcoming). *Education and the limits of reason: Reading Dostoevsky, Tolstoy and Nabokov.* New York: Routledge.
Scanlan, J. P. (2002). *Dostoevsky the thinker.* Ithaca, NY: Cornell University Press.
Scheffler, I. (1960). *The language of education.* Springfield, IL: Charles C. Thomas.
Schopenhauer, A. (1969). *The world as will and representation*, vol. 1, (E.F. Payne, Trans.). New York: Dover.
Sharp, R. (1980). *Knowledge, ideology and the politics of schooling: Towards a Marxist analysis of education.* London: Routledge and Kegan Paul.
Sichel, B. A. (1992). Education and thought in Virginia Woolf's *To the lighthouse. Philosophy of Education 1992.* Normal, IL: Philosophy of Education Society. Retrieved February 2, 2005 from: http://w3.ed.uiuc.edu/EPS/PES-Yearbook/92_docs/Sichel.html

Siegel, H. (1997). Teaching, reasoning, and Dostoevsky's *The brothers Karamazov*. In *Rationality redeemed? Further dialogues on an educational ideal* (pp. 39-54). New York and London: Routledge.

Solomon, R. C. (1986). Literacy and the education of the emotions. In S. de Castell, A. Luke, & K. Egan (Eds.), *Literacy, society, and schooling: A reader* (pp. 37-58). Cambridge: Cambridge University Press.

Solomon, R.C. (1999). *The joy of philosophy*. Oxford: Oxford University Press.

Unamuno, M. de (1972). *The tragic sense of life in men and nations* (A. Kerrigan, Trans.). Princeton, NJ: Princeton University Press.

Waks, L. (2008). The analytical revolution in philosophy of education and its aftermath. In L. Waks (Ed.), *Leaders in philosophy of education: Intellectual self portraits* (pp. 1-13). Rotterdam: Sense Publishers.

Weil, S. (1997). *Gravity and grace* (A. Wills, Trans.). Lincoln: Bison Books.

Weil, S. (2001). *Waiting for God* (E. Craufurd, Trans.). New York: Perennial Classics.

Willis, P. (1977). *Learning to labour: How working class kids get working class jobs*. Farnborough: Saxon House.

PAUL SMEYERS

A KIND OF SPIRAL THINKING

Philosophy of Education Through the Eyes of a Fellow Traveller

SOME AUTOBIOGRAPHICAL NOTES

My first exposition to philosophy of education goes back to my formation years, when I studied Educational Sciences at KU Leuven, Belgium. I registered in 1972 for a two year B.A. (Educational Sciences) degree which offered a broad introduction (more than half of the subjects out of 26 were taught from other faculties). A prominent place was given to 'pure' philosophy (one in four subjects), at the same time statistics and various courses in psychology made up the curriculum. The view behind this was a Herbartian notion of educational sciences: philosophy will give us the aims, psychology the means, the educational scientist and practitioner to be a kind of technical social engineer. Yet the profound influence of the philosophical stance should not be underestimated. Among the educational subjects three could be labelled in some sense philosophy of education. One was a general introduction into science and its presuppositions including the historical development of the educational sub-disciplines, the other two figured under the title Fundamentele Pedagogiek I and II. I am still not sure how to translate this in English. What was dealt with were various theoretical positions particularly developed within German Educational Theory bringing together views on human beings whether or not religiously (or metaphysically) inspired with their corollary, how they can live and work together, i.e., a social philosophy dealing with the state and its institutions and the place that should be given to child rearing and education. Though Illich and Freire were included it was very much a top down approach where the implications were spelled out for education in its broadest (and typically German) sense. It was about what is called in German Erziehung and Bildung, and thus not only schooling, but upbringing and the various kind of human relationships (including those between children and between adults) were focused on. Surely the paradigm of initiation into what was thought to be a worthwhile life characterized a lot we were confronted with, but so did 'self-fulfilment' and the betterment of society and the often utopian ideas on which these are based. After all, this was seen as the very reason why education and child rearing had to be studied. The formation was abstract and general; it was, to say one thing, foremost theoretical, an approach where foundations from various disciplines were offered and critically dealt with. More often than not it was criticized by colleagues and students alike for being far removed from the educational realities – a complaint that would become louder and louder in the consecutive years and which would result in the almost a-theoretical position dominated by the means-ends reasoning and evidence based rhetoric one finds oneself in today.

The two year M.A. (Educational Sciences) continued this formation along 'applied' lines: a major had to be chosen which was either Teacher Training, Special Education, or Social Pedagogy. Completion of a B.A. and of an M.A. was mandatory for all jobs which required a university degree in the educational field. Yet few positions were available when we (more than a hundred) graduated in 1976, given the aftermath of the 1973 oil crisis and its effect on the economy resulting in a high level of over-all unemployment across all university graduates but even more so in the 'soft sciences.' I was offered a part-time position at the university and combined this for three years with a lectureship in a Teacher Training College. My work at the Faculty of Psychology and Educational Sciences (KU Leuven) consisted of guidance, counselling and tutoring of first years students educational sciences of which there was no shortage (cohorts would be 300+). Challenging as this was, it did however leave little time to be involved with the academic educational discipline. I welcomed the opportunity in 1979 to get a full time position still at the same unit but with the prospect to use half of my time to make a Ph.D. Choosing a supervisor was easy: there was only one professor who taught Philosophy of Education (C.C. Dekeyser) and he himself was by the way more active in Comparative Education (having entered that field through an M.A. in Psychology coming originally from Arts where he studied more in particular Latin and Greek besides Theology and some philosophy at the seminary). It was refreshing to get in the aftermath of 1968, in a climate of action and social change (where it was almost perceived immoral to think as there was so much to do), his advice to study Philosophy – the only way he said to be able to do some real work in philosophy of education. And thus I combined my full time work at the university with a full time study of Philosophy, first a B.A. and then an M.A. As my M.A. thesis in Educational Sciences dealt with the work of the University of London Institute of Education philosopher Richard Stanley Peters, and given the manifold of references he made to the legacy of Gilbert Ryle (Oxford, U.K.), the position of the latter (and more particularly concerning 'knowing how' and 'knowing that' and the logical geography of concepts), would become the topic for my M.A.-thesis in philosophy. From both of these my Ph.D. research took shape: it centred on Wittgenstein, and more in particular on his stance concerning meaning and justification and on what this could offer for philosophy of education. I was awarded the Ph.D. in 1984, got tenured in the same year at KU Leuven, to become a Senior Lecturer in 1992, Associate Professor in 1995, and full Professor in 2000 at the age of 47. Head-hunted by Ghent University, I took up the position of Research Professor for Philosophy of Education in 2007, yet remained part-time employed by KU Leuven as Extra-Ordinary Professor; a similar position, Honorary, was bestowed upon me from Stellenbosch University in South Africa.

Looking back upon the past three decades of working in Philosophy of Education it is easy to get carried away with one or other reconstructive narrative that presents the reader with a kind of logical development of my thoughts. Though there is some of that which I will develop below, there were also many coincidences which not only shaped my career but which were also influential in my thinking. Let me mention for instance that I became at some point responsible for teaching qualitative empirical educational research (on top of philosophy of education), moreover the various work I did in international philosophy of education societies (Philosophy of Education Society of Great Britain, Philosophy of Education Society of the USA, International Network of Philosophers of Education, European Conference on Educational Research/European Educational Research Association) and for many journals (Journal of Philosophy of Education, Educational Theory, Studies in Philosophy and Education, Educational Philosophy and Theory, Ethics and Education), and further the chairing of the Research Community (FWO-Vlaanderen) Philosophy and History of the Discipline of Education; last but not least the joint authorship (and editorship) of many books, articles and chapters of which I was part over many years with my friends whose thinking has influenced me profoundly. More than anything else it is these critical engagements that have shaped my own thinking in terms of content and where I think we are now. For me, writing has always been an opportunity to formulate as precisely as possible what I think myself and then to present it to others in order to see whether it could make sense to them as well. I have always felt the need (the duty even as an academic) to do this, and such long before the present climate of 'publish or perish' came into existence. The discipline I imposed on myself to engage in this on a regular basis, was assisted by the various commitments I made to engage in projects when talking with others at conferences and seminars and which I sometimes regretted afterwards. Yet I am sure that without these it would have been even more difficult to write and to think. Some ways to structure the development of my insights are offered below.

THE WITTGENSTEINIAN LEGACY FOR PHILOSOPHY OF EDUCATION

There were not many of us in the late 1970s and early 1980s who were doing work in philosophy of education from a Wittgensteinian stance. In continental traditions in philosophy of education his insights were almost not studied, and in the so-called Anglo-Saxon tradition only few took his position as the over-all framework for their own work. Though referring to Wittgenstein at various places in their work the then dominant voices of Israel Scheffler (Harvard University, US) and Richard Stanley Peters (London University, UK) – together with those he worked closely with, i.e. Robert Dearden and Paul Hirst) – paid only lip-service to his insights but seemed unwilling to endorse radically what he argued for. With some colleagues from the Netherlands (amongst them Wilna Meijer, Ben Spiecker, Bas Levering, Jan Steutel, Siebren Miedema) quite a few papers were written and published in Dutch in the journal *Pedagogisch Tijdschrift*. Gradually some themes were developed which I took up such as 'intention,' 'radical newness,' and 'justification,' all critically relevant in educational discussions and addressed because the reproach towards the Wittgensteinian position was often that it limited itself to socialization, to initiation, and lacked to offer a place to criticize the often authoritarian passing on as well in terms of content as of processes in the area of education. Colleagues in Western Europe would see themselves as being the heirs of the Kantian, of the phenomenological, and of the critical theory tradition. They were also more interested in recent developments in philosophy such as the work of Levinas, Derrida, Lyotard, Lacan, and many other so-called post-structuralists and post-modernists. Resonances of these were to be found across the Channel and the Atlantic Ocean, but there the interest remained much more traditionally analytical. For many the problems addressed in the English speaking community seemed trivial from a Continental perspective; and being the heirs of the legacy of Russell, Moore, and as well the early as the later work of Wittgenstein, the majority of these philosophers and philosophers of education could hardly see that what their continental counterparts were doing resembled philosophy at all.

Having studied philosophy in Leuven I was obviously familiar with the work of Husserl, Heidegger, Levinas, Lacan and many others as well as with the German Educational Theory tradition. Given my own interest in Peters and Scheffler followed by studying the positions of Ryle and (the later) Wittgenstein, I felt often very lonely lacking a sounding board that critically engaged with what I tried to argue for. In some sense I had embraced the Wittgensteinian stance and even the analytical approach of philosophy of education, yet at the same time I was tempted by the Continental position and it seemed obvious to me that what they argued for was not only interesting and relevant but moreover profound. All of this came together in a particular reading of Wittgenstein's work, who is for many not only an analytical philosopher *pur sang* but as well someone who introduced several Continental themes and who set the agenda for a good part of the discussion in philosophy in the second half of the twentieth century. In the period I worked on my Ph.D. I had the opportunity to study during the academic year 1982-83 at the London Institute of Education, to take part in the weekly Wednesday seminar and to attend lectures from philosophers such as David W. Hamlyn, Peter Winch, and Norman Malcolm. This intense period of being immersed not only gave me the opportunity to take cognisance of what was the focus of the interest at that time in philosophy and philosophy of education, but brought me also in contact through their writing (and sometimes in person) with those Wittgenstein scholars who took an interest in education. Some years after the completion of my Ph.D. I attended an INPE conference in London (1990) and met Jim Marshall (Auckland, New Zealand). The both of us shared an interest in Wittgenstein (particularly in his later philosophy), worked in the area of education, but were also not insensitive towards recent so-called post-modernist writing. He and I decided to do a collection (published in 1995 by Kluwer, Dordrecht) *Philosophy and Education: Accepting Wittgenstein's Challenge*. In the preface we dealt with our reading of what philosophy of education addressed respectively in the Anglo-Saxon and in the Continental tradition and what we thought was characteristic for the Wittgensteinian stance; in the Epilogue we summed up those issues and problems which deserved further attention, amongst other issues as related to post-modernist writing. Gradually, attention to Wittgensteinian themes increased.

Ludwig Wittgenstein discussed in his *Philosophical Investigations* as well as in On Certainty what is involved in our acting, speaking and doing. The concept of the 'form of life' indicates what he considers to be the bedrock of our 'language-games.' It is 'given,' language-and-the-world,' and thus we cannot place ourselves outside of it. These unjustified and unjustifiable patterns of human activities can be seen as the complicated network of rules which constitute language and social life. In discussing the paradigmatic notion of the language-game Wittgenstein writes: "If language is to be a means of communication there must be agreement not only in definitions but also (queer as this may sound) in judgements" (*Philosophical Investigations*, 1953 – henceforth PI – PI, I § 242). Only within a 'language-game' will we be able to justify a certain inference, a certain behaviour; within a 'language-game' we can speak of justification and lack of justification, of evidence and proof, of mistakes and groundless opinions, of good and bad reasoning, of correct and incorrect measurements. And moreover, if we try to doubt everything, Wittgenstein argues in *On Certainty* we would not get as far as doubting anything: "The game of doubting itself presupposes certainty" (C, § 115). Thus, within a system of thinking and acting there occur, up to a point, investigations and criticisms of the reasons and justifications that are employed in that system. We bring this inquiry to an end when we come upon something that we regard as a satisfactory reason, and that we do so shows itself in our actions. This is the 'certainty' we are initiated into, and he insists upon the importance of the way the initiation proceeds, and on its relevance to establishing meaning: "always ask yourself: How did we learn the meaning of this word ('good' for instance)? From what sort of examples? in what language-games? Then it will be easier for you to see that the word must have a family of meanings" (see PI, I § 77). Let me draw attention to the fact that Wittgenstein's 'theory' of meaning advocates neither a position of pure subjectivity nor one of pure objectivity. From the beginning, what one could call an element of risk is present in the way communication is conceived. Though every situation is in some sense new, the different meanings of a concept are linked with each other through family-resemblances. In order to be understood, any particular use may not be radically different from previous ones. However, the consistency of meaning Wittgenstein argues for is free of essentialism. It is within the normal context that the meaning of a concept is determined. Other people and I proceed in this way. There is no absolute point of reference, neither internal nor external, neither for them nor for me. The community of language speakers forms the warrant for the consistency of meaning.

Following Wittgenstein education has to be thought of as an initiation into practices. And being part of this shared social practice constitutes the subject being inscribed in the intersubjective order; it characterizes as well knowledge and epistemology as what is right to do and ethics. Embracing a 'view from nowhere' as well as 'giving up justifying what I do' are developments exemplifying an unwillingness to live the 'scepticism' which characterizes human existence. Instead, following Stanley Cavell (1979) and his insistence that we should not try to escape from the existential conditions we find ourselves in and look for false certainties, one should embrace a particular stance. A commitment to giving substance to an ideal of 'the good life' is neither an injustice towards the other nor an ignorance of her freedom. On the contrary, here responsibility is accepted, and at the same time it is acknowledged that we always have only the particular points of departure that we contingently start from. Thus it is argued that our social practices should in some ways transcend the private concerns of individuals; my private actions should be justified with reasons to other individuals with whom I engage in public (worldly) relations.

We cannot do in education without the concept of initiation into practices. But there is a different way to think about 'practice' that consists in emphasizing first how they are learned – for instance through imitation, initiation, instruction and so forth; and secondly how they are enacted. In both cases one's relation to the practices in which one is engaged becomes crucial – that is, how one is brought into them, and how one contributes to them. Here practice is viewed in relation to human actors and not simply seen in intrinsic terms. Central here is the interrelation between the nature of the activity and how people think about and act within the practice. Of special importance is the relation that a practice encourages or discourages (through different ways of learning or enacting it), i.e. how it is intertwined with our self and sense of identity, on the one hand, and our relations and ways of interacting with other people, on the other hand. Here the way we identify with particular practices, and to what extent, is at stake. Practices transform the self, but at the same time there may be subversions of a practice that give opportunities to the self. Practices have reasons behind them, even if these are not always made explicit, but these are reasons that also can be re-examined and questioned; this may also bring forward unintended dimensions.

In the development of these insights I benefited from the discussions with a number of colleagues including Jim Macmillan, Jim Marshall, Fazal Rizvi, Michael Peters, Paul Standish, Richard Smith, Stefan Ramaekers, Nick Burbules, and my lifelong friend and colleague, Jan Masschelein, with whom I disagreed so much but from who I learned even more . At the beginning of my career I focused almost exclusively on Wittgensteinian themes, but the quest never ended: in a keynote for the Philosophy of Education Society of Great Britain conference in 2009 (Smeyers, 2012) I summarized my over-all position (which included references to Lacan and the ethics of care) and as recently as in 2012 I revisited the *Tractatus* in trying to find its message for a philosophy of educational research and the eternal pitfalls of a kind of a correspondence theory of truth.

POSTMODERNIST EDUCATIONAL PREOCCUPATIONS

In the 1990s the Anglo-Saxon philosophy of education debate became gradually ready to engage with various writings of so-called postmodernist authors. The challenge was met with great doubt whether there was indeed something there to take up. A couple of us had written about these issues in the *Journal of Philosophy of Education*, which led Wilfred Carr to ask four of us, i.e. Richard Smith, Paul

Standish, and Nigel Blake, to present our thoughts in a symposium at the PESGB Oxford conference. It was the starting-point of an intense collaboration for more than a decade which resulted in three jointly written books where we addressed how education looked after postmodernism, in an age of nihilism – rereading Nietzsche – and what kind of therapy education may be capable of offering. The quest we undertook presupposed an openness to listen thoroughly to each other's arguments which was only possible due to our friendship. In these close encounters cards had to be put on the table. Though a writing exercise and a publication project it was foremost a confrontation of similarly minded souls who jointly went on an intellectual journey to make sense of various intellectual traditions. For many years we came together three or four times a year (each time for three days) where we went again and again through the material that each of us had prepared. Our meetings resulted also in another initiative: *The Blackwell Guide to the Philosophy of Education*, published in 2003. In the introduction to that collection we diagnosed that in the Anglo-Saxon debate philosophers of education identified and exposed fallacies in reasoning, battled against fundamental errors such as ethical relativism and epistemological reductivism, and aimed for a coherent and systematic rationalisation of beliefs and practices. Due to a relentless pursuit of clarity and truth, philosophy of education came to be seen as epistemologically foundational: as the judge of matters of value and meaning, and the arbiter of appropriate theory for explaining human behaviour in the educational sphere. The criticisms of this position raised in the half of a century since then are well-known. Yet theory may still be required, not as legitimation for principles and actions but as a form of deeper reflection on the nature and implications of the very educational enterprise. Starting from seeing education as a field of study that involves a variety of approaches, we argued that philosophical analysis may still concern itself with problems rooted in the use of language in educational discourse. Though this task is not anymore that of a conceptual underlabourer, analytic techniques remain useful. Furthermore, it should still address the assumptions and values embedded in other disciplinary approaches in the study of education, whether these are explicitly promoted or tacitly assumed in policy and practice. Evidently, this is now a debate between philosophy and other disciplines on equal terms. Finally, it is clear that philosophy of education has to explore what education might be or might become. It can revisit but also problematize its canonical questions about such matters as the aims of education, the nature of knowledge and the point of particular curriculum subjects, about human nature and human practices. It requires not narrow concentration but a flexible and imaginative drawing from different aspects of the 'parent' discipline in relation to specific but typically highly complex problems of practice.

Again, for me this was not the end. I argued that part of the decline of the sub-discipline was possibly due to the entertaining by philosophers of education of a specialized jargon. To take part in the cutting-edge debate within philosophy of education is no longer enough if it ever was. Our voices are no longer heard as most colleagues lack an acquaintance with a philosophical approach. It should therefore be supplemented (as developing one's own expertise remains of the utmost importance and such is as stake when presenting one's views to one's fellow philosophers) with taking up what is at the forefront of educational discussions nowadays. And in my already mentioned 2009 address I argued that we should observe a balance in another sense as well. I found the way to proceed along the lines of Cavell, to start from reflections on how language operates, more compelling than the various routes particularly followers of post-modernist writers have taken. Cavell takes into account at the same time the danger of nihilism (implicit in looking for foundations) which looms at the horizon and the yearning for a crystalline purity that obfuscates that logic is of and thus not off the world – of which the famous story told by Lewis Carroll about Achilles and the tortoise reminds us; and recall, there was a touch of sadness in Achilles' tone. In accepting that the other is the one who I need, it becomes clear that I have to act and start somewhere – instead of indulging myself in my own narcissism (philosophical and otherwise), chasing the meaning of idle concepts such as 'the best interests of the child' (in the debate for instance concerning government intervention in child rearing). Clearly, many of the things which I try to do may not lead to the results I and we all long for; it is nevertheless a fair price for trying to make things better, as well as an antidote against the complacency of the dissatisfaction with everything one finds oneself in. Moreover, it is a remedy for being cured of the incessant demands of performativity, for the ongoing creation of needs by a greedy economy, and the means-end reasoning of a particular, though dominant, kind of manipulative psychology. All are 'like an engine idling,' sooner or later to be brought back to their true proportions and importance by the unavoidable meltdown. What is lost, however, is not to be regretted: castles of air, houses of cards. Cavell's position reminds us that there are many roads to Rome, but also that there are many other places we may want to go to; that sometimes we think that a journey deserves our efforts, but in many cases we do not know, or even cannot possibly know, either now or in the future. Thus far some of the themes I have addressed in this area over a period of ten to fifteen years and which I took up recently again in the collaborative work with Yusef Waghid (Stellenbosch University, South Africa).

QUALITATIVE AND INTERPRETATIVE EDUCATIONAL RESEARCH AND A PHILOSOPHY OF EDUCATIONAL RESEARCH

A final cluster of problems others and I have addressed deals with the nature, scope and methods which are characteristic for educational research, what their presuppositions are and how they have to be seen in relation to philosophy of education and more generally to interpretative kinds of scholarship. The Research Community Philosophy and History of the Discipline of Education established in 1999 by the Research Foundation Flanders, Belgium (Fonds voor Wetenschappelijk Onderzoek – Vlaanderen) and which involved three Belgiun units and 12 centres worldwide, has been enormously important in this respect. It resulted thus far in the publication of 9 collections (co-edited by myself and Marc Depaepe, 8 of them in the series Educational Research, published by Springer,

Dordrecht),17 special issues in leading journals and numerous other publications by members of the Research Community. Finally, with my dear friends and colleagues Morwenna Griffiths (Edinburgh), Nick Burbules (Illinois, Urbana-Champaign) and last but not least David Bridges, we are co-editing the *International Handbook of Interpretation in Educational Research Methods* (2 vols., Springer, Dordrecht).

The academics involved in this network share the belief that there is a place within the discipline of education for so-called foundationalist approaches. This is not, however, to answer a need for a (new) foundation, but to systematically study a particular area from a discipline oriented stance. Through the lenses of philosophy and history of the discipline of education we addressed: the returning reference to 'what works,' networks and technologies, the educationalization of social problems, proofs, arguments, and other reasonings, the ethics and aesthetics of statistics, the attraction of psychology, the importance and effects of institutional spaces, and material culture and the representation of educational research. The seminar form of the annual meetings guaranteed plenty of time for discussions. I have learned a lot from my colleagues in philosophy of education, and perhaps even more from those in history of education – particularly from another lifelong friend and colleague Marc Depaepe; together we selected abstracts and provided comments and suggestions for all the submitted manuscripts and wrote the introductions for the edited books. It is impossible to do justice within the constraints of this contribution to the various issues and positions that were developed; yet I believe that what is given below is a fair representation of where we are now.

To claim that educational research favours nowadays a particular methodology and the use of particular methods is an understatement. Though it loves to refer to itself as embracing 'post-positivism,' it can be asked whether it really has parted from a logical empiricism characterized by the invariance of perception, meaning and methodology. Randomized field trials and (quasi-) experiments are paradigmatically recognized as the preferred way to proceed. It is true that parts of the discipline are no longer wary of the use of qualitative methods and are sometimes even interested in 'the particular,' but it can be questioned whether this is anything more than the use of qualitative data within a design that is foremost aimed at explanation (whether causal, quasi-causal, or probabilistic) and which is looking for the general, i.e. to be able to generalize its insights. This approach is successful in the present climate of research output that almost exclusively values publications in 'Web of Knowledge' journals, as Nick Burbules and I argued. The higher the impact factor of a journal, the more prestige is ascribed to the successful author; such rankings are also applied to evaluate groups of researchers and indeed whole departments. Research and research opportunities (i.e. funding) also operate along these lines. Moreover, it is widely believed that this research can help to address the problems human beings are confronted with. It should be observed, however, that the study of education involves other theoretical approaches as well. As all of these aspects come together at the level of the practitioner and the policymaker, all of them should have a place not only in educational research that is intended to inform practitioners and policymakers, but also in the study of education and child rearing as an academic discipline in its own right.

Traditionally, education had deep roots in philosophy, religion, and more generally in questions of value and in what it means to lead a live that is worth living. Various societal processes (secularization, communication patterns, growing mobility) have weakened the importance given to these, and from this, labelled by some 'the erosion of values,' a new age has arrived, characterized by performativity, output, and efficiency. According to many scholars the debate is now more about means than it is about ends: where every element has value almost exclusively for its contribution to something else, and that other thing for something further, and so on. For some the ends themselves are no longer part of a rational debate. They are for them, to put this bluntly, just a matter of opinion (or taste). And thus education is seen as having value only insofar as it assists in acquiring a good (or a better) job, as it prepares young people for society. There is a tendency to mark out limited areas of investigation that are relatively uncontaminated by broader questions (possibly in the name of 'objectivity'). But there is always a price to be paid when investigations are pursued within very limited parameters. The result is that a lot of educational research deals with only a small, even a miniscule, part of what is at stake. But in deciding what to do (what changes to institute, what policies to put in place, what alterations to classroom practice to make) matters cannot be left exclusively to the operation of a deductive, nomological model. One can see the attraction of the kind of research that studies in laboratory conditions the relation between independent and dependent variables in the hope of achieving general insights and conclusions with the assistance of statistical reasoning. Yet the truth is that in social sciences attending to matters of meaning and intention is vital. In such a model attention must also be paid to the need for a balance between all kind of things that are important in our life (and in education), and thus to questions of value. Yet it is the model of causality and the predictability and elements of manipulation that go with it which many find irresistible. No wonder educational research has been eager to adopt such a methodology and the methods that go with it.

In quantitative research, one typically looks for a distribution of variables (how many are there with this or that characteristic) and for explanations, which can be of a deductive-nomological kind, incorporating universal laws, or be of an inductive nature, which employ statistics. Due to being subsumed under its own set of laws, quantitative research can offer either an explanation in terms of an argument (a logical structure with premises and conclusions governed by some rule of acceptance – though, incidentally, many doubt whether it is possible to find universal laws within the context of the social sciences), or as a presentation of the conditions relevant to the occurrence of the event and a statement of the degree of probability of the event given these conditions. Turning to qualitative research one can differentiate between two kinds. One may be interested in common features in different cases. Here the purpose is not only to describe categories, but also to deal with the relationships between different categories. In many cases this kind of research is generally analogous to a quantitative design (including hypotheses), with the exception that qualitative data are gathered, referring for example to what people feel about, or what their experience is with particular things, what they say that their reasons, desires and intentions are. To be distinguished from this is a second kind where, for example, the researcher arranges events and actions by showing how they contribute to the evolution of a plot. The plot is the thematic line of the narrative, the structure that shows how different events contribute to a phenomenon seen as a kind of story. The writing of it involves an analytical development, a dialectic between the data and the plot. The resulting narrative must not only fit the data but also bring out an order and a significance not apparent in the data as such. This is not so much an account of the actual happening of events from an disinterested (objective) point of view; instead it is the result of a series of (re-) constructions by the researcher. She is not only present in the conclusions, but involved all through the process (though differently as compared to the practitioner's involvement). This kind of 'interpretive research' comes close to those areas of scholarship that may be distinguished from educational research grounded in the empirical traditions of the social sciences such as theoretical, conceptual, or methodological essays, and those studies grounded in the humanities including areas such as history and philosophy of education, where in general interpretation is involved. In such a holistic approach the relation of the elements that are involved is given not only a more prominent but also a different place. Variables are not so much studied on their own, but the researcher is focused on the complex relationships between them. Here the presence or absence of any particular element may change the whole picture and, consequently, the conclusions that can be drawn from and for a particular setting.

Such a more balanced approach departs from the 'causal chain' aspired to in the dominant educational research approach. It accepts that social science does not give us fixed and universal knowledge of the social world, but rather that it contributes to the task of improving our practical knowledge of ongoing social life. It does not help to address the existential condition in which one finds oneself, a condition characterized and increasingly undermined by uncertainty and doubt, to look for laws, regularities, statistical reasoning, because these would offer only the illusion of certainty and offer us nothing in our search for existential meaning. Educational research that puts itself in the currently dominant tradition presupposes too much that normal development administers a normative background and generates aims which have to be observed and aspired at any cost. It goes without saying that there are educational researchers who apply their insights wisely and who do not exclusively rely in their advice on the limited insights particular research has to offer. But it seems that when they refer to their specific expertise (as educational experts) or when they talk about what their subject should address, they invoke a particular concept of science (laws and regularities) and use what is 'scientifically established,' thus putting themselves in danger of ignoring other relevant aspects as well as the particularities of the problem they want to address. Their help, well-intended as it is, cannot do away with the responsibility and the requirement to offer a justification for the way we interact on behalf of those who are put in our trust. In the dominant educational research approach the isolated meritocratic individual replaces the person or subject whose home is a social practice, to be understood to a large extent by focusing on reasons and intentions which explain the alternative ways in which human beings can take part.

That means that various modes of explanation may find their place in trying to understand what is involved in teaching, in child-rearing, in educational policy etc. There is indeed no need for a single method nor to prioritize one, but as Wittgenstein argues concerning philosophy: "There is not a philosophical method, though there are indeed methods, like different therapies" (PI, I, # 133). Much will depend on the problem that is studied, but also on the kind of theoretical interest one is pursuing. It goes without saying that not only reasons of an ethical or religious nature may be involved, but that there is also an appropriate interest in a more instrumental kind of reasoning. Social research does not give us fixed and universal knowledge of the social world as such, it rather contributes to the task of improving upon our practical knowledge of ongoing social life. This presupposes dialogue between all those involved. But when we realize that there are many and often highly contested versions of participants' self-interpretation, we will also see that though the latter are the only plausible starting place, more is needed for good dialogical and social scientific practice. Here science is no longer seen as disinterested and value-free: instead there do not seem to be strict boundaries between science and society. In her contribution the researcher, the interpretive pluralist, will among other things explore the operation of many different practical norms, thus through her interpretation making implicit norms explicit; she will also necessarily invoke a normative stance. Here facts are no longer seen as exclusively made to refer to objective things in the world or things in themselves, neither are values seen as subjective states of the mind. Science reveals itself instead as a performative intervention. As Winch (1958) argued, what matters is 'what is real for us.' Though the researcher's work is in this sense also of a political nature, it does not coincide with that of the practitioner or the politician. The writing of research may be seen as a case of positive slowness that prevents us from being absorbed in the chaos of unmediated complexity.

ON THE VERGE OF DISAPPEARING: THE LOGIC OF OUR TIMES AND THE INSURMOUNTABLE CONSTRAINTS FOR PHILOSOPHY OF EDUCATION.

It is fashionable to say that it is not all doom and gloom. I must say, however, that it costs me more and more effort to work in an academic environment that at most appreciates the presence of philosophers of education, but hardly takes into account their views. On the battleground one finds nowadays not only psychologists (particularly in those contexts where one has to operate within a Faculty of Psychology and Educational Sciences), but a manifold of educational researchers as well who have gone with the flow of psychologization characterized by means-end reasonings, short term-benefit, empiricism (whether in its quantitative or qualitative research modus) and for who non-empirically informed theory is a waste of time. It is all about 'follow the money' and as more money can be acquired for particular kinds of research than for others, it is easy to decide where to go. Whether it be for tenure, promotion, or funding applications, the paradigm of successful research from the natural sciences surfaces in the areas of psychology and educational research. It is almost impossible to row against that stream and it is young colleagues who suffer the most. Looking from the inside the sub-discipline is thriving. There is no lack of manuscripts sent to the home journals of this approach; there are several book series available; and last but not least, the various international conferences are well attended. But the explosion of the dominant approach in educational research and the vast amounts of money that such research is allocated signal a different story. The gradual world-wide disappearance of philosophy and of philosophy of education from the university curricula cannot be misinterpreted. My concern could be seen as a nostalgic longing, yet I would argue that this diagnosis cannot be escaped. Rather sooner than later we will end up to be a *curiosum*, an extinct species, to be studied for the time being in a zoo and later as artefacts of a museum. The irony of this remains however, that the questions continue to pop up, inescapable as they are from the human condition. Giving up on reflection upon social practices is giving up being human altogether.

FAVORITE WORKS

Selective List of Publications in English

Articles in Journals

Smeyers, P. (1998a). Child-rearing and parental 'intentions' in postmodernity. *Educational Philosophy and Theory, 30*, 193-214.

Smeyers, P. (1998b). Assembling reminders for educational research. Wittgenstein on philosophy. *Educational Theory, 48*, 287-308.

Smeyers, P. (2006). 'What it makes sense to say.' Education, philosophy and Peter Winch on social science. *Journal of Philosophy of Education, 40*, 463-485.

Smeyers, P., & Burbules N. (2006). Education as initiation into practices. *Educational Theory, 56*, 439-449.

Waghid, Y., & Smeyers, P. (2010). On doing justice to cosmopolitan values and the otherness of the other. Living with cosmopolitan scepticism. *Studies in Philosophy and Education, 29*, 197-211.

Smeyers, P. (2011). Philosophy of … Philosophy and … Taking the conditions we find ourselves in seriously. *European Educational Research Journal, 10*, 292-301.

Smeyers, P., & Burbules, N. (2011). How to improve your impact factor: Questioning the quantification of academic quality. *Journal of Philosophy of Education, 45*, 1-17.

Smeyers, P. (2012). Chains of dependency: On the disenchantment and the illusion of being free at last (Part 1; Part 2). *Journal of Philosophy of Education, 46*, 177-191; 461-471.

Books

Blake, N., Smeyers, P., Smith, R., & Standish, P. (1998). *Thinking again: Education after postmodernism.* New York: Bergin & Garvey.

Blake, N., Smeyers, P., Smith, R., & Standish, P. (2000). *Education in an age of nihilism.* London: Falmer Press.

Smeyers, P., Smith, R., & Standish, P. (2007). *The therapy of education.* Houndsmills, Basingstoke: Palgrave Macmillan.

Peters, M., Burbules, N., & Smeyers, P. (2008). *Showing and doing: Wittgenstein as a pedagogical philosopher*. Boulder, CO: Paradigm Publishers.

Smeyers, P., & Smith, R. (2014). *Making sense of education and educational research*. Cambridge: Cambridge University Press.

REFERENCES

Cavell, S. (1979). *The claim of reason: Wittgenstein, skepticism, morality, and tragedy*. Oxford: Clarendon Press.

Cavell, S. (1988). *In quest of the ordinary: Lines of skepticism and romanticism*. Chicago, IL: University of Chicago Press.

Winch, P. (1958). *The idea of a social science and its relation to philosophy*. London: Routledge.

Wittgenstein, L. (1953). *Philosophical investigations/Philosophische Untersuchungen* (G. E. M. Anscombe, Trans.). Oxford: Blackwell. [PI in text.]

Wittgenstein, L. (1969). *On certainty/Über Gewissheit* (G. E. M. Anscombe & G. H. von Wright, Eds.; D. Paul & G. E. M. Anscombe, Trans.). Oxford: Blackwell. [C in text.]

RICHARD SMITH

PHILOSOPHY IN ITS PLACE

I suppose it began when I read Plato's Apology of Socrates at school; or perhaps it began when I wrote my first philosophy essay at university, or published my first philosophy paper. In a sense it still always feels only about to begin, as if I might one day break through to the other side of this strange business called philosophy, or summon the resources to explain with magisterial clarity how philosophy is both less and more, as a form of writing, than it is often taken to be.

This is to anticipate. But is there, after all, any real philosophy (as we might call it) in the *Apology*, or the *Phaedo*, which I also read at school? Hardly any, of the sort that I later met in the work of Anglophone, analytic philosophers. The arguments for the immortality of the soul in the *Phaedo*, for example, seemed barely worth taking seriously, and in any case my classmates and I were principally concerned with understanding the Greek text to the point where we would be able to translate passages from it under examination conditions. Still, something made an impression: we had little doubt that believing in other gods than those sanctioned by the state put Socrates on the same side as us as we relished the discomfort of the British Establishment in the mid-1960s and wore Campaign for Nuclear Disarmament badges behind the lapels of our school blazers. And if the other line of Socrates' mission was to corrupt the young we were up for that too, being pretty sure (like every generation before or since) that it was the times and not us that were out of joint.

Arriving in Oxford from my little London grammar school in 1967, in my own eyes anarchic and corrupt and ready for more, I opted for all of the philosophical texts on the Classics list: Plato's *Gorgias* and *Symposium*, the *Phaedo* again for an easy ride, and the Pre-Socratics as Special Topic. The latter involved buying a ruinously expensive textbook, Diels/Kranz: *Die Fragmente Der Vorsokratiker*, which contained not a single word of English, and sitting around a green baize table in All Souls College with a dozen other mystified undergraduates while the lecturer talked dreamily and endlessly about the doxographical tradition in which the Fragmente had variously been preserved and mangled. The *Gorgias*, *Symposium* and *Phaedo* became just a handful of the overwhelming pile of Greek and Latin texts (including the whole of the *Iliad* and *Odyssey* and Vergil's *Aeneid*) that had to be mastered in the original language (or at least to the point where one could bluff successfully) in preparation for twelve examination papers at the end of the second term of the second year. It was not an experience to nurture a deep interest in philosophy, even though the green baize and its surroundings proclaimed that something timeless and invaluable was on offer. What was nurtured more than anything else was my growing suspicion that this privileged world that I had entered by virtue of luck and one of the rare egalitarian twitches of British educational politics was in many respects a fraud.

There was I imagine a faith on the part of those responsible for this relentless grounding in the Classics that proficiency in languages and their literature – particularly these languages and literature, from which much of European thought descended – was a prerequisite for engaging with the subtleties of philosophical thought and writing. Perhaps it was simply there because for so long it had been. Certainly the undergraduates I teach now are generally capable of writing respectable philosophical essays without any knowledge of Ancient Greek. In my own case I suspect that one of its long-term effects has been to put philosophy in its place: that is, to make it possible to see that the texts which are now often thought of as constituting part of the philosophical canon sit side by side with other texts of great insight, power and beauty (such as Sophocles' plays, or Tolstoy's novels) which are not necessarily or wisely to be thought of as doing anything different from them. But this too is to anticipate.

Expecting now to engage with Philosophy Itself, the Platonic Form of the thing, pure, timeless and unchanging, I set out on the second half of my four-year undergraduate programme. Immediately I was introduced to its rigours in the analytic, Anglophone mid-twentieth century style. The first essay I was required to write was on why the logical truths are logically true. The second was on why the necessary truths are necessarily true. It was some time before I realised that the setting of the second question constituted a criticism of my answer to the first. Ready discernment of this or indeed anything else was thwarted by the relentlessly Socratic style of my first philosophy tutor, David Bostock, who met any direct question with one of his own: 'Well, why do *you* think the logical truths are logically true?' The form was that the student read the essay aloud to the tutor, and then attempted to defend such argument as the essay contained for the remainder of the appointed hour. Nothing so crude as a mark or grade was offered; you quickly realised that any attempt to establish what your tutor thought of the essay would only be met with another Socratic question: 'Well, what do *you* think of the essay?' It was said to be an excellent preparation for a career in law or the civil service. I came much later to see that was a fine, if brutal, training in thinking for yourself, since no-one was going to do the thinking for you.

This part of my degree programme bore the title of *Literae Humaniores*, which Wikipedia now helpfully tells me can best be understood as meaning 'Advanced Studies in Liberal Education.' It required the close study of the *Republic and Nicomachean Ethics* (in the original Greek, naturally): that emphasis on the centrality of text again, as if to counterbalance the spoken dialogue of the tutorials. There was also a requirement to study Greek and Roman history, about which I was selective. The death struggles of the Roman Republic and the politics of Cicero and his contemporaries did not appeal to me. It was said to be another good preparation for life after university, particularly if you went into politics. I was repelled by Cicero, the chief source for the period – grandiloquent and self-justifying, even in his letters to his friends, as if forever addressing a university debating society. On the other hand Thucydides' account of the Peloponnesian War between Athens and Sparta, written in his elegaic and restrained style, transfixed me. I recall disconcerting my Ancient History tutor, Tom Braun, with an essay that compared Thucydides'style with that of Evelyn Waugh. Thucydides was of course describing the Athens which had produced first Socrates and then Plato, and increasingly I was struck by how much more sense it made to see philosophy in its historical context rather than as a series of timeless, abstract problems in the manner of the analytical school.

In my time at university one was said to be 'reading' English, or History, or Mathematics: a form of words given particular force by the fact that lectures could no more be relied on to impart knowledge than tutors to answer questions. If there was indeed a theory that we were there to read and think for ourselves it was applied with remarkable consistency. Many lecturers focused on their own research interests, which tended to be too specialised for the average student. Some were inaudible. One eminent philosopher delivered his lectures on Aristotle with such rapidity that his audience, over a hundred at his first session, was down to less than twenty at his third. There was little alternative but to use the libraries and buy many of the books that were in heavy demand. I left Oxford with two letters. One was from Blackwell's bookshop, quoting Socrates: 'How shall we recognise the truly just man? It is he who thanks a friend for reminding him of his debt.' The other was from my second philosophy tutor, John Lucas, setting out in detail my final examination results in an opaque series of alphas and betas, alpha/betas and beta/alphas, sprinkled with +, − and ? The repudiation of any idea that essays in history or philosophy can be allocated a precise numerical mark has always impressed me. The upshot was that I had done well, but not spectacularly so. Cicero, among others, had had his revenge. However I had apparently impressed the examiners with an essay that shed new light on Aristotle's account of volition. This, John Lucas wrote gleefully, was rare in a Finals essay. Of course I was pleased, and still would be if I could remember with any clarity just what I wrote.

It had been impressed upon me throughout my education that the opportunities I had been given brought with them the obligation to put such talents as I possessed at the service of my community. (My grammar school's motto was 'Rather use than fame.') Accordingly I set out to become a social worker and shortly found myself in semi-rural Northamptonshire, untrained, with a steadily rising and varied caseload. I spent an interesting year trying to cope with this; I learned a great deal − I cannot find a way to avoid the cliché − about people. It was also a frustrating year, partly because I didn't feel I was doing much for my clients; their lives, I thought, would have been more significantly improved if my salary had been divided up among them. The second frustration was that I missed, if not philosophy, then ideas and books. I decided that the answer might be to teach, if I could find the right kind of school; this would also be true to the ethos of public service. So it was that in September 1972 I started as a teacher, again wholly untrained, of Classics and English at a highly selective, partly state-funded Birmingham school called King Edward's. At the end of my first week, during which I had made more mistakes than there is space to list here, I knew I had found my vocation.

The school's Headmaster thought it would be good for my career if I undertook a part-time Postgraduate Certificate in Education (and with luck it might also mean fewer blunders in the classroom). One of my new colleagues had taken this route some years before: I bought the course materials from him and enrolled as an external student of the University of London. One of the courses that made up the Certificate was in the philosophy of education, which was at the time dominated by the 'London line,' emanating from the Institute of Education, of conceptual analysis as practised by such figures as Richard Peters, Paul Hirst, John and Patricia White, and Robert Dearden, as well as by a similar line coming out of the United States, whose most prominent member was Israel Scheffler. As I read of the aims of education, of the nature of knowledge and its connections with liberal education, of autonomy and the education of the emotions, I was struck by the clarity and confidence of this new – to me at any rate – branch of philosophy. It offered impressive critiques of some of the vapid educational theories of the time, muddled notions of progressivism and creativity in particular. Nevertheless some of my dissatisfaction with the analytical philosophy to which I had been exposed at Oxford, to which this philosophy of education owed allegiance, re-awoke and began to take more coherent form. The proponents of conceptual analysis were far from clear about what a 'concept' was. They were practising a form of legislative linguistics, declaring that 'this is how we speak,' as if there was no issue about who 'we' were, as if the diversity of the English language could be usefully tidied up with some stipulative definitions, and as if what might, but only might, be true of English usage would automatically be true of every other language of the world. Sometimes they seemed to take particular satisfaction in the very modesty of the conclusions they reached, as if this showed that they alone had arrived at the few truths about which it was possible to be certain. This new austerity, in which the philosopher could only talk about the language of morality, did little justice to the 2,500 years of western philosophy from which it descended. In its educational version it adhered uncritically to the style of what its practitioners tended revealingly to call 'pure philosophers'; it was oblivious to its own metaphoricity (for instance in having frequent recourse to mathematical tropes in which one might speak of 'teaching a particular subject, x, to any child, Y'); it generated few ideas about how education might change for the better; it was often, even in the hands of some of its most distinguished proponents, rather pedestrian.

In the story I like to tell – which may even be true – I was sharing these thoughts with colleagues in a pub near the school when I was overheard by a man at a neighbouring table. He introduced himself as Bernard Curtis, lecturer in philosophy in the Birmingham University School of Education. He had distanced himself from what he called the analytical brand of philosophy of education at its inception and was interested in some of the continental European traditions, especially phenomenology. One result of my growing friendship with Bernard was that on his encouragement I embarked on a part-time Master's degree by thesis. In this I criticised Paul Hirst's then influential claim that there was a limited number (perhaps six) of logically distinct 'forms of knowledge' into which it was the role of education to initiate the young. My argument was partly that on a charitable interpretation of his claims what Hirst was trying to distinguish were forms not of knowledge but of meaning, and that the Wittgensteinian ideas with which he progressively sought to bolster his theory presuppose a notion of meaning which cannot be separated into a limited number of different 'forms' in the way that Hirst required. I also argued that, by contrast with the very thin conception of knowledge that Hirst was using, other cognitive phenomena such as self-deception and wishful thinking, which are sometimes grouped under the 'ethics of belief,' give us a fuller conception of the nature of knowledge and hold more interest for education. The thesis might have identified itself as broadly anti-foundationalist if I had then been familiar with the idea. After Bernard moved to a post at the University of Manchester his role as supervisor was taken over by Robert Dearden, now moved to Birmingham from the London Institute, who was generous in his response to my lines of thought even though they ran counter to his own.

At around the same time that I started work on the thesis I was studying philosophy in evening classes taught by members of the Birmingham University Philosophy Department. One particular class on Wittgenstein, taught by Andrew Jones, systematically filled in some of the gaps that Oxford had left, while not obviously diminishing my ability to think for myself. It is worth noting that little of what I was undertaking at the time would be possible now. The long and distinguished tradition of adult extra-mural education in England was destroyed by Prime Minister Margaret Thatcher, who regarded adult education as no more than a hobby, like gardening, which people should expect to pay to enjoy. The fees for a Master's degree have risen to a level that I could not then have afforded. Birmingham's School of Education was for nearly a quarter of a century without anyone interested in or competent to supervise philosophical work, a lack which has only very recently been filled, but entirely due to generous funding from a charity based in the US. The increased pressure on teachers would make my extra-curricular study unlikely now. I cannot think how I managed it even then.

* * *

The imminent arrival of our first child turned my thoughts from philosophy to more basic concerns. The obvious route to a higher salary was to become a head of department, so I began to apply for suitable posts in state schools. Then among the advertisements in the trade press there appeared one for a Lecturer in Philosophy and Tutor in Classics at the University of Durham. It looked way beyond my qualifications and experience – I had not even finished writing my thesis – but the long shot paid off and in the following autumn I realised with terror that I was now a professional philosopher, or half of one, of sorts.

It would be good at this point to be able to tell a coherent story about my intellectual and philosophical development: of how I set myself a carefully thought-out research programme, selectively absorbing the influence of this and that major thinker, eventually forging that unique and distinctive approach which is unmistakably mine. (Classical Greek employs a number of small but useful particles to indicate the degree of irony with which such a sentence may be read.) But as I look back I struggle to extract configuration from succession. Unless I deceive myself the truth is that over the course of my university career, now more than thirty years in duration, I have responded to events much more than I have deliberately planned and shaped them. Philosophy has taken its place as only part of the teaching and other activities of a diverse and sometimes frenetic professional life, and if I relegate those activities to the background of the narrative here it is not out of any failure to register their importance.

A university lecturer towards the end of the 1970s in the UK was not generally confronted with a taxing work-load, certainly not by comparison with that of a school-teacher. One of my new Durham colleagues expressed surprise on finding me at my desk after lunch: 'You really don't have to be here in the afternoons, you know.' In these circumstances I was able to finish my thesis within the three years stipulated, even among the changes brought by parenthood and moving house to a different part of the country. I wrote one paper emerging from the thesis, typing draft after draft on the same manual machine on which I had prepared the thesis. When this was accepted for publication I was glad to put the thesis and the ideas that had gone into it behind me. I had submitted two bound copies of it for examination as required, but did not pay to keep a bound copy of my own. Either that was due to my desire to move on, or my motives were more complex and obscure.

There was no automatic expectation in those days, as there is now, that a lecturer should possess, or should set about acquiring, a PhD. Having recently finished one thesis I was not in a hurry to begin another, and all around me I saw, across a range of disciplines, academics who had made a narrow specialism their own through doctoral study and then turned grey as they mined their thesis for publications for ten years or even more. This did not appeal to me, though the career advantages of a doctorate were clear enough and no doubt the exercise would be stimulating given the right topic and the right supervisor. I favoured a philosophical study of memory, on which I was now beginning to publish in what some people have called, with more or less straight faces, my phenomenological phase. I was, I think, trying to do justice to some of the rich ways that remembering and forgetting work in human experience, and in doing so find a non-technical approach to aspects of learning that went beyond what increasingly struck me as the narrowness of analytical philosophy.

Two things happened as I dithered over my options. The first was that I was invited to write a book in a series edited by two colleagues, Phil Snelders and Colin Wringe, from the Philosophy of Education Society of Great Britain, which I had recently joined. From a long list of suggested topics I chose to write on issues of discipline, manipulation, punishment and autonomy. This was partly because I was irked by the way a superficially more humane attitude to children was drawing on ideas and practices from management and counselling simply in order to render children more docile and to control the classroom. The other reason for the topic was that I thought it would sell. In the event *Freedom and Discipline* (1985) sold well, and the reviews were almost wholly positive. The publishers have just brought out a second edition, nearly 30 years later; this was on condition the text remained unaltered. I would have liked to re-write the opening chapter, which offers a justification for a philosophical treatment of the book's themes in an over-confident style too reminiscent of the analytical philosophy of education from which I was trying to distance myself. I also regret not using a gender-neutral style. Some of my female education students told me the book made them feel excluded. I have I hope at least learned from that.

The second piece of chance was that the University Director of Adult Education asked me if I would like to teach a weekly evening extra-mural class, of a roughly philosophical nature. This seemed a golden opportunity to engage with more interesting ideas than were possible in my daily work in the School of Education. After much thought I offered a class called 'Philosophical problems in understanding ourselves and others,' ranging from the idea of the self, through the anti-psychiatry of Thomas Szasz and R.D.Laing, to issues arising from the work of Freud and Jung. By the end of the first evening, as at the end of my first week as a schoolteacher, I knew I had found something to believe in. Of my class of roughly two dozen adults a large handful had already explored various ways of trying to understand themselves; another group were regular extra-mural students, many of them professional people in search of more stimulus than they found in their daily professional lives. We met for two hours once a week, after which discussion would continue in a nearby pub. I learned a great deal very fast, of necessity: not least that people came to extra-mural education for a wide range of reasons. Nobody came in search of a qualification, because there was none on offer; nor for something to write on a resumé; nor to impress their friends (who, most of the students said, found the whole business nearly as odd as Margaret Thatcher did).

The outcome of this was that I taught an evening class for the next twelve years, moving steadily towards the area where philosophy and literature meet. We ranged from acknowledged philosophical novelists such as Iris Murdoch and Sartre to the philosophical ideas present in modern classics such as Robert Pirsig's *Zen and the Art of Motorcycle Maintenance*, Malcolm Bradbury's *The History Man* and Kingsley Amis' *Lucky Jim*. We studied self-deception and wishful thinking in the plays of Ibsen, the virtues and vices of character in Jane Austen and George Eliot. We explored unreliable narrators and what it might mean for a novel to be postmodern. And we wondered about the similarities and differences between literary treatments of these themes and philosophical treatments. The reading and preparation that these classes required became the welcome centre of my working week. It has been natural to me ever since to use literary examples in my writing, from critique of the ideals of autonomy and independence, drawing on D.H.Lawrence, to my growing absorption with the importance of kinds of not knowing that I have found so illuminatingly depicted by Charles Dickens. The work of Martha Nussbaum (*The Fragility of Goodness, Love's Knowledge*) helpfully began to appear just at the time when I felt in need of arguments to justify, to myself especially, the road I was taking. There was particular irony in relishing her emphasis on the inevitability of chance in human life while the educationists around me spoke insistently of school effectiveness and education as a totally reliable technology.

Eventually university extra-mural education became, as I mentioned above, the victim of cuts inflicted by a government unable to see its point if it was not the inculcation of skills for the workplace. I was at around this time increasingly sunk in administration. In addition to duties in the School of Education I had embarked on a ten year stint as editor of the *Journal of Philosophy of Education*, and towards the end of this period my colleagues in the campus trade union, the Association of University Lecturers, pressed me into taking on the Durham Presidency for two years. My research suffered, not least because it was not stimulated by my undergraduate teaching; and I felt I ought not to publish in the journal that I was editing. A handful of politically oriented articles appeared in other journals: the title of one of them, 'Remembering democracy,' indicates my view of how the UK government was treating education, and particularly universities, at the time.

Another chance meeting enabled me to develop the kind of teaching I had always wanted to do. A neighbour talked to me – I was putting out the milk bottles at the time – about his difficulty in finding someone to replace him as Director of Durham's Combined Degree in Social Sciences. This was and is an undergraduate programme which students put together for themselves from the various departments of the Social Science Faculty, with the option to take up to two modules from other Faculties. When I succeeded my neighbour I was struck by two things. One was the high quality of the students, who in addition to their academic prowess came to university with an independence of spirit that this kind of degree appealed to. The second was that they had no core module or modules to hold their programme together and from which they could survey their field of study and reflect on the idea of 'social science' which was what, at least nominally, they were students of. Accordingly I launched a new compulsory first year module, 'The discipline of social science,' which examined the aspiration of the study of the social world to be some kind of science. We traced it from the scientific revolution of the late sixteenth and seventeenth centuries, through the Enlightenment and on to Darwin, Marx and Freud. The module proved popular and the students asked for this 'core' to be continued into their second and third years. So 'The philosophy of social science' came into being, whose topics included how we can understand ourselves and others, interpretation and hermeneutics, the narrative turn, and the claims of sociobiology. This was optional, as was a third year module, 'New directions in social science,' which took the postmodern turn. I soon had roughly 100, 60 and 30 keen and committed students across the three modules: I was teaching content that I found deeply interesting and challenging (not least the ideas of Lyotard, Derrida and Levinas in the third year), and working with students who, unlike so many Education students, were absorbed in ideas for their own sake and not in the expectation that they would have any direct vocational pay-off. This happy, if exhausting, state of things continued for twelve years and, together with my duties as Course Director to over 700 students (the University having asked me to take on the Combined Arts degree too) gave me more professional satisfaction than I could ever have hoped for.

During these years a writing partnership came into being between Nigel Blake, Paul Smeyers, Paul Standish and me. Quite how this happened, beyond the fact that we met regularly at Philosophy of Education conferences, particularly the British one in Oxford, I don't think any of us can precisely recall. I see that we wrote a blurb for one of our books declaring that we 'originally came together to explore [our] shared interest in postmodern issues and poststructuralist theory in relation to education,' which sounds plausible and as far as I am concerned is testimony in important part to the stimulating undergraduate teaching I was now doing. I don't have any ready answer to people who ask just how it all worked. Certainly co-writing is unusual in philosophy of any sort. There was friendship, forbearance, patience, mutual support, generosity; there were restaurants and pubs in London; there was generally another meeting looming for which each of us had agreed to prepare draft material. The result of this collaborative work included, in various combinations of all four or three of us, five books: *Thinking Again: Education after Postmodernism* (1998); *The Universities We Need: Higher Education After Dearing* (1998); *Education in an Age of Nihilism* (2000); the edited *Blackwell Guide to the Philosophy of Education* (2003); *The Therapy of Education: Philosophy, Happiness and Personal Growth* (2006) – as well as individually written journal articles and chapters that have their origins in this partnership. It was particularly good to have philosophy of education acknowledged alongside epistemology, metaphysics and philosophy of mind as sufficiently distinctive to qualify for a Blackwell Guide.

Further collaboration was stimulated when Paul Smeyers and his Leuven University colleague Marc Depaepe set up, with generous funding from the Flanders Regional Government, an annual seminar: Philosophy and History of the Discipline of Education – Evaluation and Evolution of the Criteria for Educational Research. Meeting for the first time in 2000, this brought together philosophers and historians of education who were concerned to think beyond the prevailing assumption that research in education was essentially an empirical business, largely psychological in flavour and a matter of discovering 'what works.' It has been a continuous pleasure to be a member of this group, whose concerns matched my own as I saw educational research in Britain increasingly hostile to theory and driven largely by considerations of what will secure external funding and what can most readily be taught as 'research methods' to high fee-paying students from overseas.

Many publications have resulted from this 'Research Community,' as it has become known to its members, including several special issues of the *Journal of Philosophy of Education*. Of course it is useful to have these as evidence of one's 'productivity,' if only to keep the barbarians at arm's length. The point however is in the meetings themselves – seminars, conferences, symposia –and the friendships again and again renewed in them: in the Erasmus bar in Leuven, the King's Arms in Oxford, in a cafe in Warsaw, on a Greek island. Quite what is philosophical in these conversations and what is ordinary discourse in its many modes, or what distinguishes a philosophical text from other kinds of writing – these are questions over which there is reason to pause, but not for too long before moving on to more pressing matters. Or so it seems to me Plato himself tells us, at what we now think of as the dawn of philosophy: that we are not to be too knowing about something called philosophy, in an age much given to certainties, methods and solutions, particularly in education.

I write these reflections, so many of which seem strangely to be about someone else, in my study on the outskirts of a northern English cathedral city, as a long winter turns at last into spring. To Jenny, my wife of over forty years, and to our three children I owe the greatest of my debts, especially for keeping philosophy in its place.

FAVOURITE WORKS

Personal Favourites

Smith, R. (1999). Paths of judgement: the revival of practical wisdom. *Educational Philosophy and Theory, 31*(3), 327-340.
Smith, R. (2006). Abstraction and finitude: Education, chance and democracy. *Studies in Philosophy and Education, 25*(1-2), 19-35.
Smith, R. (2008). To school with the poets: Philosophy, method and clarity. *Paedogogica Historica, 44*(6), 635-645.
Smith, R. (2009). Between the lines: Philosophy, text and conversation. In Claudia Ruitenburg (Ed.), *Journal of Philosophy of Education* (Special Issue), *43*(3), 437-449.
Smith, R. (2013). The theology of education to come. In P. Smeyers & M. Depaepe (Eds.), *Educational research. The attraction of psychology* (pp. 147-157). Dordrecht: Springer.
Smith, R. (2013). Re-reading Plato: The slow cure for knowledge. In M. Papastephanou, T. Strand, & A. Pirrie (Eds.), *Philosophy as a lived experience*. Berlin: LIT Verlag.

Works That Have Influenced Me

Dickens, C. (1853). *Bleak house*.
Homer. *The Odyssey*.
Lear, J. (1998). *Open minded: Working out the logic of the soul*. Cambridge, MA: Harvard University Press.
Lyotard, J.-F. (1984). *The postmodern condition: A report on knowledge* (Trans. G. Bennington & B. Massumi). Manchester: Manchester University Press.
Murdoch, I. Middle period novels, especially: *The nice and the good* (1968), *The black prince* (1973), *The sea, the sea* (1978), *Nuns and soldiers* (1980).
Nussbaum, M. (1986). *The fragility of goodness: Luck and ethics in Greek tragedy and philosophy*. Cambridge: Cambridge University Press.
Plato. *Phaedrus*.
Rorty, R. (1980). *Philosophy and the mirror of nature*. Oxford: Blackwell.

BARBARA S. STENGEL

MAKING SENSE OF MOMENTS

There are moments you remember all your life.
There are moments you wait for and dream of all your life.
This is one of those moments.[1]

Life must be understood backwards ... but ... must be lived forwards.[2]

It may seem incongruous to marry Soren Kirkegaard to Barbra Streisand, but I ask you to suspend your skepticism for a moment. The controversy around Streisand's adaptation of the Isaac Bashevis Singer short story notwithstanding,[3] the original story, the Streisand lyric, and the Kirkegaard insight all provide structure for this look back at my presence in the distinctive professional world of practice we call philosophy of education. My being a philosopher of education – and the kind of philosopher of education I could be – are anchored to the moments that have enabled me to appreciate the thinking-feeling-doing nexus of experience articulated early on by John Dewey (1894, 1895) and that have been enacted for me by feminist scholars like Maxine Greene and Audrey Thompson.

It seems worth rehearsing the lines of the original Singer story and the play that emerged from it. Yentl is "the Yeshiva Boy" – except, of course, that she is not. Yentl is a girl who grows up learning to discuss and debate Jewish law with her widowed rabbi father. His death means that she may lose the practices that identify her to herself. This is not a dispassionate choice for Yentl; this choice is "live, forced and momentous" (James, 1897). She cannot give up her studies; it is in her head, in her habits, in her gut and in her heart. She dresses as a man and presents herself at a yeshiva where she studies Talmud and reinvents herself as the male "Anshel." When Avigdor (her study partner) discovers her secret, Yentl suggests that she has "the soul of a man in the body of a woman," and determines that she must live as Anshel for the rest of her life.

Fortunately for me and for my female colleagues in the field, times have changed and my studies do not challenge my self-understanding as they might have even a half century ago. Still, Yentl's story illuminates two strands of my own: 1) that I cannot avoid my calling to philosophy of education; I had it before I knew the field existed and it will call me long after I retire; and 2) that expectations – for women and men, for the privileged and the disenfranchised – that limit human potential are, for me, unthinkable. But neither the calling nor the commitment to challenging expectations was known to me at the start. This is a story I lived forward. It is a story of pragmatic attention, occasionally painful openness, and a predilection for ambiguity that accompanies – and sometimes challenges – an abiding responsibility to fix things, to find the right answer, to make it all better. It is a story of staying open, sometimes by choice, occasionally by necessity. And finally, it is a story of recognition and acceptance that staying open – moment by moment – is the only way to answer the twin call (ambiguity and responsibility) of myself as philosopher of education.

I began life as an untroubled philosopher. As early as I can remember, I was known to my father and and his friends in my Philadelphia neighborhood as "Miss Itch." The incessant questioning that earned me that moniker went with me to parochial school where I was an excellent student who talked too much – earning "medals" for academic achievement but very low marks for Self-Control. In the late 1950s and 1960s, I learned basic skills and thorough cultural literacy from highly intelligent nuns for whom the path to college and career led through the convent. I learned just as much at home from my mother who – though home with six children – followed the news, the business world and sports avidly, and from my father who – though employed as an engineer/business executive – read fiction voraciously and recommended books to me to read that were always just beyond my competence. My parents' conversations with each other were models of reason, action and affection – with a remarkably high level of common sense. In high school and in college at Bucknell University, I was privileged to live in close connection to other young men and women – and many talented and dedicated teachers – who both shared their passions and left me alone to find mine. That array of shared talents drew me in conflicting directions and it took me quite a while to find philosophy of education – but I was always on the path.

HEEDING THE CALL

I was in second grade in a parochial school in Philadelphia. I was sitting in the church adjacent to the school with my class of ninety-five six year olds. Our teacher, a Catholic nun, was sharing the value of our faith with us by telling us that only children who were Catholic could go to heaven; non-Catholic children would go to hell. I remember thinking to myself: "That can't be right. Why is she telling us that?"

Obviously my respect for authority was leavened by critical skepticism. When my own intuitions and authoritative messages conflicted, I found myself searching for some more systematic and defensible basis to make a decision. It seems I learned this from my father.

Walt Senkowski sold heavy construction equipment, managed those who did the same work and eventually became the CEO of a privately held corporation that distributed and serviced the huge cranes and payloaders that you see in major construction sites. He also taught engineering courses at Drexel early in his career. He often told me that he was not a manager, but a teacher whose task was to help his sales and service force understand what they were doing and how to do it. He was constantly called on as a consultant and motivational speaker for others in the industry and developed a tool that he called "A Credo for Success" that appeared in all his talks and workshops. The Credo appeared on slides, handouts and business cards. As I was leaving for college, he gave me a card. It read:

CREDO FOR SUCCESS

A true sense of urgency
A demand for excellence in yourself and in others
A compelling curiosity to know the things you don't understand
A driving desire to do the best you know how TODAY
A healthy disregard for the way things have been done in the past

It has occurred to me on multiple occasions since that time that these attributes are not about business or engineering, but broadly useful. It has also occurred to me that these broadly useful qualities are dangerous, that "demand for excellence" and "driving desire" can become (pathologically) destructive, while the others can get you into more trouble that you can handle. Still, they have served me well and there is no question in my mind that my own "compelling curiosity" and "healthy disregard" were the drivers that took me past other distractions to ultimately find philosophy of education. I didn't find it on my own however. It took "a little help from my friends."

In my final semester as an undergraduate political science major, I was headed for a career in business. Growing up in a household where *Forbes*, *Business Week* and *The Wall Street Journal* were the coffee table reading will do that to you. But in that last semester, I was studying *Acting*, the German *Novella*, *American Art*, and *Ritual, Symbol and Celebration*. I was in the office of my religious studies seminar instructor, Joe LaBarge, discussing my final project. I had studied with him in an earlier course and become friends with him and his wife. Out of the blue he said to me, "You would be good at this." I looked at him blankly and said, "Good at what?" He said, "Academic work, religious studies." I laughed.

But I didn't forget. I chewed on that offhand comment for months. It had never occurred to me to study further, to pursue a life of the mind. It became a bone I couldn't let go of. I did take a good job as a banker and pursued it successfully for just nine months. All the while I was birthing a plan to return to a Ph.D. program in religious studies at Catholic University in Washington, DC, just a little over a year after I left Bucknell. It was utterly stimulating and the site of a fabulous grounding in the field of phenomenology. But I realized that religious studies as a field was a little too esoteric to be my steady diet (at about the same time they realized that I was not orthodox enough to garner a Ph.D. from The Catholic University of America) and left my program after a calendar year with a masters degree – and no clear idea of what was next.

I became a high school social studies teacher in a parochial high school, pushed there by a positive experience as a teaching assistant in an undergraduate class. I was also an assistant basketball coach in a small college nearby. (Did I mention I was really good at driving the baseline as a high school and college player?) I continued this combination for several years, moving from Lancaster, PA to Pittsburgh where my then-husband entered Pitt Law School. I very much enjoyed high school teaching, perhaps ironic in that education was the only major at Bucknell that I steadfastly avoided. And I learned over time – with the help of many wonderful colleagues – how to do it well. But I was also open to a career as a college basketball coach and thought that a masters degree in sports psychology might be just the right credential. So I enrolled at Pitt while teaching during the day and coaching in the afternoon, taking courses at night and in the summers. Two years later, I had the degree and coaching experience, but also the growing realization that babysitting 12 college women would not be esoteric enough for me. The coaching career door closed, but another opened.

My sports psychology degree required a substantial research project for graduation. Professor Mike Sherman was the instructor of my research seminar and the one who fielded ideas for my empirical research. In the course of one of these conversations (that ranged pretty widely and included some discussion of my background), Mike said, "You ought to talk with Dave Engel over in Foundations of Education. His background is like yours and you talk like he does. You would have a lot in common."

So I did. Dave was a professor of philosophy of education with a doctorate from Teachers College, Columbia. He came to the field through an M.Div. from Union Theological Seminary. I found out that there was a field called philosophy of education and that I could study it. I could learn Dewey from Dave Engel and existentialist thought from his colleague Margaret Anderson, and I could go over to the Cathedral of Learning and study with Wilfrid Sellars and others in what some considered to be the best philosophy program in the country. Several years later in 1984, with a Ph.D. from the ed school and another M.A. from the philosophy department, I would be a philosopher schooled in both pragmatism and analytic philosophy. My taste of existentialism and my background in phenomenology from Catholic U leavened both as I struggled with the task of wrestling the three major strains of early 20th century philosophy into a personal stance. My dissertation that became a book, *Just Education: The Right to Education in Context and Conversation* (1991), was an effort to do just that. Intentionally written in an idiom that my mother could follow, I employed linguistic and phenomenological analysis rooted in reality-based 'hypothetical scenarios' culminating in a pragmatist's response. This was a way of working that I found neither too esoteric nor too concrete, and I would continue to speak philosophy in this way. Post-modernism and post-structuralism were not yet on my radar.

I found my way to philosophy of education through banking and coaching and teaching, through political science and religious studies and sports psychology. And it took a phys ed professor to get me there! All I did was stay open to possibilities I had not planned.

BUILDING A CAREER UNWITTINGLY

By the time, I finished my doctorate, I was Tim's mother. I had little thought of "building a career" because my husband and son formed the frame of my life and priorities. Still, I knew that I was a philosopher of education; I might as well get paid for it. My first full-time position – and one where I would flourish for 25 years – was at Millersville University in Lancaster, PA. Millersville is part of the state system in Pennsylvania and a place where very fine faculty members who generally identify as teachers-who-are-also-scholars educate the sons and daughters of the truly middle class. Because of its roots as a normal school, and despite (or perhaps because of) its accomplishments in establishing strong liberal arts majors, hundreds of teachers graduate and are licensed each year. Working at Millersville University meant teaching four courses a semester, usually three sections of a required social foundations course and one of masters level philosophy of education. Without actually intending to, I became a teacher educator and that "day job" would ground much of my philosophical reflection. That work would move me from an interest in teacher knowledge and the philosophy of teaching to a focus on pedagogical responsibility and the moral dimensions of teaching and learning to my present concern with emotion as a factor in educational experience.

TEACHER KNOWLEDGE

I had not been formally educated into teaching. I found myself in that place unexpectedly and used the experience as an opportunity to grow. As I moved into a career as teacher educator, I turned to my own practice as a teacher to inform my practice as a teacher educator. I wanted to make sense of my creating active learning environments in response to no dictate except the perceived needs of my students. And the push to think through my own experience to illuminate that of my students was piqued by a dean who arrived in my third year at the university.

I walked into a colleague's office and encountered the recently-arrived dean. She was the first woman to hold an administrative position at Millersville, replacing a dean who had been there for more than twenty years. I introduced myself to her and she asked what I taught. I replied "Philosophy of Education." She said, "Sometime you'll have to tell me what philosophy of education has to do with teacher education."

We became close friends and collaborators, the dean and I, working to figure out and articulate the relationship between content and method in teaching, and, in the process, to structure a teacher education program that would reflect the missing paradigm in teacher knowledge that Lee Shulman (1986, 1987) was calling "pedagogical content knowledge." This work, always both practical and intellectual, both professional and philosophical, resulted in pedagogy seminars and programmatic collaborations with arts and sciences colleagues through a Carnegie-funded effort known as Project 30 and, eventually, in a Spencer Post-Doctoral Fellowship for "Teaching Knowing: Knowledge in Use." All of this work marked a further step toward my use of the concrete, pedagogical and empirical as grist for the mill of philosophy. I employed edited videotapes of novice teacher practice as interview prompts for the teacher educators (both ed school and arts and sciences faculty) who worked with them in order to frame a theory of teacher knowledge in terms of functional ways of knowing (logical, cultural, pedagogical and professional) through which teachers draw on funds of knowledge.

My work in teacher knowledge and the philosophy of teaching connected me personally and theoretically to Shulman, then a Stanford professor and later President of the Carnegie Foundation for the Advancement of Teaching. It also returned me to some ideas that had been important in my study of religion and moral development, specifically, the ethical theory of Christian pragmatist H. Richard Niebuhr (1963), and was the proximate cause of my professional collaboration with teacher educator Alan Tom (following a chance meeting after an American Educational Studies session related to the work). Shulman's ideas about pedagogical reasoning (1986, 1987), Niebuhr's image of an ethic of responsibility, and Tom's focus on the Teaching as a Moral Craft (1983) prompted a perhaps predictable development of interest in pedagogical responsibility.

PEDAGOGICAL RESPONSIBILITY

I was ten years old and playing football in the side yard with my brother and his friends. They always needed extra players but never let me actually carry the football. So I should have been suspicious when my number was called. Instead, I was overjoyed. I gathered in the ball after the handoff and headed up field only to be tackled by Nicky Macko playing for the other team. As I hit the ground, I realized that all the other players had scattered. I was set up. Looming above me, Nicky, a seventh grader, asked me if I would wear his tie-clip, the 1960s Catholic school version of "going out." I took it confused and went into the house where I found my mother ironing in the basement. I told her, "Nicky Macko wants me to wear his tie clip." She said, "What does that mean?" I said, "I'm not sure." She said (without a trace of smile), "Well, you'll have to make this decision because you will have to live with the consequences."

In that moment, I formed a prospective theory of responsibility that has stayed with me to this day and emerges in my own work and in response to the work of others. It is the kind of theory of responsibility that Dewey espouses and the kind that flies in the face of so much of the Calvinist accountability that infects modern American social and political rhetoric. And it is very much at home in Niebuhr's view of the responsible self, the person who responds to ethical demands only partly of her own making, interprets what is actually going on, conjectures and imagines the consequences of possible action, and then acts in context, that is, in a community of value and practice of which she is and chooses to be a part. For Neibuhr, ethics is not following rules or optimizing outcomes – though both rules and outcomes are part of responding deliberately. The moral life is a life of determining the fitting response at every turn. (In case you were wondering, I gave Nicky back the tie clip.) This understanding was given concrete form as Alan Tom and I worked through multiple collaborative efforts starting with "Taking the Moral Nature of Teaching Seriously" in *Education Forum* (1995) and eventually resulting in *Moral Matters: Five Ways to Develop the Moral Life of Schools* (2006).

Responsibility had a face that was not purely pragmatist however and my thinking was complicated accordingly. I was drinking deeply of feminist theorizing about ethics and education including Carol Gilligan, Mary Belenky et al., Jane Roland Martin, Nel Noddings, and others. Natasha Levinson, Gert Biesta, Denise Egea-Kuhne and Ann Chinnery introduced me to Emmanuel Levinas and his understanding of ethics as first philosophy and response as constitutive of one's being. Other colleagues in the Philosophy of Education Society brought me face to face with Jacques Derrida and Michel Foucault as well as their feminist shadows Judith Butler and Nancy Fraser. As I would put it in 1997, "I'm not a postmodernist, but ...." My encounter with my colleagues thinking through this continental tradition was cracking me open, reshaping what I was able to say. This resulted in a series of presentations, responses and publications that all had "responsibility" in the title (see Stengel, 1994, 1999, 2001, 2003, 2013a, 2013b) and that fleshed out a conception of "pedagogical responsibility."

The last essay in that series, "Teacher Responsibility: Practical Reasoning in a Pedagogical Wonderland" is one developed for a Carnegie Foundation-sponsored multi-year symposium on practical reasoning in the professions in 2004. Lee Shulman and Gary Fenstermacher invited me to participate in this dialogue with teacher-theorists from medicine, law, ministry, engineering and education along with teacher-theorists of the liberal arts. It was a joy for me to encounter practitioners of various professions who took this kind of prospective view of responsibility seriously and who were working to make it a reality in the professional preparation of novices.

AN INTERLUDE: RECOGNIZING MYSELF AS OTHER

We usually took the El to Margaret and Orthodox and then walked or took the R bus the rest of the way home, but this day my mother decided to take the bus from downtown. As we rode north on 11th, all the Whites folks got off the bus and only Black folks got on. By the time we got to Hunting Park, my mother and I were the only White faces in sight. I lived in a White neighborhood, attended a White Catholic school and church, and though I knew a few Black men and women, I had never been the only White face in the space. I was on alert – until my mother and the woman sitting next to her struck up an easy conversation that lasted all the way up 11th. When we got off the 23 and boarded the R, the situation was the same, but my discomfort was gone.

That moment is the first time I can recall being the Other. (I probably should have felt it as a young woman, but patriarchy was so entrenched as to be invisible and my parents were remarkably even-handed in their treatment of their sons and their daughters.) I have since had similar experiences – as the only White woman living in an all Black apartment complex when I enrolled in graduate school in Washington, DC, or as the only woman in a room full of men making decisions about business or academic programs, or as a White teacher in a classroom full of Black and Brown children. And I have been "pulled up short" (Kerdeman, 2004) in the face of my own privilege on more occasions than I can recall.

In a required social foundations course during my masters study in sports psychology at Pitt, I first encountered revisionist social and political theory and learned a language to express the reality of a world in which someone is always Other. I thought I knew that world, but it became a vivid and compelling place after I acquired affect- and action-laden concepts that shaped my perception of everything I encountered.

My associations with Carole Counihan, Tracey Weis and Rita Smith-Wade-El in Women's Studies and African-American Studies at Millersville led me to W.E.B. DuBois' formulation of "double consciousness" (1903), to Pat Hill Collins "standpoint theory" (2000), to bell hooks' transgressive teaching (1994), to Kimberle Crenshaw's "intersectionality" (1998), to Charlotte Perkins Gilman's 1915 humorous and deeply disturbing portraits of patriarchy and women's place in it, to Gerda Lerner's deconstruction of the creation of patriarchy (1986), and all this reinforced a commitment to multicultural education and culturally responsive pedagogy that seemed like common sense when working with diverse children in public school settings.

But not until I realized that I could love a woman as a partner did I inhabit what it meant to live as Other. The ideas about equity and diversity that had been made vivid in my social foundations study and subsequent reading and teaching became immediate and unavoidable in my daily living. I was stunned by the subtle ways my life changed. Where I had once been visible and respected, I was invisible or disrespected. My contribution was inexplicably discounted; my presence subtly unwelcome. Nobody who had liked or loved me didn't like or love me anymore, but for some, for many, I was an embodied reminder of something not quite right.

I was also comforted by all the ways nothing changed. I was still Tim and Emily's mother, but my parenting was infused with a humility I could not have known previously. I was still a philosopher of education, but one whose thought could never again offer a simplistic answer to any question. And fortunately, those who both loved me and found me a puzzle have since figured out that I am still a person worth their investment. Today's world is a different place than the world I came out into. Twenty years and a change of location have made a significant difference. While living as a lesbian has its ever-present complications, they are relatively minor and getting more so every day.

Just as the birth of my first child (a story too long to tell here) radicalized me to the reality of subtle and overt forms of misogyny, the end of my marriage to a good man who remains my friend and the later process of coming out radicalized me to the reality that there is no making the world better without also making it worse. That which is useful – and even necessary – is always also dangerous, politically and personally. That insight, one that Cris Mayo helped me to frame, would become part of my theorizing fear in educational experience.

FEAR AND EMOTION IN CONTEMPORARY EDUCATION

I cannot for the life of me remember when and why fear moved to the center of my philosophical consciousness. It was already there before 9/11 before "Be very afraid" became the watchword of the War on Terror. It was already there before the creep of No Child Left Behind and AYP turned schooling into the timid approximation of education that we see today. It may have been the confluence of Christian and Wiccan ideas that I encountered in readings as various as Martin Luther King, Jr. ("Antidotes to Fear," 1977) and Starhawk (*Dreaming the Dark*, 1982). I just know it grabbed hold of me. When we completed the manuscript for *Moral Matters* in 2002, fear was waiting for me. To learn enough to think fear through, I designed a first year seminar, a "passion course" that Millersville faculty teach to new students. I could chose any content I wished as long as, in the process, I coached students into better habits of mind and inquiry.

Each year the course attracted a full complement of students and each year those students taught me what I needed to think about. When I applied for sabbatical – and a Fulbright Award to the Universidade de Évora in Portugal, the task of understanding fear as it figured in educational experience at all levels was at the center of my proposals. Both the sabbatical year and the Fulbright experience (in 2008-09) proved helpful in setting up time to think about my own experience of living alone – and learning constantly.

It was my second night in Mitra, in a tiny three-room casa that would be home for four months. I knew no one who lived in the small circle of dwellings seven miles outside Évora, a fabulous and fascinating "museum city" in the Alentejo region of Portugal that dates to the Roman Empire. Mitra had been the Bishop's residence in the 16th and 17th centuries. The casa was constructed of thick stucco walls without windows, accessible by thick wooden doors without sils. There was no radio, no TV, no internet. The gap at the bottom of the door welcomed ratos and cobras, and, of course, cold air. But in the late summer, the air was warm and the thick walls kept the living space from becoming too warm.

I was near sleep when I was startled awake by a pounding on my door. I laid motionless and, after about two minutes, it ceased. I got out of bed and peered out the small porthole like window in the front door. I saw nothing. I was wary and confused – and my heart pounded long after the bater a porta ceased.

The next night the same thing happened, but this time I got out of bed and cautiously moved to the door, convinced that whatever this was, it was not human. Eventually, I saw a harmless looking Collie trying to enter my new home.

Two days later, I went out into my quintal, a scrubby backyard larger than my house and encountered my first neighbors – and with them, the Collie, Aqua! Susanna (a nurse) and Vitor (a professor of informatics) and Miquel (their son) became my new friends and helpful neighbors. When I told them the story of Aqua pounding on my door, they explained that he was just coming home after a night roaming the countryside and got confused because Vitor had lived with Aqua in my casa until just a week earlier when Susanna and joined him.

What might have become crippling fear became curiosity and interest that generated support and empowerment. This happened over and over in my time in Portugal and gave me much to think about.

My experience in Évora – finding my way, forging relationships, working in schools, talking with teacher educators, teaching psychology and leadership students in pidgen português – was the basis of my Kneller Lecture for AESA in 2009, "Schooled to Fear: Case Studies of Educative Feeling and Miseducative Emotion." That essay was the first in a series (see, for example, Stengel, 2010, 2010b, 2013) that will, I hope, inform a book-length manuscript on the topic.

My interest in fear has lead me to work on a theory of emotion that distinguishes affect, feeling and emotion, relying on Dewey's concept of experience as inevitably integrating affect, cognition and behavior into habits of perception and response (1894; 1895) and on Sara Ahmed's (2003) notion that affect circulates by sticking to objects. We associate objects with affect and react with automatic affect to those objects. But affect is not emotion or even feeling. I use the term "affect" for involuntary and unnamed bodily excitation, "feeling" as consciousness of the excitation, and "emotion" as the name (concept) properly placed on the state of excitation once it becomes conscious as a state felt and also defined by the action state that accompanies it. In other words, a math phobic student doesn't shut down because he is afraid of math; we label him 'phobic' because he shuts down. We cannot control the affect associated with mathematics because of "past histories of association." But we can accept affect as just that, an automatic physiological reaction that prompts but does not compel the avoidance behavior that would designate that affect as fear. A good teacher knows this and can use the affective energy in constructive ways to reconstruct habits of reaction and response.

All of this is spilling out into analyses of the emotional terrain of various educational issues. To date, just one published essay addresses this, "After the Laughter" (2013), an entry in a special issue on humor in *Educational Philosophy and Theory*, but I am working now on a piece that applies my thinking about educational affect to questions of gun violence. More such pieces are, I suspect, on the way.

My interest in fear seems to be the culmination of a lifetime of (small and large) openings to difference – and the subsequent discomfort and interruption that makes the new possible. From the inconsequential (learning to play the violin – and doing it badly – at the age of forty) to the substantial (leaving the comfort of heterosexual privilege), from the exciting (living in Portugal quite on my own) to the mundane (living vegetarian for one year in 1991), from the voluntary (having a child) to the involuntary (losing both my parents at what seemed like too early an age), I found that I could not predict what was good for me ... or how it would affect my being a philosopher of education.

Perhaps that is why I left Millersville after 25 years – at the urging of my trusted friend and colleague Marcy Singer-Gabella – to take a position as a Professor of the Practice of Education at Peabody College, Vanderbilt University. I am still a teacher educator, still a philosopher of education, but my being in Nashville, TN is opening me up at the same time that it is opening up new possibilities for practice and thought.

OPEN TO THE GIFT(S) OF OTHERS

Philosophy of education has been, for me, a relational practice. At every turn, it involves encounters with texts, with others, with myself, and with myself as Other. These encounters have never been only intellectual, purely cognitive. They have always been embodied and emotional. Whether I use my daughter Emily's experiences as a source for my analysis and speculation or find inspiration in the madness that passes for educational policy in Tennessee right now, my thinking bears both the weight and the generative energy of my feelings. Relations matter and relations invoke idea, affect and disposition. As I write this in retrospect, as I understand backward, I am acutely aware that my "career" is a gift from those (people, events and texts) who called me to responsibility and challenged me with ambiguity. They cracked me open and kept me open until I could understand. This is one of those moments.

NOTES

[1] This is a lyric from "This Is One of Those Moments" from the score of the movie, Yentl, produced and directed by Barbra Streisand (1983).

[2] The complete original: "It is quite true what philosophy says: that life must be understood backwards. But then one forgets the other principle: that it must be lived forwards. Which principle, the more one thinks it through, ends exactly with the thought that temporal life can never properly be understood precisely because I can at no instant find complete rest in which to adopt the position: backwards" (Kirkegaard, 1996, p. 161) (43 IV A 164).

[3] Barbra Streisand's film adaptation of "Yentl" veered dramatically from the original short story and play by allowing Yentl to reveal her true feelings for Avigdor and having her return to her female self and sail for the United States at the end. The film received a scathing review from author Singer but went on to do quite well both financial and with many critics.

FAVORITE WORKS

From My Own Work

Stengel, B. (2001). Teaching in response.
Stengel, B. (2004). Knowing is response-able relation.
Stengel, B. (2010). The complex case of fear and safe space.
Stengel, B. (2011). Feelings of worth and the moral made visible.
Stengel, B., & Casey, M. (2013). To grow by looking: From moral perception to pedagogical responsibility.
Stengel, B. (2014). So open it hurts: Enabling "therefore, we can ... " in the dangerous, secure world of education.

Most Influential Work

Ahmed, S. (2003). *The cultural politics of emotion*. New York: Routledge.
Berger, P., & Luckmann, T. (1963). *The social construction of reality*. New York: Doubleday.
Dewey, J. (1910). *How we think*. Lexington, MA: D.C. Heath.
Dewey, J. (1921). *Human nature and conduct*. New York: Henry Holt.

Follett, M. P. (1995). *Mary Parker Follett: Prophet of management* (Pauline Graham, Ed.). Boston: Harvard Business School Press.
Foucault, M. (1995). *Discipline and punish*. New York: Vintage Press.
Goodman, N. (1978). *Ways of worldmaking*. Indianapolis: Hackett Publishing.
Niebuhr, H. R. (1963). *The responsible self*. New York: Harper and Row.
Scheffler, I. (1991). *In praise of the cognitive emotions: And other essays in the philosophy of education*. New York: Routledge.

REFERENCES

Ahmed, S. (2003). *The cultural politics of emotion*. New York: Routledge.
Collins, P. H. (2000). *Black feminist thought*. New York: Routledge.
Crenshaw, K. (1991). Mapping the margins: Intersectionality, identity politics, and violence against women of color. *Stanford Law Review, 43*(6), 1241-1299.
Dewey, J. (1894). The theory of emotion I. *Psychological Review, 1*(6), 553-569.
Dewey, J. (1895). A theory of emotion II. *Psychological Review, 2*(1), 13-32.
DuBois, W. E. B. (1903). *The souls of black folk*. Rockville, MD: Arc Manor.
Gilman, C. P. (1915/1979). *Herland*. New York, NY: Pantheon Books.
hooks, b. (1994). *Teaching to transgress: Education as the practice of freedom*. New York, NY: Routledge.
James, W. (1897). *The will to believe and other essays*. London: Longmans, Green, and Co.
Kerdeman, D. (2004). Pulled up short: Challenging self-understanding as a focus of teaching and learning. *Journal of Philosophy of Education, 37*(2), 293-308.
King, Jr., M.L, (1977). Antidotes to fear. In *Strength to love* (pp. 115-126). Cleveland, OH: Collins and World
Kirkegaard, S. (1996). *Papers and journals* (Alastair Haney, Ed.). New York, NY: Penguin Books.
Lerner, G. (1986). *The creation of patriarchy*. New York, NY: Oxford University Press.
Niebuhr, H. R. (1963). *The responsible self: An essay in Christian moral philosophy*. New York, NY: Harper and Row.
Richardson, R. (2006). *William James: In the maelstrom of American modernism*. New York, NY: Houghton Mifflin.
Starhawk. (1982). *Dreaming the dark: Magic, sex, and politics*. Boston, MA: Beacon Press.
Stengel, B. (1991). *Just education: The right to education in context and conversation*. Chicago: Loyola University Press.
Stengel, B. (1994, October). All things considered: Prolegomena for a response mode(l) of teaching. *Philosophical Studies in Education, 25*, 64-75.
Stengel, B. (1995). Taking the moral nature of teaching seriously. *Education Forum, 59*(2), 154-163.
Stengel, B. (1997a). "Academic discipline" and "school subject": Contestable curricular concepts. *Journal of Curriculum Studies, 29*(5), 585-602.
Stengel, B. (1997b). I'm not a postmodernist, but .... *Philosophical Studies in Education, 28*, 140-148.
Stengel, B. (1999). Pedagogical responsibility: Dewey and Buber lay the groundwork. *Philosophical Studies in Education, 30*, 147-162 .
Stengel, B. (2001). Teaching in response. In *Philosophy of Education 2000*. Champaign-Urbana, IL: University of Illinois.
Stengel, B. (2002, April). *"As if we were called": Response-able teaching and learning*. Paper presented at the American Educational Research Association Annual Meeting.
Stengel, B. (2004). Knowing is response-able relation. In C. Bingham & A. Sidorkin (Eds.), *A pedagogy of relations* (pp. 139-152). New York: Peter Lang.
Stengel, B., & Tom, A. (2006). *Moral matters: Five ways to develop the moral life of schools*. New York, NY: Teachers College Press.

Stengel, B. (2009, November). *Schooled to fear: Case studies of educative feeling and miseducative emotion.* Presented at American Educational Studies Association Annual Meeting, Invited Kneller Lecture.

Stengel, B. (2010). The complex case of fear and safe space. *Studies in Philosophy and Education, 29*(6), 523-540.

Stengel, B. (2011). Feelings of worth and the moral made visible. In J. DiVitis & T. Yu (Eds.), *Character and moral education: A reader* (pp. 321-333). New York: Peter Lang.

Stengel, B. (2013a). Teaching responsibility: Practical reasoning in a pedagogical wonderland. In M. Sanger & R. Osguthorpe (Eds.), *The moral work of teaching: Preparing and supporting practitioners* (pp. 44-59). New York: Teacher's College Press.

Stengel, B. (2013b). After the laughter. *Educational Philosophy and Theory, 45*(1), 1-12.

Stengel, B. (2014). *So open it hurts: Enabling "therefore, we can ... " in the dangerous, secure world of education.* Presidential Address, Philosophy of Educational Society Annual Meeting, Portland, OR. Philosophy of Education 2013.

Stengel, B., & Casey, M. (2013). To grow by looking: From moral perception to pedagogical responsibility. In H. Sockett & R. Boostrom (Eds.), *NSSE yearbook: A moral critique of American education* (pp. 116-135). New York, NY: Teachers College Press.

Stengel, B., & English, A. (2010). Exploring fear: Rousseau, Dewey and on fear and learning. *Educational Theory, 60,* 521-542.

Streisand, B., Ashby, J. M., & Peters, J. (Producers), & Streisand, B. (Director). (1983). *Yentl* [Motion picture]. USA: MGM.

SHARON TODD

LEARNING FROM AND LIVING WITH LIFE'S ROUGH THREADS

In the development of a life it is not always easy, in effect, to distinguish what comes from one source and what comes from another. (Irigaray, 2002, p. 49)

When writing an autobiographical essay, the past's explanatory power has a tendency to create a coherency through which the self seems to emerge like a silken tapestry with all the rough threads fully smoothed over – and some excised altogether. However, a life is full of rough threads, and the question is, to what degree can a narrative such as this allow them some freedom to stray from the density of the weave and create a more textured fabric? It is not that these threads don't have sources, but that each cannot be easily separated from all the others, and they repeat back on themselves before they move forward, like a split stitch begins from the midst of the previous one. As Irigaray remarks, it is not easy to distinguish (never mind to put into a 'proper' narrative) the sources that go into making a life: what I have learned or not from my encounters with various traditions, ways of thought, works of art cannot be sewn together according to some pre-outlined intellectual pattern. I have never felt that my own intellectual curiosity or engagement has had a progressive or developmental trajectory to it. Of course, that might be saying something about the limitations of my intellect, but I would also like to think it says something about serendipity and change, about transformation and the shifting nature of attachments.

I have long entertained a pet theory that a scholar's desire to specialize in certain topics rather than others is reflective of personal discomfort and/or difficulty with those same topics: the communicationalist who cannot seem to listen to others, the moral educator who has a history of sleeping with students, the critical theorist who tells everyone how to think for their own good. I am no different. My concern for ethics, affect, and conflict are very much indicative of my struggles with myself throughout my life. What has shaped my scholarly fascinations has been fuelled not so much by some Aristotelian desire to know, but by trying to have some insight into (dare I say, control over) what it is I am fearful of or uncomfortable with. For me, at least, this has meant some unpleasant facing of myself and it has undergone changes over the years, changes that prevent me from depicting my intellectual life along a straight temporal seam. And so, in thinking about the changes in facing what has haunted (and haunts) me, which has largely driven my scholarly work, I want to pick up some rough threads and offer a reading of them in the spirit of keeping them stray and unironed, although I fear that I won't be able fully to help doing a bit of stitching together in spite of myself.

READING

My work to date (see, e.g., Todd, 1997, 2003, 2009, 2010) has been concerned with pedagogical relationships and educational demands, about the idea that pedagogy concerns how we learn to become subjects and persons, women and men, and about how this becoming is invoked in ethical and political contexts, such as classrooms, where various forms of violence, conflict, and suffering take place, alongside and sometimes intertwined with pleasure, desire and love. I have explored such interests through a number of topics, from identity to cosmopolitanism, from desire to human rights, from eros to democracy, and from different philosophical positions: feminism, post-structuralism and psychoanalysis, to name a few. With each twist of interest, I have sought a language that seeks to shed some light on the 'mystery' of human becoming and its stakes in education. For it is this, if anything, that I have spent my life (not just my academic life) interested in: what is unsaid – or unsayable – in life's encounters: the silent currents that lie just under the surface of what it is we think we are revealing; the movements and gestures of bodies that seem to live a life independent of speech; the almost imperceptible shift in the air we are breathing as we stand close to one another.

Initially, from childhood, such interests were a matter of survival, growing up as I did in a poor, working class family in Montréal, in a neighbourhood that didn't brook dissent, particularly from timid girls with glasses like me who were easily intimidated. I learned therefore to read. Reading, as I mean it here, is more than just decoding type on a page, it is a way of feeling your way into situations and allowing them to 'speak' to you, about being vulnerable and susceptible to what goes on unsaid. As Simone Weil (1947/2022) describes it, reading is akin to a mode of emotional inquiry: of sussing out a situation, interpreting what is at hand and making a judgement. In this sense, I did indeed learn to read rather well, keeping body and soul largely intact on the schoolyard was no doubt due largely to this kind of reading, out of fear and necessity. Yet, what enabled me to read these 'real life' situations was also my capacity to read fiction; for it was – and still is – my immersion in literature that opened up spaces of mystery, of the complexities and layers of human contact, of the affections that propel us toward and away from others.

In fact I cannot remember not reading, as I read by the time I was 4 years old, and so the world of my memory is filled with the Brothers Grimm and Mother Goose alongside the hurts and humiliations suffered at the hands of the bigger kids in the back lanes, and my falling in love with the new friends I made down the block. The two aspects of my life go hand in hand. The stories that made up my early world have also been allied with my then budding social life (rather more Grimm than Goose at times), and since then I have never been entirely capable of separating fact from fiction.

This intertwining of passions for both real and fictional others, and the avoidance of harm at all costs, have informed the kind of authors, philosophers and educationalists I read. Such passions were reflected in a spurt of freedom experienced when I entered CEGEP at the age of 17. Then, I turned from physics and mathematics as my chosen subject areas and threw myself into the humanities. I remember telling myself it was because humanities courses offered answers to the questions about life that concerned me, but I now wonder if it was just because I could keep reading the stuff that I liked to read: Freud and psychoanalysis; French Existentialism; Russian Literature; English Poetry. What these subjects offered were windows into suffering, tragedy, sexuality, love, existence and anxiety. My life. The fictional and the philosophical came together in my education, but it would be a long time before I ever thought schooling and education were anything of relevance to study, even if I thought they were central to my existence and to my escape from the confines of the neighbourhood.

POLITICS AND CLASS

Around this time in my late teens I discovered a whole set of voices with which I could identify my disappointment and anger, and they have stayed with me, acting as conversational partners over the years whenever I confront questions of social justice. Having been acutely aware of the discrepancies between rich and poor for all of my life (and I can remember the television programmes I watched did make it seem as though we were the only ones not part of the relative affluence of the North America of the 60s and 70s) I always thought that if I worked hard enough the life of my parents didn't have to be mine. Then, I became fascinated with the philosophy of Marx and Engels, Lenin and Mao. I began to see new patterns emerging concerning who I was, for they talked not just about a life, but about shared lives, connecting my one singularity to a history of oppression and exploitation, and more excitingly, to change and purpose. I became part of the histories of working people and their struggles with the everyday. I had another way of understanding my own grandmothers as immigrants from Northern Ireland and Scotland in the early part of the 20th century, and the conditions of living in the 'old country,' as they called it, which seemed to be worse than those they were living in now. I understood better the tensions my mother faced, working as a typist in a large, faceless company while raising three children single-handedly. I read Rosa Luxemburg and Leon Trotsky, who for very different reasons both spoke of heroism to me, and passion: a passion for politics and for life. From Rosa, it was a woman's life and its precariousness in a world of capital and patriarchy, and from Trotsky it was that raw uncompromising intellect in his writings that I so admired (indeed to the point I think I actually developed a crush on a man who was over 40 years dead). What I loved was the power in their writings and a commitment for justice that made my own preoccupations with myself seem almost beside the point.

While teaching me so much about the very political nature of my existence, I never became revolutionary, although I sometimes wanted to think it was because I was born in this time, my time, and not theirs. But having grown up with straightjacket attitudes and values, which as in many working class neighbourhoods were both sexist and racist, I had no illusions about some grand working class that I wanted to be part of even as I felt eminently tied to its history. Then, I wanted away from it, unlike others I knew who travelled more noble paths toward their vision of radical change. I lived instead in ambivalence. Being proud of my background and at the same time wanting to leave it behind me was an excruciatingly painful process which put my own sense of belonging in a family and in a community at risk. When I became an elementary school teacher in 1988, I only wanted to work in schools and in neighbourhoods not unlike my own; I felt more comfortable there than in middle class schools whose cultures I had trouble reading. I continued to seek to allay this ambivalence with my much later interest in critical and feminist pedagogy and other educational theories of social justice, and I became influenced by the early work of Henry Giroux, Roger Simon and Deborah Britzman. However, despite wanting to engage critically with my students about issues like poverty and racism, I could never accept the group mentality that seemed to reduce singularity and uniqueness entirely to effects of social and political factors. Surely, I thought, education is more than a political mission, and the pain I experienced in living at the crossroads of the classes and therefore belonging to none with a full heart means that for me education created risks for students. It has been my contention that the risk of education carries with it an onus of responsibility, for if we, as teachers, are trying to create spaces of transformation for our students, spaces for them to become, then we need to bear in mind what unpredictable effects this can have. The risk I experienced is like a sore that has long ago scabbed over and healed, leaving only the faintest of scars, but a scar nonetheless.

MYSTERY, IN PICTURES AND BEYOND

One of the most influential books in my life has been the Bible. Not just any Bible, though, but the copy belonging to my father, which he received as a present from a relative one Christmas in 1956. It is leather bound, printed on onionskin, with gilded edges and adorned with sumptuous images. The paintings that illustrate the text are sometimes in the rich palette of Rubens ("The Betrayal of Samson" still stands out here), and sometimes in the Turner-like translucency of whites and blues in the portrayal of the Ascension. I did not understand the Old and New Testaments as the word of God, but as images conveyed by God, filled with magic, horror, and benefaction. I do not remember having a child's bible, and since my family was not particularly religious, I never attended Sunday School as some of my Protestant friends did, nor did I go to the big church down the corner, as some of my Catholic friends did, filled as it was with incense and candlelight and stained glass. (Other of my friends who were Buddhist and Greek Orthodox had to go to temples and churches far outside the borders of our neighbourhood and so such places of worship were unknown to me at this time.) When very young, I asked my father to read to me now and then, to translate the foreign lyricism of the King James text, to which I had little access on my own. Then, I seemed to hear the timbre of those painted images. To me they created a sensibility for all things ephemeral and transcendent.

I remember being mesmerized my first time in a Catholic church at the age of 5, having accompanied my friend who was a year older than me. We just walked in one fall day (I don't remember why we weren't at school; kids seemed to do a lot more on their own then) and it is my first recollection of being overwhelmed and quite a bit scared in that thrilling way that children often like. Filled with pictures on glass and canvas, the chill of the stone, the scent of votives and a light suffused with dust motes, we sat down in a pew and Karen showed me how to pray. The crucifix over the altar seemed gargantuan, and I immediately thought the figure was watching every move I made, even though he looked like he should be paying more attention to his own suffering. His perceived concern for me was puzzling and troubling, given the pain he seemed to be in. I remember trembling with what I now read as awe under his gaze and wanting to run away. But I also remember wanting to stay, relishing the feeling of being submersed in something ineffable. I don't remember leaving, but I remember I had a strong desire to return.

Such feelings make their way into my fascination with art to this day and with its power to move me in ways that speak to me of that same mystery I encountered in the Bible and in that church. To a large degree art has indeed become intertwined with the divine for me. Taking a Bachelor's Degree in Art History at McGill University was perhaps one of the ways I had of resuscitating these early feelings and of embracing them with my then current interests in English, history and philosophy. It was the romanticism of Beethoven, Shelley and Delacroix, introduced by Peter Sinclair, a dear teacher in my CEGEP, which initially captivated my longing for formal study. But it was what art made me feel that has had the most lasting impact.

That sense of mystery in our encounters not only with art, but with each other – things I cannot fully articulate and which seem to defy easy expression – have always captivated me. My much later scholarship on the work of Emmanuel Levinas (1961/1969, 1974/1998) has largely been shaped by my struggles to put into words things for which I never had a language. His notion of the face to face encounter as a relation with infinity; the sacredness of the other's otherness; and the humility that this calls forth in me, are not merely intellectual ideas, but like acts of faith, provide structure and guidance. Levinas, perhaps more than any other philosopher, or artist for that matter, gave me a way of expressing what I think is valuable in education, gave me a way to think beyond my own ambivalence, and truly face the difficulty of radical difference as an existential break with who it is we think we are. In facing the Other, I transcend the borders of myself. A space opens up to become someone different than I was before, bearing with it an ethical sensibility. This has become for me the very model of what it means to learn and teach. That is, pedagogy, like any transformational event, is about learning *from*, not *about* otherness, no matter how disruptive to my own sense of self I believe it to be.

VIOLENCE AND CONFLICT

In October 1970, when I was 8 years old, martial law was declared in Québec. The Front libération du Québec had kidnapped British high commissioner, James Cross, and later a member of the provincial assembly, Pierre Laporte, who would soon be found dead. The regular programming on television, which I watched at lunchtime and after school, was constantly being interrupted with news updates about the kidnappings. No doubt my memory has made this seem a rather longer period than it was, given the brevity of the period in comparison with the import it has taken on for me. But I grew up with regularly reported bombings, at least a half dozen every year for a 5-year period leading up to this time. I remember seeing armed militia and tanks roll down the street and parents and teachers talked about the violent dangers that always seemed to be lurking around the corner. Coming from an Anglophone family and school, although living in a predominantly Francophone area, such warnings were often accompanied by some condemnation of "those Frenchies," and old prejudices like parasites sought to find a host in a new generation. Such tensions translated for us kids in back lane struggles, English versus French, and harassment on both sides was the game of the day. It was only when I was in high school, at the height of the Parti Québecois separatist campaign under the leadership of René Lévesque, that I finally understood the shaded contours of the struggle for liberation, and the PQ's then largely socialist agenda which complicated the nationalist aspirations far more than our parents had let on about. Sympathising with the PQ, I was a couple of months shy of my 18th birthday and was not able to vote in the first referendum on sovereignty-association – a bitter disappointment to me at the time.

It is thus that I have always seen politics as something that is about struggle and about the difficulties of transforming ingrained social divisions. It has never been for me about merely going to the polls or reaching some kind of consensus. Violence was not something simply to be avoided (although I certainly did my best to dodge it personally), but something to face and confront and understand. Here, my reading of left wing literature seemed to find some tangible resonance. Looking back from my vantage now, I could be writing about how these two threads became intricately woven together. Yet, I know it is not that way. Although my childhood experiences (however indirect they were) of political violence have made me largely agree with Chantal Mouffe's (2005) agonistic view of democracy, of which I have written about in the context of education (Todd, 2010, 2011a; Todd & Säfström, 2008), these do not neatly fit into a tapestry. Instead, the continuing search for facing violence as an existential encounter infused with mystery, as something captured in that first crucifix and those Bible pictures so long ago, has mitigated my outlook, to the point that violence for me is not only political, but part of the human condition, part of life itself, which philosophers such as Levinas (to say nothing of Freud) understand all too clearly. To hold such a view of violence, then, is in no way to suggest that it is benign, but unless we come to confront the vulnerabilities it conceals, the humiliations it causes, and the humility it can lead to, then I think we are missing how to learn from it. I recently gave a talk (Todd, 2013) at the National College of Art and Design in Dublin in conjunction with an exhibition by Jonathan Cummins that dealt with IRA prisoners who were non-supporters of the Good Friday Agreement. It was part of a public series entitled "Impossible Conversations" that led up to the opening of the film-based installation. There, in that context, it became clear to me the urgency of facing violence, and the importance both art and education have in constructing possibilities for communities that might never find common ground. The answer is not to focus exclusively on conflict resolution by turning those who commit violence into moral pariahs – or worse yet, into those who have no moral subjectivity altogether. Instead, the real challenge is to create spaces where one becomes implicated in the act of listening to others – not agreeing with, but attending to, as Deborah Britzman (1998, 2006) would say, what it is we cannot bear.

EDUCATION AS SECOND BIRTH

It takes years to be able to cast a glance backward without, hopefully, being turned into a pillar of salt, without, that is, being punished for gazing upon what one has left behind, for disobeying the law that prevents us from longing for the irretrievable past. But we all begin somewhere and the only event that is absolutely needed in order to start us off on life is life itself. As novelist Jeanette Winterson (2011) writes, "My advice to anybody is: to get born." Without birth, there is no life – a nauseatingly obvious point, perhaps, but one too often forgotten. The history of philosophy has been filled with the existential anxiety surrounding our mortality, but those philosophers who dare speak of natality, such as Irigaray (1985), Hannah Arendt (1959), and Adriana Cavarero (2000), hold a special place for me, for they acknowledge not only the certainty of death, but the happenstance – indeed miracle – of birth. For I have no illusions that one of the rough threads of any life has to do with chance and serendipity. It is a wonder not only to have been born at all, but to be so at a time when I had options, to be born in a place that enabled my survival with access to the basic necessities of life and more, without which no biography is possible. One might think this is karma, or the result of some universal design; but for me it is a kind of luck that could just as easily be misfortune.

What these women philosophers speak of is not only biological birth, but the importance of what they refer to as a 'second birth' – a birth that can only be realized in relation to others. That is, I become someone in relation to the narratives I tell and that are told about me; I become a 'who' in a web of relations that I have not always chosen. What a second birth gestures towards is the learning at work in becoming. That is, for me, the emergence of subjectivity is a pedagogical act par excellence. Not that schooling necessarily leads to this kind of becoming, but that the event of becoming is properly pedagogical. For example, I was fortunate enough to be schooled by a few teachers in the 60s and 70s who were idealists; who didn't think because I was poor, or a girl, or any other such category, that I was condemned to live a particular kind of life (although I also had my share of teachers who made me feel ashamed of who I was and made it clear that they didn't think we would amount to anything). These, however, were the days of alternative education, of protest, of freedom of expression, of experiential learning and new forms of classroom decision making. I learned from these other teachers that the value of learning was not about what I was, but ought to be connected to who I was, and who I was had to something to do with challenging perceptions and modes of thought, of breaking down prejudices and structures that held a girl of my social standing in a particularly oppressive constellation of 'oughts.' It was many years later that I could relate this orientation to education to the 'art of teaching,' of which Maxine Greene (1973, 1978) writes so eloquently. Without the fortune of being part of the reformist attitudes of the 60s, who knows whether I would be in any position to be writing this now. This is why, it seems to me, that the unpredictability of life is so central both to my scholarship and to how I conduct myself as a teacher with my students. There is no other time than this one; no future to hide behind, no past that conceals us. Teaching is an exposure that can never follow patterns, and attempts to regulate the act of teaching demean its power as a potential source of transformation. Living a life, with all its rough threads, is integral to all our human activities, including teaching and learning. It is not that life is a separate issue, or that students somehow either only have a "life outside" the classroom, or that education is about preparing students for a "future life;" students lives are here and now, living out their fullness in time.

* * *

The threads of life are not held together by any overarching plan, and there are many strays still waiting to be discovered. There is no predictable path, no foreseeable pattern; who each of us becomes is truly a wonder, serendipitous and irreducible to a singular event or cause. It is what Irigaray would call "the alchemy of becoming" – that magical mix of ingredients that goes into forming and reforming and transforming a life, and whose recipe can never be replicated. Finding coherency and patterns is something we do afterwards; it attempts to sew up the gaps, keeping us on a single track, and forcing us to 'read' with tunnel vision. I wonder, if we take away much of our anxious efforts to subdue the roughness of life would we not find new ways of paying attention to what, in fact, comprises life? As Nicole Kraus (2010) puts it so beautifully in *Great House*: "We search for patterns, you see, only to find where the patterns break. And it's there, in that fissure, that we pitch our tents and wait" (p. 89).

FAVORITE WORKS

Influential Texts

Arendt, H. (1959). *The human condition.* New York: Anchor Books.
Britzman, D. P. (1998). *Lost subject, contested objects: Toward a psychoanalytic inquiry of learning.* Albany, NY: SUNY Press.

Castoriadis, C. (1997). *World in fragments: Writings on politics, society, psychoanalysis, and the imagination* (Transl. D. A. Curtis). Stanford: Stanford University Press.

Dostoevsky, F. (1979 [1866]). *Crime and punishment*. London: Penguin Books.

Freud, S. (1954 [1900]). *The interpretation of dreams* (Transl. J. Strachey). *Vol. 4. The standard edition of the complete psychological works of Sigmund Freud*. London: Hogarth.

Irigaray, L. (1985 [1974]). *Speculum of the other woman* (Transl. G. C. Gill). Ithaca: Cornell University Press.

Levinas, E. (1998 [1974]). *Otherwise than being or beyond essence* (Transl. A. Lingis). Pittsburgh: Duquesne University Press.

Simon, R. I. (1992). *Teaching against the grain: Texts for a pedagogy of possibility* Toronto: OISE Press.

Favourites from My Own Work

Todd, S. (Ed.). (1997). *Learning desire: Perspectives on pedagogy, culture and the unsaid*. New York: Routledge.

Todd, S. (2003). *Learning from the other: Levinas, psychoanalysis and ethical possibilities in education*. Albany, NY: State University of New York Press.

Todd, S. (2008). Welcoming and difficult learning: Reading Levinas with education. In D. Egéa-Kuehne (Ed.), *Levinas and education* (pp. 170-185). London: Routledge.

Todd, S. (2009). *Toward an imperfect education: Facing humanity, rethinking cosmopolitanism*. Boulder, CO: Paradigm.

Todd, S. (2011). Going to the heart of the matter. *Studies in Philosophy and Education, 30*(5), 507-512.

Todd, S. (2011). Becoming present in context: The politics of the gap in educational transformation. *European Journal of Educational Research, 10*(3), 363-366.

Todd, S. (2011). The 'Veiling' question: On the demand for visibility in communicative encounters in education. In *Philosophy of Education 2010* (pp. 349-356).

Todd, S. (2013). *Difficult conversations, or The difficult task of facing humanity*. Presentation as part of the Impossible Conversations Series, National College of Art and Design, Dublin, April 9th

Todd, S. (Forthcoming). *Pedagogy as transformative event: Becoming present in context*. Festschrift for Kenneth Wain.

REFERENCES

Arendt, H. (1959). *The human condition*. New York: Anchor Books.

Britzman, D. P. (1998). *Lost subject, contested objects: Toward a psychoanalytic inquiry of learning*. Albany, NY: SUNY Press.

Britzman, D. P. (2006). *Novel education: Psychoanalytic studies of learning and not learning*. New York: Peter Lang Publishers.

Cavarero, A. (2000). *Relating narratives: Storytelling and selfhood* (Transl. P. A. Kottman). London: Routledge.

Greene, M. (1973). *Teacher as stranger: Educational philosophy for the modern age*. Belmont, CA: Wadsworth Pub. Co.

Greene, M. (1978). *Landscapes of learning*. New York: Teachers College Press.

Irigaray, L. (1985). *This sex which is not one* (Trans. C. Porter & C. Burke). Ithaca: Cornell University Press.

Irigaray, L. (2002). *Between east and west: From singularity to community* (Trans. S. Pluháček. New York: Columbia University Press.

Krauss, N. (2010). *Great house*. New York: W.W. Norton & Company.

Levinas, E. (1969). *Totality and infinity: An essay on exteriority* (Trans. A. Lingus). Pittsburgh: Duquesne University Press.

Levinas, E. (1998 [1974]). *Otherwise than being or beyond essence* (Trans. A. Lingis). Pittsburgh: Duquesne University Press.
Mouffe, C.. (2005). *On the political*. London: Routledge.
Todd, S. (Ed.). (1997). *Learning desire: Perspectives on pedagogy, culture and the unsaid*. New York: Routledge.
Todd, S. (2003). *Learning from the other: Levinas, psychoanalysis and ethical possibilities in education*. Albany, NY: State University of New York Press.
Todd, S. (2009). *Toward an imperfect education: Facing humanity, rethinking cosmopolitanism*. Boulder, CO: Paradigm.
Todd, S. (2010). "Can there be pluralism without conflict?" In *Philosophy of Education 2009* (pp. 51-59).
Todd, S. (2011a). Educating beyond cultural diversity: Redrawing the boundaries of a democratic plurality. *Studies in Philosophy & Education, 30*(2), 101-111.
Todd, S. (2011b). Going to the heart of the matter. *Studies in Philosophy and Education, 30*(5), 507-512.
Todd, S. (2013). *Difficult conversations, or The difficult task of facing humanity*. Presentation as part of the Impossible Conversations Series, National College of Art and Design, Dublin, April 9th.
Todd, S., & Säfström, C. A. (2008). Democracy, education and conflict: Rethinking respect and the place of the ethical. *Journal of Educational Controversy, 1*, http://www.wce.wwu.edu/Resources/CEP/eJournal/.
Weil, S. (1947/2002). *Gravity and grace* (Trans. E. Crawford & M. v. d. Ruhr). London: Routledge.
Winterson, J. (2011). *Why be happy when you could be normal?* London: Jonathan Cape.

LEONARD J. WAKS

AFTERWORD: A PATH FORWARD

In his chapter in the first volume of *Leaders in Philosophy of Education*, Paul Hirst (2008) provided a manifesto for our field going forward. He stated:

> Academic philosophy has in the 20th Century faced the challenge of two major movements, those of analytical philosophy and post-modernism. The positive significance of both has, I consider, now been absorbed into the historical development of Western philosophy and there seems to be a slowly increasing consensus on the broad conceptual framework within which we can now best make sense of human nature and what constitutes a good life … Its major implications for educational aims and practices I have however so far only outlined in the most general terms and their working out in much greater detail I think the most important task for contemporary philosophy of education. There is in many Western societies a feeling that the upbringing of children and much institutionalised education have lost their clear sense of purpose and hence also of how best to decide their means. It seems to me philosophers of education are increasingly in a position to help significantly in elucidating those aims and practices in a way appropriate for the institutions of modern secular and pluralist liberal democracies that are at least in principle committed to the pursuits of reason in all their affairs. Little such work has so far been done in any detail …

The chapters in this second volume show that the 'consensus' Hirst refers to has not been reached in philosophy of education. The split between analytic and postmodern approaches in philosophy of education persists. Despite the spread of postmodern ideas in English language philosophy of education, it may be some time until they are fully domesticated and absorbed within Anglo-American philosophy. The easy and wholesale rejection by postmodernist authors of the work of analytic philosophers of education, while no doubt useful from a programmatic point of view, does not help in working toward a pragmatically useful if provisional working consensus for public interventions; nor does the wholesale rejection of the practical value for the field of any such working consensus.

For example, Smith, in his chapter in this volume, notes that he had from his student says at Oxford rejected analytic philosophy as a "fraud." This attitude was reinforced when he was exposed to the "London Line" of Peters-Hirst and company as well as their American counterparts. He found them practicing "legislative linguistics" and attempting to "tidy up" concepts with merely "stipulative definitions." He saw analytical philosophers as asserting that "philosophers could only talk about the *language* of morality, rather than adding normative insight" and hence as "generating few ideas about how education might change for the better;" and, "even in the hands of some of its most distinguished proponents, rather pedestrian." This makes for a good reform platform, but as scholarship I doubt if it could be sustained. To my eye it misrepresents even the analytic philosophy of the 1960s upon which the new philosophy of education was built, and bears little relationship to developments in the analytic tradition after the 1970s and 1980s.

But more to the point, this sort of divisive posture is outdated and now stands in the way of the public work Hirst proposes – work that "significantly elucidate(s) those aims and practices in a way appropriate for the institutions of modern secular and pluralist liberal democracies." Post-modern critiques of grand narratives may make us cautious about grand general theories of educational aims and best practices, but they should help guide, not hinder, our case-by-case practical work of critique and reconstruction.

In this spirit, I want to acknowledge the recent rebirth of interest in Richard S. Peters' philosophy of education, demonstrated e.g. by the recent publication of the book *Reading Richard S. Peters Today* (Cuypers & Martin, 2011), particularly the chapter by M. Luntley, "On Education and Initiation," as well as Kelvin Beckett's (2011) article, "R. S. Peters and the Concept of Education." Close reading of these works demonstrate how overdrawn is the dichotomy between 'initiation' on the one hand, and 'natality' and 'openness to newcomers' on the other. Surprisingly Biesta, who has been a leader of the battle against the initiation image of education, does not in his essay "Education, Not Initiation" take up Peters' own formulations nor even mention Peters in his critique of education as initiation.

Biesta (1996) claims that initiation is tantamount to transmission in that it conceives of bringing newcomers into an already established world, as providing a requisite commonality for newcomers with those who have preceded them. Biesta counters the initiation image with an 'agency' conception stressing education as individual growth in uniqueness or difference from what has existed before them.

'Initiation vs. agency' is, however, an 'untenable dualism.' The "worthwhile activities" intended by Peters are not static but self-transforming, and Peters makes explicit place for newcomers in re-shaping and transforming these activities.

Education as initiation allows for the radical differences and new identities regularly exhibited in intellectual, artistic and technical craft fields. In art education, for example, it is a given that newcomers bring unique perspectives and practices. They do this by working through art traditions and conventions, as filtered through their unique life experiences and those of their generation, discarding outmoded forms while extending their fields in new ways. They enter on-going practices and study past masters to learn from competing contemporary paradigms in the process of qualifying themselves as insiders or initiates – as creative members of the artistic community, agents positioned to manage and advance the tradition in creative and unexpected ways.

Michael Luntley and Kelvin Beckett help explain how this takes place. Beckett notes that for Peters, initiation is a two-step process. In the first step, teachers bring learners into worlds of cultural activity and teach them basic moves. Luntley notes that this first stage is possible because the young learner's thoughts and behaviors prior to education as initiation are not foreign to, but rather continuous with, cultural activities, a point that Peters' formulations often obscure. Young learners are not "barbarians" and there are no "gates" separating them from cultural practitioners. For example, a young girl, a newcomer, moves her body naturally in response to music. Her dance teacher – if she is any good – already grasps that dance arises from such natural impulsions. She gives them full consideration in coming to grips with this young learner, and then builds on the learner's native expression, in the course of inviting her into traditions and practices of dance.

In the second step of education as initiation, as Beckett observes, after newcomers have acquired provisional vocabularies and operational tools, teachers and learners explore these ever-evolving cultural worlds together. Newcomers inevitably have new interests shaped by new generational life situations. Drawing upon tools acquired in the first step of initiation, the newcomers as agents question the judgments and emphases of their teachers and move beyond them in unpredicted ways. Initiation in Peters' sense thus *implies* agency and establishes transitional roles for newcomers. If a putative emancipatory project for education prohibits teachers from drawing on the most relevant cultural resources, then it is hardly clear just what – if anything – they would have to contribute to a newcomer's growth.

Looking ahead, philosophy of education in English cannot advance beyond outdated polarities without practicing in our teaching and writing appreciative close reading of both older Anglo-American analytic and post-modern texts and setting them into constructive dialogue. This is a daunting challenge – working across and through competing paradigms to forge something new and useful for our times. But we may discover that we have more to contribute to one another – and the bewildered educational public – than we ever thought.

We cannot, however, succeed in contributing "as citizens with a special expertise and obligation to bring pedagogy into the broad public discussion," as Lovlie puts it, if we can't find even minimal agreement about where our expertise lies and cannot work toward an appropriate and accessible public diction. To succeed in this public task philosophers of education will need all of the resources our philosophical (and rhetorical) traditions – pragmatist, analytic, postmodern and others – have to offer.

REFERENCES

Beckett, K. (2011). R. S. Peters and the concept of education, *Educational Theory*, 61(3) (June), 2329-2355.

Biesta G. (1996). Education, not initiation, *Philosophy of Education*, online at http://ojs.ed.uiuc.edu/index.php/pes/article/view/2247/942

Cuypers, S. E. & Martin, C. (Eds.). (2011). *Reading R. S. Peters today: Analysis, ethics, and the aims of education*. Wiley-Blackwell.

Hirst, P. (2008). Philosophy of education in the UK: The institutional context. In L. Waks (Ed.), *Leaders in philosophy of education* (pp. 305-311). Rotterdam: Sense Publishers.

Luntley, M. (2011). On education and initiation. In S. E. Cuypers & C. Martin (Eds.), *Reading R. S. Peters today: Analysis, ethics, and the aims of education*. Wiley-Blackwell.

CPSIA information can be obtained at www.ICGtesting.com
Printed in the USA
BVOW01s1602231014

371982BV00002B/22/P

9 789462 097568